HOW TO PRINT T-SHIRTS FOR FUN AND PROFIT!

By
Scott and Pat Fresener

U.S. Screen Printing Institute

605 S. Rockford Drive
Tempe, Arizona 85281 USA
Corp. Office: (602)929-0640   Order Line: 800-624-6532   Fax: (602)929-0766
Email: sales@usscreen.com   Web Site: www.usscreen.com

Revised and Expanded

Printed in the U.S.A.

ISBN: 0-9639474-0-0

(Previous IBBN: 0-9603530-0-3)

Printing history
   Last digit is the print number: 10 9 8 7 6 5 4 3

Published by:
Union Ink Company, Inc.
453 Broad Ave.
Ridgefield, NJ 07657 USA
(201)945-5766 Fax (201)945-4111

Dedication:

This book is dedicated to our wonderful kids, Mishelle, Michael and Sandy. The first version was dedicated to you in 1978 when you "got stuck with the dishes while mom and dad wrote the book." You are still the joys of our life and dedicate the totally revised book to you since you helped run the business while mom and dad rewrote the book!

Contents

Contents

Contents

Introduction

Congratulations!

You're entering one of the few businesses that can be started with very little capital. Interest, enthusiasm and self motivation is the real capital needed to build this business. Many of the big companies started out this way, in fact many started in their garages! This book provides all the information necessary to print T-shirts. Put your new-found knowledge to work and add a second income, or build up a full-time business. *It's up to you!*

Of course, you don't have to limit yourself to T-shirts. Other screened items are everywhere. Objects you don't think about are screen printed: bottles, cans, computer control panels, labels in clothing, graphics hanging in your home, the tiniest printed circuit in your watch, to large billboards.

How To Print T-shirts For Fun And Profit! contains a good basic knowledge on screening techniques, and totally covers screen printing T-shirts, fashion items, athletic wear, and most fabric type printing.

Whether you're a beginner or already do screening, this book is an excellent technical guide and will be used constantly for reference, so keep it handy! A fairly respectable printed shirt could probably be done by just following the photos in this book - *but don't do it that way!* Read this book completely before you even start to do any printing. Once you've read it, you'll have a basic knowledge and understanding of the *entire* screening process, and many of your unanswered questions won't even have to be asked!

One fact in the screen print industry: *screen printers don't like to share their knowledge.* They are a rather secretive bunch and rightfully so! For many, their techniques were developed through trial and error and a lot of sleepless nights. Why should they spread their hard earned secrets around? Some simple time and money saving techniques might have taken months to discover! Wait until you've been printing awhile. You won't want to give the competition any handy little tips either.

That's where this book comes in! When we see poorly printed shirts it hurts *all* of the industry. When we see energetic and inventive people trying to develop a screening business, and using completely *archaic* methods, it's time for a book that discloses *modern, easy, time and money saving techniques.*

Indeed, there are screeners still using old techniques, still spending more time and money than necessary. Virtually, no two printers will do things exactly the same way. In doing research for this book, we found numerous books on screening that totally contradicted each other in technical methods!

Admittedly, it's hard to change methods that are already in use. They become comfortable and familiar. At times, it's hard to decide which way is best. Some methods in this book were developed through trial and error; some were developed by observing other printers and then, if necessary, changing or improving on their techniques. *All* the techniques in this book have been *proven* in actual daily use! *They work.* They make it possible for *you* to start a screen printing business and make a *profit!*

Throughout this book you're urged to experiment! That's because seeing is believing. Often, very technical information that tends to be confusing when just read, becomes crystal clear when actually, physically, done. Experimenting will also help you build the confidence necessary to develop your own techniques and ideas!

There are various stages in the printing process and we have tried to take them in the order that they actually occur. We will first teach you how to prepare the artwork, then cut a screen and print the order. After all this, you'll learn how to buy shirts for the jobs, how to print other items, how to sell the order and how to run your business!

Remember, this book contains everything you need to know. Putting it to use is up to you.

Welcome to the exciting world of T-shirts!

Scott and Pat Fresener

Authors' Post Script:

The original *How To Print T-shirts for Fun and Profit!* was pubished in 1978 and was 160 pages. The first revision was in 1988 and the book grew to 176 pages. The book was totally rewritten and updated in 1994 and increased in size to 260 pages. There have been additional revisions to this 1998 version.

We had to chuckle a bit when we began to rewrite the old introduction (from the 1978 version) and discovered that it didn't need rewritten! Everything we said then *still* holds true today and so we decided to leave it exactly as it was written in 1978.

From our humble entry into the education arena in 1978, we had no way of knowing that this little book would be the beginning of a lifelong career. We knew the industry needed an excellent, albeit simple book on screen printing T-shirts, but we didn't realize how much it would be *appreciated!*

We had no idea that 20 years later, *How To Print T-shirts for Fun and Profit!* would have sold over *115,000 copies* and been the recipient of dozens of industry awards. We had no idea that it would be the launch pad for the *U.S. Screen Printing Institute* (our school in Arizona since 1979) or for our next book *The Encyclopedia of Garment Printing* (a 1000 page technical T-shirt extravaganza), or for dozens of educational video tapes.

We had no idea that we would build a base of loyal followers, who, even 20 years later, never fail to come up just to say "hi" at industry trade shows. We had no idea that this little book would take us to foreign lands to speak about screen printing and we never thought that it would provide us with friends in almost every city in the United States and friends in so many foreign countries. And so dear friends and associates (you all know who you are) let us take this opportunity to give a formal, written, great big *thank you!*

And to our future new friends, be assured that the report on the future of T-shirt printing is even *better* than it was in 1978! Through the years we have heard that printed T-shirts is a fad. Well guess what. After 20 years we don't hear that very much any more! Indeed, our industry has finally come into its own, and with it the respect, profitability and satisfaction that it has always deserved to have.

Scott and Pat Fresener

Learn More at the *T-Net* Web Site!

This book covers just about everything, but you can never stop learning or keeping up with the latest trends. To keep on top of the industry, check out the *T-Net* web site at **www.usscreen.com**. It has a very active Message Board with dozens of topics and thousands of active messages. If you have a technical question, this is the place to get an answer! There is also a FREE Classified Ad section with thousands of ads for equipment for sale.

The *T-Net* site also has dozens of technical articles, a complete calendar of trade shows and hundreds of links to other industry sites. The *T-Net* site is the #1 bookmark for the screen printing industry and is brought to you as a service to the industry by Mike Fresener and the U.S. Screen Printing Institute.

Commonly Asked Questions

How much money do I need to start?

You can start your business on a shoestring or invest thousands. A very small basic shop can be put together for $300–$500 if you can build a few pieces of equipment yourself. On the high range, a $30,000 investment buys a large, completely self-contained, professional shop. Add $20,000–$100,000 if you want to go with giant automated printing presses.

How much money can I make?

Of course, this is in direct relation to your original investment. However, on the smallest level, working just weekends you could add $200–300 per week to your income.

What kind of things can I print?

Although this book expounds mainly on printing T-shirts, the techniques used for shirts are the *same techniques* used for all screen printing–from artwork to screen making to printing. Usually, printing other items just entails finding the right ink. Items such as posters, bumper-stickers, signs, decals, vinyl binders, decorative mirrors and tiles are just a few of the other items that are often decorated by screen printing techniques.

How much space do I need?

When we first began, we printed in our very small dining room. From there, we progressed to the garage (you would be surprised how much work can be produced in a garage!) and progressed to industrial buildings as large as 10,000 sq ft.

Do I need to have art talent?

No. There are a host of techniques and art aids to help you with this chore. Of course, if you're one of the many with a great graphics computer, artwork practically creates itself!

Isn't screen printing messy?

Yes. However, so is cooking when certain people try to do it. The good news is that like cooking, the mess can be cleaned up. The secret, as in cooking, is to clean as you go and put things away as you use them! Of course, not everyone minds a little mess, however, if you're one of those people who wear rubber gloves to dust, you should probably keep your day job.

Isn't screen printing hard to do?

The actual process of printing is very easy and with *How To Print T-Shirts For Fun and Profit!,* everything else is easy too! Each step involved in producing the printed product is explained in easy-to-understand step-by-step detail that incorporates *professional techniques and products,* not old-fashioned artsy college-course methods.

How A Shirt Is Printed

T-shirt printing is fairly simple. The following six steps give a quick overview of the process. Just follow the procedures outlined in this book and you'll be on your way!

1. Artwork

A design is drawn, traced, scanned or called up from computer clip-art.

2. Screen

A screen frame is stretched with poly-ester screen fabric.

3. Stencil Preparation

The fabric is prepared with a photo-graphic stencil and the artwork is transferred to it by exposing it to ultra-violet light. The artwork is developed on the stencil by rinsing it with water.

4. Printing

The screen is placed on top of a garment and the ink is transferred through the stencil with a squeegee.

5. Curing or Drying

The printed shirt is run through a dryer or hung to dry (if water-based ink is used).

6. The Finished Shirt

The shirt is ready to present to the customer!

CHAPTER

1

ARTWORK PREPARATION

This chapter is designed, as is *every chapter* in this book, to give you a broad overview of the screen printing process *and* plenty of easy-to-follow step-by-step techniques to get you started in the "hands-on" application of the techniques.

Good artwork is the first requirement for a quality end product and there are many ways of producing good artwork. In this chapter we'll discuss the practical ways of creating artwork in-house, as well as where to find and how to deal with amateur and professional artists. We'll also cover how to use art materials and tools, techniques for tracing and creating multicolor overlays, graphic arts camera work, and the role computer graphics, copy machines and overhead transparencies play in art preparation.

Setting Up An Art Department

When setting up an art department, try to find an area where your artists can work undisturbed. It will also be helpful to assemble as many tools and supplies as possible. Artwork is much easier to create if you have the right supplies.

A good, comfortable chair and drawing board will be a real help. Place a light over the work area, too.

As you accumulate a lot of camera shots and original art, you will need to establish a filing system. Buy a supply of 12 x 14 in. manila envelopes and file each job separately with the customer's name on the envelope. By keeping these in a box in alphabetical order, the art will always be at your fingertips when you need it.

Tools and Supplies

There are literally thousands of different art tools, materials and supplies. Visiting a local art supply store and collecting a lot of supplier catalogs will show you just how many different items there are.

Some of the devices are well worth the money. Some tools are easy to use, while others are not worth the trouble. It really boils down to personal taste. If something looks like it will save you time and frustration, then go ahead and buy it (**1.1**). You'll never know unless you give it a try! (But then you could always ask other artists for their opinions!)

A Word About Computer Graphics

The ideal art department would not be complete without a computer graphics system (**1.2**). It is not listed here because there is a separate section in this chapter about computer graphics.

Although a great portion of the artwork being done by professionals is on the computer, there are still many companies doing all or part of their designs "the traditional" way using drawing paper, hand-cutting color overlays and applying lettering by hand. There are also as many new "computer artists" who have never touched a drawing pen or hand-done anything.

This section of the book is designed to provide a listing of the traditional art tools that are still used for piecing together work and doing simple jobs even if you have a computer graphics system. The computer is just another tool that will certainly make life easier, but can be cumbersome when working with complicated designs or when original artwork needs a lot of hand work in order to be usable in the computer.

1.1

1.2

1.1 This can be your complete art department. A small supply of tools and materials is all you really need to do simple designs.

1.2 Computer graphics systems are now very common and have replaced many traditional tools in the modern art department. Designs that took hours by hand can now be done in minutes on a computer - with very little art talent!

Shopping List

Now, Let's Get Started!

The following list of supplies is geared toward the small shop. However, the materials listed are used by all sized shops. Do not expect the art store clerk to be able to answer questions on what works well for screen printers! Like screen printing supply sales people, many have never used the products they are selling!

    X-Acto® Compass
    X-Acto® Knife with a #16 angled blade
    Swivel Knife
    Drawing Board - inexpensive wood
    T-square - wood with clear plastic edges
    Templates - French curves, squares, etc.
    Triangle Templates -
        One of 45-45-90° 12 in.
        One of 30-60-90° 12 in.
    Ruler
    Scissors
    Tweezers
    Technical Pens
    Black Felt-tip Markers - assorted tip sizes
    White-out Correction Fluid
    Opaquing Pen - with red and/or black ink
    Non-Reproducing Blue Pen or Pencil
    Rubber Cement Pick-Up
    Rubber Cement - with brush applicator
    Rubber Cement Thinner
    Artist Sketch Pad
    Vellum Paper - heavyweight 12 x 18 in. pad
    Non-Reproducing Blue Graph Paper
    Rubylith® - flat sheets or roll
    Frosted Acetate
    Clear Acetate
    Percentage Wheel (Proportional Scale)
    Transparent Tape
    Masking Tape ¼ or ½ in.
    Clip-Art Books
    Formatt® Catalog
    Lettering Sheets
    Halftone Screen Tints (Tint Screens) and
        Texture Sheets
    Computer Graphics System

The Basic Drawing Tools

Drawing Board

Investing in a good drafting table (drawing board) will save eyesight and prevent an aching back. Since they are rather expensive, why not be creative and put a makeshift one together? Using a piece of wood that is tilted up with books in the back will serve the purpose. Perhaps even an old cutting board would do. If the surface is rough or uneven, cover it with posterboard.

T-square

T-squares are used to keep horizontal work straight and parallel. When putting a design together (such as applying traced artwork as discussed in "Drawing on Vellum Paper"), don't rely on eyesight to straighten anything! Always use a T-square. A portion of the lettering may only be ¼ in. off, but after the design is printed, someone is sure to notice.

Triangles

Triangle templates are used with a T-square to keep vertical work straight and parallel (**1.3**). Using triangle templates is also a quick but accurate way to center artwork.

Just like triangle templates, *variety templates* are usually made of a transparent plastic and most art supply stores carry a large variety. They are one of the handiest tools ever invented and very inexpensive! There are templates with circles, squares, rectangles, French curves (very handy), geometric symbols, architectural symbols, chemistry symbols, etc. These templates work like a stencil in that the circles, squares, etc. are stamped through the plastic, allowing tracing inside with a pencil or pen.

Circle Compass

An *X-Acto® compass* (**1.4**) is another often used item. Besides making perfect circles, a compass can make different shapes just by moving the point to different positions.

The beauty of the X-Acto compass is that it can accommodate the width of a wide felt-tip marker as well as a cutting knife.

Vellum Paper

Vellum paper is a specially made paper that is semitransparent, has a fairly stiff body, smooth texture and virtually eliminates any problem with ink bleeding into the paper. We recommend it highly for use with technical pens, ink pens or felt-tip markers.

Don't confuse this vellum paper with the vellum paper that we will talk about for use in a laser printer. They are very similar with the exception that the laser vellum is cut to fit in a laser printer paper tray and has the grain going the correct direction to not jam in the laser.

Opaquing Pens

Opaquing pens are used when drawing or tracing on clear films such as clear acetate, film positives and stripped Rubylith. Purchasing the wrong opaquing pen can lead to frustration! Many will dry up before you even get them home! We have found that one of the best pens on the market is the *Film-opaque* pen (**1.5**) by Mar-Tex Corp., Englewood, NJ. This pen has the terrific feature of a pump tip which prevents it from ever drying out. Also, it comes with an extra replacement tip. They can be purchased in opaque black and transparent red. The black is the best to use when you are drawing freehand. The red is best when tracing items because it is helpful to be able to see through the red ink to the artwork being traced.

Photomasking Film (Rubylith®)

This material, often referred to as *Ruby*, is a soft, red film, that is adhered to a clear plastic backing sheet. It is used for tracing designs (by cutting the design into the film) (**1.6**) and for overlays for multicolor work. Artwork made with this material can be used for screen exposure. An orange film called Amberlith® is also available and is easier to see through when cutting overlays. However, the red film works better because it blocks more UV rays during screen exposure.

Photomasking film is available from all art stores and is a standard item used throughout the graphic arts industry.

Technical Pens

Technical pens are available as either an ink cartridge-loading type or a refillable cartridge. The tips are unusual in the respect that they are not pointed, but flat, round circles (**1.7**). Very narrow through very wide tips are available. The major advantage of using a technical pen is uniform ink deposit.

1.3 A T-square, good drawing board and triangle templates are the basis of a good art department.

1.4 A circle compass can be used with a technical pen or felt tip pen to draw circles. It can also be used with a razor knife to cut circles in red overlay film.

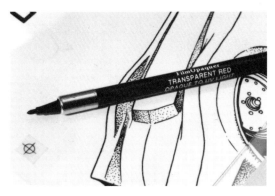

1.5 An opaquing pen or film opaquer is a must for drawing on film and touching up artwork. (Photo courtesy Mark-Tex Co., Englewood, NJ.)

1.6 Photomasking film is used for tracing, to hand-cut overlays and when masking around areas for perfect color overlays. It is sold by the roll or by the sheet.

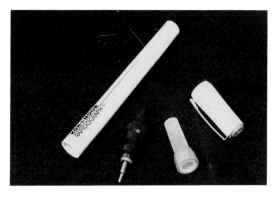

1.7 Techical pens are precision drawing pens that can be used to make very accurate lines at specific widths.

Once you are experienced with these pens, they will probably be quicker and easier to work with than pen and ink. The major disadvantages of working with technical pens are clogging and the general inconvenience of working with a wet surface. (It's so easy to accidentally smear wet ink.)

If necessary, you can scrape away mistakes (ink blobs, crooked lines, etc.) with a razor knife after the ink has dried.

Clear Acetate

Clear acetate is exactly what it sounds like: a sheet of clear plastic film that is resistant to fluid spills (ink, water, etc.). You can purchase acetate at art supply stores in flat sheets or rolls. Flat sheets are easier to work with and allow you to buy only the amount that you need. For general use, such as applying cut-out letters, the most inexpensive acetate will work well. For tracing, use frosted acetate since it accepts and holds ink better than the clear variety. Before you buy, ask the salesperson what types of acetate they carry and the best use for each.

1.8 A variety of halftone screen tints and special texture sheets can be used to add interest and depth to a design.

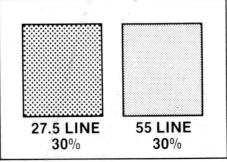

27.5 LINE
30%

55 LINE
30%

1.9 Large dots are easier to expose on a screen. Both of these dot patterns are 30% but the one on the left is 27.5 lines (dots) and easier to expose than the right 55 line halftone dot pattern.

Art Aids

Guideboard

Before beginning the different applications of basic lettering, it is most useful to have a lettering aid called a guideboard.

A guideboard generally consists of a piece of cardboard or a drawing paper that has circles and grids marked off to make basic layout easier. Some brands of artist's vellum have a guideboard printed on the cover sheet.

You can make the board yourself. A compass, T-square, triangle, ruler, paper and clear shelf paper for covering is all that's needed. Measure carefully as you are working. The circles can be in ½ in., ¾ in. or 1 in. increments. Vertical and horizontal lines are also fine in these same increments. After the guideboard is finished glue it to a sturdy piece of posterboard or thin cardboard and cover it with clear shelf paper to protect against ink spills, tape, etc.

A guideboard won't be used for all lettering methods, but it will see a lot of use for basic straight line copy and for arching words and doing circle text. With many methods, the guideboard will allow copy to be centered by sight, provide nice arches above or below a design and keeps lettering good and straight.

Borders, Decorations, Halftone Screen Tints and Textures

Add a little interest to designs with any of the great borders, flourishes, halftone screen tints and textures (**1.8**). These nice finishing touches are made by most of the lettering companies, and are available at art supply stores.

Flourishes, halftone screen tints and textures are usually printed just like the cut-out lettering and used the same way. Just cut lightly, peel it off the backing sheet and apply to the artwork. You can use all of these decorations on clear acetate (they are opaque enough to expose a screen), a film positive of the artwork, vellum paper or add them to any work you've done on drawing paper.

Use the halftones to add shading and depth to a design. Be aware that air-dry inks will clog in the screen easily when printing designs with halftones. Clogging is no problem when using plastisol ink.

A fairly large dot, such as Formatt style #7002 (27.5 line) (**1.9**) will be easier to print than a smaller dot. You can also do irregular shading by hand with pen and ink or a felt-tip pen. Give it a try!

Relationship of Artwork to the Screen Stencil

Before we talk about how to do artwork, it is helpful to understand how the art is used to make the printing stencil. In this book, as in the professional screen printing shop, we will deal mainly with photographic stencil making. In-home shops can also utilize photostencil techniques to achieve results that are superior to old-fashioned hand-cut stencils.

Artwork should be prepared so that it can easily be converted into a medium that is used to make the printing stencil. You can prepare simple artwork using manual techniques and materials that do not need to be converted before making the printing stencil such as just drawing a design on a piece of clear acetate. Other, more complicated artwork will need to be changed to the correct format before it can be used to make the printing stencil. This may require doing a special camera shot or scanning the artwork into the computer.

The following section will give you a brief overview of the screen making process. This process is covered in detail in Chapter 2.

What is a Photostencil?

A photostencil is a stencil created by exposing an image onto a screen that has a light sensitive coating.

Photostencil materials come in two forms: *direct emulsions* and *capillary direct films.* Direct emulsion is a liquid form of photostencil material, Capillary direct film is a clear "plastic" backing sheet that is coated with photosensitized emulsion. To use direct emulsion, you coat it directly onto the screen fabric (**1.10**). Capillary film is adhered to the fabric with water (**1.11**).

Exposing or "Burning" a Screen

Photographic emulsions are sensitive to light sources containing ultraviolet (UV) rays. These UV rays "expose" the photographic materials just as the emulsion on the film of a 35mm camera is exposed when the lens opens to take a picture and lets light in.

Sunlight contains an abundance of UV light compared to some plant "grow-lights" and photoflood bulbs that produce much smaller amounts of UV output. Professional screen-exposing units also contain light sources that are high in UV output such as mercury vapor lamps (street lights) and metal halide lights (warehouse lighting).

How Does the Artwork Create the Stencil?

The artwork, providing it meets photostencil requirements, is placed directly onto the emul-

1.10 Direct emulsions are light sensitive liquids that are coated on a screen.

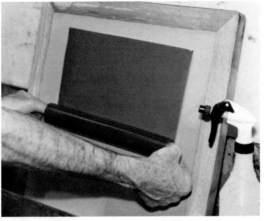

1.11 Capillary direct films are similar to direct emulsions except they consist of a clear carrier sheet with the coating already on it. They are adhered or "applied" to the screen with water.

1.12 A screen can be exposed from anything that will keep UV light from hitting the photostencil material. You can even use your hand!

sion-coated screen and exposed to a light source that contains UV rays. Wherever the emulsion receives light, it becomes exposed. Exposed emulsion becomes water *resistant;* areas that were shielded from the light are not exposed and remain water *soluble.*

To simplify this, let's consider an example (**1.12**). If you were to place your hand over the emulsion on a screen, and go into the sunlight for 20 seconds, the light would hit (and expose) all of the emulsion *around* your hand, but your hand would prevent the emulsion *underneath* it from receiving light. The emulsion *under* your hand would *not be exposed* and would therefore be *water soluble and wash away when rinsed with water.* The emulsion that received light, however, would remain on the fabric because it had been exposed and became water resistant. This would create an open stencil in the shape of a hand that ink could now pass through.

What Type of Artwork Works?

With this knowledge, you can see that any material that prevents light from passing through it could actually be used to create an image on the screen - from your hand to black electrical tape to coins! However, not too many jobs will have such simple art requirements!

Actually, to be technically correct, a material does not have to prevent all *light* from passing through, but rather has to *block all UV transmission.* Some materials (such as your hand in the previous example) block all light and therefore all

1.13 A simple "film positive" can be made by drawing on a piece of clear acetate with an opaquing pen.

1.14 You can even expose a screen from the vellum printout of a laser printer or copier.

1.15 Artwork can be made into a film positive with a process camera.

UV; other materials, such as Rubylith, *will* allow light to pass through but blocks UV transmission.

To create a stencil, in addition to the art material's ability to block UV transmission, the emulsion surrounding the artwork must be free to receive light as in the hand example. This means that you cannot simply draw a design on heavy white paper and try to expose it on a screen. The result would be an unevenly washed-out area in the shape of the paper. This is because drawing paper is generally dense enough to filter out a good portion of the UV rays, preventing the emulsion from becoming exposed. *Remember, unexposed emulsion is water soluble* and will wash away when water is applied.

Converting Artwork

Sometimes artwork is fairly simple and can be prepared using materials that already meet the photostencil requirements (screen-ready materials). For instance, if you draw on clear acetate with an opaque marker, this artwork can be used to make the stencil (**1.13**).

Computer-generated art can vary from simple to highly detailed, and if printed on vellum paper with a high quality laser printer, can be used for screen exposure (**1.14**).

Often, designs might be too complicated to be produced by hand with screen-ready materials. For example, you might need to work with a pen and ink drawing on a heavy white drawing paper. Or perhaps a customer will supply an existing logo on a business card or letterhead! You must convert this type of art before it can be used to make the stencil.

By converting it, we mean changing it to a solid, dense format on a clear or transparent carrier. This is quite different from a pen and ink drawing on white paper. Typically, artwork is converted to the right form for screen exposure by having it made into a film positive (**1.15**) at a graphic arts camera house, or by scanning it into a computer and printing it out on vellum paper or a clear receiver. Other methods are also used, although they are either slower, more difficult or don't produce great photostencils without taking extra steps. Some of these techniques include tracing the artwork with materials that meet the photostencil requirements and using overhead transparency film in a copy machine.

Lettering

Although the easiest way to create basic lettering and designs is with the help of a computer graphics system, we will examine how to create artwork using traditional methods first, since some of you may not have access to a computer system.

Using Cut-Out Letters

1.16 There are hundreds of type styles and sizes available in cut-out letters.

1. Cut around the letter lightly. Do not cut into the backing sheet.

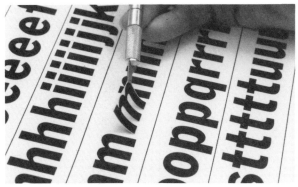

2. Lift the letter off the backing sheet with your knife blade.

3. Apply the letter to artwork, clear acetate or vellum paper.

Cut-Out Letters

Cut-out letters are printed on a transparent, self-sticking film which is adhered to a smooth-coated carrier sheet (**1.16**).

Hundreds of different styles and sizes are available and can be found at any art supply store. Pick up a copy of each company's catalog so you'll have instant reference to the different lettering styles. When purchasing them, buy different styles and letter sizes. Formatt® and Artype® are both good brands (see Appendix A). The average cost of these letters is $4.00 to $7.00 per sheet.

Burnish Letters

Burnish letters are rubbed or burnished directly onto the paper. They can crack during use and cannot be repositioned after placement.

The lettering methods in this chapter deal with cut-out letters rather than the burnished type because we've found that cut-out letters are much easier and quicker to use and have a multitude of other advantages.

Using Cut-Out Lettering

To use cut-out letters, lightly cut a small square around the letter, just deep enough to go through the translucent film layer but not hard enough to cut through the carrier backing sheet. Lift the letter off the backing paper with the tip of the blade and place it on the artwork (**1.17**).

Cut-out letters can be applied to any of the art receiver materials such as drawing paper, graph paper, vellum, clear or frosted acetate, stripped Rubylith® and film positives. If the letters are applied to transparent materials such as clear or frosted acetate, thin vellum, film positives or stripped Rubylith®, you can use the artwork to expose the printing stencil without converting it to a film positive.

Lettering on Papers

Place each letter of the word on graph paper or white paper that has been marked with guidelines in non-reproducing blue pen or pencil. Work from left to right, keeping the letters spaced closely together. After laying out all the words, cut them apart and put them in the correct position.

1.17 Cut-out letters are still used if you don't have access to a computer graphics system.

Glue the words on drawing paper that has been marked with non-reproducing blue pencil or another piece of graph paper (**1.18**). Use rubber cement since it will allow you to reposition the words. Space letters closely for a neat and professional look.

Lettering on Clear Acetate or Vellum Paper

You can do direct layout on clear acetate or vellum paper and go right to exposing a screen if you have the exact size of lettering the design requires and the design is not too complicated. Cut-out letters work well for this and require no artwork conversion before screen exposure.

To letter directly on clear acetate, simply lay a piece of acetate or vellum paper over the guideboard or a sheet of paper that has been marked with guidelines and layout the lettering.

1.18 Paste-up is still a valid technique in the art department.

Film Letters

Expect a little trouble finding cut-out letters that are large enough for direct layout. Cut-out letters come in large sizes, but often a design will require even bigger letters than are available, especially when dealing with athletic work. If your shop is located in a rural area or you simply do not have access to a graphic arts process camera or computer, it might be advisable for you to make a set of film letters. You can do this by enlarging cut-out lettering using a process camera and transferring the image to film.

After the films are made, cut the letters apart with scissors, trimming very close at the sides. This will allow the letters to be placed very closely together without overlapping. Leave a ¼ in. tab at the top to allow for taping the letters in place.

To use film letters, position them on clear acetate that has been placed over the guideboard. Tape them in place with clear tape at the top of each letter (**1.19**). One of the main advantages of film letters is that they can be used over and over again. After you have exposed the design, remove the letters from the acetate and file them for future use.

1.19 Film letters can be used on simple lettering jobs and are easily made by making film positives of cut-out lettering sheets.

Art Sources

Clip-art

One of the best sources of good artwork is *clip-art books* (**1.20**), which are available at art stores and screen printing supply companies or can be purchased from various clip-art services (see Appendix A). These books contain page after page of professional stock artwork and cover almost every subject imaginable. It's like having a complete art department at your fingertips! Clip-art books are copyright free and add a professional touch to your work.

Most clip art books are also available on computer disk and CD-ROM for easy access with a computer graphic system.

With the exception of clip-art books, beware of infringing on copyrighted material. If you have a question on legality, definitely consult a lawyer. Stealing and unauthorized use of artwork or designs is a legal and ethical no-no!

Tracing

Whether or not you have art talent, you can produce artwork through the wonderful world of tracing. Tracing is perfectly acceptable and should not be thought of as anything less! There are certain jobs where tracing may be the only way to provide customers with the artwork they want.

All professional artists have a library of reference material that they use for ideas and to trace from. If the customer wants a rose on a shirt you can easily find a rose in a gardening magazine

and do a simple tracing from it.

Maybe their logo is very small and will not englarge without becoming ragged. You can make an enlargement in your copier and then trace the logo to clean it up.

Tracing on Acetate

Tracing on acetate is not easy, but it can be done with an opaquing pen or a technical pen with black acetate ink. You normally trace on acetate if you don't have a camera and want to expose a screen directly from the tracing.

Place the article or artwork to be traced under a sheet of clear acetate and tape it securely in place. As mentioned earlier, an acetate that is frosted on one side will be easier to trace on. Make sure the frosted side receives the ink.

When finished, untape the acetate and hold it up to the light. The tracing should be uniform in relation to the amount of ink laid down. Be sure there is a solid layer of ink (either acetate ink or opaquing pen) with no thin spots showing through. If part of an area is dense and another part is thin it won't produce a very good screen. Again, this method is only for simple designs, and remember that the screen can be exposed from artwork done with these materials.

Drawing/Tracing with Rubylith

While working on clear acetate has its place, you may find that working on Rubylith® is faster, cleaner and easier, and produces a better quality stencil. Often, two techniques are used for tracing on Rubylith; larger areas are actually cut rather than drawn, and after the surrounding film is

1.20 Clip-art can make anyone an artist. There is a wide variety of artwork available in books and on computer disks and CD ROMS. (Book courtesy U.S. Screen Printing Institute, Tempe, AZ., CD-ROM courtesy Smart Designs, Tempe, AZ.)

1.21 Simple designs can be cut out of red overlay film and then used to immediately expose a screen.

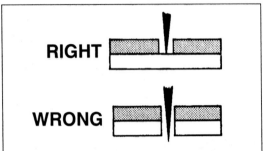

1.22 Red overlay film consists of a red top coating on a clear carrier sheet. To cut the top layer do not use too much knife pressure or you will cut through the backing sheet.

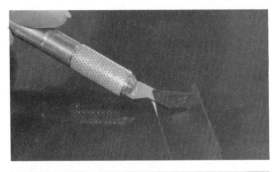

1.23 Lay the knife blade low to slip it under the film easily.

1.24 You are actually making a mechanical "film positive" with red overlay film. When peeling, you want to peel the red film around the image area.

peeled away, finer detail is added by hand with an opaquing pen or pen and ink.

Notice that the clear acetate backing is very shiny, while the red film side is dull. Make sure that you work on the dull red film side.

For practice, cut a few shapes into the film (**1.21**). Use light but even pressure when cutting just enough to go through the film but not through the clear backing. Putting too much pressure on the knife will cause you to cut through the film

and the clear backing sheet. Too little pressure will make a noticeable line in the film, but not cut deeply enough to actually penetrate the red film (**1.22**).

After cutting the area, slip the tip of the razor knife blade under it and lift it off the backing sheet (**1.23**). If you cut with the right amount of pressure, the red film will lift off the backing sheet and leave a clear area surrounded by a field of red film. Try several more shapes to get the feel of it.

Next, take another piece of the film and cut a "T" in it. Peeling off the film that surrounds the "T" should leave a red "T" surrounded by a field of clear backing. When working with photomasking films, it's important to remember that the areas to be printed with ink are cut on the film and *left in place* - and the *surrounding* film is peeled off (**1.24**).

These are the same techniques you will use to cut multicolor overlays later on in this chapter.

A Word About Vellum Paper

Vellum paper is a pleasure to work with compared to acetate, graph or regular drawing paper. It is inexpensive and produces a sharp edge to lines when used for drawing. It is transparent enough that it can be used to expose a screen if the image is dark and dense.

Although vellum is a great paper to draw on, because it is fairly transparent, the ink from the opaquing pen or technical pen may not leave a dense enough image to really block all the light when exposing a screen.

You may need to make a camera shot before you can expose the copy onto the screen. You can expose a screen directly from the vellum copy, but only if the lines are solid and opaque, the design is not too detailed, the art is done on one page (not traced, cut out and applied), the screen has been coated evenly (we'll get to screen coating soon!) and luck is on your side!

As you've already heard and will continue to hear throughout this book, *you will have to experiment!* Go ahead and try exposing a screen from the vellum copy. It won't take long before you're capable of deciding what art will make a good screen and what won't. Don't forget that in this section we are talking about the problems of exposing a screen from a hand-drawn vellum. It is *very* common to use vellum paper that has been processed in a laser printer or copier to expose a screen because the toner deposit is fairly dense.

Tracing from a Photograph

Often, your customer's artwork may be in the form of a photograph. You can create an excellent design from a photograph by having it reproduced as a halftoned film positive (changing it to small

dots that you can expose on a screen) or by simply converting the photograph to a "line drawing" (like a coloring-book drawing) using tracing techniques (**1.25**). You can then add spot colors and print a similar looking design on a shirt. Tracing a photograph is difficult at first, but a few tricks make it easier. Your first tracing attempt will probably look very plain or very cluttered.

Slip the photograph under a sheet of vellum and secure it in place. After taking a good look at the object to be traced, trace the basic outline first, using a non-reproducing blue pen or pencil. If you are going to do a camera shot of the drawing the camera shot will *not* reproduce the light blue because of the type of special film that is used. If you plan to make a laser or copier copy of the design then use a very light pencil that can be erased later.

If the lines look good, go over them with a medium-width felt-tip marker. Felt-tip markers are the best type of pens to use for this task. You may have to eliminate or add some detail depending on how detailed the photograph is to begin with. A good rule to follow is to put as much detail as possible in the design but don't overload it. Leaving out a little detail is better than a cluttered, busy or heavy design.

For ideas on tracing, look at designs of race cars to see how the artist adds reflections, highlights and other subtleties to a simple tracing to make them look real.

Tracing from a photograph can be used for almost any design from race cars, boats, animals, and flowers to pictures of people. You'll be surprised at how good you become as a tracing artist!

Camera Work

Although you can expose a screen using a design produced on a transparent film or vellum paper from a copy machine or laser printer, using a camera-made a film positive (**1.26**) is a more traditional method. A film positive is made using a "process camera" that creates a sharp, dense image on clear film (**1.27**).

Process cameras have been an essential piece of equipment for many screen printing shops, but are now slowly being replaced by computer graphics systems and laser printers that print dense black images on film.

Most large shops have both pieces of equipment. They use their computer system to create the design and then use their camera to create a

1.25 You'll be surprised at how good you can be as a tracing artist when converting a photograph into a line drawing.

1.26 A film or paper positive of the artwork is made with a process camera.

1.27 Process cameras are still widely used but are being replaced by the power of compter graphic systems and laser printers.

film positive. Smaller shops sometimes use either vellum or an overhead transparency to make a simple stencil and send their more difficult or large designs to an outside service to shoot the film positives.

The "PMT" Process

The most economical type of film positives are made with "diffusion transfer" materials. This process is often referred to as *PMT*. PMT is a Kodak trademark that stands for *photo mechanical transfer*. This process uses an inexpensive paper negative that produces a positive image on either film or paper in *one* camera shot. Sometimes camera shots are called "stats" or "veloxes."

To find a source for your film positives, contact your local offset printer (the ones who do letterhead, brochures, etc.) first. They can normally do camera shots for you or refer you to someone who does. Many times, a blueprint company offers camera shots.

You can expect to pay from $6-$10 for an 11 x 14 in. film positive. Most camera shops will be able to do shots up to 20 x 24 in. for you.

Make sure the camera shop you choose uses the diffusion transfer process. It is much cheaper than the conventional method printers use to make a *negative* first and then a positive from the negative.

Using a Copy Machine

One alternative to making a film positive is to make an overhead transparency of the artwork on a standard copy machine. Since overhead transparency material is clear, a good copy machine will render a dense black image that will expose a respectable screen. Most copiers can also enlarge and reduce artwork, and the cost for this kind of film is less than $1. You can also use a copier to make paper enlargements and reductions for paste-up.

If you don't have a copier, there are local copy services in most towns. In fact, their larger copiers can make bigger enlargements than most business copiers.

Using Vellum Paper

Another alternative is to use special vellum paper that is designed for a copier or laser printer. This is generally a 17 lb. vellum paper that is available from many blueprint supply companies and screen printing and computer graphic suppliers. Don't expect your local office supply to carry vellum paper (or even know what it is)!

Vellum paper will actually give a smoother, and often more opaque black image, than overhead transparencies and is very widely used to expose screens. However, it is very important to use a copier or laser printer that lays down a heavy amount of toner. Certain laser printer and copiers only put down a thin deposit of toner and it may be necessary to make *two* copies of the artwork and actually expose the screen using *both* copies stacked together!

Another tip to make the toner darker is to run a printed vellum through your shirt dryer or place it under a flash heater for a few seconds. The black will actually get darker! You can also spray the vellum with a matte fixative spray (available from all art stores) to make the image darker.

When exposing screens using a design on vellum, you may need to increase the exposure time. Do *not* use vellum when you're trying to expose very fine detail or fine halftone screen tints. Of course, most copiers and laser printers will only print in sizes 8½ x 14 in. Therefore, you may need to tape parts of images together (also called "tiling") to make the design large enough.

Overhead Transparency Film

Overhead transparency copies film is available for your copier or from local copy services. It is generally used with an overhead projector for sales presentations, meetings, etc.

Although it would appear that these would be better "films" than a paper vellum, they are not very dense in large block areas of copy and the image is not durable enough to take much handling.

If you must use an overhead transparency as your film positive, try printing two copies and stacking them together to give you a very dense image that will expose the screen better than just one light image. This technique also works with vellum if your copier doesn't put enough toner on the paper!

Art: The Final Check

Before making a camera shot or transparency of a design, be sure the artwork is neat and clean. Scrape ragged areas with a razor knife or cover them with typewriter correction fluid (**1.28**). If correction fluid is used, the art must be converted even if screen-ready materials (acetate, Rubylith, etc.) were used to prepare the art.

Don't worry about all the lines you'll have when pasting different parts of the design together if you are going to do a camera shot. The film used in the camera process is sensitive to black and white areas only. This means that the "gray" area, or lines formed when pasting-up artwork will not show when making a camera shot. This black and white artwork is called "line art."

It is common to lay out each item in a piece of artwork separately and then paste it all in place. When you make a camera shot, the lines where these have been pieced together will not appear. The only thing that does is what the camera sees as solid, black areas.

Unfortunately, a copy machine or scanner may "see" these cut marks and paste-up marks. If you are going to copy scanned artwork, it will need to be a little cleaner than for a process camera shot.

Professional Touches

When having an outside service shoot artwork, you will tell them what size of enlargement or reduction the artwork needs. This figure is always calculated as a percentage (**1.29**). You can purchase a simple percentage wheel or proportional scale from an art store. Both items convert the size of enlargement or reduction to a percentage. For example, if a design is going to be the same size, it is shot at 100%. If a design is going to be twice the original size, it is shot at 200%.

After you figure the correct percentage, write it in a corner in non-reproducing pen or pencil - and don't forget to specify if it's a PMT film positive or a PMT print. To be professional, tape or rubber cement the artwork to posterboard or cardboard and tape a cover sheet over the artwork to protect it. Write your company's name and phone number on the back. This will guard against loss and the camera operator can reach you easily if there are any questions.

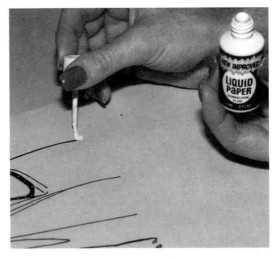

1.28 White-out correction fluid can be used to clean-up designs and cover any unwanted areas.

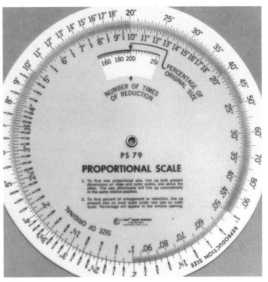

1.29 A proportional scale or percentage wheel is used to find the correct percentage of enlargement or reduction for a design.

Checking the Final Films

The finished film positives, vellums or copier transparencies may require some clean up before you expose them on a screen. Hold them up to a light and check for black specks, smudges and ragged edges. These can be scraped away with a razor knife. A light table is very useful when checking the quality of your final "films."

Check the copy area (black area) to be sure all black parts are evenly dark, with no light spots or scratches. If some areas don't look dark enough or are scratched, go over them carefully with an opaquing pen.

Remember, the art on the film positive is exactly what will be printed on the garment. If it looks clean and neat, so will the printed garment.

1.30 For multicolor artwork, each color to be printed is created separately, including the "outline" color.

Multicolor Overlays

Up until now we've been talking about artwork for one-color printing. After you've printed one-color designs, it's time to go on to the real fun: *Multicolor artwork!* Don't let multicolor confuse you. If you just focus on the fact that a multicolor print is nothing more than a number of *one-color* prints, it will make it easier to understand.

For practical purposes, this section will deal with four-color work, but it will also show you how to get a lot more than four colors in a design when printing with only four colors of ink!

Multicolor printing is going to require multicolor artwork, right? *Wrong!* So don't sit down and draw a nice design filled with all those rainbow colors. In multicolor printing, each color, including the black artwork, is drawn or created separately (**1.30**)!

Spot-Color and Overprinting

Often, a design will be printed as a simple spot-color design. This is where separate colors of ink are printed next to each other, as in figure **1.31.**

Other times, the printing technique will incorporate "overprinting" inks directly on top of one another to create more colors (**1.32**).

Inks are overprinted to produce extra colors - called *"Secondary Colors."* You will overprint inks when the design requires more colors than you can print with your press.

A Word about Color

Here is the fun part. Primary ink colors are red, black, blue and yellow. When you print two primary colors on top of each other you get a secondary color. Basically, we will concern ourselves with how to make secondary colors (i.e., blue + yellow = green, red + yellow = orange, red + blue = purple, red + yellow + blue = brown.).

The important thing to remember is that the ink must be transparent for this to work. Also, this overlaying is only recommended for light-colored shirts (yellow, blue, white, tan, etc.). Using transparent ink on dark shirts will *not* produce good work.

At first, design the artwork using only these colors: black, red, blue, yellow, purple, green, orange and brown.

Later on, as you get more experienced you will try printing halftone screen tints to achieve different *shades* of primary and secondary colors. You can create very nice effects by mixing halftones. *Experiment!* Also, analyze other people's work. You can learn a lot from looking closely at designs in stores!

1.31 Spot colors are generally colors that are printed as solid areas of ink on a design as in this two-color print.

1.32 This design has "spot colors" that have been overprinted in certain areas to achieve "secondary" colors. This design is printed with just four colors of ink.

Creating Color Overlays

In multicolor printing, you will need a piece of film or artwork for *each color to be printed* (**1.33**). These are generally called "color overlays." You can create color overlays manually or by computer. Although computers are widely used, hand-cut overlays are still used to create many designs because of the size limitation of the laser printer.

Trap Color

The first step in making color overlays is to create the design using one of the previously mentioned methods (lettering on paper, lettering on acetate, ink on vellum, etc.) and have it made into a film positive, vellum, overhead transparency, etc. This "film" positive counts as one of the colors to be printed (usually in black ink). In multicolor work, the film positive is often referred to as the "*trap color*" if the artwork is to be *filled-in* with other colors. This is because it is used as the guide to "trap" or "outline" the other colors printed.

Cutting Color Overlays

The next colors are cut separately with a razor knife from photomasking film which is often referred to as *"Ruby."* This separate piece of artwork is called an "overlay." Each color to be printed requires one overlay of this film.

Cutting Overlays to a Trap Color

Before we go further, take a good look at the original film positive of the design and decide what color will go where.

The next step is to decide how close of a cut your four-color press can handle. If it will hold tight registration, cut the overlays close to the inside edge (**1.34**) of the line. If it does not hold precision registration, cut the overlays a little more to the center (**1.35**) or outside of the line.

The best overlays are perfectly cut to the inside edge of the outline. This is called *"butt-cutting."* When using this method, the overlay is cut flush with the very inside edge of the outline and the press must be able to hold good registration.

Butt-cut overlays print better because other ink color under the trap color is minimized. The prints will be much sharper and you will *not have to flash-cure* as often.

Butt-cutting the overlays will help maintain sharp multicolor prints throughout the entire job and will help minimize the problem of ink buildup, which will be discussed in the "*Printing*" chapter.

1.33 Overlays are created for each color that is going to be printed.

1.34 If your press will hold tight registration, cut the overlay right to the edge or with a very slight overlap into the trap or black outline.

1.35 If your printing press is a little sloppy or you can't hold tight registration, then cut the overlay with an overlap over the outline color. This will allow for any slight out-of-register you may get when you print the job.

Let's Get Started

The film positive is usually for the black outline and referred to as the "trap" or "keyline" color as mentioned earlier. That leaves three colors to go for a four-color design. Cut three pieces of the masking film each as large as the design. One piece will be for the red ink overlay, one for yellow ink and one for the blue ink.

In this example, we will be cutting overlays for a design that will use transparent inks and overprint colors to achieve secondary colors. We can also use halftones to produce different shades of colors.

Tape a piece of regular drawing paper to the drawing board and then tape the film positive over it. To line up the overlays, place registration targets at the top, bottom and on the side on the film positive or vellum (**1.36**).

Next, tape a piece of the masking film over the film positive. Be sure the film has the dull red side up. Now, you're going to use the underlying

1.36 Registration targets are placed on the film positive ~~or~~ vellum.

1.37 The overlay for blue ink will represent areas to print as blue, green, purple and brown.

1.36

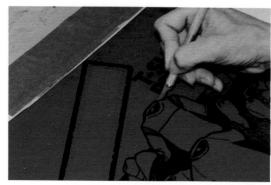

1.37

1.38 The film surrounding the art areas is peeled away.

1.39 The red film represents areas of solid color. Apply halftones and textures after the overlay has been stripped of the surrounding film.

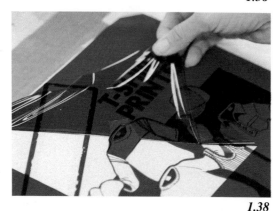

1.38

1.39

1.40 Detail can be added with an opaquing pen.

1.41 Using the targets on the film positive as a placement guide, place new targets on the overlay.

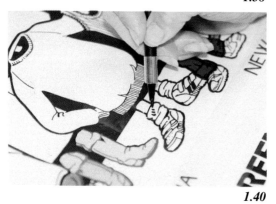

1.40

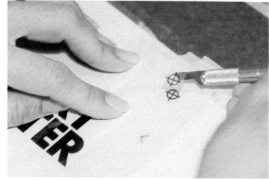

1.41

artwork much the same way as a coloring book design. But instead of coloring it in, you're going to cut *around* the area to be "colored."

Let's make the overlay for blue ink first. You will cut around all areas where you want to print blue ink and all areas where blue will need to be overprinted to achieve secondary colors. So, you will cut all areas to appear as blue, green, purple and brown (**1.37**). Remember, to make a perfect overlay you should cut just to the *inside* edge of the outline.

Work Carefully

When you're finished cutting, peel off all film from the *surrounding* area (**1.38**). You can now use halftone screen tints to give you different shades of color (**1.39**), and you can even draw on the overlay with an opaquing pen for added detail or simply use an opaquing pen for touch-up (**1.40**).

Now, put registration targets on this overlay, using the targets underneath, that were placed on the film positive as a guide (**1.41**). Then, in a corner, write the color of ink to be used. Many shops actually place the job name, ink color, color sequence and mesh count on each overlay. This information will be exposed on the screen so that everyone knows how the job should print. It is then taped over before the production run begins. Leave the first overlay in place.

Next, tape another piece of photomasking film over the film positive and your first overlay (**1.42**). This next overlay can be for yellow ink. Cut all areas to be printed with yellow ink - this means all areas to print as yellow, green, orange and brown. Then strip away the *surrounding* film (**1.43**). Next, place registration targets just as you did on the first overlay.

Following the same procedures, cut the overlay for red ink (**1.44**). On this overlay cut all areas

1.42

1.44

1.43

1.45

1.42 *A new piece of film is secured over the first overlay.*

1.43 *The overlay for yellow ink represents all the areas to be printed as yellow, green, orange and brown.*

1.44 *The overlay for red ink represents all the areas to be printed as red, orange, purple and brown.*

1.45 *The finished work is examined carefully.*

to appear as red, purple, orange and brown. Strip away the surrounding film and place registration targets just as you did on the first and second overlay.

Since you have left all the overlays in place over the film positive, you can now examine each overlay to see how they line up to each other (**1.45**).

Double Check

Examine all overlays to be sure that you cut the right area for each color and remove any pieces of the red film that might have clung to the backing.

If you have accidentally cut away areas that are supposed to be printed, you can remedy this problem in one of two ways. Cut a patch from a piece of masking film using just the red film (not the plastic backing), stick it over the area and recut it or use an opaquing pen to ink-in the area (**1.46**). You already know from *"Tracing on Acetate"* that it will still make a good screen.

Perfect Overlays

For the best print quality you should create perfect overlays. These are ones that have no color under other colors and are butt-cut with color-next-to-color (you can put color-on-color where necessary to create other colors but do not put any color under black). This is called *under color removal*, and will keep your prints very sharp when printing wet-ink on wet-ink.

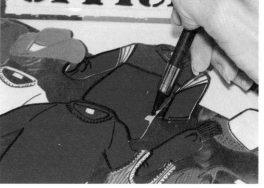

1.46

1.46 *Correct errors by filling in the area with an opaquing pen or by using a patch of red overlay film.*

This means that even areas with small lines on the black or fine detail should not have any color underneath. It is to difficult to cut around each and every little dot or fine line just to remove any color that might print under the black ink. There is a special product called Fotostrip® (made by the Autotype Company) that can be used to make "perfect overlays."

It is basically a light sensitive overlay film that can be exposed on your screen exposure unit and washed out with water just like screen making.

After exposure, you have created a perfect negative of the design that can be peeled and drawn on just like red overlay filmand cut if necessary. A negative of a design area is a perfect overlay for that design area!

Since Fotostrip is harder to peel than standard red overlay film, it is much easier to create a red

Stack the film positive, the mask and Fotostrip.

Wash out with water after exposure.

Spray on UV block, rinse and let dry.

The final perfect overlay.

1.47 Fotostrip is great for making perfect overlays without color under black.

overlay film mask around the area you are trying to make a perfect overlay for and then expose the film. The mask will block the light from hitting the Fotostrip around the image and will produce a perfect overlay of just the area you want to remain (**1.47**).

Using Halftone Screen Tints and Textures

Halftone screen tints and textures are easy to use: just cut an area larger than needed, lift it off the backing paper, apply it to the art and trim away the excess (**1.48**).

Halftones can be applied directly to a film positive, vellum, acetate and other materials. If they are used on overlays, you will *not* cut the red film over areas where the halftones are to be applied. This is because the halftones are applied directly to the clear backing. Apply them after the areas to receive solid color are cut and the entire overlay is stripped of the *surrounding* film.

Halftone dots are popular because they are sold in a variety of sizes and percentages. You can mix different size dots on overlays and print

"dots-on-dots" to create shades of other colors.

The size of dot is referred to as the line count. The line count is the number of dots per inch. Dot sheets are also specified by the percentage of coverage. You can see from figure **1.49** that a smaller percentage is a smaller dot and a higher line count is a smaller dot.

It is best to stay with low line counts (32.5) and medium percentages (20% to 60%) when first starting because it is hard to expose smaller dots on the screen.

The same number system applies to halftones generated by the computer. Line count is also called "frequency" in computer graphics.

Using Halftones on Multicolor Overlays

Halftone dots are great on multicolor overlays because of all the additional colors you can create. It is hard to know what colors you will achieve when using dots on overlays. It is almost a guessing game when you put a 30% royal blue dot on top of a 50% scarlet red dot. What shade of purple will you get?

1.48 Screens and textures are applied, trimmed to the proper area and the excess peeled away.

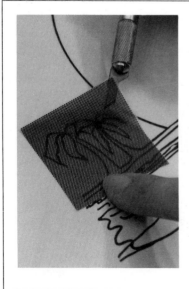

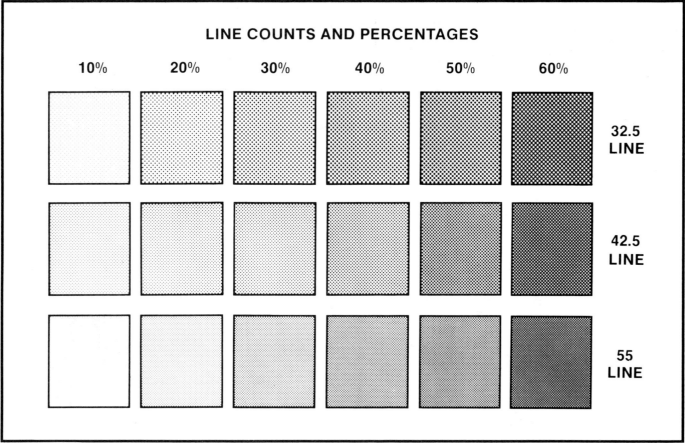

LINE COUNTS AND PERCENTAGES

10%   20%   30%   40%   50%   60%

32.5 LINE

42.5 LINE

55 LINE

1.49

Artist's Color Guide

There is a tool available called the Artist's Color Guide (**1.50**) that allows you to determine what colors you will get when overprinting dots-on-dots.

The Color Guide consists of a set of four film positives with halftone dots ranging from 10% to 80% for the four primary colors. When the guide is printed in *your* shop with *your* screens you can see how to achieve over 600 color combinations - with just four colors of ink!

Mixing Various Techniques

Don't be afraid to mix the various art techniques in this chapter. For example, lettering can be done directly on a film positive if all the customer wants is his logo and a slogan around it. To do this, make a positive of the logo, lay it on the guideboard and place cut-out, or film letters directly on it.

You can also tape different film positives together and a expose a screen from the composite films. This will occur when you enlarge a logo to one size and lettering to another size. Make a camera shot of each and tape them together to make the final design.

A word of caution: Don't tape too many layers of acetate together in one spot. The *less con-*

tact the film positive has with the screen, the *less sharpness* the stencil will have. Each layer of acetate will keep the image area from making perfect contact during screen exposure!

1.50 The Artist's Color Guide is a useful tool in determining color combinations. (Photo courtesy U.S. Screen Printing Institute, Tempe, AZ.)

1.51 Dark shirts require special artwork and are generally printed with a number of colors and one or two flash-cures.

1.52 A Dark Shirt Printing Kit is available that teaches advanced dark shirt techniques from computer generated artwork to printing techniques. (Photo courtesy U.S. Screen Printing Institute, Tempe, AZ.)

1.53 Some jobs require an underbase print of white ink to make the colors on-top stand out from the shirt and be bright and opaque.

Special Artwork for Dark Shirts

This is a whole topic in itself and will be covered here only briefly. A dark shirt presents the problem of light colored prints not being opaque enough to stand out without an *underbase* or *underlay* of white ink.

Also, it is common to let the color of the shirt (black generally) be part of the design. This gives dark-shirt prints a softer feel.

Most great dark-shirt designs, such as sports and entertainment designs (**1.51**) are printed on automatic equipment using 8 to 12 colors of ink, and artwork is done using halftone dots and is created on the computer or in a process camera. That process is a little too complicated for this book but is covered thoroughly in a *Dark Shirt Printing Kit* available from the U.S. Screen Printing Institute in Tempe, AZ. This kit consists of four training videos, five computer work disks, an 80-page manual and sample shirts and films (**1.52**).

Underbase Techniques

The easiest way to print simple multicolor designs on dark shirts is to create all the color overlays as butt-cut or perfect overlays and print them with a high opacity ink and *don't* print the black outline. Let the shirt be the black in the design!

Since the colors may not be too bright this way, it is better to also print an underbase of white ink first (**1.53**) and then flash-cure it before printing the colors on top. You will need to create a piece of artwork for this underbase screen.

The simplest method to create an underbase is to stack all the color overlays together and have a *contact* camera shot made of the sandwiched

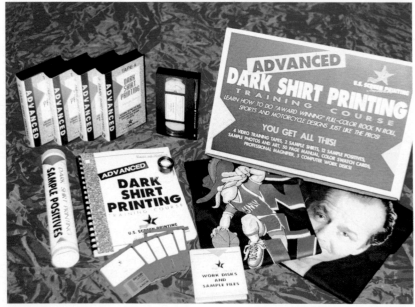

films. The new film will be black where ever there was an image on the overlays and you will basically have a single-piece underbase film that can be used to expose the screen.

Choking the Underbase

The problem with this method is that the underbase will be a perfect copy of all the films together. If you print this and then print colors on top, the top colors will have to be in *perfect* register to the white or else the white ink will show around the colors.

A common technique is where the underbase is made slightly *skinnier* or *thinner* than the top colors. This is not the same as reducing the artwork. You don't want the overall design smaller; you want it to have a thinner outline or thinner edge to it.

You can choke the underbase in the camera when doing the contact shot of all the overlays if you just tell the camera operator to choke the shot 1 or 2 points (**1.54**). This will give enough choke that you can be slightly out-of-register on the top colors and it won't be seen because they will *fall off* the underbase.

In computer graphics you can do the same thing by printing the color overlays with a 1 or 2 point outline thickness, and then, print the same overlays to be used as the underbase with *no* outline on them. Some programs actually ask if you want a choke when printing out the image.

Double Check It

This is it! The design is done and ready for the screen. But don't forget the most important step: *Checking your work!* If the design has lettering, look at the spelling. Are you sure it's correct? Maybe the customer should see the design. Customers have a way of telling you they want one thing and then saying it isn't exactly what they had in mind when they see the final product! If you have any doubts, ask the customer to initial an approval on the artwork.

Also check to see that the film positive is free of dirt and dust. These can show up later as pin-holes on the screen.

How about the overlays? Is all the masking film peeled off? Do they all line up?

Is the size of the design okay? If you are printing on children's shirts, the design should be small enough for them. If you have to print the same design on both children's and adult sizes perhaps two different size designs would work best.

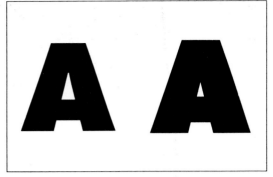

1.54 A choke is a slightly skinnier version of the artwork. The exaggerated choke on the left shows a 4 point reduction in the thickness of the outline of the letter on the right. A normal choke is only one or two points.

Hiring Artists

When first setting up shop, try to create as much of the artwork as possible yourself. If you have a computer graphics system, you should be able to create respectable designs with lettering and clip-art. Of course, the time will come when a customer will ask for an original design. If you have no real drawing talent, this could be a problem.

Believe it or not, there are a lot of artists available. Artists often have a hard time finding good jobs where they can use their talent, so many of them work other jobs and do art on the side.

Initially, try to steer clear of professional artists. Some professionals will charge $100 or more for a design - and neither you nor your customer can afford that! The time will come when some customers will be willing to pay a higher price for a good design, but use "semi-professional" artists for starters.

Where to Find Artists

Try your local college. Call art instructors to see if they can recommend a few good students. Many art students have good, raw talent! That is, they can draw, but you'll have to give them some directions as to what you want. If you find a student with real talent, hang on to him/her. As your company grows, there talents will grow with you. A talented student is sometimes better than an artist who thinks everything he/she does is a Rembrandt!!!

There are some pitfalls in dealing with artists that you should be aware of. Many artists come out of school and think they know it all. Sure, maybe they can do a nice watercolor, but when you ask them to cut an overlay, they say "what's an overlay?" What we are trying to say is that schools do not always teach people what they need to know in the "Real World" of commercial work! Don't assume that just because artists have-had schooling and has a nice portfolio that they can do layout, overlays or a quick cartoon!

1.55 Computer graphics system like this will do designs in just minutes with no previous computer experience necessary!

It is not uncommon to pay $500 to $1,000 or more for a great piece of artwork done by a "T-shirt" artist who will guarantee that the artwork will print well and look great on a shirt!

Where to Get Designs

If you have to generate your own artwork, look around for ideas. Go into stores and look at other printed shirts. Start to become aware of design, layout and lettering styles. Buy books on specific subjects. Your art store should have books on lettering, basic layout, drawing, etc.

Almost anything that can be photographed can be used for a design. In most cases, all the customer will have is a business card or letterhead with a logo on it. That's okay. You can enlarge a small logo to the needed size with just one or two camera shots.

Remember, the bigger the enlargement, the rougher the film positive will be! If you take a 1 sq. in. logo and enlarge it to 10 in. that's 1000%! The design will definitely need some clean-up to look sharp again.

Always try to get the largest and cleanest copy of the art possible. If the quality of the finished enlargement is really rough, try tracing from the enlargement. This will give you a clean piece of art to work from and will probably take less time than cleaning up the original enlargement!

Copyrighting Designs

Copyrighting a design is not as hard as you might think. Copyrighting and trade standards are covered in Chapter 11 on *The Business*.

Paying Artists

Many larger shops have their own art department and pay artists by the hour. This is probably the cheapest way if you have a lot of work and can keep them busy. If not, then you should pay them by the job on a freelance basis.

Words of caution: Artists love to be creative and while there is definitely a place for creativity; if the customer wants an elephant on a design, don't let an artist tell you he needs a mouse! Get the picture? Tell the artist exactly what the customer wants, give him as much information as possible and then let him be creative.

Always discuss money up-front! If all you want to spend for a design is $15, tell the artist that. This will avoid any misunderstandings when the artist returns with a Picasso and thinks it's worth more than you had in mind.

Also, don't try to haggle for a lower price on every design. Some designs take hours, days or even weeks to finish. Pay the artist what the time is worth and realize that many larger customers *will* pay good money for artwork!

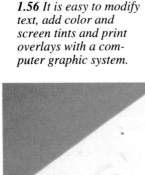

1.56 It is easy to modify text, add color and screen tints and print overlays with a computer graphic system.

Computer Graphics

Computers have certainly changed the face of the art department. While artists still perform much of their work at drawing boards, artists in modern art departments hold a mouse in one hand while looking at the computer screen!

This section will briefly discuss the advantages of computer graphics with a quick overview of hardware and software needs.

IBM Compatible or Macintosh?

This question has become less important as many software programs are now available for both platforms. Most trained artists use Apple Macintosh computers, while most business people use IBM's and IBM compatibles because they have been exposed to them in the workplace.

Frankly, both systems will create excellent graphics and the choice is more an issue of personal preference. Obviously, IBM compatibles are a more "open system" and more readily available and less expensive than a Macintosh.

Overview of Computer Graphics

Computer systems are now very inexpensive. You can purchase a complete system including a scanner and laser printer for $5,000 to $6,000 depending on whether you purchase a complete system (**1.55**) or put together your own pieces. In fact, you can put together a "bare-bones" system without a scanner for less than $3,000.

Computer graphics make the job of creating artwork painless and allow you to create more designs in less time. If you are an owner/artist, you will find your art skills greatly enhanced with a computer. And computer graphics systems *are very easy to use.* You can be doing simple designs the minute you get the system set up!

Designs that once took hours to do now can be done in *minutes!* Overlays that once had to be painstakingly cut by hand can now be automatically generated by the computer with a click of the mouse.

Computer graphics systems consist of a main computer (called a CPU), a mouse, a scanner and a laser printer. By simply moving the mouse, you move the "pointer" or "cursor" on the screen and basically "point and click" on the selection you want.

You can also easily type text on the screen, arch or modify it, add color and then print out sharp imaged color overlays in just a few minutes (**1.56**).

Computer Clip-art

The real value to the computer is clip-art. Most programs have literally *thousands* of built-in stock clip-art designs. In fact, many of the designs are in *full color!* Clip-art can be called up and modified, colored and merged with text to create quick designs (**1.57**).

Even simple designs can be made terrific with clip-art and stock graphic backgrounds and there is a wide variety of clip art on disk and CD-ROM (**1.58**).

Hardware

On the hardware side, you should put as much money as you can into computer speed and extra memory whether you are buying an IBM compatible or Mac. Your system should have a fast microprocessor with at least 32mb of RAM (temporary memory) and 2 to 3 gigabytes of hard disk storage. These are actually bare minimums!

Software

Software programs can be categorized into *drawing* and *paint* programs. Drawing programs are used for lettering and drawings. These programs are also called "vector" or "object" programs. With a drawing program, the computer knows the math coordinates between point A and

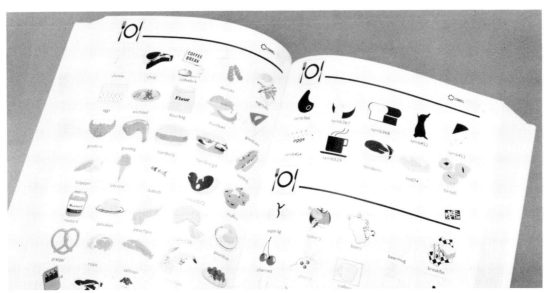

1.57 Clip art is available in full color that can be modified and text added to to make a complete "custom" design for the customer.

1.58 Clip art is available with programs and as separate packages that contain thousands of designs on disk or CD-ROM. (Photo courtesy Smart Designs, Tempe, AZ)

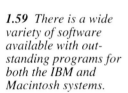

1.59 There is a wide variety of software available with outstanding programs for both the IBM and Macintosh systems.

point B and can make a design any size you want. Drawing programs generally "fill" closed shapes with color.

Paint programs are made up of small "pixels." With a paint program, you can airbrush, erase, smooth and fill images. Paint programs are generally used with one-color or multicolor scanned images.

On the Macintosh side, the most popular drawing programs are Adobe Illustrator™ and Aldus Freehand™. On the IBM side, all programs work with a graphic interface program called Windows™. The most popular IBM compatible drawing programs are Corel Draw® and Arts & Letters.

The most popular paint or image manipulation program on both the IBM and Mac is Adobe Photoshop™.

Granted, there are a few other great programs and you may be using one that is not listed here. This list simply includes the most widely used programs that have become standards in the art department (**1.59**).

Scanner

A scanner is somewhat like a copy machine. You can scan customer supplied artwork into your drawing or paint program, add text, or manipulate the image (if it has been traced with a tracing program) and print out one-color or multicolor overlays.

Small hand scanners are available, but try to purchase a full-size flatbed *full-color* scanner.

Laser Printer

For many years, the standard resolution of a laser printer was 300 dots per inch (dpi). For screen printing, the slight ragged edge on a 300 dpi laser output was acceptable. Most manufacturers now offer 600 dpi and higher resolution laser printers for the same price as the older 300 dpi models.

If possible, buy a 600 dpi laser printer that has a program in it called PostScript. PostScript is an optional program for some laser printers that will allow you to print out your color overlays.

The main drawback to a laser printer is the page output size. Most desktop lasers only print up to 8½ x 14 in. paper. Newer laser printers can print onto 11 x 17 in. paper which will help minimize the need to tile images together. These laser printers are now fairly affordable for the average screen printing shop.

Should You Buy a Computer?

The computer has become a staple of the art department! If you want to be competitive and creative, you should consider a computer a standard piece of equipment just like the printing press and conveyor dryer. Customers have come to expect great designs, but still don't want to spend much money. Computers allow you to create designs quickly and economically.

In many shops, the art department is the bottleneck in getting jobs to production. A computer graphics system will allow you to process more jobs per hour and get more jobs to the screen making and production departments.

PREPARING THE SCREEN

A screen consists of a carrier frame that holds the screen fabric and has a stencil of the design imaged on it (**2.1**). The process of making a screen is actually fairly simple, and if you just follow a few rules, you will find that it's not difficult to get professional results.

The Screen Making Area

Screen making is the one part of the process that has special requirements. You will need a sink, laundry tub, shower stall or bathtub with running water to degrease, wash out, reclaim and develop screens. You will also need an area where you can reduce the light level to work with the photographic emulsions and a dark room where you can dry the screens that have been coated with a light-sensitive emulsion. Don't worry. The emulsion is not extremely light sensitive, and as long as it is kept from daylight (watch out for windows, skylights, etc.) you can use it in a windowless room (or one with windows that have been covered) or even in your shop with the lights turned low. In fact, you can store the screens in a light-tight box or storage cabinet until you are ready to use them.

The Screen

The screen is the heart of the process. Unfortunately, there is some confusion in the industry about what type of screen to make. Since garment printing encompasses everything from simple lettering on uniforms to very detailed multicolor prints, there are times when a simple screen is all that is needed and times when the "perfect" screen is important to obtain a high-quality print.

2.1 The screen consists of a carrier frame with fabric and a stencil of the image on it.

2.2 Fabric that is loose will ripple in front of the squeegee blade as the print is made.

You will need to determine what type of work you will be doing and make your screen accordingly. Keep in mind that the screen is the carrier or printing plate for the image and the better the printing plate, the better the quality of the final print. Remember, the tighter the screen fabric the better the final print. Loose screen fabric will tend to ripple in front of the squeegee blade as the print is made (**2.2**). This ripple effect will cause the print to be slightly blurred.

The movement or shifting of the fabric may actually distort the print. This is not a problem for

2.3 Screen frames are made from either wood, rigid aluminum or special frames that you can retension.

2.4 If you make your own frame make sure to miter and glue the corners.

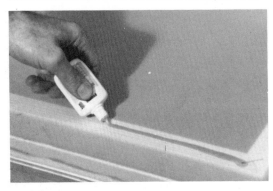

2.5 One of the most popular methods for attaching the fabric is with a glue called "frame adhesive."

one-color printing, but can cause a multicolor design to print out of register. (The colors will be slightly out of alignment because the fabric changed shape slightly.)

If the job calls for a one-color print on 12 shirts, you should spend less time and money on the screen than for a six-color, close-registration job on 1,000 shirts.

The Screen Frame

The function of the frame is to act as a supporting stretcher and holder for the screen fabric and to provide a holder for the ink.

Screen frames are generally made from either wood or aluminum (**2.3**). Wood frames are the least expensive and are ideal for general printing and shorter print runs. Retensionable aluminum frames allow you to re-tighten the fabric between printing jobs. Since the fabric on the screen loses tension with use, retensioning is the only way to keep the fabric tight. In fact, fabric can be tensioned tighter after it is used, thereby making a *better* screen.

Wood Frames

Wood frames are widely used by small shops. Since they are inexpensive, you can use them on a job and then save and reuse them when the customer reorders.

The drawback to wood frames is that the fabric will lose tension through use and cannot be retensioned. For most average printing, this really isn't a problem. Many shops have a selection of both wood and retensionable frames for more critical jobs.

Wood frames can also warp and change shape as they react to humidity, water, solvents and wear and tear. This can make it impossible for them to hold perfect registration on multicolor jobs.

Although it is not too difficult to make your own frame, it can be time consuming. Years ago, we recommended that you make your own frames when you are just getting started. Today, most screen printing supply companies (see list at the back of the book) offer premade wooden frames that are very inexpensive. In fact, dozens of companies sell wood frames for as low as $10 to $15 with fabric already prestretched on them! If you decide to use wooden frames we highly recommend using prestretched ones. They are well made and the fabric is stretched very tightly.

Making Your Own Frames

If you decide that for economy's sake you want to make your own frames at first, use 2 x 2 in. (5.08 x 5.08 cm) kiln-dried pine or better yet douglas fir. These are fairly light woods that will not warp too much. Make sure to miter the corners and secure them with a waterproof glue and screws or corner fasteners (**2.4**). To keep them from warping we suggest treating them with a polyurethane spray or varnish before you put the fabric on.

Attaching Fabric to Wood Frames

The best way to attach fabric to a wood frame is by using a stretcher to tighten the fabric and a frame adhesive to glue the fabric in place (**2.5**). This method may be too expensive when you first start because of the expense of a stretcher. Another option is to buy *one* oversized retensionable frame and use it as your stretcher. Simply stretch the fabric on the retensionable frame and then lay it over the smaller wood frame and glue or staple the fabric in place. Take a razor blade and cut the fabric from the retensionable to transfer the tight fabric to the wood frame.

The least expensive method is to staple the fabric in place. Since the head of the staple can break and tear the fabric, the tension will suffer.

Stapling the Fabric to the Frame

Staple up the first side using staple tape.

Staple across the second side.

Pull the fabric tight on the last two sides.

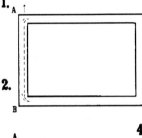

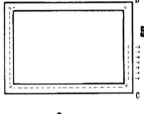

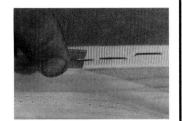

Trim off the excess fabric.

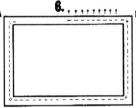

2.6 Although the staple method will not hold the fabric very tight you can use it when you first start if you can't purchase pre-tensioned screens. Just follow these steps and get the fabric as tight as you can!

This method has lost popularity with the advent and availability of inexpensive pre-stretched wood screens. If you want to try the staple method, follow the steps in figure **2.6**. Make sure to use a hammer to drive the head of the staple deep enough to hold the fabric. A pair of screen-stretching pliers will help pull the fabric tight when using staples.

Retensionable Aluminum Frames

By far, the biggest change in this industry has been in screen frames and fabric tension. Retensionable screen frames are now used by both small and large shops and offer better print quality and more control over the screen printing process.

A number of companies offer retensionable screen frames which are designed to be used over and over for different jobs (**2.7**). After a job is printed, the image or stencil is reclaimed (removed) from the screen fabric. If the customer reorders, the design is re-imaged onto the screen fabric. This helps reduce the amount of space needed for screen inventory. Large shops that have switched from wood to aluminum frames have gone from storing thousands of wooden frames to just dozens of retensionable ones.

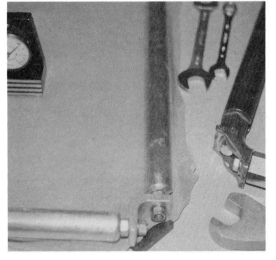

2.7 Retensionable frames are by far the best because they hold the fabric tight and allow you to re-tension between jobs to maintain proper tension.

How Retensionable Frames Work

Most retensionable frames operate the same way. They are made of a round bar that is rotated with a wrench to tighten the fabric. They generally have round bars on three sides and a flat or square tube on one end that fits into the holder of a standard T-shirt printing press.

Frame Size

Regardless of the type of frame you use, it will have to be large enough to hold a standard T-shirt size design. Designs can vary from all-over images to small over-the-heart prints. A general

Close-up View of Screen Mesh

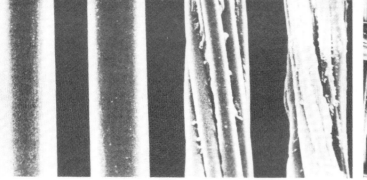

Nylon Monofilament Multifilament Silk   **Multifilament Polyester**

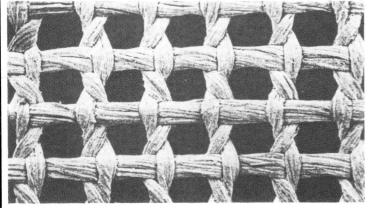

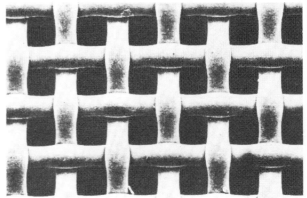

Silk Bolting Cloth   **Monofilament Polyester**

2.8 Closeup view of the various types of fabrics.

T-shirt screen is 18 x 20 in. (inside dimension) (45.72 x 50.80 cm). This frame size will hold most images and still fit on a manual T-shirt press.

Screen Fabric

Screen fabric is called mesh and comes in a wide variety of types and materials.

Silk

Although the screen printing process is still referred to as "silk screening," silk is very rarely used anymore. It is much more expensive than synthetic fabrics and dimensionally unstable, making it hard to use on detailed tight-registration prints. Also, direct emulsions cannot be reclaimed (removed) from silk.

Polyester

The most popular screen fabric is polyester. It is sold in two thread types: monofilament and multifilament (**2.8**). Unlike silk, polyester is almost completely unaffected by atmospheric humidity changes, and it is considered the most stable fabric.

Monofilament Polyester

Monofilament polyester is woven from a single thread, as opposed to a twisted multiple-strand thread. It has the advantage of a uniform mesh opening and will permit a more consistent flow of ink. It is also very durable and can be stretched to very high tensions. Due to the smoothness of the thread, monofilament polyester can be easily reclaimed. Monofilament polyester is by far the most popular screen fabric on the market.

Multifilament Polyester

Multifilament polyester is woven from a twisted multiple-strand thread, making it less uniform in weave, but giving it more tooth or edge so the stencil will have something to adhere to. It is about half the price of monofilament mesh and was the standard fabric until retensionable screens became popular.

Mesh Count

The mesh count of monofilament fabric is determined by the number of threads per linear inch (or cm). A lower number such as a 60 mesh count (24 cm) will allow more ink to pass through than a higher number such as 305 (120 cm) mesh.

FABRIC SELECTOR CHART

Type of Work	Manual	Automatic
Thick athletic printing	30 - 60	50
Broad coverage on a dark garment	60	74
Detailed coverage on a dark garment or as an underbase	86 - 125	125 - 160
Average print on light garment	110 - 140	140 - 180
Multicolor print on a light garment	140 - 200	200 - 230
Very detailed multicolor print on a light garment - halftones	200 - 260	230 - 305
4-color process (process-color)	305 - 330	355 - 380
Overprint colors on underbase	200 - 230	230 - 260
Hot-peel heat transfers	86 - 125	86 - 125
Cold-peel heat transfers	60 - 86	60 - 86
Puff ink	60 - 86	86 - 110
Suede ink	200 - 230	200 - 230
Metallic ink	86 - 110	86 - 110
Nylon Jackets - light material	180 - 230	
Nylon Jackets - dark material	110 - 125	
Crystaline overprint and glitter	30 - 60	30 - 60
General non-textiles (posters, etc.)	200 - 305	230 - 330

These mesh counts are based on a standard "T" (medium) thread and are given in the number of threads per inch. To convert to centimeters consult the conversion chart in Appendix B. Similar mesh counts may give good results also. Some manufacturers have different numbers that are close to these. For printing on soft or coarser material like sweatshirts or aprons, use a 10 to 20 lower thread count.

2.9 This fabric selector chart shows the best mesh to use for each particular type of print.

Coarser or lower counts are also made of thicker thread and will leave a thicker deposit of ink. Think of the lower number as being like screen-door wire and the higher number feeling like a fine silk scarf.

Multifilament fabric is usually measured by a mesh number followed by an X, XX or XXX. The number of X's denotes the thickness of the thread used. Multifilament numbers start at 2 and range to a high of 25. The numbering system has no relation to the number of threads except that the higher the number, the finer the mesh. If you decide to use multifilament mesh check with your supplier for a conversion chart to find out what mesh number equates to the monofilament mesh count you're used to.

Importance of Mesh Count

We cannot overemphasize the importance of using the correct mesh for the job! This is one area where beginning printers often want to cut corners and where industry suppliers often give poor advice. Often, poor-quality prints can be attributed to incorrect mesh selection.

The mesh count and ink thickness determine how much ink is deposited on the garment. For athletic-type prints, the customer wants a very heavy deposit of ink. For a detailed soft-hand print, a very thin deposit of ink is necessary for the print to not have any noticeable feel to it. For average single-color jobs, it really won't matter if the print has a heavy or soft feel to it. As long as the customer is happy with the quality, then you too should be happy. The correct mesh count is more critical when trying to print on dark garments and when trying to do multicolor prints on light shirts!

The chart on the previous page (**2.9**) shows the recommended mesh counts to use for various jobs. You will note that the chart distinguishes between automatic and manual printing. Although most readers of this book probably print manually, many large shops use this book as a guide for new employees.

Please *do not* worry if your supplier does not have the exact mesh count we suggest. Fabric is made in both Asia and Europe, and often the numbers are not exactly the same when converted from centimeters to inches. As long as you use a number that is close, you will be on the right track. For example, if we recommend an 86 (34 cm) monofilament and your supplier only carries a 92 (36 cm), it should be close enough. A few threads will not make a difference. On the other hand, if we recommend a 125 (49 cm) mesh and all you can get is a 200 (78 cm), it is too great of a difference.

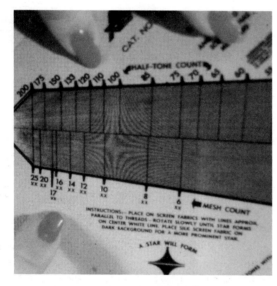

2.10 A mesh determiner will tell you what mesh you are using. Simply place it on the mesh and then rotate it until a "star" appears.

2.11 A tension meter is the only accurate way to test the tension of the screen fabric. They sell for $250 to $500 and are almost a must when using retensionable screens.

If you look at the chart, you will see that you can print almost any type of job with just four or five mesh counts. Since we do not recommend using multifilament meshes we have not included them on the chart.

What should be obvious from the chart is that when printing on a dark background or where you need a thicker deposit of ink, you should use a coarser mesh count. When printing multicolor jobs (especially when printing with the wet-on-wet technique covered in the Printing chapter), use a finer mesh count. When trying to print very fine detail (halftone dots and fine lines), go to a much finer mesh.

All fabric is sold by the yard and usually comes in stock widths of 42, 52, 66 and 72 in. (106.68, 132.08, 167.64 and 182.99 cm). Start off with 42 in. (106.68 cm) material. If you are going to make your own screens, just buy a few yards of each material. Coarse mesh counts like 86 (34 cm) costs as little as $9 per yd (US) while fine mesh counts of 305 (120 cm) can be as high as $35 per yd. If you are buying prestretched wood frames, just buy a few of each mesh count.

Mesh Color

Screen mesh is available in either white or dyed mesh such as amber, orange and yellow. Dyed mesh is much better because it helps to hold finer detail when exposing the screen by absorbing the light from the exposure unit and preventing it from burning around (undercutting) the detail in the image.

Mesh Counter

Once you accumulate a supply of fabric, it may be impossible to determine what mesh count the various fabric is. It's easy to tell the difference between 86 (34 cm) and 305 (120 cm), but try to tell 125 (49 cm) from 195 (77 cm) when they are side-by-side! A useful aid is a plastic gauge known as a *mesh counter* or *mesh determiner*. You can quickly find the mesh count by placing the mesh counter on top of the fabric and rotating it until a "star" points to the proper count. Try it and you'll see what we mean (**2.10**).

About Fabric Tension

One of the most talked-about topics among high-quality printers is tension. As mentioned above, tighter fabric makes a better screen and a better print. You can measure the tension on a screen with a device called a tension meter.

This meter measures the deflection of the fabric when it is placed on the screen (**2.11**). Tension meters are not essential to an operation but do make it easier to make consistent screens when doing high-quality prints.

Stretching Retensionable Screen Frames

Retensionable screen frames allow the fabric to be retensioned between jobs. For the best results, do an initial tensioning following the steps here or those supplied by the frame manufacturer. Allow the fabric to relax for 10 to 20 minutes and retension. Do a second retensioning and then use the screen on a job.

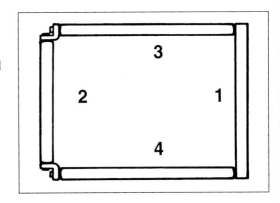

After the screen is reclaimed retension it again. By doing this a number of times, you will *work-harden* the screen and get it to the highest tension possible. Frame suppliers provide a chart to follow giving the ideal tension levels for the first tensioning, second tensioning, etc.

1. Attach fabric to the frame using the appropriate locking strip. Make sure the fabric is parallel to the frame bar.

2. Soften corners so you can touch the table through the fabric. The softer they are, the tighter you can get the screen.

3. Turn frame over and tighten side #2 at least 60° depending on the mesh count. You will not get a reading on the meter yet.

4. Tension side #3 to ½ of final first tension. Consult the tensioning chart supplied by the manufacturer.

5. Tension side #4 to the proper first tensioning level. If you feel the wrench stop or "stall," then you have gone far enough.

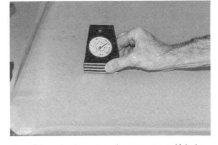

6. Check the tension to see if it is even. Let the fabric relax 10 - 20 minutes and retension. Let it relax again and retension. Re-soften corners if necessary.

In the beginning, don't worry if you don't own a tension meter. If you start to use retensionable frames, you should put a meter on your wish list of things to have someday. They range in price from $250 - $500.

Fabric tension is measured in newtons per centimeter – commonly called N/cm or just referred to as *newtons*. The higher the number of newtons, the tighter the screen. Suppliers of retensionable frames can provide charts showing the recommended tension for different mesh counts.

As a starting point (if you have a meter), you should try to achieve a minimum of 15-20 N/cm. With a retensionable screen, an average mesh can go as high as 40 or 50 N/cm by retensioning between jobs! Some printers actually take the mesh off the screen and throw it away if the tension drops below 5 N/cm. Many shops have 25 newtons as the standard mesh tension.

Besides getting a sharper and more in-register print with a tight screen, you will see a reduction in fatigue when printing a lot of shirts. The squeegee has less drag on the fabric. You will also have to use less pressure to drive the ink through the screen and will use less ink. If you're printing a multicolor job wet-on-wet, you will have less ink picking up on the bottom of the screens and will get higher production.

Degreasing

Before the stencil material is applied, you should wash or degrease the screen fabric. The oil, dust and impurities on it need to be removed so the stencil system will stick to it properly. If the screen was used for a previous job, it may have ink, solvent or reclaimer residues on the fabric.

Although suppliers carry standard degreasers, they are generally just concentrated cleaners and soaps that can be purchased from hardware stores or janitorial supply companies. Do not use household products like dishwashing liquids (they contain perfumes and hand softeners) or scouring powders (they contain bleach and the particles will embed in the fabric).

Regardless of whether you use a standard degreaser or industrial cleaner, simply spray or wipe it on both sides of a wet screen and work up a lather. Rinse the screen off with warm or hot water and let it dry (cold water is OK). Make sure to get all of the soap out of the fabric, and do not touch the screen after you have degreased it (**2.12**)!

2.12 The screen fabric should always be degreased before an emulsion or stencil is applied. Simply scrub the screen on both sides and rinse thoroughly.

Some suppliers still recommend using a grit or roughening agent to give the slick monofilament fibers a rougher edge to them. This was the way to prepare a screen in the old days of indirect films that had a hard time adhering to the fabric. This *is not* necessary when using direct emulsions and actually weakens the fabric!

Stencil Systems

Once the fabric is stretched and degreased, you need to make a stencil that will mask the open areas of the screen and allow just the ink to pass through where desired.

There are various kinds of stencils including hand-cut paper, hand-cut film, direct photo emulsion and capillary film. The stencil system you choose will depend on the amount of detail in the print and the size of the printing run.

Other than paper stencils for athletic numbering (discussed in the Printing section), direct emulsion and capillary direct film are the most popular stencil systems. We will not discuss hand-cut films because they are antiquated and very rarely used in garment-printing shops.

Photostencil Systems

Don't let this throw you. Direct photostencil systems are used by *everyone* and they are very easy to use! They are simply light-sensitive liquids or films that are coated or adhered to the screen fabric and then exposed to ultraviolet light with a film positive of the image on top of them. The area where the light hits the emulsion becomes water resistant. The area where the image on the film blocks the light, the emulsion remains water soluble and washes away or develops with water.

Direct Emulsions

Direct emulsions are simply glue-like liquids that are light sensitive. They are coated on the degreased (and thoroughly dry) screen with a special tool called a *scoop coater*. Scoop coaters sell for less than $20 and are a must for applying direct emulsion!

There is a wide variety of direct emulsions. Some suppliers offer dozens of varieties, which can confuse the new printer.

Dual-Cure Photopolymer Emulsions

For years, we used standard diazo-sensitized emulsions. Diazo emulsions have been slowly replaced with *dual-cure* emulsions that are also called photopolymer or diazo-sensitized photopolymer emulsions. These emulsions have less water than the older diazos and do not shrink as much when they dry. This gives a sharper edge to the screen and makes screen making faster. They are also more durable when used with water-based ink systems.

Besides dual-cure emulsions, some large shops use pure photopolymer emulsions or one-pot photopolymers. Pure photopolymer emulsions are premixed and have a very fast exposure time. They are also expensive. Don't let all of this confuse you, though, because you can simply call your supplier and ask for a standard dual-cure emulsion. These are standard products carried by all screen printing supply companies.

Some brands offer thicker and thinner versions called *light deposit* and *heavy deposit* emulsions. For average T-shirt printing, use the heavy deposit because it is a little thicker.

If you will be using water-based inks for longer print runs (500 or more impressions), you will need a special water-resistant emulsion. Standard dual-cure and pure photopolymer emulsions are fairly water resistant, but will not hold up for longer print runs.

Mixing the Emulsion

Dual-cure and general diazo emulsions are supplied unmixed in two parts (**2.13**). One part is the glue base and the other part is the light-sensitive sensitizer. You simply add warm water to the little bottle to dissolve the powder and then add this mixture to the base emulsion (**2.14**). Stir this mixture together, let it stand for a few hours to allow any air bubbles to escape and then just use it!

Emulsions are *very* heat sensitive. They should be kept below 95° F (35° C). If your shop is hot, then store the emulsion in a refrigerator. After they are mixed they will last for three to four months before they become clay-like and do not work.

Pure photopolymer emulsions are supplied premixed and have an almost unlimited shelf life.

Advantages of Direct Emulsions

Direct emulsions are extremely durable and can be used with any kind of screen mesh. They are practically impervious to all inks, including water-based textile dyes. Because the emulsion actually embeds in the fabric, the screen will hold the finest detail.

Direct-emulsion screens can be cleaned and then stored between printing without fear of damaging the image. In most cases (except emulsion with hardeners), the screens can be reclaimed by using household bleach (diluted with water) or reclaiming or stripping solution.

Handling Direct Emulsion

Direct emulsions are fairly light sensitive. This does not mean you have to work in total darkness though. You can work under subdued light such as a 50 watt bulb or yellow bug light. Do not use emulsion near a window or in any area where there is a lot of ultraviolet light. If you are working out of your home you may need to put a shade or cover on the windows when using direct emulsion.

Coating the Screen

There are various ways to coat the emulsion on the screen. While you can use a sharp squeegee or stiff piece of cardboard we *highly* recommend purchasing an inexpensive scoop

2.13   *2.14*

2.13 & 2.14 The emulsion is supplied in two parts. Simply add warm water to the powdered sensitizer and mix it with the emulsion base.

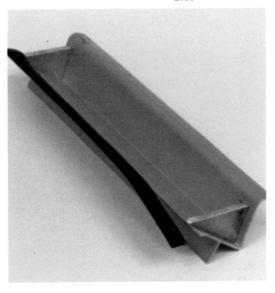

2.15 Use a professional scoop coater to apply the emulsion to the screen fabric.

coater (**2.15**). Available in a variety of lengths, the coater should be slightly smaller than the *inside dimension of the screen*. This way, it will only touch the stretched fabric and not be held off the fabric by the frame. Some coaters have both a round and a sharp edge. Always use the *sharp* edge!

Working under subdued light, pour enough emulsion into the coater to almost fill it up. If the emulsion was stored in the refrigerator you may want to let it warm to room temperature since it will be thicker when cold. If the coater came with a protective rubber edge, remove it *before* you use the coater! Hold the screen in a vertical position, place the coater edge against the fabric at the bottom of the screen (*on the outside of the screen*), tilt the coater *slightly* forward so that the emulsion touches the fabric and slowly pull the coater up the screen (**2.16**).

Sound hard? It really isn't once you get the hang of it. Now repeat this process on the *inside* of the screen. Most manufacturers recommend coating two or three times on the outside and another two or three on the inside. This is actually too thick a coating and can cause problems with underexposure and loss of fine lines.

2.16 Place the edge of the coater against the bottom outside of the screen and slowly pull the coater to the top. Repeat this procedure on the other side.

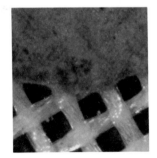

2.17 Capillary direct film produces the sharpest edge definition on the stencil.

Put any unused emulsion back in the container and then make sure to clean the coater right away after you use it. If you don't, the emulsion will dry and form a skin over it just like white glue. Take care not to nick or damage the edge of the coater. A nick will leave a streak in the coating.

Once coated, the screen is now ready to be dried in a dark area in front of a fan – preferably in a horizontal position with the bottom of the screen down. If you have high humidity, the screen may take all day to dry all the way through. Normally the screen will dry in 30-60 min.

The coating process may have to be repeated again, depending on how coarse the fabric is. If you are using a very fine mesh, one application may be enough. With dual-cure or pure photopolymer emulsions, *one* or *two* coats on both sides should be enough. If using a normal diazo emulsion you may need to coat again after the screen is dry to build up the thickness and help prevent having to spend an hour blocking out pinholes.

After the screen is dry you can store it in a dark cabinet or light-tight box for up to *three months* before using it. (Remember to keep the screen from getting too hot!) This allows you to coat a batch of screens at one time for future use.

Capillary Direct Film

Another popular stencil system is called capillary direct film or capillary film. This is simply a clear acetate carrier with a direct emulsion precoated on it. This stencil film is adhered or stuck to the screen mesh with water.

Capillary direct films are actually easier to use than direct emulsions because there is no mixing and much less mess. They do not work as well on fine mesh counts, though, and will occasionally fail if not used properly.

The beauty of capillary direct film is that it gives a *very sharp* edge to your stencil (**2.17**). This is because there is no shrinkage when it dries

and you only adhere the film to the bottom of the screen. Capillary direct films are *great* for printing on non-textile items like decals, bumper stickers and posters where you need a very sharp edge to the print.

Capillary direct films are sold by the roll or cut sheet. They are also sold in various coating thicknesses. For average T-shirt printing a 38-micron film is fine. These films are light sensitive just like direct emulsions and need to be handled under subdued light and kept cool when stored. Screens with capillary direct film can be prepared and not used until months later.

Adhering Capillary Films

Capillary direct film is adhered to a wet screen that has already been degreased. The real secret to getting it to work is to thoroughly degrease the screen. In fact, it actually helps to roughen-up the fabric slightly with an *abrading solution* – especially on high mesh counts. Many manufacturers sell a combination liquid degreaser/abrader that is put on the bottom of the screen and worked around in a circular motion with a brush.

Another chemical, called a *wetting agent*, greatly improves adhesion by helping the screen to hold more water. To use it, simply squirt the wetting agent on the screen, wipe it in with a sponge and then rinse it off just prior to adhering the film.

After you have degreased, roughened (optional) and wet the screen, simply roll or lay a piece of the capillary direct film onto the bottom of the screen with the dull side against the screen mesh. The water in the screen fabric actually draws the emulsion up around the screen mesh by a process called "capillary action."

You can take a squeegee and squeegee the inside and outside of the screen to push the water from the screen and aid adhesion. If some areas have not adhered well just spray some water (very fine mist) on the inside of the screen. You may need to wipe excess water from around the frame.

Using Capillary Direct Film

Capillary Direct film is very easy to use. Simply follow these directions or those supplied by the manufacturer. Proper screen prep is very important for proper film adhesion.

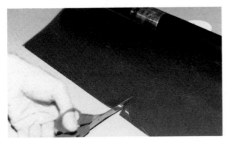

1. Cut a piece of film from the roll or use a pre-cut sheet. The film is light sensitive just like emulsion and should be handled under subdued light.

2. Degrease the screen fabric. On higher mesh counts use a combination degreaser/roughener and thoroughly rinse the fabric.

3. For better adhesion to higher mesh counts, use a wetting agent to help the fabric retain more water while you are appying the film.

4. Immediately after degreasing and rinsing, and applying the wetting agent and rinsing, roll the film onto the wet fabric on the bottom of the screen.

5. Keep a spray bottle handy for small areas that did not adhere. Squeegee the bottom and inside of the screen to remove excess water.

6. Dry the screen in front of a fan. When dry in 20 minutes, peel off the clear backing sheet and you are ready to expose the screen.

2.18

Each manufacturer has their own directions and you should read the instructions accompanying the capillary direct film you use.

After adhering the capillary direct film, dry the screen in a dark area with a fan blowing across it. The screen should dry in 30 minutes or less. When dry, peel off the clear carrier sheet. You are now ready to expose the screen (**2.18**).

Many printers prefer capillary direct film to direct emulsion. If you have any failure with the film, it will probably be on mesh counts of 200 (78 cm) or higher. It is also a little easier to hold fine halftone dots with a direct emulsion (regardless of what the manufacturers say).

Screen Exposure

There are a number of ways of exposing a screen from something as simple as sunlight to units that cost $5,000 and more. The funny thing is that you can get about the same quality screen from either one!

The light source you use must be high in ultraviolet light. The difference in light sources is that some have higher UV output than others. A regular light bulb is too low, but a quartz light (backyard light), blue fluorescent (unfiltered blacklight) grow light or sun lamp has enough UV to expose a screen in a few minutes.

More professional units use mercury-vapor (street lamps) and metal-halide lamps because they are more powerful.

If you are on a tight budget you can use sunlight, a quartz backyard light or unfiltered blacklight fluorescent tubes.

Sunlight

To expose a screen in sunlight you'll need a 2 or 3 in.-thick (5.08 or 7.62 cm) foam pad that is approximately 14 x 14 in. (35.56 x 35.56 cm) covered with black cloth. The black cloth prevents the light from bouncing off the foam and exposing from behind the screen. You'll also need a piece of glass about 14 x 14 in. (35.56 x 35.56 cm) with the edges smoothed and a film positive or vellum of the design (**2.19**).

Lay the screen over the foam pad, fabric side up. Place the film positive or vellum on the screen so that it is centered and square with the frame.

2.19

2.20

2.21

2.19, 2.20 & 2.21
A sunlight set-up can be made from a piece of glass, foam rubber, black cover and vellum or film positive. Tape the vellum or film to the bottom of the screen and lay the screen over the foam with the glass on top.

The film positive must be wrong reading as you are looking down at it.

Tape the film positive in place and lay the piece of glass over it (**2.20**). If the sun is out (that's the drawback to this method) take this setup outside and hold it in the sun for approximately 30 seconds (**2.21**). You may have to experiment with this time. After you have exposed a few screens, you'll know whether to increase or decrease the time.

Figure **2.22** show an illustration of a screen holding set-up.

If it is cloudy, or early or late in the day, you will have to expose for a longer time. Try doubling the time as a test.

If this sounds too simple to be true, give it a try! Of course this is very low tech and may be unreliable if you don't have bright sun every day. Keep this method in mind as a back-up source or for oversized screens.

Quartz Backyard Light

A quartz backyard light can be used also. Place the screen, positive and glass together the same as for sunlight and expose under the light for 6 to 8 minutes. Consult the *exposure chart* at the end of this section for approximate exposure times. The exposure time may vary depending on the distance from the screen to the light and on the *age* of the light. In general, when using a point light source the lamp should be about 20 in. (50.80 cm) away from the screen. If the light is too close it will undercut around the detail on the film positive and the heat from the light may harden the emulsion or film.

This same technique works for a sun lamp or photoflood bulb (available from photo supply stores). Be careful not to look directly at the light when exposing the screen. These lights are high in UV output and can burn your eyes.

Exposure Box

A more uniform way to expose screens is to build an unfiltered blacklight fluorescent tube exposure box (also called blue fluorescent). As you get into exposing screens for multicolor, you will need to be more precise in placing the design and overlays on the screen.

The next page shows a simple exposure box you can make. It consists of four wood sides, four rows of unfiltered blacklight tubes, a ¼ in. plate-glass top and an on-off switch. This box can be built for under $100 (**2.23**).

You may not be able to find a source for the fluorescent tubes, since many lighting companies don't carry them in stock. However, most department stores do carry grow-lights for house plants. These are similar to the unfiltered blacklights, produce a similar amount of ultraviolet light and work just as well. Don't confuse *unfiltered* blacklights with *regular* blacklights! The regular blacklights are very dark purple in color and won't

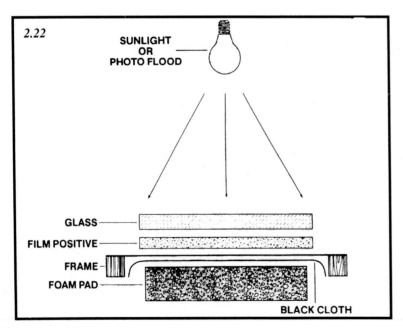

2.22
SUNLIGHT
OR
PHOTO FLOOD

GLASS
FILM POSITIVE
FRAME
FOAM PAD

BLACK CLOTH

EXPOSURE BOX PLANS

Materials List

1 – 18 X 30 in. (45.72 x 76.2 cm) – ¼ in. (.64 cm) plate glass.
1 – 18 x 30 in. (45.72 x 76.2 cm) – ½ in. (1.27 cm) plywood bottom.
2 – 9 x 28½ in. (22.86 x 72.39 cm) – ¾ in. (1.91 cm) pine front and back.
2 – 9 x 18 in. (22.86 x 45.72 cm) – ¾ in. (1.91 cm) pine ends.
1 – 24 in. (60.96 cm) – double-fixture fluorescent light.
1 – 24 in. (60.96 cm) – single-fixture fluorescent light.
3 – 24 in. (60.96 cm) –unfiltered blacklights or Gro-Lights.
1 – 10 ft. (3.048 m) – electrical cord with switch.

Note: More tubes can also be used than shown here. A larger box can be made that will expose two screens at once. Make sure that the top of the lights are no more than 3 to 4 inches away from the glass. This makes a shorter exposure time. Gro-Lights have a little less output than standard unfiltered blacklights.

Side

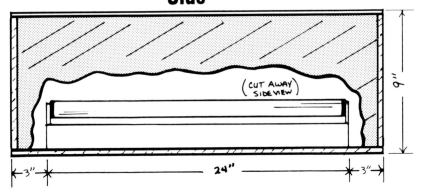

(CUT AWAY)
SIDE VIEW

9"

3" — 24" — 3"

Assemble sides, ends and bottom using glue and wood screws.

Use plastic or duct tape to hold the glass in place.

Top

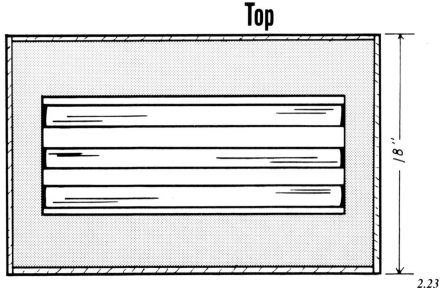

18"

2.23

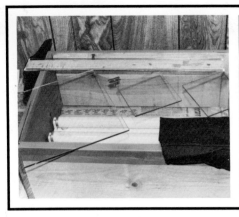

2.24 Lay the film on the glass, place the screen on top, and lay a black cloth inside the screen with a weight on top.

2.25 Professional exposure units have powerful point light sources and rubber vacuum blankets that draw down around the screen to make perfect contact between the film, the glass and the emulsion on the screen.

work. Unfiltered blacklights look almost like regular fluorescent tubes, except they are bluer.

When using the tube exposure unit, you will need to place the film or vellum on the top of the glass right reading and then put the screen on top of it. Lay a piece of black cloth inside the screen and then a flat piece of wood, glass or steel weight on top of this (**2.24**). This will help press down on the film and provide good contact between the emulsion of the film and the emulsion on the screen. Even ink cans can be used for extra weight.

The only drawback to the fluorescent tube exposure unit is that you will not be able to expose really fine halftone dots because you are using a diffused light source rather than a point

light source. You get a little more undercutting around fine lines with a diffused light source.

Professional Exposure Units

Professional exposure units have powerful point lights and a rubber vacuum blanket that comes down around the screen to provide good contact between the film and emulsion (**2.25**). These units generally sell for over $1,500 and offer a very consistent exposure and the ability to hold very fine lines and halftones.

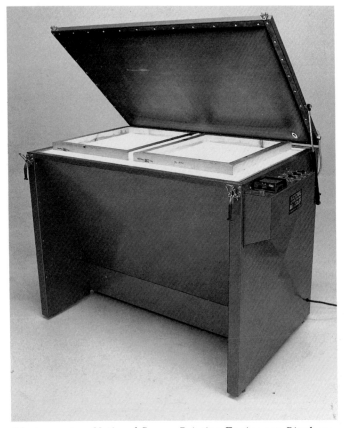

Photo courtesy National Screen Printing Equipment, Pittsburg, KS.

Photo courtesy nuArc Company, Chicago, IL.

Exposure Chart for Dual-Cure Direct Emulsion

Light Source	Mesh Count 30-60	70-100	120-180	200-275	305-350
Sunlight	60 sec.	45 sec.	30 sec.	25 sec.	20 sec.
Unfiltered Blacklights	6 min.	5 min.	4½ min.	4 min.	3½ min.
Photoflood or Sunlamp (24 in.)	18 min.	15 min.	12 min.	11 min.	10 min.
1000 Watt Quartz	6 min.	5 min.	4½ min.	4 min.	3½ min.
1000 Watt Mercury Vapor	5 min.	4 min.	3½ min.	3 min.	2½ min.
5000 Watt Metal Halide	75 sec.	60 sec.	45 sec.	40 sec.	35 sec.

Increase the time 30% when using dyed fabric. Times will vary between brands. Use an exposure calculator to determine correct time. Increase times 30% to 50% when using vellums. If trying to expose fine detail, shorten time slightly and *post expose* screen after wash-out. For 40 micron capillary direct film use the 120 mesh times increased by 50%.

2.26

Exposure Times

The chart in figure **2.26** shows estimated exposure times based on the most common stencil systems. For general work with little detail, the exposure times can be off a little and the screen will still wash out fine. If you are trying to hold fine lines or small halftone dots you will need to be more precise.

If you underexpose a screen, the emulsion does not harden all the way through and it may actually wash off during development. If it is only slightly underexposed. It will be a little slimy when the screen is washed out.

If you overexpose a screen, the light will actually burn through the film positive or vellum and expose the emulsion under it. If there are fine lines in the design, the light will burn around them and they will just disappear and not wash out of the screen.

To determine the correct exposure, you will have to expose a couple of screens to see how they turn out. Obviously if the emulsion washes away, the time is too short. Since emulsion is a relatively slow-speed material you will need to adjust the test times to give you a good sampling of what is too short and too long. As an example, if you expose with a backyard light for 10 min and the emulsion is soft, try going for 13 min. If you only increase the time a few seconds, you won't really know if it worked.

Exposure Calculator

A simpler method is to use a tool called an exposure calculator (**2.27**). This is a piece of film that has *five* exposure times built into it. Simply expose it onto the screen. With this one exposure you will be able to see a range of five different exposure times. Don't let this confuse you!

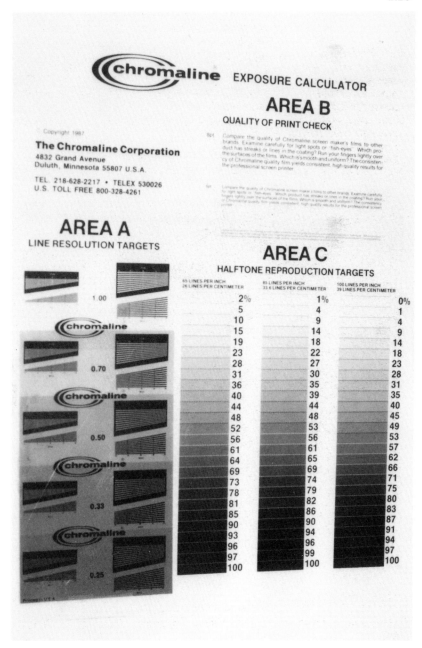

2.27

2.28 *After exposure, place the screen in a washout sink and get it wet on both sides with light water pressure.*

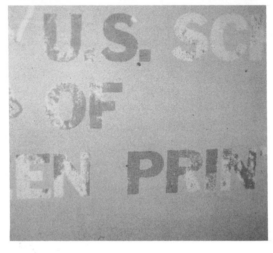

2.29 *After about one minute of washout, the unexposed emulsion starts to wash away.*

Once you establish the correct time, it really never changes unless you change to a different (or newer) light source or change brands of emulsion or film.

Keep in mind that with a finer mesh you must expose the screen for less time (for direct emulsion only) because the coating is thinner. For capillary direct film, the time remains constant from mesh to mesh because the coating is always the same thickness.

The idea is to be consistent and to *document* the correct times for future reference. Use the wall chart in Appendix B.

Exposure Tips

Direct emulsions and capillary direct films are actually very forgiving. For general-purpose screens, you can overexpose or underexpose them and they will still work. However, you might run into problems when trying to hold fine lines and halftone dots. For more detailed screens, use a thinner coating of emulsion or a thinner capillary direct film. Try exposing them for a little less time than normal. This underexposure will result in a stencil that has all the detail but may be soft or slimy when washing out the screen.

An underexposed screen may not reclaim properly because any solvent in the ink will mix with the softer emulsion coating. If you underexpose a screen to try to hold fine detail it is *very* important to *post expose* it after the screen is developed and dried. This means putting it back on the exposure and exposing the developed screen again. An easier method is to just set the screen outside for a few minutes to dry and *post* expose.

Washout

After exposure, take the screen to the washout sink and rinse it off with water (**2.28**). Make sure there isn't too much light in this area (from windows) because the emulsion that was covered with the film positive is still light sensitive and can actually expose while you are washing it out.

Using a sink sprayer, shower sprayer, garden hose or whatever, wash out the screen from the *inside*. Just don't use too much pressure in the beginning. In a few minutes, the image area will start to wash away where the film positive kept the light from hitting the emulsion (**2.29**).

If there are spots that don't seem to want to wash out, take a sponge or your finger and gently wipe these areas. You may have to increase the water pressure to remove stubborn spots. If you have underexposed the screen, the stencil may be very soft at this point, so be careful!

The washout process should only take a few minutes. If it takes longer, the screen may have gotten too hot during drying and storage or you may have fogged the screen by getting light to it while it was drying or just by walking from your exposure unit to the washout sink. Remember: if you can expose a screen in 30 sec in sunlight, you can partially expose it by just walking past a window!

You will find that washout is easier if you have a low-level ordinary fluorescent light behind the sink so you can see the image develop.

Blotting and Drying

After washout, and once you are sure that all the image areas are developed, you will need to blot the screen dry. You can use paper towels, newsprint (available from your local paper as an end roll), a chamois cloth or compressed air or a hair dryer. Simply lay the screen on top of the blotting paper (bottom side down) and blot the inside at the same time.

If the screen was underexposed you should always blot it dry to prevent scumming in the image area.

The screen is now ready to dry in front of a fan, outside, or in a drying cabinet.

Blockout and Touchup

Pinholes

When the screen is dry, it is ready to be prepped for printing. This includes covering up any small, open areas in the stencil called pin-holes. To spot the pinholes, simply hold the screen up to a light and look for little dots of light coming through the stencil. Pinholes are generally caused from dusty glass or film, underexposure, too much water pressure or not enough coats of emulsion if using a standard diazo emulsion.

Pinholes are covered or blocked on the *bottom* of the screen with a solution called blockout. Blockout is a liquid that is used to fill in areas of the screen where ink should not pass through. Pinholes can also be covered with scotch tape or masking tape if the print run is short (100 shirts or less).

To block-out pinholes, simply hold the screen up to the light and put a drop of blockout over the pinhole with a small paint brush or the tip of a pencil (**2.31**).

You can also use a special *block-out pen* that dispenses blockout when you depress the tip (**2.32**).

The fabric edges near the frame where the mesh is not covered with emulsion also needs to be covered with blockout. Simply pour a small amount on the *bottom* of the screen and spread it around the edges (**2.33**).

Taping the Screen

After the blockout is dry, you can tape off the bottom of the screen and the inside around the frame (**2.34**). Although you can use standard masking tape or plastic packaging tape, a higher-grade screen printer's tape will adhere better and not leave a sticky residue when reclaiming the screen.

Other Screen Prep Considerations

If you are using retensionable frames, be careful not to get blockout in the locking strip groove. In fact you will use less blockout and a lot more tape with retensionables.

For short print runs, you may not want to use any blockout. Just tape the screen on the *inside only* and print the job. This will make it easier to clean up afterwards.

Another option is to use a frame liner on the inside of the frame. They are available from most suppliers and are simply laid in the screen and taped in place (**2.35**).

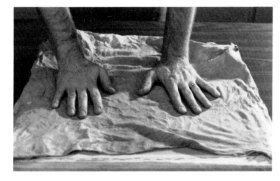

2.30 Blot the screen dry with a paper towel or newsprint after you have finished washing out the image.

2.31 Cover up any pin-holes in the emulsion with a small drop of screen blockout or filler on the bottom of the screen.

2.32 Pinholes can be easily touched up with a blockout pen.

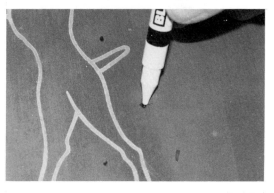

2.33 Pour a small amount of blockout on the bottom of the screen and spread it around the edges with a stiff piece of cardboard.

2.34 Tape off the bottom and also the inside of the screen with a special screeners tape, plastic packaging tape or masking tape.

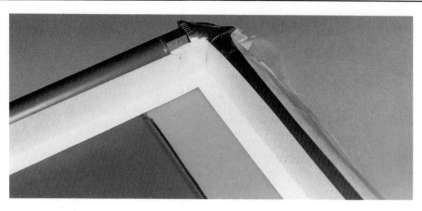

2.35 Screen frame liners are cardboard squares that are folded and placed inside the screen to line it. These work well on wood frames and on retensionable frames and make reclaiming easier. (Photos courtesy Ron Smith & Associates, Dallas, TX.)

Reclaiming

Emulsions can be removed from the screen by using standard household bleach or special reclaiming liquids or pastes sold by suppiers. To reclaim the image from the fabric, first clean all of the ink out of the screen and remove any tape. If you used a water-soluble blockout, you can remove it with reclaimer. Solvent based blockouts will need to be reclaimed with a solvent.

Spray or wipe the reclaimer on both sides of the screen and let it sit for 1 - 2 min. Next, use a garden hose sprayer or high-pressure washer to remove the emulsion from the screen. *Do not* allow the reclaimer to dry on the screen. It will harden in the mesh and totally block the screen.

It may take a number of applications of reclaimer to get a screen really clean. Expect to have a ghost of the previous image on the screen from where the pigment in the ink dyed the screen fabric. As long as the ghost does not clog the fabric, there should be no problems with future use. Eventually you will have so many ghosts that you will need to remove the fabric from the frame and restretch the screen.

Sometimes there will be stubborn spots or clogs and you may have to resort to a harsher paste called a haze remover to get these spots out. Haze remover is *very caustic* and should be used in small amounts. It is so strong that it will actually eat a hole in the fabric if left on it too long!

Certain brands of emulsion that are totally *water resistant* are generally not reclaimable.

Health Aspects

There are obviously some products that are more toxic than others. In screen making, the more harmful products are the reclaimers and haze removers. If you are on a septic system and making just a few screens a week, you should be okay as long as you minimize reclaiming and *do not* use haze removers. If you have any questions concerning disposal or safe handling procedures, contact the emulsion manufacturer for assistance or your local water company.

If you are reclaiming a lot of screens, you may want to provide respirators for employees to wear if they are spraying reclaimer on the screen. To minimize misting of the solution into the air, we suggest that you wipe the reclaimer on the screen rather than spraying.

Special Techniques

Multicolor Exposure

After you have mastered the simple techniques in this book, it's time to move into the more advanced area of multicolor printing.

We've already discussed cutting overlays for multicolor printing, but the screens have to be exposed *in register* also. What this means is that the distance from the bottom of the screen and the end of the artwork must be the same on all the screens in a multicolor job. If the main outline color is exposed on one screen, the overlay colors must be exposed in the same spot on their screens *in register* with the outline.

The reason for this will be obvious when lining up the first multicolor job! The outline screen is placed on the press first and a print is made. The second color is then placed on the press and lined up on the print that was just made. What if that color is 2 or 3 in. (5.08 or 7.62 cm) too low or high? It won't line up! It must be in register with the outline color in relationship to the bottom of the frame.

A simple method is to just measure the distance from the bottom of the design to the frame and place each film or vellum the same distance on each screen (**2.36**).

Gang Screens

As your business grows and you're doing more and more work, there will be times when you want to put more than one design on the same screen. This is called a gang screen and will save money (**2.37**)!

If you have a lot of small designs to print, put them all on one screen. (Remember to use the correct mesh for the ink color and type of print.) When it comes time to tape the screen, tape over the designs that *will not* be printed first on the *inside of the screen*. As one design is printed, move on to the next by untaping it and taping over the old one on the *bottom of the screen*.

Torn Screens

Every now and then a screen will tear – usually when least expected, like right before it's going to be used! Making a temporary patch is a fairly simple operation.

Cut a piece of screen fabric larger than the tear. Coat the area around the tear on the outside of the screen with blockout and then lay the fabric

2.36

2.37

2.36 To line-up each positive in the same location from screen to screen, simply measure the distance from the bottom of the frame and the design. Place each overlay in the same location as you expose the screens.

2.37 You can save money by ganging more than one image on the same screen.

over the blockout, kind of like fixing an inner tube. After letting this dry, the screen will be good as new unless the tear is in a design area! In this case, a new screen will have to be made.

Clogged Areas

Occasionally, a screen will get washed out, dried, blocked out and taped before you discover a tiny dot or two that didn't wash out. Take a straight pin or push-pin and poke the dried emulsion out. It may damage the fabric slightly but it shouldn't affect the print. If the clogged emulsion is in an open area you can also put a small drop of reclaimer on a Q-tip and carefully apply it the clogged emulsion. Rinse this area when done.

Filing System

As screens are exposed and if they are going to be kept for a reorder, place a number and title on the end of the frame. Now, instead of just placing the screen in a stack, file it numerically with the rest of the screens.

Try keeping a file card for each customer. On this card, you can keep important information about the customer and the job, including the screen number. When they reorder, you can check the card and find the screen easily. This system also works if a stencil is going to be filed. Even the artwork can be assigned this number.

If you reuse frames a lot, it might be wise not to write the name of the customer on it. Just use the number and keep a separate sheet of the frame numbers and what is on each particular screen. Then, as a screen is reclaimed or restretched and used for different jobs, you can change the name of the customer on the screen *sheet*.

If you use retensionables, it is *very* important to permanently mark the mesh count on the frame. Since you will be using this screen for a variety of jobs, simply place a piece of masking tape on the frame with the job name on it. This can be removed easily during reclaiming, but the mesh count will remain permanent.

Screen Storage

While we're on the subject, screen storage can be a problem. Hopefully, the more work you do, the more screens you will accumulate. A simple 2 x 4 in. (5.08 x 10.16 cm) shelf will do for screen storage. Try building shelves up high and out of the way and storing screens vertically. This will keep them from getting torn or warped.

Other Information

It's a good idea to start a file of the instruction sheets that come with the different capillary direct films and emulsions. Sometimes they'll come without instructions and you'll have to ask for them. All chemicals are required by law to be supplied with Material Safety Data Sheets (MSDS) that tell how to handle them safely. Make sure you read these and make them accessible to your employees.

Troubleshooting

Copy the charts on the next two pages of this chapter and post them in the screen making area. They cover common problems you will encounter and suggested solutions and remedies.

The Future is Here

Screen making is one area where great changes are in the works. It is now possible to expose a screen without using any film or vellum paper. A system called a Screen Jet ™ (Gerber) allows you to send a computer file directly to a machine that paints the image on the emulsion coated fabric with a special black ink. The screen is now exposed and washed out as usual.

This system totally eliminates the need to shoot films or print out vellum paper, plus it speeds up the entire screen making process.

While these units are fairly expensive ($20,000 + as of this writing), they are becoming almost a standard item in bigger shops that produce large volumes of screens. As the price of a Screen Jet drops, it may replace film and vellum!

Photostencil Troubleshooting Chart No. 1
This chart applies to Direct Emulsion (DE), Capillary Direct Film (CDF), or Both

Problem	Stencil	Cause/Remedy
Excessive Pinholes	*Both*	– Dust or dirt on film, exposure glass or uncoated screen. Improve housekeeping in screen area.
	Both	– Improper degreasing. Dirt or grease still on screen.
	Both	– Underexposure. Increase exposure time. Use an exposure calculator. Expose longer with vellum or dyed screen mesh.
	Both	– Washout water pressure to high. Reduce spray.
	DE	– Emulsion coating too thin. Use higher solids emulsion, slow down coating speed, or coat more than one time on coarse mesh.
	DE	– Emulsion not thoroughly dry before second coat. Use a fan to speed drying and add a dehumidifier to drying box.
	DE	– Air bubbles in emulsion. Allow emulsion to settle for two hours after mixing.
	CDF	– Film too thin for mesh. Use higher micron film or increase mesh count.
	CDF	– Not enough fabric wetness during adhering. Adhere film immediately after degreasing and use a wetting agent.
	Both	– Agressive solvents or water in ink. Use more water or solvent resistent stencil system.
Washout Breakdown	*Both*	– Underexposure. Use exposure calculator to determine correct time.
	Both	– Excessive water pressure. Decrease water pressure and wash out time.
		– Poor coating technique. Coating too thick or uneven. Use the sharp edge of a professional scoop coater.
	CDF	– Improper film adhesion. Use an abrading agent when degreasing the screen. Use a wetting agent to make the water "wetter."
	Both	– Outdated film or emulsion. Check package date.
	CDF	– Film fogged before use. Handle under very subdued light and keep film container light-tight before use.
Early Stencil Breakdown	*Both*	– Underexposure. Use an exposure calculator. Screen should not feel slimy or soft on inside during wash out. If purposely underexposing to hold detail make sure to post expose screen. Vellum exposure times need to be longer to expose through translucent paper.
	DE	– Emulsion coating too thin. Use one coat on the underside and one coat on the inside (pure photopolymer or dual-cure). Thoroughly dry and coat again on the underside if using coarse mesh or standard diazo emulsion.
	Both	– Screen not thoroughly dry prior to exposure. Use a dehumidifier or fan.
	CDF	– Stencil too thin for mesh. Use recommended stencil thickness.
	Both	– Excessive humidity. Maintain humidity in printing room at 45-65%.
	Both	– Aggressive solvents or water in ink. Use correct stencil system for ink system. Change to more durable stencil for longer run jobs with solvent or water based inks.
	Both	– Mesh not tight enough. Excessive rippling of stencil during printing. Use a tension meter to properly tension mesh.
Scumming or Hazing	*Both*	– Incomplete washout or underexposure. Increase exposure time.
	Both	– Incomplete blotting after washout. Blow screen dry with air if necessary.
	Both	– Light scatter causing undercutting. Use dyed mesh or reduce exposure.
	Both	– Poor positive. Weak positive or vellum will cause burnthrough. Improve quality of film or vellum or use two pieces stacked together. Decrease exposure time.

Photostencil Troubleshooting Chart No. 2

This chart applies to Direct Emulsion (DE), Capillary Direct Film (CDF), or Both

Problem	Stencil	Cause/Remedy
Difficult Wash Out and Loss of Detail	*Both*	– Overexposure. Decrease exposure time and use an exposure calculator to determine correct time.
	Both	– Weak film or vellum. Excessive burnthrough exposes stencil under image area. Reshoot film, improve toner deposit of vellum, or double-up film or vellum. Running a vellum through dryer or using a spray fixative improves density.
	Both	– Fogged screen. Keep screen in a light-tight area prior to exposure.
	Both	– Excesive heat during drying and storage. Do not exceed 110° F (43° C). For best results do not exceed 85°-95° F (30°-35° C).
	Both	– Coated or filmed screen stored too long before exposure. For best results do not store coated or filmed screens more than two or three months. Maintain proper room temperature and keep screens light-safe when in storage.
	Both	– Poor stencil-to-film contact. Use a vacuum frame or additional weight or pressure on exposure unit.
	Both	– Layered or taped positive causing loss of detail in certain areas. Minimize taping or overlapping of films or vellums, especially in halftone dot areas. Reshoot as single piece.
Sawtooth Edge	*Both*	– Too much water pressure and temperature. Reduce pressure and keep water temperature below 95° F (35° C).
	Both	– Underexposure. Use exposure calculator to determine time. Increase exposure for dyed fabric and vellums.
	DE	– Incorrect coating technique. Emulsion must be thicker on underside of screen. Dry screen horizontally, underside down, and do last coat on inside to push the emulsion to the underside. If coating after drying, coat on underside only.
	Both	– Stencil too thin. Use more coats or thicker film.
Image Distortion	*Both*	– Excessive heat build-up on the exposure glass during multiple exposures may distort the film or screen fabric. Let glass cool between exposures.
	Both	– Loose screen fabric. Use a tension meter to insure proper tension.
	Both	– Uncoated (sealed) or loose wooden screen frame. Use a well-made, sealed wooden frame or properly tensioned retensionable screen frame.
Difficulty Reclaiming	*Both*	– Mesh count high. Fine meshes are more difficult to reclaim. Use increased water pressure from pressure washer.
	Both	– Multifilament fabric. Multifilament fabric will not reclaim as easy as monofilament.
	Both	– Old screen. Stencils will harden with age and be more difficult to reclaim.
	Both	– Underexposure. Unexposed emulsion will lock in screen when a solvent is used to clean screen. Use proper exposure or post expose screen after wash out.

CHAPTER

3

ALL ABOUT INK

There are a lot of different ink manufacturers with different trade names for their inks. The ink of choice in the garment printing industry is plastisol. It is used on 95% of all imprinted sportswear on the market! Water-based ink can also be used on T-shirts, but it's mainly reserved for fashion items, yard goods and beach towels.

This chapter will cover plastisol and water-based inks. Other inks and special additives are covered in Chapter 6 - *Jackets, Caps and Other Printables*, and Chapter 7 - *Special-Effects Printing*.

Don't let this chapter confuse you. Once you start to use inks, they become an everyday item. But it is important to know about various inks, what you can add to make them work better and how to dry or cure them.

As with many products in the printing industry, most inks come with no directions. Screen printing inks are no exception. Don't expect to see a lot of data on the containers other than health and safety warnings. Make sure to start collecting technical data sheets (TDS's) from ink companies. They contain a wealth of information about each particular ink and will be a good resource to help you learn what you can and can't do with each product (**3.1**).

Plastisol Ink

Plastisol is the most popular ink in the industry because it will work on practically everything you print. It is a very stretchy, durable ink that does not dry in the screen, making it easy to print. It can be printed thick on athletic uniforms and thin on fashion items. It can be used to make heat transfers, print puff designs, print on 100% cotton, and polyester/cotton blends, print light and dark shirts and even print nylon jackets if you add a special bonding agent. What else could you ask for?

What you can't do with plastisol ink is dry-clean or iron it. This limits its use on fashion items or any garment that needs to be ironed. (However, you can turn a shirt inside out and iron it.)

A true plastisol is a solventless ink, one that is 100% solids. The majority of plastisol is made up of plasticizer, a liquid with a very high and safe flash-point of 440° F (225° C), and polyvinylchloride resins (PVC).

What Can You Print Plastisol On?

Plastisol ink can be printed on virtually any substrate that meets two requirements: the material must be able to withstand a curing temperature of 300° F (149° C) and must be porous enough to permit good ink penetration.

3.1 Collect all of the ink manufacturers catalogs and technical data sheets.

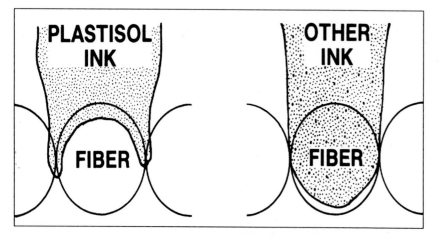

3.2 Plastisol ink wraps around the garment threads and does not dye or penetrate the fibers.

3.3 All-purpose plastisols work best on light shirts or printed over an underbase of white ink.

3.4 High opacity inks are designed to cover dark backgrounds.

Plastisol does not actually dye the fabric by penetrating into it like a water-based ink does. Instead, the ink wraps *around* the fibers in the material. It is really classified as a surface coating because it makes a *mechanical bond* with the fab-

ric (**3.2**).

Because plastisol has no real adhesive power, it is not used on nonporous materials such as plastic, metal and glass. It will also not work properly on waterproofed nylon without adding a special bonding agent.

Types of Plastisol

A wide variety of plastisol inks are available in dozens of standard colors. To make things easier, we have grouped the types of plastisols into four major categories. Some manufacturers offer a variety of inks for every application so that you could conceivably have eight to ten different whites, blacks and colors. Your ink inventory could really get out of hand! When possible, try to use multipurpose inks to reduce your ink inventory.

All-Purpose Inks

This is the ink you will use on most items (**3.3**). All-purpose plastisols are fairly creamy and good for printing on light-colored shirts and as the overprinting ink on a underbase white (for dark shirts). Your main ink inventory will be AP plastisols. They are not opaque enough to work on dark substrates, though.

High Opacity Inks

High opacity inks (HO) are specially formulated to cover dark backgrounds (**3.4**). They are thicker than AP plastisols and have fillers to give them better hiding power when printing on dark items. HO inks are available in a more limited range of colors, the most popular of which are white and golden yellow.

High Opacity Low-Bleed Inks

When printing high opacity inks on shirts with polyester and polyester blends, the dyes in the polyester will often bleed into the ink. This is what turns white ink pink on a red shirt. The problem is more severe with certain brands of ink and can happen over a period of weeks after the shirts are printed.

Ink companies offer special low-bleed white inks designed to eliminate this problem. You can also print low-bleed inks on 100% cotton shirts but it is not recommended by the ink companies. Make sure to read any warning notices on the low-bleed containers regarding curing temperatures and possible ghosting problems.

High Opacity Fast-Fusion Inks

In the category of high opacity inks, are special white inks that can be semi-cured in a second or two without any tack to the surface (**3.5**). These are designed to be used as an underbase and are often called underbase or flash-cure whites.

Athletic Plastisol Inks

Athletic uniforms require a more durable ink to withstand industrial washings and abrasion. Special athletic plastisols are much more durable and stretchy, and cure with a glossy finish (**3.6**). If you do any athletic printing, this is the ink to use.

Athletic plastisols are also great for other stretchy items like Spandex® and Lycra® used in bicycle jerseys and aerobics outfits (**3.7**). They will also work fairly well on wetsuit material and bathing suits. (A little bonding agent will help the ink withstand chlorine better.)

Process Plastisol

Process printing is where you print the four specific colors of process red (magenta), process blue (cyan), process yellow and black to create all the shades of the rainbow (**3.8**). These inks are very transparent and creamy. They are too thin to make good transfers and only work on very light fabrics. You don't have to use these inks just for process printing. The colors are very bright and they will work as an all-purpose ink, too.

Curing Plastisol Ink

Plastisol is different from other screening inks in that it does not dry by air as most do. It can sit uncapped or be left in a screen for days, weeks or even months without drying. This property is what makes it such a pleasure to print with. The ink will not dry and clog the screen.

The full *cure* of plastisol is attained by the *application of heat.* When plastisol is subjected to heat, the PVC resin particles swell and absorb the surrounding liquids (plasticizer). As the resins swell, they merge with each other and form a continuous film called an elastomer.

Plastisol will start to become *dry to the touch* or softcure (also called semi-cure or gel) between 180-250° F (82-121° C). It *fully cures* at between 280-320° F (138-160° C) depending on the type of plastisol. The temperature at which the ink becomes fully cured is called the fusion temperature.

For all practical purposes, don't worry about overcuring direct plastisol prints because the overcure temperature is beyond the scorching point of the garment.

Curing Units

If you are going to print T-shirts with plastisol ink, you must have a curing unit. Whether it be your oven at home or a large flameless gas dryer, you must have a "heater" somewhere in your shop.

This section will detail some of the features to look for when purchasing curing equipment. If

3.5 High opacity fast-fusion inks cure quickly and are designed as an underbase color on dark garments.

3.6 Athletic plastisols are more durable and designed for nylon mesh and other uniform material.

3.7 Athletic plastisols also work on stretchy material like lycra and spandex.

3.8 Process plastisols are very transparent and are designed for printing 4-color process on light shirts.

just about to make your first purchase then hopefully you will find some tips you can use to stump the salesperson.

Flash-Curing Units

You really must have a flash-curing unit (**3.9**). Even if you have a dryer, you will need to flash cure between colors on some jobs. The reason they are called flash- or spot-cure units is because if you put them close to the ink, you can soft-cure it in only a few seconds. Generally, a flash-cure unit is set so that the element is 1½ to 2 in. (3.81 to 5.08 cm) above the garment.

Before we talk about the features of flash-curing units, let's clarify one major point. You *can* use a flash-cure unit as a full-cure unit! Some suppliers will tell you that a flash-cure unit can only be used for curing between colors and not to achieve a full cure, but this is absolutely not true. There are thousands of printers who use a flash-cure unit to *fully cure* shirts everyday.

A flash-curing unit is the *same heater that's in a conveyor dryer* without the conveyor or tunnel. And, since these are infrared heaters that do not heat the air but only heat what the infrared radiation touches, you really don't need a tunnel to contain the heat.

Important Flash-Cure Unit Features

Heater Size

Since so many customers want large prints nowadays, if you buy a unit with a curing area of less than 16 x16 in. (40.64 x 40.64 cm), you are kidding yourself. Invest in a 16 x 20 in. (40.64 x 50.8 cm) or even a 24 x 24 in. (60.96 x 60.96 cm) unit if possible (**3.10**). The larger units are 220 volts, but the size is worth it. If the flash-curing unit will be your main heater, you will have less undercuring problems around the edge of the prints with a larger model.

Size of Stand

If you have ever tipped over a flash-cure unit, you know that a sturdy, wide-leg stand is a must. Wheels are also indispensable because you always need to move it around. Larger wheels are better because they don't get caught in cracks and on cords.

Automatic Cycle Feature

You will never know how great this feature is until you try it.

The automatic cycle is controlled by a foot switch, and you can set the amount of time the heater is over the garment so you get a consistent cure every time (**3.11**).

Okay, so it's like buying a Cadillac, but this feature is *really* worth the money.

3.9 A flash-curing unit can be used as your "dryer" and to cure between colors.

3.10 Oversize flash-cure heaters cover the print area more evenly and will help minimize undercuring around the edges of the prints. (Photo courtesy Hopkins International, Berkeley, CA.)

3.11 Flash-units that cycle automatically over the garment for a pre-set time are much easier to use and give a more uniform and consistent cure. (Photo courtesy Black Body Co., Fenton, MO.)

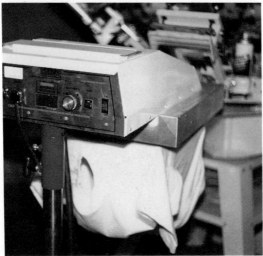

3.10

3.11

Heat Controller

Since you are generally going to run your flash-cure unit on high, you may not need a heat controller. Many units just plug in and are always on. However, this feature might be used occasionally when printing in heat sensitive substrates.

Are All Units the Same?

You can actually buy a heater, make your own stand and have the same unit as those supplied by the manufacturers (**3.12**). What you will not have is a protective covering, a heavy-duty stand, a heat controller, the auto-cycle feature, etc., but you will have a curing unit for less than $400!

Conveyor Dryers

Dryers come in all sizes (**3.13**) and range in price from $2,500 for a small infrared dryer to over $15,000 for a gas-fired dryer. Remember, as you grow the dryer is the first piece of equipment you outgrow!

One shop's small dryer is another shop's giant dryer! Look at the following list with your overall production and *future growth* in mind. If you plan to print only a few dozen shirts a week, then a flash-curing unit will do the job forever. If you have lofty goals of being the T-shirt tycoon of your area, then get a dryer that can handle larger quantities and higher production.

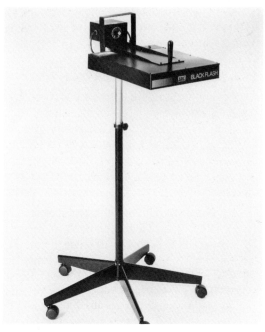

3.12 A simple heater on a stand is really all you need as a flash-curing unit. (Photo courtesy Black Body Co., Fenton, MO.)

Important Dryer Features

Conveyor Size

By our standards, a small dryer is 6-8 ft. (1.829-2.438 m) long with a 24-in. (60.96 cm) wide conveyor belt. These dryers are just one step above a flash-cure unit and will handle from 8 - 12 dozen shirts per hour (regardless of what the manufacturer says). They are great for small shops, but will not be able to keep up with the production of more than one printing press feeding it shirts.

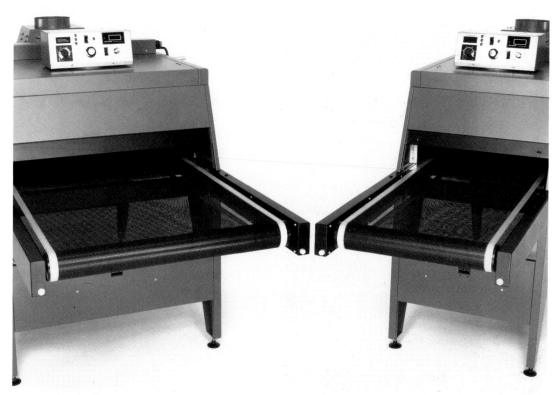

3.13 Dryers are available in a wide variety of sizes. (Photo courtesy Chaparral Industries, Phoenix, AZ.)

3.14 Adjustable heater height is an excellent feature that allows higher production and the ability to run thicker items through the dryer.

If you can afford it, buy at least the next largest dryer. If you are looking at a 6-ft. dryer, see if you can swing an 8 or 10 ft one. If you are looking at a 24-in. wide belt, try to move up to a 30 or 36 in. (76.2-91.44 cm) belt. *You can almost double the amount of throughput by just increasing the length a few feet!*

Adjustable Heater Height

This feature is a must, especially if you have a *small* dryer. By simply lowering the heating element, the ink gets hotter faster. (There is a point where you will burn shirts, though.) This allows you to increase production on shirt jobs, and still fit puffy jackets and tall caps through the tunnel when needed (**3.14**). Having this feature will keep you from being locked into a set heater height and a set amount of production.

Ease of Maintenance

Sooner or later, you will burn out a heating element or a temperature controller. You need to be able to *easily* get inside the dryer to drop out a

heater or do other electrical repair. Even if you aren't the one who will fix it, keep in mind that someone has to be able to take it apart. Some dryers have so many "pop rivets" and twists and turns that it takes days to get the thing apart. Again, you will never know how much you need this feature until you realize that somehow you have got to get the dryer fixed *quickly* so you don't lose too much production time!

Forced Air

This feature is important only if you will be printing air-dry inks on towels, non-textiles, etc. Although forced air *may* help minimize scorching, you will find that forced air flowing through the dryer may also cool the ink and keep it from curing properly. Although many manufacturers claim you must have forced air (and preferably hot air) flowing through the dryer, millions of shirts have been cured at high production rates without forced air.

Can You Build a Dryer?

Yes, you can actually build a dryer. Figure **3.15** show a variety of pictures of a homemade dryer. Heater manufacturers will sell the heaters direct, and you can buy the heat controllers and conveyor belts from industry suppliers. There are really no plans available for building a dryer so you will have to look at commercial dryers to get ideas. Unless you are experienced in 220 volt wiring and have a knack for building things, you should stick with buying a new or used commercial dryer.

3.15 These photos of a typical homemade dryer will give you some ideas on how to make your own.

TYPICAL HOMEMADE DRYER

Curing in Your Home Oven

Yes, this will work. Just put the shirt on a cookie sheet, place it in the oven at 450° F (232° C) and cook the shirt for about 2 minutes. It may be slow and low-tech, but it will work. These times are just estimates and you will need to experiment.

Heat-Transfer Press

This is probably the best investment you can make. Not only will a heat-transfer press work like a dryer and flash-cure unit, but you can use it to apply transfers and athletic numbers.

Although you can cure a print on a heat-transfer press by bringing the element down directly on the print (if you cover the print with blank heat transfer paper), the cured print will have a rubbery feel to it.

The best way to solve this problem is to adjust the pressure of the heat-transfer press so that the heater doesn't touch the shirt. Then bring the element down and lock it in place for 10-15 sec with the element set at 375° F (191° C). If you can't get the press to adjust to a light enough pressure, place a thin piece of wood or a ruler on the shirt before lowering the element (**3.16**).

How Long for Full Cure

It is a popular belief that plastisol must be brought to the full cure temperature and then remain there for 2-3 minute to attain a full cure. In commercial use, plastisol is generally cured in an infrared oven or under a flash-curing unit operating at a much higher temperature that brings the ink rapidly up to the desired curing temperature.

Once the entire ink film thickness reaches the proper cure temperature, the ink becomes a continuous film and is fully cured. This means that with a high enough temperature coming off the heater, the ink could actually be cured in a matter of seconds!

What Happens if the Ink is Undercured?

If the *entire thickness* of the ink is not brought to the correct curing temperature, the ink will be undercured (the resin will not have absorbed all of the plasticizer) and the ink will *crack and flake off the garment when washed.*

How to Adjust the Curing Time and Temperature

It is very important to understand how to set the drying unit to achieve the desired temperature at the garment. Since the ink will cure when the entire ink film reaches the full fusion temperature, you must be able to measure the temperature of

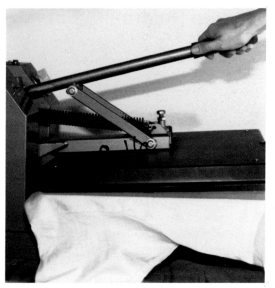

3.16 A standard heat transfer press can be used as a curing unit for wet plastisol. Simply bring the element down until it almost touches the ink. Leave it there for 5 to 15 seconds.

the ink film. It is a common misconception that you should measure the temperature of the *heating elements.*

Generally, the temperature of the heating element is set much higher than the temperature that is required to cure the ink. This higher temperature allows the ink to be brought to the cure temperature fairly fast, allowing higher production.

Very Important Concepts!

The amount of heat a print receives is controlled by two things – Time and Temperature! Curing temperature is controlled by a combination of the time the garment is under the heater and the temperature of the heater!

For example, if the heater temperature is set at 800° F (427° C), then of course, the element temperature will be at 800° F (427° C). Let's say you print a shirt, put it on the dryer and turn the belt speed up as fast as it will go. Odds are good that the print will *still be wet* when it comes out of the dryer. However, what happens if you turn the belt speed down to the slowest speed? Odds are good that the shirt will scorch (and may even catch fire!). There is the *time* factor – the element temperature did not change in this example, only the length of *time* the print was subjected to heat.

Obviously, one way to control the amount of heat the print receives is to adjust the *time* the print was in the dryer by increasing or decreasing *belt speed.*

With a *high* temperature combined with the *correct belt speed* it is possible for the ink film to reach the full-cure temperature in a matter of 20 - 30 seconds (or less)!

Obviously, the temperature setting *will influence* the time needed to achieve a full cure. A lower temperature setting means that the belt must run more slowly. With a higher temperature setting, the belt can run faster.

How to Determine Full Cure

Although washing the garment is the first, and the definitive test for curing, there are other methods you can use to determine if the ink film has fully cured. The most popular method is to simply stretch the print. If the print cracks badly and does not retract, the ink is probably undercured. In this case, the print needs to reach a higher temperature and the belt speed should be slowed down. By increasing the amount of time the garment is under the heaters the ink film will reach a higher temperature. Of course, you might also be running the heater temperature too low. If this is the case, increase the temperature.

The stretch test does not always work on thick deposits of ink such as athletic prints. The top layer may stretch, but the ink deep down in the fibers may still be undercured.

Measuring the Ink and Dryer Temperature

Paper Thermometers

You must get in the habit of checking the dryer or flash-cure temperature on a consistent basis. A popular item to measure the temperature

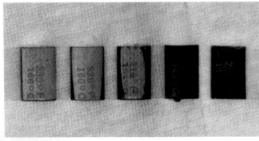

3.17 Paper thermometers can be used to measure the surface temperature of the ink.

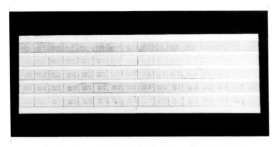

3.18 Place a paper thermometer strip on the shirt and run it through the dryer or under the curing unit. A small section or edge will turn black at the temperature the garment achieved.

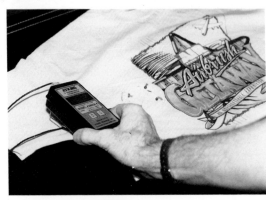

3.19 Temperature probes or "donuts" can be run through the dryer to get a reading of the temperature at the belt.

at the ink is a paper thermometer (also called heat tape) (**3.17**). These heat-sensing paper strips turn black at whatever temperature they reach. Paper thermometers are sold in six different ranges and are available from most suppliers and ink companies. They should be used daily to safeguard getting a full cure. For direct printing plastisol ink, you need a #5 tape that reads from 290-330° F (143-166° C). When undercuring ink (as with heat transfers) you'll need a #3 paper thermometer – it will read temperatures of 190-230° F (88-110° C).

To use these tapes, simply place a strip on the garment and run it through the dryer or place the tape on a shirt under the flash-curing unit. Note that the tapes are only accurate within + or - 15° (**3.18**). To conserve money, you can cut the tapes in half before using them. Paper thermometers cannot be reused. Once one goes through the dryer, take a reading and throw it away.

Temperature Probes

You can also measure the temperature of the ink (also called the *belt temperature*) with special heat sensing temperature probes that you run through the dryer (**3.19**).

Quick Setup Recommendations

Flash-Cure Unit

Let the unit heat up (this will take about 15 min). Set the heater 2 in. (5.08 cm) above the garment for 10 sec. Check the curing time with a paper thermometer.

Dryer Setup

Let the dryer heat up for 15 min. Set the heaters at 6 in. away from the belt (they can be preset) at a setting of 500-600° F (260-316° C). Adjust the belt speed so that the garment will be in the dryer for 20 or 30 sec. Check this setting with a paper thermometer.

Curing Tips

1. Let the garments or transfers fall into a box at the end of the dryer. This is how most shops do it, and that is the reason for the cool-down section at the end of the dryer belt.

2. If the ink isn't fully curing, (especially if it's plastisol) run the garments through a second time. It may be necessary to run white plastisol through two or three times. Make sure to do wash tests!

3. Turn the dryer belt speed down slightly for thick prints and light-colored prints on dark shirts.

Properties of Plastisol

Plastisol inks are very *thixotropic*. This big word means that the ink will stiffen when not in use. This phenomenon is also called *false body*. When you stir or squeegee the inks, they reduce slightly and become creamy.

Plastisol Additives

This is a very important area to understand. Plastisol inks are generally supplied *ready-for-use* (also called *RFU* or *press ready*). This is not always true, though, and they may need slight modification to work properly. There are special additives available that will make the ink work better. Do not be afraid to use them.

Viscosity Reducer

This is a thinner for the ink. If the ink is too thick, it will not flow properly through the screen and can make printing difficult. Reducing an ink so that it prints better is very common.

There are two types of reducer. The older version is based on a liquid plasticizer and is clear and oily. If you add too much, the ink will not cure because there will be too much plasticizer for the resin to absorb! The most popular reducer is called a curable or balanced reducer. It has both resin and plasticizer and will not affect the balance of the ink.

Before reducing the ink check its consistency by stirring it first! Because it has a false body, you really won't know if you need to reduce it until you stir it. If you determine that it is too thick, mix in a small amount of curable reducer. You don't need to stir the entire container; just mix the top portion. When printing light-colored shirts, the ink should be smooth and creamy. For dark-colored shirts and athletic prints, it should be thicker.

Very Important Point

If you reduce the ink slightly, it will flow through the screen and be easier to print. It will also result in a sharper print with good ink penetration. This penetration will help minimize the buildup on the bottom of the screen. Any detail in the print will be sharper because of less squeegee pressure, and you will get higher production – all from simply reducing the ink slightly (if necessary).

Extender and Transparent Base

Extender base is a cheap ink base used to make an ink less expensive and go farther. Transparent base is a clearer base used to make an ink more transparent when overprinting colors. Special versions of extender are also called a soft-hand base or soft-hand additive.

It is common for a supplier to recommend using extender base or soft-hand additive to reduce an ink. We recommend you use a *reducer* to reduce an ink!

Should You Reduce Opaque Inks?

It is a common misconception that if you reduce opaque inks, the *coverage* will be affected. In reality, if the ink is too thick, you need to use more pressure on the squeegee to get the ink through the screen and, in turn, drive the ink into the shirt.

If white ink is reduced slightly (if it is too thick to print) less squeegee pressure is required and the print may actually be more opaque!

Other Additives

There are a variety of other additives that may never be used or will be used very sparingly. These include thickening powder, flattening powder (gloss remover), buildup minimizer and toner.

Special-effects additives such as puffing agents, nylon bonding agents, phosphorescent powders, metallics, etc. are covered elsewhere in this book.

Mixing Colors

The first word of caution in mixing colors is to *go slowly!* Mixing colors is like thinning: once you've gone past the color you wanted, there is no turning back! It only takes a small amount of red to turn a gallon of yellow into orange.

You usually need to mix colors when a customer requests a special Pantone® shade. The Pantone Matching System® (PMS) is the international color-matching system that everyone uses. To find out what color your customer is specifying, you need to purchase a Pantone Matching Color Guide® from an art store (**3.20**). The guide shows the formula for mixing thousands of colors from just a few basic colors.

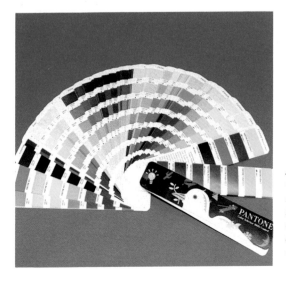

3.20 A Pantone® Color Matching Guide has the formulas for mixing thousands of colors. They are available from art stores and ink companies.

Most ink companies offer special mixing systems of their own. Some of these are based on Pantone® colors. Some matching systems that are based on the Pantone® colors even work on dark shirts (**3.21**). Mixing systems usually consist of 10-15 basic colors plus plastisol base. The formulas are measured out on a gram scale in small quantities for the first batch and then those quantities can be scaled up to weigh out the desired amount of ink.

When you're first starting out, a mixing system may be more than you need. It also can be one more area of confusion. If you don't have a mixing system, you can still mix non-critical colors from the basic primary colors of ink.

Beginning Ink Colors

Start your ink collection by at least buying the four basic colors of black, red, yellow and royal blue.

These are called primary colors. With them you can mix almost any color or shade. Here is the basic formula:

1. RED + YELLOW = ORANGE
2. BLUE + YELLOW = GREEN
3. BLUE + RED = PURPLE
4. BLUE + RED + YELLOW = BROWN

Remember – *always use a small amount of the dominant color.* A little red and a lot of yellow will make orange. A little blue and a lot of yellow will make green. Different proportions will vary the shade and adding white to primary and secondary colors will give a more pastel shade. As before, *experiment!*

You should also buy a high-opacity low-bleed white for shirts that contain polyester and an all purpose white for mixing colors. Buy more of high-opacity low-bleed white and black than the other colors. Although you can make orange, green, brown, purple by mixing primary colors, you really should just buy them. Mixed secondary colors will be a little "dirty" or dull in color compared to purchased secondaries because you will be using two different pigments to make the color and the ink company is using the specific pigment color.

Tips for Mixing Colors

If you don't have a Pantone® mixing system then use the following guides as a starting point for mixing colors. Even if you don't purchase a Pantone® system you can actually use the Pantone® Mixing Guide with plastisol colors that come close to the Pantone® basic colors. Your final mix will be fairly accurate!

1. If you don't have a gram scale (they can be purchased for less than $200) then start with a spoonful of this and a drop of that. Then you will know what proportions to use on a larger scale when you find the right color.

2. Spread or print a small sample of the mix on a swatch of the garment to be printed. Dry this sample and compare it to the color you are trying to match. Ink colors will change slightly when printed on the cloth and dried!

3. Buy a color wheel from a local art supply. It's a helpful aid when finding and mixing colors.

3.21 Pantone® Matching Systems are available for both light and dark color garments. (Photo courtesy Union Ink Co., Inc., Ridgefield, NJ.)

Water-Based Textile Inks

If you don't have a dryer, this may be the ink to use. Although water-based textile inks withstand washing better if they're heat cured, some brands have catalysts that eliminate this need.

Water-based inks come in a wide range of pre-mixed 100% aqueous systems and systems that contain both water and oil. Although you can actually make your own water-based ink using a base and pigments, you should probably buy it premixed in the beginning.

Although the softest water-based inks are the water-in-oil, they have become less popular because they contain a solvent.

Advantages of Water-Based Ink

Water-based ink certainly has its advantages. It penetrates into the shirt's fibers, giving the print a much softer hand. Some manufacturers claim water-based prints wash better than plastisol.

Because most water-based inks can be dry cleaned and ironed, they are ideal for fashion items. Because of their soft feel, they are widely used in the yard-goods industry. Water-based inks are also the ideal choice for beach towels – where a soft print is important – because the ink penetrates into the garment.

Water-based inks don't require as many solvents, and the squeegee and screen can be cleaned with water. In most cases, the ink can be washed down the drain. (Check with your ink company and the local water department first!)

Disadvantages of Water-Based Inks

Water-based inks are not as popular as plastisols because they dry in the screen. This means you need to start the job and keep printing in order to keep the screen open. Once the screen clogs it may be impossible to remove the ink.

Although clogging is common with non-textile inks, the average T-shirt printer is so used to plastisol that lazy habits make using water-based ink a little foreign.

Another disadvantage is that water-based inks are not as opaque as plastisols. Although they do not work as well on dark garments, some manufacturers offer a wide range for both light and dark colored garments (**3.22**).

Because of the aggressive nature of these inks, you will need a water-resistant stencil. Dual-cure emulsions are fairly water-resistant for printing runs of less than a few thousand. For longer print runs, you will need to purchase a permanent emulsion that cannot be reclaimed.

3.22 Some companies specialize in water-based inks for both light and dark garments. (Photo courtesy CHT North America, Lynchburg, OH.)

How to Print with Water-Based Inks

Water-based inks work well when printed through meshes ranging from 110-160 (43-63 cm). They will clog faster on high mesh counts and will practically run through low mesh counts.

Flood Stroke

The main difference between printing with water-based inks and plastisols is that you must do a flood stroke after you do the print stroke. This coats the image area and keeps the ink from drying in the open mesh (see Chapter 4 - Printing Techniques).

If you must stop printing – even for a few minutes – you will need to wipe the image area and make sure the ink is in the back of the screen. You can also cover the ink with plastic wrap to keep it from skinning over.

Because water-based ink dries so easily, it is helpful to keep a spray bottle of water near the press. Positioning a humidifier next to the press will help on dry, hot days.

Additives

The main additive for water-based ink is retarder. It slows the drying process and helps minimize ink clogging. Retarders are usually glycols. (You can purchase glycol glycerine from a drug store.) Although you could us automotive antifreeze as a retarder, the ink manufacturer will sell you a much safer retarder. Use it sparingly!

Other additives for water-based inks include low crock (to improve rub resistance),screen opener (to minimize drying in the screen), extender bases for mixing and catalysts to improve washability if you can't heat set the ink.

Drying and Curing Water-Based Ink

It is important to understand how water-based inks dry. Water in the ink is just the vehicle or carrier for the pigment and binders. This water must evaporate from the ink before the ink will actually cure or dry.

Conveyor Dryer

For best results, use a dryer or drying system with good airflow. Ideally, a conveyor dryer with heated *forced air* is the best choice. Even a small dryer will work, but it may take two trips through the tunnel to achieve a full cure. The first trip is enough to evaporate the water from the ink; the second trip heats up the rest of the ink and fully cures it.

If your dryer does not have any airflow (do not confuse an exhaust fan with an air-flow system), you will find that it may even take three trips through the tunnel to fully cure.

Flash-Cure Units

Flash-cure units can cure water-based prints, but again, you need airflow. Try placing a fan next to the unit and letting it blow across the shirt as you heat it with the flash-cure unit. Some flash-cure units have built-in airflow systems.

Other Drying Systems

If you don't have any way to heat the printed shirt, then you will need to add a catalyst to the ink to make it washfast. You can also use the following more simple methods of drying and curing.

Clotheslines

Don't laugh, it works! If the ink is strictly air-dry, try hanging a clothesline in the shop. Run as many lines as possible, and then simply drape the printed shirts over them. This is how they do it in foreign countries where water-based ink is much more readily available than plastisol.

Heat Lamps

Heat lamps will do wonders with air-dry inks. Don't place them closer to the shirts than about 10 in. (25.4 cm), though, because they tend to have a hot center and might scorch them.

A good arrangement is to space six or seven lamps so that you can fit shirts under each lamp. Laying them out, one at a time, will allow the first print enough time to dry so that you can stack it (2 or 3 min). Then you'll will have a production line going!

You can also use heat lamps to cure plastisol, but it is a tricky proposition! Besides needing more than one lamp per garment, it's hard to get them up to 300 or 350° F (149 or 177° C) without scorching the garment because of their hot centers. Try them and then do a few wash tests.

Hand Ironing

Ironing does an excellent job of heat setting air-dry inks. Try using heat lamps to dry the ink enough for stacking and then iron the print (place a piece of heat-transfer paper over it first) for about a minute. If you don't have transfer paper, iron the back of the shirt. The heat will penetrate to the front and set the ink.

Clothes Dryer

As with an iron, first dry water-based prints by hanging or using heat lamps. Do some wash tests to see how hot to run the dryer and how many shirts it will handle at a time.

Important Rules to Follow

Remember three basic rules when using ink:

1. Follow the directions for use and mixing! Always ask for the ink manufacturer's catalog and technical data sheets.

2. Pretest if you aren't sure. Pretesting means making a few trial prints, washing them, washing them again and then picking at the print. If you feel confident that the prints will stay on the garment and hold up well, you'll sleep better at night!

3. If you have a problem, it is rarely the result of bad ink. Undercuring, improper mixing or adding too much additive is usually the culprit.

CHAPTER

4

PRINTING TECHNIQUES

Printing is the real payoff for all the previous work. People are actually surprised to find that printing is at times the easiest part of the process. Let's take a look at the equipment, tools and materials used in the printing process.

Printing Equipment

You can either build some of your equipment or purchase a ready-made press. There are plans in Appendix B for a 4-color press you can build for less than $150. There are actually thousands of these homemade presses in use (**4.1**). They are good if you are on a budget and want to get into the business without much of an investment.

Generally, it is common to build some equipment in the beginning and then as you grow, purchase a professionally made press (**4.2**).

There is a wide variety of equipment on the market ranging from a low of $750 for a no-frills 4-color manual press to over $5,000 for a heavy-duty press with all the bells and whistles.

The next two pages have plans for a simple one-color press you can build for less than $50. It will be a good starter press and you can see how well you like the process.

If you progress up to a multicolor press you will still use a one-color press for simple jobs, jackets, and one-color athletic and numbering jobs.

4.1 You can build a simple 4-color press for less than $150. The plans are in Appendix B.

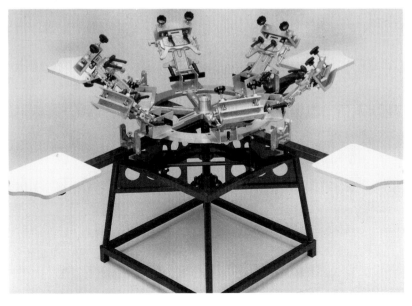

4.2 Professional presses will hold tighter registration and are easier to set-up. (Photo courtesy Hopkins International, Berkeley, CA.)

BUILD A ONE-COLOR PRESS

This is a simple one-color press that can be built for under $50!

SIDE

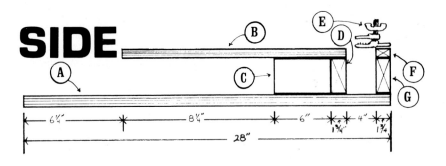

Materials List

Drawing	Quantity	Size	Material
A	1	24 x 28 in. (60.96 x 71.12 cm)	¾ in. (1.91 cm) Plywood
B	1	14 x 16 in. (35.56 x 40.64 cm)	¾ in. (1.91 cm) Plywood
C	1	6 in. (15.24 cm)	2 x 4 in. (5.08 x 10.16 cm)
D	1	14 in. (35.56 cm)	2 x 4 in. (5.08 x 10.16 cm)
E	1 pr.		Jiffy Hinges
F	1	14 in. (35.56 cm)	1 x 2 in. (2.54 x 5.08 cm)
G	1	14 in. (35.56 cm)	2 x 4 in. (5.08 x 10.16 cm)

Tools and supplies: Hammer, drill, screwdriver, wood screws, wood glue, clear polyurethane spray, magic marker, sanding block and sand paper.

Jiffy Hinges

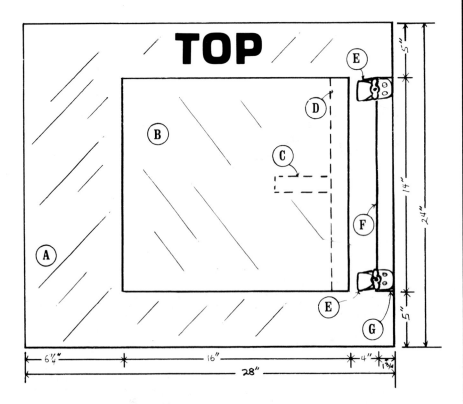

TOP

Steps in Assembly

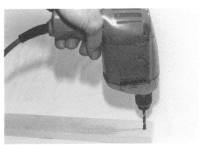
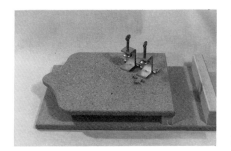

The above printer is a professionally made version of the home-made press. (Photo courtesy Backdoor Shop, Phoenix, AZ.)

Drill a hole in the kick-leg so it will hang free when nailed to the side of a screen. To protect the press wood from ink spills, solvents and humidity, spray it with a coat of clear polyurethane spray.

Squeegees

The tool used to push the ink through the mesh is called a squeegee. Squeegees consist of a wooden handle with a rubber or plastic blade. The handle is designed to fit into the palm of your hand and keep your fingers extended away from the ink, allowing you to apply heavy, even pressure to the blade (**4.3**).

Sharp, clean prints depend to a great extent on a good squeegee. The blade must be resistant to all solvents and thinners used in screen printing and be compatible with the items being printed.

Squeegees can be purchased already assembled with the blade in the handle. Most suppliers carry large stock lengths of squeegees and will cut to any size you want. If you buy a squeegee from an art store, you may have to choose from the stock sizes they carry.

4.3 The squeegee is the tool used to push the ink through the screen. It consists of a wooden handle with a rubber or polyurethane blade.

The Handle

Squeegee handles are generally made of wood and are available in either 4- or 5 in. (10.16 or 12.7 cm) lengths. A 5 in. (12.7 cm) handle will keep more ink off the finger tips.

Special *ergonomic* handles are available (**4.4**) that help minimize strain on the wrists which causes carpal tunnel syndrome (repetitive motion disorder).

The Blade

Blades are available in either rubber or polyurethane plastic. Polyurethane blades will stay sharp longer, but are more expensive than rubber.

The hardness of the blade is measured in durometers.

> *Extra-Soft*   40-45 durometers
> *Soft*   50-55 durometers
> *Medium*   60-65 durometers
> *Hard*   70-75 durometers
> *Extra-Hard*   80-85 durometers

For most general T-shirt printing, you will need a medium squeegee, 14-16 in. (35.56-40.64 cm) wide. The flex, or firmness of the blade will determine how much ink is deposited on the shirt.

After you've printed for awhile, try other squeegees. A medium durometer works well for the average job. A slightly rounded blade will lay down a thicker deposit of ink, which is good when printing white ink on dark shirts or when trying to achieve a thick athletic print (**4.5**). A sharp, hard blade is good for extremely detailed prints, but will deposit a lighter coat of ink. Don't be afraid to experiment with different kinds. You'll soon find "your favorite" that seems to work for most jobs.

There are also triple-durometer blades that have a harder center. One popular triple-durometer squeegee is a 70/90/70 (70 durometers on the outside with a 90-durometer center). Triple-durometer blades do not flex as much, yet they have a soft enough edge to lay down a clean deposit of ink.

4.4 Special squeegee grips call ErgoGripstm are available to help widen the hand's grip on the squeegee (increasing the gripping power) and padding the handle. These have proven to greatly reduce carpal tunnel syndrome. (Photo courtesy Squeegee Plus, Eugene, OR.)

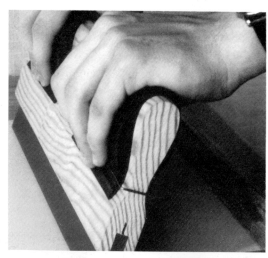

Care and Feeding

It is extremely important to take care of squeegees. A good one should last for years.

The first step in proper care is to always clean the squeegee thoroughly after each job. Take special care around the crack where the blade fits into the handle. Don't let squeegees soak in a solvent tank or a pan of thinner too long. The blade will eventually warp and lose some of its hardness from sitting in the solvent.

4.5 A sharp squeegee blade lays down a sharper and thinner deposit of ink. A slightly rounded blade deposits a thicker print.

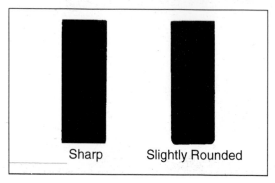

Sharp   Slightly Rounded

4.6

4.7

4.6 You can make a simple squeegee sharpener with two pieces of wood and some sand paper.

4.7 Store the squeegees on their backs so the blades won't get warped.

It is actually easiest to designate a squeegee for each primary color of ink. Then, getting them thoroughly clean is not as important.

After extended use, a squeegee will start to get dull and will require sharpening. You can build a simple squeegee sharpener by buying a belt-sander belt (not too coarse), splitting it and stapling it to a piece of wood. By running the squeegee back and forth on the paper, you will be able to sharpen the edge. To keep the squeegee straight, nail a piece of wood to the side of the sharpener as a guide (**4.6**).

Try not to store the squeegees on the blade. To keep the blade from warping or bending, simply drive a few nails in the table or board and store the squeegees on their backs (**4.7**).

Eventually, a blade will wear out, get nicks or be so badly warped that it needs to be replaced. Screen printing suppliers sell lengths of blade for replacement purposes (see Appendix A).

Printing

Well, the time has come. Now that you know about artwork, screens, squeegees, ink, textiles and drying and have hopefully even built a one-color press, you are ready to go!

You still need a few more supplies before your first print is made (**4.8**). The following list should get you started.

Supplies List

Mineral Spirits – for screen and tool cleaning.
Screen Opener – to open clogged screens.
Stirring Sticks – wooden spoons work great!
Rags – cotton rags work the best.
Masking Tape – for taping off screens.
Plastic Packaging Tape – for taping screens.
Screeners Tape – for taping screens.
Paint Scraper or Stiff Cardboard – to scrape ink from screens.
Cans for Mixing Ink – start saving!
Newspaper – to cover counters and clean screens.
Spray Adhesive – to hold the garments in place.
Apron – you may get dirty.
Test Squares – for screen lineup and samples.
Rubber Gloves – to keep it off your hands.
Hand Cleaner – don't forget this one.
Tools – for fine-tuning the equipment.
T-square – for lining up jobs on press.

4.8 Just a few of the supply items to keep handy when getting ready to print.

Setting up the Press

Put the screen on the press, frame side up, with the design facing away from you. Make sure the screen is centered and square on the centerline of the press. If the screen was exposed centered and square, the print will fall into the right place on the shirt. Clamp the screen down tightly with the hinges.

If you're using a homemade press, attach the kick leg to the left or right side (whatever feels comfortable) with a small box nail about halfway up the side (**4.9**).

Off-Contact Printing

The screen should be set from 1/16-1/8 in. (.16-.32 cm) above the garment. This is called off-contact printing and keeps the screen from touching the shirt until the actual print stroke is made. You will have much sharper prints if you print off-contact (**4.10**).

4.9 Clamp the screen in place on the press so it is square to the shirtboard with the image facing away from you. Hold the screen up with a kick-leg on the homemade press.

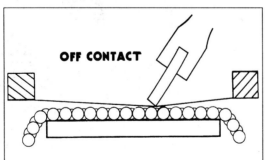

4.10 For sharper prints set the screen 1/16-1/8 in. off-contact.

4.11 On some presses you may have to use a small cardboard shim under the screen.

4.12 Square the image on the screen to the shirtboard using a t-square.

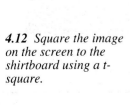

To adjust a homemade press to print off-contact, you may have to tape or staple a small piece of cardboard to the underside end of the screen. This cardboard shim will hit the shirtboard as you print and hold the screen a little off-contact (**4.11**).

Although the one-color press plans call for a square shirtboard (it's easier to build that way), it is easier to set the screen off-contact if the board has a tip on it that helps guide the shirt into place.

Some professional presses have automatic off-contact adjustments.

Make sure the image on the screen is square to the shirtboard before you clamp the screen in place. This can be done by placing a t-square under the screen and lining up the image to the edge of the square (**4.12**).

Making a Print

Place a small amount of ink in the ink reservoir along the back of the screen and lay the squeegee in the reservoir area. You can put nails on both ends of the squeegee to keep it from falling in the ink. Figure **4.13** shows the entire sequence.

Spray the shirtboard (platen) with a light coat of spray adhesive. This will keep the shirt from pulling up after you make the print and lift the screen. The spray will wear off after 20 or 30 prints and another light coat will be needed.

If you are doing sweatshirts you may need to use more spray or a special *web spray* that deposits a thicker coating on the boards or use special pallet covering called pallet tape that has adhesive on one or both sides. This can be taped to the board and then sprayed. It is removed when it gets too covered with lint and spray.

Slide a shirt over the platen. The platen should go between the front and back of the shirt. Most shirts have a natural center-line crease down the middle. Line this crease up on the center line of the platen. For the first print, place the shirt on far enough so that the collar just touches the end of the platen. You may have to vary this placement

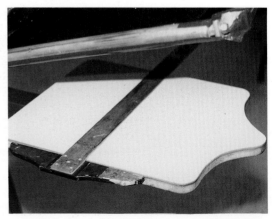

This is how you print a shirt!

1. Place ink in the back of the screen.

2. Use nails in the ends of the squeegees to keep them from falling in the ink.

3. Spray the board with adhesive.

4. Load the shirt on the shirtboard. Place the crease in the shirt down the center of the board.

5. Position the collar on the neck of the board.

6. Work some ink in front of the squeegee and pull it towards you with good downward pressure.

7. Don't apply so much pressure that you flatten the blade.

8. Pick up the squeegee at the end of the print and return it to the back of the screen.

later, depending on how high or low the print is on the screen and on the size of the garment. Generally, most designs are placed on the center of the chest or in the center of the back.

Pull the kick leg out of the way and lower the screen to the shirt. If you have a professional press just lower the screen frame. Grab the squeegee firmly with both hands and work it into the ink so that ink is in front of the blade. Pull the squeegee toward you with an even stroke.

When you reach the end of the screen, pick up the squeegee and return it to the ink reservoir. Pretty simple!

Lift the screen and let the kick leg fall into the down position. How does the print look? Chances are, the first print will be light (**4.14**). Some inks will require more squeegee pressure than others, and you may need to use more than one stroke to get a good, solid coat of ink. If the print is light, lower the screen and make another pass with the squeegee. Try to clean all the ink off the screen and make another pass. No ink should be left on the screen where the squeegee has passed.

4.14 If you don't apply enough downward, even pressure, the print may be light on one side. Lower the screen and make another stroke.

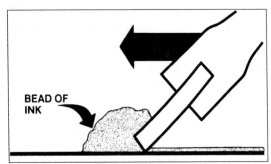

4.15 You can also push the squeegee away from you. This stroke may be less fatiguing on longer printing jobs.

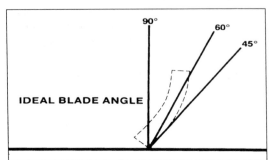

4.16 The squeegee blade should be at a 45° to 60° angle.

Proper Squeegee Handling

The squeegee can be used in a variety of ways. Not only can you pull the squeegee toward you, but you can also push it away (**4.15**). The idea is to apply just enough downward pressure to slightly flex the blade. The angle of the squeegee should be from 45° to 60° (**4.16**). The lower the angle, the more ink you will deposit on the garment. Ideally, the blade should just shear off the ink. Too much pressure and you will actually flatten the blade and cause it to skim across the screen.

Problems

Shadow or Double-Image Prints

This phenomenon can be caused by a number of factors. The screen fabric could be loose, allowing it to ripple in front of the squeegee as the pass is made (**4.17**). The screen may not be fastened down properly or tightly. The frame could be loose or warped. If the fabric is loose, try to make a good stroke in one direction only.

If you have a shadowed print, don't print any more shirts until you wipe the bottom of the screen with a cotton rag (**4.18**). One shadow print will lead to another because part of the shadow will be on the bottom of the screen and deposited on the next print!

When wiping the bottom of the screen, make sure no ink is in the open areas. Wiping will just draw this ink through the screen and you'll never get the bottom clean. You may have to put a little mineral spirits or screen opener on the rag to get the excess ink off the bottom. Always wipe the bottom with a dry cloth after using a solvent-soaked rag! Otherwise, you may still have ink and solvent on the bottom of the screen that will transfer to the next garment printed.

Pinholes

The first thing to do after checking for ink evenness and print quality is to check for pinholes. These will show up as tiny dots or "freckles" on the garment. While you should try to block out all the pinholes after the screen is exposed, they are easy to miss and occasionally will develop after you start printing. If you are ready to print an order and don't want to apply blockout to the new pinholes, just use a small piece of masking tape or even transparent tape as a temporary block (**4.19**).

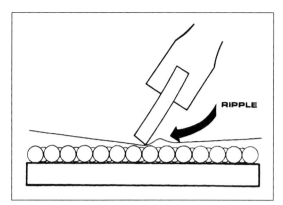

Flood Stroke

4.17

A flood stroke is a squeegee pass that is made with the screen in a partially up position and lays a thin coat of ink on the image area. It is generally used by printers who do a back *push stroke* and need to get the ink to the front before the stroke is made. It is also used when printing with air-dry inks after the stroke is made to keep the image area from drying-in and clogging.

To make a flood stroke, position the screen approximately 3 in. (7.62 cm) above the platen, lift the squeegee and pull it towards you using light, even pressure. Don't try to push ink through the screen; you just want it to lay *on* the screen (**4.20**).

A flood stroke is *not* necessary when using plastisol ink because it will never dry in the screen. Some printers feel a flood helps lay down more ink because the screen already has ink in the image as the stroke is made. You be the judge whether you want to use a flood stroke or not.

The ink should be fairly creamy and not runny for a flood stroke to work. If the ink is runny, it might run right through the screen before you make the next print! As before, *experiment!* It takes practice to get the feel of a good flood stroke. Too much pressure and you'll push the ink through; too little and the ink won't cover the screen.

Experiment

Printers have their own techniques. Plan to ruin a few shirts or rags trying different strokes, holding the squeegee differently and just plain getting the feel of it. It will take time to get your own techniques down and keep your fingers out of the ink. Keeping your hands clean is important because not only will you be printing, but handling the shirts as well.

Number of Strokes

Generally, you can make a good print by using a flood stroke followed by a print stroke in

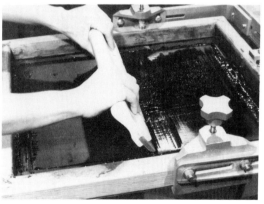

4.17 Shadow prints can be caused by loose fabric that ripples in front of the squeegee.

4.18 To remove a shadow from the screen wipe the bottom with either a dry cotton rag or a rag soaked in mineral spirits or screen opener.

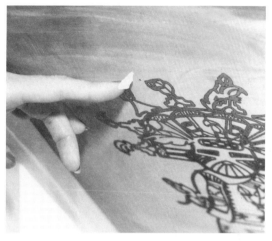

4.19 After the first print check for any pinholes that you missed. These can be blocked-out with a small piece of clear tape or a drop of block-out from a block-out pen.

4.20 A flood stroke is a light stroke that just coats the inside of the screen. It will keep the ink from drying in the screen when using air-dry inks.

the same direction. If you are using plastisol or *slow* air-dry ink, the flood stroke can be eliminated. Two or more strokes can be used if you're having trouble getting good coverage or if you're printing on a dark background. You can make strokes in both directions to deposit more ink, but you may lose some print detail. Strokes in both directions should really only be used if trying to make a thick print on nylon mesh or other open weave material. You may also get some shadowing if the screen mesh is loose or if the press has excess movement.

If possible always try to do the strokes in the same direction!

A Word About Plastisol Ink

Remember from Chapter 3 on Ink, that if the plastisol ink is too thick it will not flow very well and you may have to make more than one stroke. If you simply reduce the thickness (viscosity) of the ink slightly it will flow better and you can reduce the number of strokes and the pressure you have to apply. *This means sharper prints with less work!*

Basic Printing on Dark Material

One stroke with plastisol may not deposit enough ink to adequately cover a dark garment. In order to get a good, thick deposit, try using one clean stroke and one light stroke (with the screen down, of course). The second, light stroke, will leave a thin film of ink on top of the first coating. Again, experiment. If the ink isn't opaque enough, you may need to use three or four strokes and a light flood stroke. The light stroke also helps keep the last coating of ink on top of the garment (**4.21**).

A common misconception about ink for dark shirts is that the ink shouldn't be thinned. This is not really true because if the ink is too thick you apply too much downward pressure to make it go through the screen, and in turn drive the ink too deep into the garment.

4.21 You may have to do more than one stroke to get good coverage on a dark shirt with high-opacity ink.

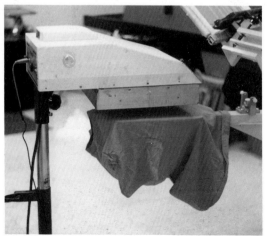

4.22 For the brightest print, you can print a color, flash-cure it, and then print it again!

By simply reducing the viscosity of the light colored ink slightly, you can use less squeegee pressure and leave a thicker coating of ink on top of the shirt.

Flash Curing

It's easy to tell you to do a number of strokes and reduce the ink slightly to get good coverage, but if you want a great looking print on a dark garment, you may have to use the flash-cure unit.

You can actually print a color twice and cure in between the prints to build up a layer of ink.

To do this, simply make a normal print on a dark shirt. Next, take the flash-curing unit and place it over the platen for about 10 seconds (**4.22**). This is enough time to *skin cure* the ink. Now you can print the same color *again* directly over the first print. The print will be very opaque now!

When printing on dark garments, remember to use a coarse mesh such as 60 or 86 (24-34 cm) monofilament. You can also use a slightly rounded squeegee. The coarser fabric will allow more ink through the mesh, and the roundness of the blade will lay down a thicker deposit of ink.

Some manufacturers offer a special flash-cure spray adhesive that will not lose its tack when heated with a flash-curing unit.

Clogging

When using air-dry inks, clogging or "freezing up" can be a constant problem. As mentioned earlier, using a flood stroke will help keep the ink moist, but you still must make a print at least every minute. The longer the ink sits in the screen with no motion, the more clogging!

What happens when the screen starts to clog? With most air-dry inks, you can remove the clog by wiping or scrubbing the clogged area with a rag that's been moistened with mineral spirits (or water if you're using a water soluble ink). If this doesn't remove the clog, use a harsher solvent like lacquer thinner or screen opener. Spray or blot a small amount on the clog, let it sit for a minute and then make a print or two on a rag. This should open the screen. As a last resort, try dipping a toothbrush in lacquer thinner and scrubbing the area lightly.

If you allow the screen to stay partially clogged in areas while printing, the ink may dry permanently in the fabric and not be removable. Then the only solution is to remake the screen! There are commercial sprays on the market similar to lacquer thinner that will soften stubborn clogs. Always use proper ventilation when using these sprays.

What happens when you want to take a break and you are using a water-based ink? Flood the screen heavily or push all of the ink back into the reservoir end and clean out the image portion of the screen.

When printing a job, try to get a routine down so that the screen and ink are almost always in constant motion. Having someone put on and remove shirts will help *and* keep inky hands off garments.

Position of Print

The position of the print on the shirt should be in the same place every time. Hold a shirt up and see where the center of the chest is. If a design is full size – approximately 12 x 12 in. (30.48 x 30.48 cm) – position the top of it about 1½ in. (3.81 cm) down from the neck. This will vary with the shirt size – small shirts will be placed a little higher; extra-large shirts a little lower.

A back print should go across the center of the back. Try putting the top of the design about 4 or 5 in. (10.16 or 12.7 cm) down from the collar. Again, this will vary with the size of shirt and the size of the design. The thing to remember is to keep each order *uniform.*

Print Placement and Uniformity

The press you build is mainly designed for printing adult-size T-shirts. When printing kids' sizes, such as 6-8, you'll find that it takes a little stretching to get them on the platen. It may even be impossible to get the shirt on far enough for the print to be high and close to the collar. Try laying the shirt, unopened, on *top* of the platen (not *around* it). If the platen has spray adhesive on it, or ink buildup, put an old, clean shirt over it and lay the kids' shirt on this.

This method also works when printing ladies' tops and other items that are too small to fit around the platen. One of the problems with stretching kids' shirts or ladies' tops is that the print won't look the same when the shirt is removed from the platen and returns to its normal shape. If there are any straight lines in the design, they'll look like a roller coaster.

As a general rule, don't stretch a shirt to fit over a platen. Instead, lay it on top of the covered platen. This is not applicable to multicolor work. *A word of warning!* When you lay the shirt on top of the platen, it will pull up with the screen and you *won't* get a second chance on the print! If possible, have someone hold the collar or sleeves down while you raise the screen.

Printing Both Sides

When an order calls for printing both sides of a shirt, handle one side at a time. Print the first side of all the shirts, drying and curing as normal, and then print the other side.

Heart-Size Prints

Some orders will call for a small heart-size print on the front, and a large full-size print on the back. This is where a gang screen comes in handy. Remember to watch the placement on the front print. Don't put it too low or too far to the left. If it's too far to the left, it may look fine when printed, but be under the arm when someone is wearing it.

Tip: If you're going to print a heart-size print *on* a pocket, the placement is critical! Draw an outline of the pocket on the platen with a felt-tip marker right where the pocket has to go for the print to fall into place (**4.23**). When putting the shirt on the platen, position the *top* of the shirt pocket on the top of the drawing.

Another easy technique is to spray glue a piece of cardboard to the shirtboard in the same position as the pocket. Line up the screen to print on the cardboard and use spray on top of the cardboard to hold the shirt in place. When loading the shirt you can feel the cardboard underneath and you will load the shirt so the pocket or heart print loction is in the correct spot (**4.24**).

You can do the same thing when printing above the pocket by using the cardboard as a guide.

Band Designs

A band design (also called a wrap design) is a print that goes all the way across the chest of the shirt to the edge and might be continued on the back.

4.23 Draw a mark on the board where the heart or pocket print needs to go and load the shirt using the mark as a guide.

4.24 A piece of cardboard glued to the shirtboard can also be used as a guide for pocket or heart prints.

4.23   *4.24*

To print a band design, you need to make a larger frame. The total width of the design should be from 20-24 in. (50.8-60.96 cm). Allow 3-4 in. (7.62-10.16 cm) on each end of the screen reservoir. The frame size should be approximately 38 x 20 in. (96.52 x 50.8 cm). Remember that you'll be printing small shirts and extra-large shirts with the same screen, so keep intricate artwork to a minimum towards the end of the band (**4.25**).

You should print most bands by hand on a flat table. Place a stack of open newspapers on the table and lay the shirt on the papers. Smooth out wrinkles under the arms and along both side creases. Try to start the top of the band under the arm of the shirt. You should be able to see through the screen to position it in the proper place.

Once you've got it in position, lay the screen down and have someone hold it in place. Assuming it already has ink in it, make a good solid stroke from left-to-right or right-to-left (**4.26**). If you aren't sure of the quality of the stroke, do it again. Since the shirt will pull up when you lift the screen, you only get one shot at making a good print! Lift the screen slowly, starting at one end, and let the shirt peel itself off the screen. Dry and cure the shirt as normal.

4.25 *Band designs need to be longer than the largest shirt and exposed on very wide screens.*

4.26 *Print band designs on a stack of newspaper with the screen hand-held.*

After removing the shirt, you'll see why the newspaper is necessary. The ink that ran off the edge will be on the newspaper. Remove the inky sheet of paper, lay down the second shirt and repeat the process for the next print.

Tips: Print the larger shirts first and work your way down to the smaller sizes.

If you also have to print a band on the back, you will have to line up the prints on the edge of the shirt and see where the front print is. Mark the paper with a magic marker where the print starts on both sides. Look through the screen to align the top of the back print with this line.

Positioning the design square to the frame will make printing band designs much easier.

Blends

Sooner or later, one-color prints will get a little boring. But there is a way to add a little spice to "one-color" prints. A blend is a very simple process of putting more than one color of ink in the screen to allow you to get a three- or even four-color effect. As you pull the squeegee, the different colors will start to blend together in the middle making a third color.

Try placing a small amount of red in the ink reservoir on the left-hand side. Place a small amount of white to the right of the red and then small amounts of red, yellow, royal and white (**4.27**). By making two or three passes with the squeegee, the ink should start to blend together nicely giving you a multicolor print with just *one screen*. The more strokes you make, the more the ink blends until the gradation becomes even. Eventually, the ink may mix and become all one color. That is the reason for using a small amount of ink. As the blend loses its color definition you will have to add more ink.

If the design you're printing is wide enough, it's possible to use three or more colors of ink in one screen.

Tips: If the blend becomes too muddy after 40 or 50 prints, scrape all the ink out of the screen and start over.

Use a small amount of the dark color and more of the lighter color and use a squeegee that is almost the same width as the inside of the screen. Any excess sideways squeegee movement will decrease the number of prints you'll get before you have to replace the ink.

Save the ink that you scrape out of the screen and put it in a "junk" can. You can add black to this to make more black or use it to mix brown.

Generally, run blends vertically. If you run them horizontally, the ink will tend to run together when the screen is in the up position.

Don't get too carried away with blends. They can get a little boring if they're used on every job.

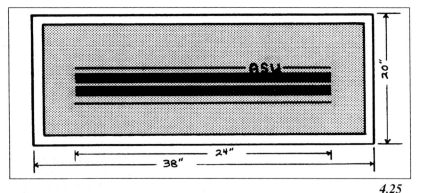

4.25

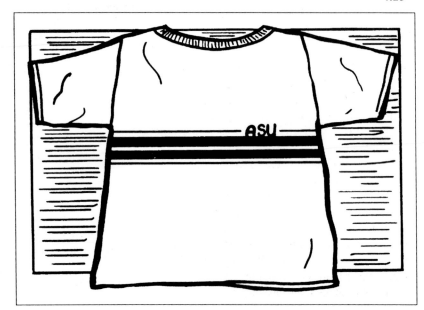

4.26

Printing A Blend

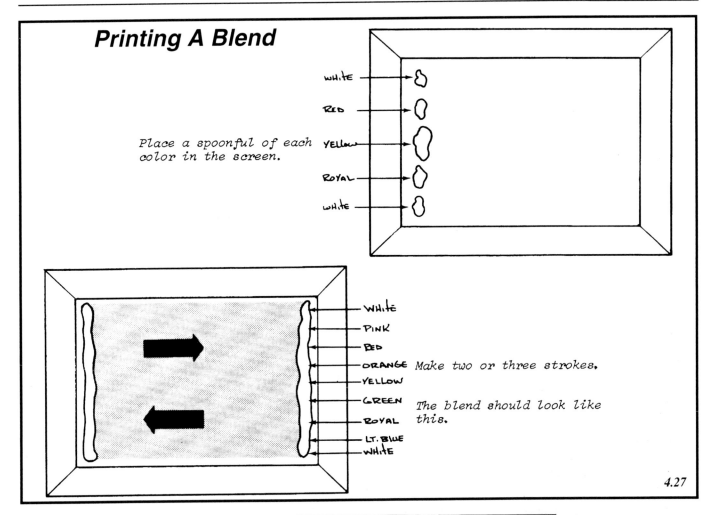

Place a spoonful of each color in the screen.

WHITE
RED
YELLOW
ROYAL
WHITE

WHITE
PINK
RED
ORANGE Make two or three strokes.
YELLOW
GREEN The blend should look like
ROYAL this.
LT. BLUE
WHITE

4.27

Try to stay away from a blend if the design has a lot of lettering. It might make it harder to read. The blending technique lends itself to designs with a lot of large, solid ink areas.

Gang Screens

As described in the *Screen Making* chapter, you can gang three or four different designs on the same screen to save time, screen storage room and money.

To use a gang screen, you must block off the portion you don't want to use so that the ink will only be pushed through the design you want. The unused designs should be taped off on top of the screen. If you tape them off on the bottom, the ink and mineral spirits will start to react with the adhesive in the tape and may clog the design.

When you're finished printing with the first design on a ganged screen and ready to do the next one, untape the second design from the top and tape the first design on the bottom (**4.28**). Repeat the process with each design.

When you're through with the screen, remove all the tape over design areas and clean it thoroughly.

4.28 Gang multiple designs on one screen to save time and money. Tape them off on the top before you use them and then tape off each image on the bottom after you are done with it.

Imprinting

It may be necessary to print something on or around a design that has already been printed. This could happen, for instance, if a word, date or something belonging in the design was forgotten. Perhaps a customer wants his logo printed on T-shirts and wants only five shirts with "Fred" above the logo, ten shirts with "Bob," etc.

You may have customers who buy stock designs from you but want them customized with their city or state. This is called a *name drop* and is an easy way to make a multicolor design work for a variety of customers. The easiest way to do these jobs is to imprint the additional information after you print the main design.

Start by printing the basic design on the whole order, dry or cure the ink and then set up the imprint screen. Position the additional information to be printed on the imprint screen so that the wording will fall in the proper location on the shirt and then do the imprinting.

You can use a gang screen for imprinting the name drops and just tape and untape as described earlier.

Athletic Printing

Generally, athletic printing requires a thicker deposit of ink and is usually only one or two colors. For the highest quality athletic printing, you should use a special athletic plastisol that is much more durable and elastic than an all-purpose plastisol.

Printing on uniforms is different than T-shirts because the athletic customers want a lot of ink on the garment so it will be durable. They also prefer a glossier finish to the ink (a common characteristic of athletic plastisols).

For heavy uniforms and jerseys that are nylon mesh or porthole mesh, you can use low mesh counts 30-60 (13-24 cm) monofilament in order to deposit a thick layer of ink (**4.29**).

It will also take a number of strokes and maybe even strokes in both directions to get ink down around the material. A softer squeegee with a rounded edge may help.

Don't worry about having to use a nylon jacket bonding agent with nylon mesh. The bonding agent is designed for waterproofed nylon.

Some printers do add a little bonding agent to their athletic inks to make them more durable and industrial wash resistant!

4.29 Athletic prints are thicker and use a special athletic plastisol printed through coarse mesh counts.

When printing on mesh, you will have little *dimples* of ink on the shirtboard after each print. You can either wipe them off after the print, or you can place a piece of blank heat transfer paper on the board and let the paper stay with the garment and go through the dryer. This will let the ink fill the holes in the mesh. After the print is dry you can peel the paper off.

For the smoothest and thickest prints on heavy uniforms you may have to do the print, flash-cure and then print again.

A Word of Caution

Although athletic printing sounds easier, it can actually be much more frustrating because you a generally printing on an expensive jersey that needs to have specific colors, team names, numbers and maybe players names – all on the correct garment size. If you make a mistake you can't just tell the customer you are sorry. Who is going to pay for the garment if it was special ordered from the sporting goods store?

Athletic printing requires patience and a clear understanding that a lot of work goes into making sure the garment is printed correctly.

Also, when printing with thick inks it is common to not get a full cure. You get accustomed to curing normal thickness prints and now you are trying to cure much thicker prints with the same dryer setting. Make sure you get the plastisol cured to at least 320° F (160° C) down deep where the ink is bonding to the material.

It may be necessary to place a paper thermometer *inside* the garment to get a good reading down deep where the ink needs to fully cure!

Numbering

If you get into athletic lettering, there will be times when individual or consecutive numbering will be needed. You can do this by various methods.

Heat Transfer Numbers

Although you can buy special die-cut vinyl heat transfer numbers, they can be fairly expensive. You can easily make your own transfer numbers by following the directions in the chapter on *transfer making*. This is handy if you do a lot of Little League uniforms every year. Just make gang sheets of the various size numbers in all of the athletic colors (**4.30**).

Paper Stencil Numbers

The easiest way to do numbering is by using ready-made paper stencil kits that are sold in a variety of sizes and styles, and in two-color numbers (see Appendix A). They are easy to use and cost less than making up hundreds of screens for all of the number sizes (**4.31**).

4.30

4.30 *You can easily make heat transfer number sheets for your athletic numbering needs.*

4.31 *Paper stencil kits are available in a variety of number styles and sizes.*

To use paper stencils, simply make a master frame that has a large, square, open mesh area. The size of the area will depend on the number size. Generally, a 14 x 14 in. (35.56 x 35.56 cm) area is fine.

Now, lay the paper stencil in the proper location on the garment (**4.32**). If you have two digits, simply line them up on the garment by eye. You may need to lay masking strips around the number to make sure you don't get excess ink on the garment.

Next, bring down the master screen and make a print in the desired color. The paper acts as a stencil and allows ink to go on the garment only where the opening in the *paper* is. The ink will act like an adhesive, holding the paper stencil to it when the screen is lifted and allowing you to make dozens of prints of the same number (**4.33**).

With this method, you only need a set of numbers and a screen (with a coarse mesh, such as 30-60 monofilament on it) for each color of ink.

Standard Screens

You can also screen print numbers using conventional screens. The easiest way is to make a screen for each number. This is okay if you are doing a lot of 1-15. Unfortunately, the customer often wants random numbering.

In that case, you can make a special numbering screen where one side of the frame is made of thin metal. The fabric can then be glued to the metal side and stapled on the others. These frames should be made to slip easily into a master frame (**4.34**). You will need two frames for each number – one left and one right. Of course, you will need a set of numbers for each size number you are going to print.

Numbering Equipment

Some manufacturers make numbering easy with special printers that are designed specifically to number on garments.

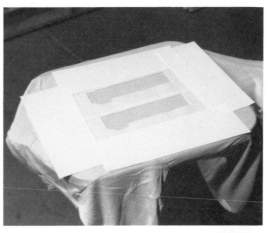

4.32 *Lay the paper stencil in the proper location on the garment. If necessary, put masking pieces around the number.*

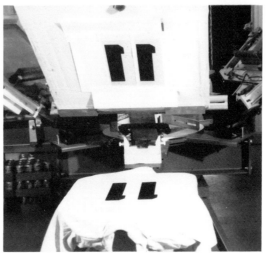

4.33 *A paper stencil can be used for dozens of prints because the ink acts as an adhesive and holds the paper on the screen.*

4.34 *If you do a lot of numbering then invest in a set of number screens so you easily direct screen print numbers.*

Multicolor Printing

Sooner or later someone will want you to print a multicolor job. As time goes on, you'll find that a lot of multicolor work is available, so you might as well gear up for it!

Multicolor printing is done by putting a screen for each color to be printed on a special carousel printing press that lets the screens rotate (**4.35**). The prints are then done one-after-the other with wet-ink-on-wet-ink (some jobs require flash curing between colors).

Equipment

If you are just starting out and can't afford to buy a professional press, simply build one from the plans in Appendix B (**4.36**). You can build a press for under $150 that will work fine for beginning level work.

Sooner or later, you will want to purchase a commercially made press. They range in price from $500-$5,000 or higher for an eight-color model with all the features. You can purchase a good four-color press for $2,000-$3,000 (**4.37**). In fact, some manufacturers make basic models for less than $1,000 (**4.38**).

If possible, try to get a sturdy printing press that can print at least six colors (**4.39**) and has a micro-adjustment feature for registering screens (**4.40**).

An often overlooked feature is called a speed table. This is where the base of the press that holds the platens rotates separately from the top printing head section (**4.41**). This feature allows higher production because someone can be loading a fresh shirt while the printer is printing. This feature also makes flash-curing between colors much easier.

If you plan on doing a lot of high production printing then by all mean purchase a press that allows all of the printing heads to come down at once. This is called an *all-heads-down* press and allows more than one person to print at the same time. *Not all presses are all-heads-down.* Some of the less expensive models only let you bring down one head at a time.

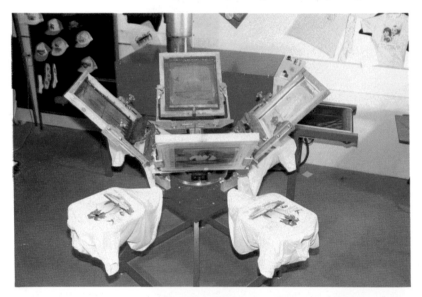

4.35 *Multicolor printing is done on a carousel press that lets the screens rotate and print one-after-the-other.*

4.36 *A simple 4-color press can be built for less than $150 from plans in Appendix B.*

4.37 *Commercial presses are available for $2,000 to $3,000. (Photos courtesy Hopkins International, Berkeley, CA. and Chaparral Industries, Phoenix, AZ.)*

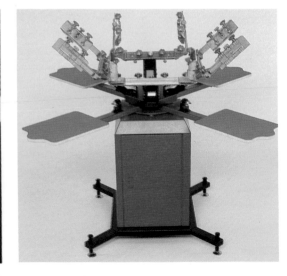

4.38

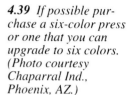

4.38 *4-color basic presses are available for less than $1,000. (Photo courtesy Dynamic Screen Equipment, Charlotsville, W.VA.)*

4.39 *If possible purchase a six-color press or one that you can upgrade to six colors. (Photo courtesy Chaparral Ind., Phoenix, AZ.)*

4.40 *It is much easier to setup a job with micro-adjustments to fine-tune the registration.*

4.41 *Shirtboards that rotate help increase production and make flash-curing easier. (Photo courtesy Hopkins Int., Berkeley, CA.)*

Set-up

As discussed in the *Screen Making* chapter, it is very important that you expose all multicolor screens in register to each other. Make sure to use the correct mesh. Generally, you should use a finer mesh for multicolor printing on light shirts to allow for a thinner deposit of ink and less buildup on the bottom of the screens.

Line-up to the Outline Color

Start setting up the press by putting the *black*, or outline color screen on the press first. If there is no real outline color, then put the screen that has most of the design elements on the press. The following section is illustrated in figure **4.42**.

Square up this screen to the platen so that the design will print in the right location.

Adjust for Off-Contact

Next, set the screen to print *off-contact* through press adjustments. If you're printing on a homemade or inexpensive press, simply place a shim under the screen where it attaches to the screen clamp and another thin cardboard shim on the underside of the outside edge of the screen. These shims will now hold the screen about 1/8 in. off of the platen. Make sure the screen is firmly clamped in place.

To allow for error when exposing the screens, make sure the first screen you set up is placed from ¼-½ in. (.64-1.27 cm) out from the back of the screen clamp.

Put ink in this screen and make a print on a piece of test print material or an old shirt. If you're going to be printing on light shirts, you may need to reduce the thickness (viscosity) of the ink with a curable reducer. This will help the ink penetrate into the garment and not just lay on top. This will also help minimize buildup.

Use plenty of spray adhesive on the platen because you will align the other screens to this print.

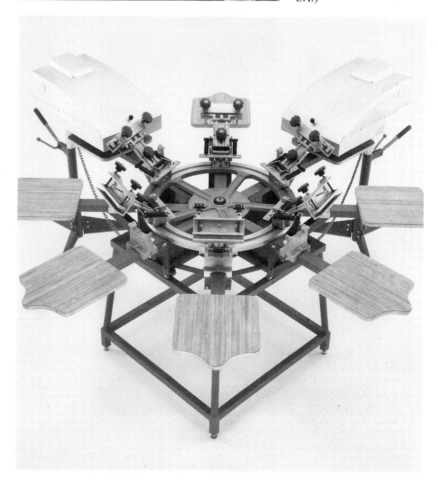

This is How You Set-up a Four-Color Job!

1. Put the outline or black screen on the press.

2. Set the screen for off-contact or use shims.

3. Make a print of the outline or alignment print.

4. Line-up the next-to-last color to the alignment print. The normal color sequence is light to dark.

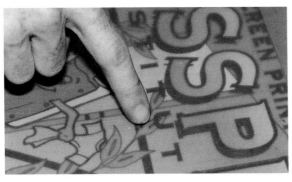

5. Line up the rest of the screens in the correct printing order.

6. Ink the screens. Reduce the viscosity slightly if the ink is too thick.

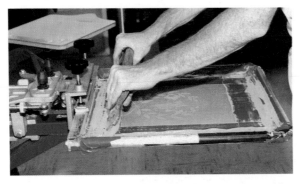

7. Use medium or medium hard squeegees with sharp edges.

8. Make a test print on a fresh rag or test square. Try to use just one stroke on each screen.

Determine the Color Sequence

The outline or black screen will always be the *first* screen lined up but the *last* color printed! Always set up screens in the *reverse* order that you will print them. Now, decide which color you want to print *next-to-last*. Normally, the next-to-last color should be one with a lot of open print area (i.e., if there is a lot of red to be printed, print it next to last). This is the second screen you should set up.

Rotate the screens one position to the right and set up the screen for the next to last print color. You should be able to see the black print just made through the screen and see where the next color should fall. Line up this screen, using the black outline just printed as a guide, and clamp it down tightly. Do not put ink in this screen yet.

Once again, move the screens to the right, leaving an open position above the platen. Take the color you wish to print *second* and place that screen on the press. Line the screen up on the black print, the same as you did for the previous screen. Again, do not put ink in this screen yet.

Now it's time for the first print color. This should be the screen with either the lightest ink color (yellow?) or the smallest print area. Place this screen on the press, line it up on the black print and clamp it down.

Now, before inking the screens, recheck the registration. Make sure the screen for black ink lines up perfectly on the black print already made. Check the rest of the screens to see that they also line up perfectly.

Ink the Screens

If everything checks out, you're ready to ink up. Start with the first screen, which we'll assume is for yellow ink. This is the first color to be printed. Don't run the ink too thick and try to use a fairly sharp squeegee. Place the ink in the screen.

Now, move on to the second screen to be printed. Let's assume this is blue. Again, don't print the ink too thick and use a fairly sharp squeegee. Ink this screen.

The third print color is next and we'll assume this is red. As before, don't print the ink too thick and use a fairly sharp squeegee. Ink this screen.

The black screen already has ink in it but the black ink should be a *little thicker* and requires a squeegee that is fairly sharp.

Make Your First Test Print

Now, remove the black sample print. Put a clean shirt or rag on the platen and make a print, starting with the *yellow!* Try to make one stroke, going only one way on the yellow screen. Leave the shirt on the platen and swing the blue screen into position. Again, make a good solid stroke in one direction. Do the same with the red. When

4.43 A multicolor print that was printed wet-on-wet.

4.44 When printing wet-on-wet you will get a build-up of ink on the bottom of the screens. Buildup can be minimized by using a higher mesh count and a slightly reduced ink with only one or two squeegee strokes.

4.45 Buildup can be removed by wiping the bottom of the screen with a dry cotton rag or a rag that has a slight amount of mineral spirits or screen opener.

you get to the black, you may need to do the stroke a little slower because the ink is thicker. It also may take a couple of strokes to get good coverage (**4.43**). Congratulations, you have just printed four colors wet-on-wet.

Buildup

Why is there all the concern about ink thickness, color sequence and squeegees? Multicolor printing presents a lot more problems than you had with the simple one-color print. The main problem is buildup.

Look on the bottom of each screen (**4.44**). The blue screen will have a little shadow of yellow, the red screen will have a little shadow of yellow and blue, and he black screen will have a little of each color. This isn't so bad on the first few prints, but wait until you've done four or five dozen shirts. The buildup will get worse and worse and start to affect the sharpness of the prints.

If you have used the correct mesh, reduced the ink a little and printed with one or two clean strokes, you should have minimal buildup that really won't affect the quality of your prints.

If you do encounter excessive buildup (some colors like fluorescents tend to build up more than others), the remedy is to stop and wipe off the bottom of all the screens in order to restore the print sharpness.

If the buildup gets too bad, you may have to wipe the bottom of each screen with a dry cotton rag (**4.45**). If this doesn't remove it, you may need to put a little mineral spirits or screen opener on a rag to remove it. Another way is to try to clean the buildup off before it gets too bad. With each screen, make four or five clean, hard prints on a rag *bringing no ink forward* with the squeegee; use a new rag for the next screen. This will help transfer the buildup from the bottom of the screen to the rag.

4.46 A flash-cure unit can be used to cure between colors or just before the last color on a multicolor job.

4.47 To help colors stand out on a dark garment, print an underbase or underlay of white ink first and then flash-cure it.

4.48 Print all purpose plastisol on top of the underbase white to achieve bright colors on dark shirts.

Flash-Curing

If necessary, you can flash-cure each color or print all of the undercolors and flash just before printing the black outline. This will help minimize the buildup but will *greatly decrease* production! A flash-cure unit should not be used as a solution to improper mesh, ink and technique (**4.46**)!

To flash-cure, simply swing the unit over the board after you have made a print. For higher production use a press with a speed table and make the print and then rotate the platens under the flash-cure unit. While the print is curing you can be making another print.

It should only take a few seconds to quickly skin over the plastisol ink.

Try printing the jobs without flash-curing first, and then, if necessary, just flash before the last color. If all else fails, flash every color.

Multicolor Printing on Dark Shirts

This is quite a bit harder to do but can give an outstanding look. To print multicolor designs on dark shirts, you will need to use a lower mesh count such as 86 (34 cm), along with a high opacity ink.

To get a bright print, you will need to make a number of strokes and possibly flash-cure between colors.

Print an Underbase of White

A popular method is to print a base of white ink first; this is called an "underbase" or "underlay." You can print this with a normal high opacity white ink or a special underbase white that flash-cures quickly (**4.47**). The underbase is generally printed through an 86 to 125 (34 - 49 cm) mesh.

Once you flash cure the underbase, you can print on top of it with all-purpose plastisols

through a much higher mesh count such as 180 to 230 (70 - 90 cm). The prints will be very bright and appear to be opaque. You may still need to flash-cure certain problem colors (**4.48**).

Use the Black of the Shirt as a Color

By creating perfect overlays you can actually just print them with an underbase *and not* print the black outline for a design. It will feel much softer on the shirt and the actual shirt color becomes the black (**4.49**).

Creating the Underbase Art

The best dark shirt printing is done with the underbase *choked* slightly to be a little thinner than the colors on top. This allows a design to be slightly off register yet appear to be in register because the top colors fall "over" the underbase slightly when printed.

Choking artwork and creating underbases is covered in Chapter 1.

Most of the great sports and entertainment characters on black shirts are created on the computer and in the camera and printed with 8 to 12 colors on automatic presses. This work is more difficult to do and requires special artwork that has been converted into halftone dots (**4.50**). It is now possible to do some of these designs with a standard computer graphics set-up and a six or eight-color manual press.

Ideas

Try using puff ink as one of the colors in a multicolor job. Print the puff ink last to avoid any buildup problems and to allow it to puff properly.

You can also incorporate some of the other specialty inks covered in Chapter 7 on Special Effects Printing with a standard multicolor design.

Four-Color Process Printing

This is a topic that is a little too advanced for this book. We are mentioning it here to make you aware of it and so that you will understand the potential of four-color process.

Four-color process is a method where a fully colored piece of artwork is sent to a color separator who separates out all the colors in the design into the four basic process colors of black, yellow, cyan (process blue) and magenta (process red) and creates four film positives. By exposing these special film positives on high mesh count screens (generally 305 and higher) and printing the job with the four special process colors of ink, all of the colors in the original art are resproduced *fairly* closely (**4.51**).

4.49 Create perfect overlays and print them on an underbase of white using the shirt color as the black outline.

4.50 This image was taken from a color photograph and created entirely with a computer graphics system. This is only a five-color print.

4.51 True process color consists of designs that are separated by a professional separator and then printed with the four process colors of ink. (Photo courtesy Union Ink Co., Ridgefield, NJ.)

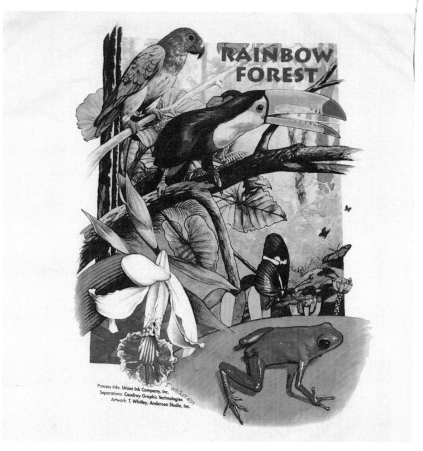

4.52 *These designs were created from full-color photos that were scanned into Adobe Photoshop and printed out onto vellums that were used to expose the screens. This method only works for non-critical jobs.*

The drawback to the process is that the separations cost between $200 - $500. This cost eliminates this process for most small customers.

Although you can make process color separations using a computer graphics system and a laser printer, the quality is not as good as those created by separators. For non-critical jobs such as nature scenes, animals or cartoons, you can do your own separations for much less than a professional separator (**4.52**). To learn more about this process, consult the *Encyclopedia of Garment Printing* or the video tape *Process Color Printing*. Appendix A has a list of color separators who specialize in making separations for textile printers.

General Tips

Buy a large supply of test squares (see Appendix A) to do the first sample prints. It will save money and you won't have to ruin a good shirt to make a test print.

Always save a sample for yourself! Having good samples of your work is very important. When that big customer calls and wants to see what kind of work you do, you'll have lots of impressive samples to show.

If the print size is larger than the press you

built can handle, cut a piece of 1/8 in. Masonite™ to the size you need and tack it to the existing platen. If the design is really big, print the shirt on a table, the same way as described for printing band designs.

Clean-up

This is always the worst part of the job! That's why we left it for last. An important point to remember is that it is illegal to just wipe down screens with rags and throw the rags away. You may be *generating* hazardous waste products!

Start by scraping all the excess ink back into the can with a stiff piece of cardboard or paint scraper. Clean as much of the ink from the screen as possible (**4.53**).

The more ink you scrape back into the container, the safer and more legal the process is. It is important to minimize the use of solvents that are not only flammable but emit VOC's (volatile organic compounds) into the atmosphere.

In the old days, we would take the screen off the press, pour mineral spirits into the screen, and wipe the ink residue out with a rag. The problem today is what do you do with the rag?

You may find that in your area you can actually use this method as long as the rags are rented from a rag service who will come and pick them up.

A more popular option is to clean the screen with water! Yes, you can actually clean plastisol ink from the screen with special water-wash-ups (**4.54**). Simply spray them on the screen (after you have removed as much ink as possible) and wash the residue down the drain with water.

There are also companies who specialize in very safe products for screen clean-up and reclaiming and who will put their claims in writing for you to show the local municipality (**4.55**).

Tips: By taping off the inside edges of the screen before printing, you can keep ink from seeping between the frame and the fabric. This is very useful if the screen will be reclaimed. Just remove the tape and the excess ink with it. Use rubber gloves when cleaning to keep the ink and solvents off of your hands.

4.53 *Scrape as much ink as possible back into the container.*

4.54 *Plastisol ink can be cleaned-up with special water wash-ups. (Photo courtesy Union Ink Co., Ridgefield, NJ.)*

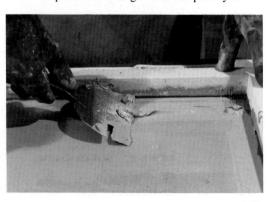

4.53

4.54

One popular method for professional printing shops is to use a special clean-up sink called a *Safety Kleen* unit. This is just a parts washer that is used by automotive repair shops (**4.56**). You can rent these units by the month. Although you can buy a parts washer, it's better to rent one because then the chemical solvent is not totally your responsibility. The company you rent from removes the old solvent, properly disposes of, or recycles it and brings a new solvent drum.

Clean all of the tools, squeegees, stir sticks, scrapers, etc. Clean the squeegee very well and try to get all the ink out from around the area where the rubber meets the wood. See the section on *Care and Feeding of Squeegees*.

An option for screens that you will use over and over is to just store them wet with a small amount of ink left on them. Just scrape them out, wipe the frame clean and store it. The ink will never dry and you don't have the worry of the hazardous waste or chemicals. When the customer re-orders just pull the screen and you are ready to go!

Repairing Reject Prints

Let's face it. Some misprinted shirts are destined for the rag box. But, you can fix other mistakes by using special *spotting guns* that shoot out spotting fluid at very high pressure. They will even shoot out cured plastisol!

Spotting guns sell for $130 and up and are a worthwhile investment for a serious printer!

To use a spotting gun, simply place a rag inside the shirt and spray the fluid on the outside of the shirt directly on the spot (**4.57**). If the shirt is printed be sure to cure or dry the print first, otherwise the ink will run and spread.

Packaging

It looks very impressive for the customer to pick up the order and find that each shirt is individually folded and bagged six shirts per bag. Some people may think this is too much work, but believe use, it makes the difference between the amateur and the professional.

Packaging has a psychological advantage, too! If all the shirts are tossed in a box unfolded, the customer may start picking through and look at each shirt. Actually, they will *inspect* each shirt, and you can bet that if a marginal print is in there, they'll find it. On the other hand, if the shirts are folded and bagged, it will look like a very professional job and the customer will only be able to look at one or two shirts!

Another tip on packaging, is to *always* pull out the best print and leave it loose on the top.

Always tell the customer how great the order looks. Again, you are getting a psychological advantage. The first impression will be of that *excellent* print and your *enthusiasm*. Try it! Most industrial supply houses have stock size polybags. The best size for shirts is a 1-mil-thick 12 x 16 in. (30.48 x 40.64 cm) bag. If you can't buy the bags from a supplier, try a grocery store. They usually have plastic bags that are 11 x 13 in. (27.94 x 33.02 cm). This size will work.

4.55 *Many companies offer environmentally safe products and will back up their claims in writing. (Photo courtesy I.C.C., Cincinnati, OH.)*

4.56 *Safety Kleen units are basically parts washers that have found wide popularity in the screen printing industry. They are available in every community and are a common item in gas stations. (Photo courtesy Safety Kleen, Elk Grove, IL.)*

4.57 *A spot removal gun is an essential piece of equipment for repairing mistakes and marks on shirts.*

The Future is Here

What is your next step? As you grow you will want to have higher production. You could certainly farm out any large jobs to printers with automatic presses, but a small automatic is not totally out of the question. As the cost of labor and keeping employees rises, many small shops make the move the automatic equipment rather than put more people on payroll.

Most equipment companies now offer starter automatic presses for less than $25,000 (**4.58**). Yes, that is a lot of money, but on a lease plan, may only be a $600 per month payment! Cheaper than a full time employee and it won't call in sick.

Automatic presses can generally produce from 25 to 50 dozen prints **per hour** with only two or three operators! The following photos show the more popular starter automatic presses on the market.

4.58 Automatic presses are available for under $25,000. (Top photo courtesy Tuff Products, Houston, TX., bottom photo courtesy M&R Screen Equipment, Elgin, IL.)

Printing Troubleshooting Chart

One-Color Printing

Problem	Cause/Remedy
Print loses detail or gets shadowed	– Use a finer mesh. Consult *Fabric Selector Chart*. – Too many strokes. Keep strokes same direction. – Screen fabric loose. – Squeegee too soft or not sharp enough. – Printing press loose. Tighten press. – Not printing off-contact.
Ink coverage too thin	– Mesh too fine. Consult *Fabric Selector Chart*. – Use more strokes. – Ink too thin. – Stroke too fast. Slow down print stroke to let ink flow. – Loose weave shirt. Use a thicker ink.
Ink color on dark shirt looks weak and not bright	– Ink not high opacity. Change ink. – Improper screen mesh. Consult *Fabric Selector Chart*. – Not enough squeegee strokes. Dark shirts may require more than one stroke. – Squeegee too hard. Use medium blade. – Squeegee too sharp. Use slightly rounded blade. – Stroke too fast. Use much slower stroke for ink to flow.

Multicolor Printing

Problem	Cause/Remedy

Excessive buildup on screen bottoms on light shirt print	– Too much ink on top of garment.
	   – Reduce number of squeegee strokes.
	   – Reduce ink viscosity for better penetration.
	   – Stroke too slow. Increase squeegee speed.
	   – Mesh to coarse. See *Fabric Selector Chart*.
	   – Squeegee too dull. Use sharp edge squeegee.
	– Wrong color sequence. Print light to dark if possible.
	– Screens not off-contact. Set screens for slight off-contact.
	– Artwork too loose. Use perfect overlays and more under-color-removal.
	– Job may need flash-curing. Flash-cure before black.

Prints don't remain sharp	– See above "Excessive buildup." – Too much squeegee pressure. Reduce pressure to lay down cleaner deposit of ink. – Squeegee angle too low. Raise angle to make sharper print. – Black ink too thin. Use thicker black to lay on top of undercolors.
Print on dark shirts not sharp	– Ink too thick. Reduce ink *slightly* and use less squeegee pressure with a slower stroke. – Too many strokes. Reduce number of strokes. – Squeegee not sharp. Use sharper squeegee with slower stroke. – Underbase not smooth enough. Keep underbase smooth and clean.

CHAPTER

5

HEAT TRANSFERS

eat transfers – also known as an Iron-on or Iron-on Decals – are a very popular method to decorate a T-Shirt. Contrary to popular belief, heat transfers are not a new item. The Kaumagraph Co. in Delaware has been making hot-melt gravure transfers since 1902! In the mid 1970's, transfers became a standard method used to decorate T-Shirts.

Although customers may feel that a transfer is not as good as a direct print, the improved quality of inks and printing technology have made transfers a very popular and durable method of decorating garments. In fact, it is now hard to tell the difference between a direct print and a hot peel heat transfer.

What Is a Heat Transfer

Basically, you can make a plastisol heat transfer by screen printing plastisol ink on a special release paper. The transfer is then applied to a garment or fabric using a heat press that applies pressure and melts the ink so it will bond with the fabric (**5.1**).

Types of Transfers

Hot-Peel (Hot-Split)

There are two basic types of plastisol transfers: hot-split and cold-peel. The term "hot-peel" or "hot-split" comes from the fact that you actually peel the transfer paper off the garment while it is hot. Part of the ink stays on the garment while part remains on the paper (**5.2**). This gives the design a screen printed feel. Hot-split transfers are the most popular transfer system and are very easy to make and apply.

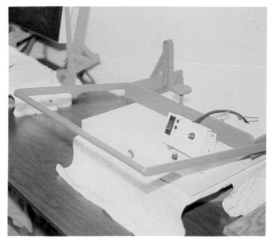

5.1 A heat transfer is applied with heat and pressure to garments and other imprintable items using a heat transfer press.

5.2 A hot-peel transfer has a soft direct screen print feel because the ink splits during application and only part of the ink stays on the garment and the rest remains on the paper.

5.3 A cold peel transfer deposits all of the ink on the garment and generally has a rubbery feel to it. Cold-peel transfers are once again popular because foil will adhere to them.

Cold-Peel

A cold-peel transfer is made similar to a hot-split except that you peel the transfer paper after it has cooled. With a cold-peel, all of the ink transfers to the garment (**5.3**). The final product has a more rubbery and slick feel to it. Cold-peel transfers are not popular for large T-shirt prints because they are hot to wear and do not let the shirt breath.

Cold-peel and hot-peel transfers are actually made the same way with the exception of how you apply them. They are popular for athletic lettering and for foil applications.

Puff Transfers

Puff ink is a special ink that will expand and puff when heated. It is popular on T-shirts and caps and can be printed as a heat transfer.

Foil Transfers

Hot-stamping foil is very popular on shirts. It can be applied with a heat press to direct screen printed plastisol or a cold-peel transfer.

Sublimation Transfers

You can make special sublimation transfers that will work on metals, mugs and cloth with a sublimation copier, full-color copier or full-color laser printer.

This chapter does not deal with how to make sublimation transfers or litho/screen plastisol transfers.

5.4 Transfers have a wide range of uses from baseball caps, to mugs, short runs and athletic numbering.

Why Make a Heat Transfer?

If a heat transfer can feel identical to a direct screen print why not just print the *garment* and eliminate the extra steps of making the transfer and applying it?

It's a good point, but let's look at applications where heat transfers can provide benefits (**5.4**).

Baseball Caps

Transfers are great for baseball caps! Even though you can print directly on baseball caps, heat transfers work very well if the design has fine lines or if you are printing on a dark front cap. Sublimation transfers on light front caps have a very bright appearance and soft feel.

Small Orders

Transfers are also perfect for customers who want to order small quantities on a regular basis. If you make extra designs and just stock the printed transfers, you can quickly and easily print small shirt orders and make more money on them!

Event Shirts

If you work fairs, festivals or events, then you already know the value of heat transfers. It is much easier to "eat" printed paper than it is to take home pre-printed shirts! Hot-peel transfers will give customers the quality look and feel they want, and make things financially less risky.

Stock Designs or Preprinted Shirts

This is where hot-split transfers really shine! If you make your own line of T-shirts (called "preprints" or "stock designs") for either retail, mail-order or small order wholesale businesses, then transfers are the way to go. You can print all the designs on transfer paper and then just match the proper shirt and size to the proper design when the order comes in.

Startup Business

If you are just getting into the business and are looking for the quickest way to offer multicolor designs on shirts without the expense of a multi-color press, making hot-split heat transfers is the least expensive route. Read on and you will see why.

Athletic Printing

A lot of athletic printing requires you to print team names and numbers on shirts and jerseys. Heat transfers are great for your Little League orders. Just make up transfers with team names and numbers and use them over and over every year!

Mugs, Metals and Signs

Sublimation transfers are great for mugs, metals and signs and have created an entire industry within the awards, trophy and ceramics trade.

Aren't They Hard to Make?

In reality, making heat transfers (either cold-peel or hot-split) is really quite simple if you already know how to screen print. The only extra items needed are the proper inks, special papers and a vacuum table to print on. (You can use a T-shirt press, but printing multicolor is a little harder.)

Transfers are printed just like other non-textiles items such as a posters, decals, etc. You print one color at a time, but not wet-on-wet as you would for a direct print on a shirt. After printing and semi-curing (undercuring) all of the first color using special plastisol ink on heat transfer paper, you print all of the second color and semi-cure it, then the third, etc.

Making Plastisol Heat Transfers

The Paper

Plastisol heat transfers are printed on special transfer paper. There is only a handful of specific papers for this process and they are readily available from your local screen print supply company.

Transfer papers need to have good *release* characteristics to let the ink release from the paper during application. They also need good *hold-out* characteristics to keep the ink from absorbing into the paper during storage.

They also need to be very stable to moisture and heat to minimize paper shrinkage when the transfers are run through the dryer to semi-cure the ink.

Most transfer papers are sold under a variety of standard names and trade names. Some suppliers re-package the paper and give it their own name. We have tried to give as many of the various names that we know of for the same products (**5.5**).

T-75

T-75 is also known as *French paper* or Transfert-75. It is available in 11 x 13 in. (27.94 x 33.02 cm) sheets and larger. The cost is approximately 6-8 cents per 11 x 13 in. sheet. It can be printed on either side, is fairly stable and will not shrink too much when printing multicolor designs. This was the original paper designed specifically for this industry.

5.5 There is a wide variety of specially made heat transfer papers.

T-75 can be used for both cold-peel and hot-peel transfers and is the paper of choice if you are going to make a transfer that needs to be applied both ways.

T-55

T-55 is also call *soft-trans*, *trans-soft* and *trans-55* and is designed specifically for printing hot-peel transfers.

T-55 claims better hold-out characteristics, meaning that the plasticiser in the ink will not migrate into the paper as much as it will with off-set or bond papers, providing better shelf life.

Although some suppliers recommend using T-55 for both hot and cold-peel transfers, it does not peel cleanly enough to produce a good cold-peel transfer.

Super Trans

This paper is designed to work for many applications including hot-peel, cold-peel and with plastisol puff ink where excellent hold-out is important. When hot-peeled it transfers more ink to the garment and is an excellent choice when making hot-peel transfers for dark garments.

Super Trans is not recommended for water-based puff ink.

Parchment

In the old days, we used to buy Patapar from baking supply companies to make transfers. It was a parchment paper that would shrink ½ in. (1.27 cm) in both directions on a 25 x 38 in. (63.5 x 96.5 cm) sheet. However, it had excellent release characteristics and was great for one-color transfers!

This paper almost disappeared when Transfert 75 was introduced over 20 years ago but it has now gained popularity as a good translucent paper that is great for team names, numbers and for cap transfers, where it is helpful to see through the paper.

Sparkle

This is another paper like parchment that was popular in days of glitter and combo transfers (later 70's and early 80's). It has a very shiny surface and gives the surface a glossy look when the transfer is applied.

This paper is also called *Glitter Strip,* and *Trans Gloss.*

Like parchment, it is again popular for use with glitter inks, crystalina or shimmer inks and other inks where a high gloss is needed.

Paper Size

Transfer papers are sold in a wide variety of sizes. T-75 is generally available in 11x13 in. (27.94 x 33.02 cm), and 12-1/2 x 12-1/2 in. (31.8 x 31.8 cm), while other papers are sold in 12½ x 12½2 in. (31.75 x 31.75 cm) to 25 x 38 in. (63.5 x 96.5 cm). Most papers are sold in 1000 sheet cartons.

Which Paper To Use

If you are confused by the number of papers, simply use T-75, or Super Trans in the beginning. They work for all types of transfers and are readily available. When making puff transfers use a paper with better hold-out such Super-Trans.

Papers are also available with different grains. If you are printing multicolor transfers you need to specify *long grain* paper for less shrinkage.

Heat Transfer Plastisol

Most general plastisols can be used to make good cold-peel transfers, but when making hot-split transfers, use a plastisol designed for this purpose. Some ink companies make an all-in-one ink for direct printing *and* hot-split and cold-peel transfers (**5.6**).

High-opacity ink designed for dark shirts generally will *not* work well for transfers because it doesn't re-melt properly. Most ink companies make a special high-opacity heat transfer ink.

Some manufacturers offer a *hot-peel additive* that can be added to their regular plastisol to make it a hot-split.

It is important to lay down a thick deposit of ink when printing a transfer. Because of this, you should avoid thinning the ink, if possible.

If you want to use the thin and transparent process colors for transfers you must first print and under-cure a special splitting clear plastisol on the paper. Then print the process colors.

5.6 For less inventory, use an all purpose ink that will work for both direct printing and transfer making. (Photo courtesy Union Ink Co., Ridgefield, NJ.)

The Artwork

Artwork for transfers should not be too detailed. If the artwork has a lot of detail, try to put a backing color such as white behind the detailed area to hold this ink on the garment. If there is no backing color, it may be necessary to make the lines on the artwork heavier.

Artwork for hot-peel transfers should not use heavy trapping. Since the ink film splits in half during application, under-colors will show through.

It is possible to use halftone dots, but care must be taken when handling the paper between colors not to rub the dots off the sheet.

If you must use halftone dots, keep them large such as 22 to 32 lines per inch (**5.7**).

When making puff transfers, be careful of small letters and art areas that will close up. The puff will expand slightly and you may lose detail. It may be necessary to choke the puff art 1/32 inch to compensate for the *gain* you will get when the ink expands.

The Screen

Since the ink film splits when making a hot-peel transfer, it is important to lay down a thick deposit of ink. Screen meshes will be in the range of 60 to 125 (24 - 49 cm).

Wrong Reading Stencil

A transfer screen is exposed *wrong reading* so that when the transfer is applied it becomes right reading. To make a film positive wrong reading, it is re-shot in the camera wrong reading. This is recommended for detailed designs. If the films are not wrong-reading, you will not have emulsion-to-emulsion when exposing the screen, causing undercutting around any detail or halftone dots. *You need a wrong-reading emulsion-side-up film positive.*

If you have a computer graphics system, simply *flip* the design over before printing it out.

Use Direct Film

Although direct emulsion works well, capillary direct film is a much better stencil choice because it provides a thicker stencil (for a thicker ink deposit) and has better edge definition for a sharper print with less sawtoothing.

For best results use a 40 to 80 micron capillary direct film.

Mesh Selection

The mesh selection will vary depending on the type of ink and transfer you are making. The following guide gives the recommended meshes:

Standard Plastisol**	86 to 110
	(34 - 43 cm)
Detailed Plastisol**	92 to 125
	(36 - 49 cm)
Opaque Plastisol**	60 to 74
	(24 - 30 cm)
Water-based or Plastisol Puff*	60 to 74
	(24 - 30 cm)
Glitter+	20 to 33
	(10 - 13 cm)

** Hot or cold-peel
* Hot-peel only
+ Cold-peel only

5.7 This hot-peel transfer is a good example of the type of detail that can be held with careful handling of the printed sheets and good artwork. (Shirt courtesy Modern Designs, Bristol, TN.)

Screen Frame and Tension

Obviously, the better the frame and tension the better the print. In some cases you will be ganging a number of designs on one sheet or possibly printing oversize sheets. Use a sturdy screen frame and properly tensioned fabric.

Gang Screens

When printing baseball cap transfers, save money by ganging a number of images on one screen.

Printing Equipment

Transfers can be printed on an existing T-shirt printing press. In fact, a T-shirt press is more than you need because a transfer is printed one color at a time. A simple one-color press will do.

If you plan to print a lot of transfers buy or build a vacuum table that will hold the paper in place. This is how most non-textile items are printed. You can either build a simple vacuum table from the plans in figure **5.8** or you can buy an attachment for your printing press (**5.9**).

Larger manufacturers use semi-automatic flat-bed presses for higher production and better quality prints (**5.10**).

5.9 A vacuum attachment is available that will fit most manual printing presses.

5.10 Larger manufacturers print transfers on semi-automatic flat-bed presses. (Photo courtesy Lawson, St. Louis, MO.)

Printing Technique

Unlike T-shirts, heat transfers (and other non-textile items)are printed one color at a time. If using a standard T-shirt press you will need to use a light coat of spray adhesive to hold the paper in place.

The reason they aren't printed wet-on-wet is that the paper does not absorb the ink and the uncured colors will smear. It is common to print all of the first color and then re-register and print all the second color, etc. Transfers should always be printed *off-contact* for the best print quality.

If this sounds difficult or too time consuming, it really isn't. Since you are not *loading* a shirt you will find that production rates of 200 to 300 prints per hour are possible. Even lining up the additional colors is quite fast using simple registration methods.

One-Color Transfers

These are easy (**5.11**)! Simply clamp your screen on the press (the image should be wrong reading) and ink the screen with a hot-peel plastisol.

Use a medium squeegee with a *sharp* edge and set the press for off-contact, with either the standard adjustment or the cardboard shim, under the end of the screen.

Spray the board lightly with spray, or if using a vacuum table simply turn on the vacuum. If possible, attach a foot-switch to the vacuum so it can be turned on and off as needed.

Next, place the paper in the correct location on the board or vacuum. Once the correct location is determined, mark the board with thin pieces of masking tape so that the paper can be positioned in the same basic location every time .

Now, simply lower the screen and make a good, clean stroke. Try to do just one stroke and if you need to do another, make sure it is in the same direction. This is not as hard as printing on a shirt where the ink is driven into the garment. You are just laying the ink on top of the paper. Place the print on the dryer or under a flash-unit and make the next print (**5.12**).

Curing

After printing, the goal is to *only partially cure* or *soft-cure* the ink. This is also referred to as *under-curing* the ink. Soft-curing happens at around 220° F (93° C). The soft-cure stage is achieved when the ink just passes the wet point. To find the proper soft-cure temperature, use paper thermometers to get the proper belt speed on a conveyor dryer or time under the curing unit. If you are not sure, find the point where the transfers come out wet and start *slowing down* the belt

Vacuum Table Plans

Drill 1/16" holes every 1½ in. in the top piece of plexiglass only.

Drill a 1½ in. (approx.) hole in the bottom piece of plexiglass and use epoxy glue to attach the vacuum hose to this hole.

Use a ¾ in. square strip of wood as the spacer between the top and the bottom.

Any household or shop vacuum will work. If possible attach a foot switch that can be used to turn the unit on and off when in use.

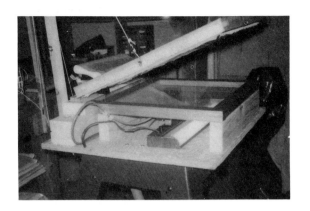

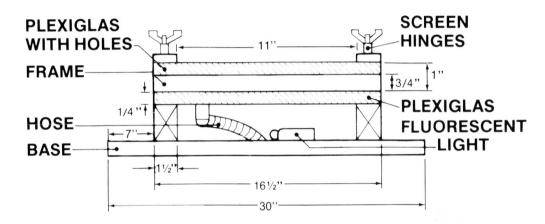

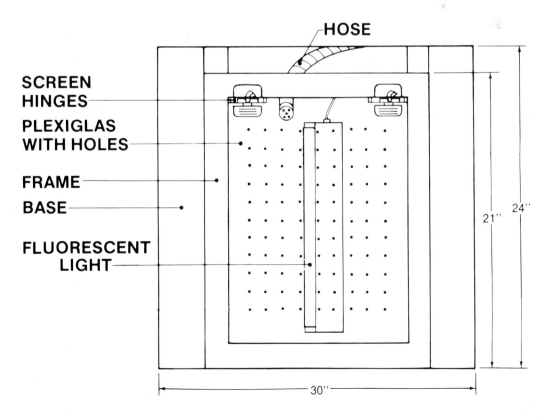

5.8

5.11 *Set your wrong reading screen on a press, adjust for off-contact, use a light mist of spray under the paper and make a print!*

5.12 *Place the printed transfer on the dryer or under a flash-cure unit. Make sure to only partially cure the ink.*

5.11

5.12

5.13 *Use a standard heat press to under-cure the transfers. Simply block the element open and slip the printed paper under it for a few seconds.*

or increasing the time under the curing unit until you get just past the wet stage.

It is *hard* to tell the difference between under-cure and full-cure! The best way is to apply the transfer to a piece of material and see what happens. If it has been under-cured properly, the ink will re-melt when applied and it will penetrate into the cloth. An over-cured transfer (full-cure) will not re-melt properly. It will sit on top of the garment and can be easily picked off!

On multicolor jobs, there is a potential for overcuring the first colors down. If the job calls for more than four or five colors, try to put a backing color (usually white) behind all the other colors to hold them on the garment even if the first colors are overcured.

Generally, you can get away with a little over-curing of a hot-peel transfer. They can even get up to 240° or 260° F (116° or 127° C) and still work.

You can also under-cure transfers with a flash-cure unit or even a heat transfer press by simply setting the element so that it has a ½ in. (1.27 cm) opening when it is closed. Then, slip the wet transfer under the element for 4 or 5 second making sure to only get the print just past the wet stage (**5.13**).

If you're using a conveyor dryer, just set the prints on the belt and let them fall into a box at the end of the dryer.

Multicolor Plastisol Transfers

Multicolor transfers are printed the same as one-color except the additional colors must be lined up to the first colors printed.

The *darkest* or outline color is printed first because it will be the color *on top* of the print *after* the transfer is applied.

Three Point Registration

The most popular method of registration is the three-point registration system commonly used when printing decals, posters, etc. Simply tape three thin cardboard stops or guides (two across the back and one on the side) to your printing surface. These can be a simple "Z" that is folded and taped in place (**5.14**). Commercial registration tabs are available from screen print supply companies. Position each piece of transfer paper snugly up against these stops before printing (**5.15**).

If you print all the sheets in the stops the same way, then your images will all be in the same exact location from paper to paper.

After you have printed and under-cured the first color, tape one of the first color prints to the board in the guides and line-up the second color screen to it. Remove this alignment transfer and ink up the screen (**5.16**).

Now, if you slip each first print under the guides and make a print, the ink will go in the correct location on each print (**5.17**). Again, this is how all non-textiles items such as posters, decals and signs are printed.

For additional information on this procedure, talk with your local screen printing supply company.

Vacuum Table Registration

Although you can use a three-point registration system, the easiest way to print multicolor transfers on a vacuum table is to place a print on the table (this becomes the registration print) and line up the images to it. To do this, take one of the soft-cured black prints and position it on the vacuum table in the same position as it was printed. Place a sheet of clear acetate over this print and tape it in place (**5.18**). Use a pen or nail to poke holes in this acetate to allow the vacuum to still hold paper down.

The reason for the clear plastic top with a light underneath should be obvious now. You will be able to register the second color on this print when a light shines through the clear plastic and through the paper of the black print.

Here's how it works:

As just mentioned, run all of the first color as if the job were a one-color print.

Turn on the vacuum table light, line up the second color screen using the black print that has been placed under the acetate as a placement guide. Secure the screen. Pour the proper ink color in this screen.

Now turn on the vacuum and place one of the already-printed first-color prints directly on top of, and in register with the print taped to the vacuum table. Lower the screen and make a print. The color should be in the proper place and in register on this sheet.

Don't let the description bog you down. It is very simple once you've tried it.

Positioning the black prints with the vacuum going may take a little getting used to, but with a little practice you can make the prints almost as fast as the first color!

Print all of the second color in this manner. When you're finished, remove the screen and line up the third color on the black print taped to the vacuum table (the same as for the second color). Print all of the third color. If there is a fourth color, print it next, following the same steps.

Registration Problems

Since transfers are printed one color at a time, the paper is subjected to a number of passes through the dryer. Paper will shrink when it is heated for the first time, which may cause registration problems on multicolor designs. To compensate for this problem, avoid artwork with heavy trapping around the colors if possible. When ganging multiple designs on one sheet, don't fill up the entire sheet because the transfers along the outside edge of the paper will be more out of register than the inside transfers.

The most common solution is to *preshrink the paper*. You can easily do this by running the paper through the dryer one sheet at a time. If you don't print the entire job in one day, wrap up the transfers in a plastic bag to keep the moisture in the air from being reabsorbed into the paper and allowing it to grow to it's original size.

5.14 *Make three thin cardboard "Z's" and tape them in place across the back and one on the side.*

5.15 *Slip each piece of paper against the cardboard guides as you make the print.*

5.16 *Align the screen to one of the prints.*

5.17 *Bring it down and make a print and the second color will be in register to the first. It's that easy!*

5.18 *Place one of the first prints on the vacuum table and cover it with a protective piece of acetate.*

If the job has tight registration you will need to carefully pre-shrink each sheet of paper by laying them individually on the conveyor belt and running them through the dryer. Paper can grow back to it's original size in less than 10 minutes so make sure to either wrap the paper up and work in small batches or do what the professionals do and have a small *hot box* next to the press that keeps the paper at 110° F.

Another solution is to print only one color per day (on a multi-color job) and allow the paper to sit out in the air overnight to grow back to it's original size.

It is not uncommon to run all the first color and then have the artist create the overlays from an already printed and shrunk sheet in order for the overlays to lineup.

Transfers for Caps

A special powdered adhesive can be applied to wet transfer ink prior to soft-curing that will help hold the transfer on unusual surfaces such as nylon mesh (not jackets!) and baseball caps. The powder is available in two grades – fine and coarse.

To use the powder simply pour it into a shallow box and pull the wet transfer through the powder (**5.19**). Then run the transfer through the dryer as normal to under-cure the ink.

5.19 Apply powder to plastisol transfers by pulling them through the powder and then soft-curing them.

5.20 Sublimation transfers work well on caps, metal signs, and mugs.

For multicolor transfers, use the fine powder and apply it after each color *or* use the coarse powder and apply it *only* to the last color. The powder transfers are *cold-peel only* and should not be used on T-shirts because the ink is *not as stretchy* and it tends to sit *on top* of the material rather than being *driven into* it.

The powder also helps make the ink much more opaque on dark front caps.

Powdered adhesive is available from most suppliers for approximately $10 per lb. One pound will coat 500 - 1000, 11 x 13 in. (27.94 x 33.02 cm) transfer sheets.

Puff Ink Heat Transfers

Puff transfer ink is available in either water-based or plastisol. It is generally used as a backing behind a standard hot-peel transfer although you can make stand-alone puff transfers.

To make a puff transfer you will need to use the correct paper as covered earlier. You will also need to back the puff portion of the transfer with either coarse powdered adhesive or a clear adhesive coating.

If using the water-base puff as a backing to a regular plastisol hot-peel transfer, you will need to powder the transfer after you have printed the puff and then let the ink air dry before application! Using puff ink as a selective backing in this fashion will add a terrific three-dimensional look to your designs.

If using a special plastisol puff transfer ink, you can make the print, and either back it with a coarse powdered adhesive, or a clear printable adhesive coating and then run the print through the dryer to partially cure the puff (make sure not to puff it yet!).

Because these inks are more specialized from manufacturer to manufacturer, make sure to consult their technical data sheets about the correct use.

Sublimation Transfers

Sublimation transfers are made from special sublimation dyes that penetrate synthetic materials like polyester when you apply heat and pressure. During the transfer process, the dye heats up and turns into a gas that bonds with the synthetic portion of the fabric. These transfers only work well on material with *at least 65% polyester!* In addition to synthetics, sublimation transfers can also be applied to specially coated metals (for trophies and awards), coated mugs, tote bags, polyester satin jackets, synthetic bumper stickers and lots more (**5.20**)!

You can make sublimation transfers using screen printing methods or standard offset printing methods (the process used to print business cards, letterhead, etc.).

Sublimation transfers can also be printed on wax thermal printers that use a special sublimation ribbon. This means you can create a quick design on the computer and immediately print a full-color heat transfer (**5.21**). Although expensive to make, this process has revolutionized the instant T-shirt business and is great for short runs, events and retail type sales (5.22).

Full-Color Copiers

Another popular method is to make T-shirt transfers using high-end full-color copiers and special heat transfer paper. These are generally done at copy services and are fairly expensive. Like the wax thermal printers, they are great for short runs.

Foil Transfers

If you ever saw a shirt with a mirror-like foil print on it, it was probably just a cold-peel transfer that had hot-stamping foil applied to it with a heat press (**5.23**).

Special foils are available that will stick to plastisol and foil adhesives. The process is quite simple to produce and the look is stunning!

To apply foil to a transfer, simply apply a cold-peel transfer to the shirt as normal (**5.24**). For best results, try to apply a transfer that is a color similar to the foil. If the foil flakes off slightly after a few washings, it will not be as noticeable if the ink color underneath is the same.

Next, lay a sheet of foil over the cold-peel transfer with the colored side facing up (**5.25**).

5.21 Images can be made in any computer graphic program and printed as sublimation transfers on wax thermal printers with special ribbons. They can be applied to a wide variety of items. (Photo courtesy D&D Distributing, Tempe, AZ.)

5.22 The sublimation process is great for creating vibrant full-color images in small quantities.

5.23 Shirt designs can be made mirror-like by applying a special hot-stamping foil to a cold-peel transfer or direct screened adhesive.

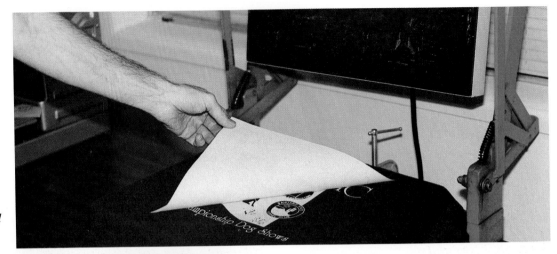

5.24 Apply a cold peel as normal.

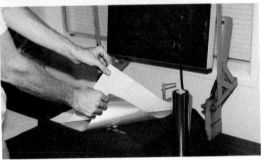

5.25 Lay a piece of special foil over the transfer with the colored side up. Place a piece of cloth over the foil.

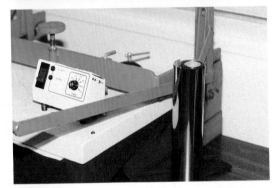

5.26 Apply the foil for 2 to 5 seconds with medium to heavy pressure at 350° F (177° C).

5.27 Let the foil cool and peel it away. It will only stick to the plastisol.

5.28 Foil is available in a wide variety of colors. (Courtesy Union Ink Co., Ridgefield, NJ, and Transfermania, Hialeah, FL.)

Cover the foil with a protective sheet of blank transfer paper or piece of cloth. This prevents the edges from curling during and after application.

Now, simply close the press for 2 to 5 seconds (**5.26**).

Open the press carefully and thoroughly cool down the print. Peel away the foil and it will have stuck wherever there was plastisol (**5.27**)!

You can also get creative and crinkle the foil for an antique look, or apply different colors of foil in different locations!

Washing Directions

For best results you should give your customer specific washing directions for foil shirts. Although they wash well, you may experience a slight dulling after the first washing and the foil may eventually start to flake.

Simply use wording similar to the label below and print it on a sticker and apply them to *every* shirt that you foil.

Garment Care Instructions

This garment has been carefully printed with a special foil process.
Turn garment inside out and wash in cold water on delicate cycle. Line dry. Foil print will soften and dull slightly after the first washing.
DO NOT DRY CLEAN
DO NOT BLEACH
DO NOT IRON DESIGN
(Your Company Name)
(Your Toll Free Number)

Where to Get Foil

Foil is available by the roll from a handful of suppliers. It comes in a wide range of colors including pearlescent and rainbow. The average cost is 15 to 25 cents per foot.

5.29 There are thousands of excellent stock designs available as transfers. A listing of suppliers is in Appendix A.

Stock Designs

There are dozens of companies offering stock designs as heat transfers (**5.29**). This part of the industry has exploded with thousands of hot graphics. You may find that there is a lucrative market in just buying stock designs and imprinting a name drop of your city, resort or state on them!

5.30 Die-cut letters and numbers can be used on athletic uniforms. (Photo courtesy Stahls, St. Clair Shores, MI.)

Athletic Transfers

You can also purchase special die-cut transfers that can be used to number athletic uniforms and jerseys (**5.30**). These transfers are very durable and are widely used by sporting goods stores.

Heat Transfer Equipment

There is a wide range of heat transfer presses on the market, from very low priced manual units, to large, high production presses that cost thousands of dollars.

You generally get what you pay for in heat presses. If you pay less than $500 for a T-shirt press you will probably get a light-weight press that will do a marginal job of applying a transfer.

Most presses will apply a cold-peel transfer, but you need good pressure and even heat to apply a hot peel properly.

Lower priced presses may also have warped heating elements or not enough rods in the element to give even heat. Stick with the companies who have been in the business for a long time and you can't go wrong (**5.31**).

You may also need a baseball cap press. These can be used for sleeve prints and a variety of odd sized items. You also get what you pay for in a cap press. The heating element must fit the curved surface of the cap holder and apply even pressure (**5.32**).

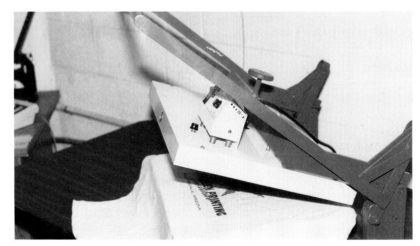

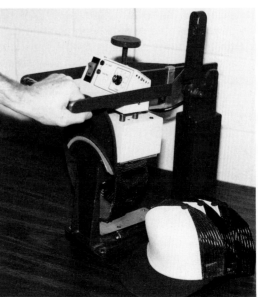

5.31 & 5.32 Well built T-shirt and baseball cap presses are worth the extra expense because they will apply a transfer properly. (Photos courtesy Geo. Knight Co., Brockton, MA.)

Application of Transfers

The following listings are application times for the various types of transfers. You will find that when you buy stock designs or die-cut letters you may be given different times and temperatures. Consult your ink company for their specific recommendations.

Plastisol transfers apply well to 100% cotton, 50/50 cotton-polyester blends, and any other porous surface. They do not apply well to waterproofed nylon jackets!

Sublimation transfers apply to anything that has a high percentage of polyester or synthetic fiber.

Powdered adhesive transfers apply well to baseball caps and open weave materials such as nylon mesh, golf shirts, jerseys, etc.

Cold-Peel Transfers

1. Use on 100% cotton, cotton-polyester blend or 100% polyester fabric. Do not use on waterproof nylon.

2. Set your transfer machine at 350-375° F (178-191° C).

3. Lay the garment over the Teflon pad of the heat press. Smooth out wrinkles and remove any lint or foreign material from the surface of the garment.

4. Place the transfer in the desired print position with the printed side down against the fabric.

5. Lock the heating element into print position for 15 sec, making certain that the pressure setting is fairly heavy for good adhesion.

6. Release the heating element and return it to the open position. Do not raise the element too quickly since this may lift the paper and separate the ink from the fabric while it is in a hot and soft state.

7. Cool the paper with a rag shirt or a chalkboard eraser for 10-20 sec.

8. Remove the transfer paper in a slow, even motion by pulling from a corner diagonally across the design.

9. Garments decorated with heat transfers should be laundered without the use of bleaching agents.

Hot-Split Transfers

1. Use on 100% cotton, cotton-polyester blend or 100% polyester fabrics. Do not use on waterproof nylon.

2. Set your transfer machine at 375-400° F (190-204° C).

3. Lay the garment over the Teflon pad of the heat press. Smooth out wrinkles and remove any lint or foreign material from the surface of the garment. Preheat the garment by lowering the heat press onto the shirt for a few seconds.

4. Place the transfer in the desired print position with the printed side down against the fabric.

5. Lock the heating element into print position for 10 seconds, making certain that the pressure setting is fairly heavy for good adhesion.

6. Release the heating element and return it to the open position. Immediately reach in and smoothly pull the paper off the transfer. (If you wait too long, the transfer will peel like a cold peel.)

7. Garments decorated with heat transfers should be laundered without the use of bleaching agents.

Application of Transfers

Powdered-Adhesive Transfers

1. Set the cap press to 325° F (163° C) with *fairly light pressure.*

2. Place the cap on the cap heat transfer press.

3. Lower the heating element and preheat the cap for a few seconds. (Some caps shrink slightly under heat and preheating will preshrink the cap.)

4. Lay the powdered transfer on top of the cap. If it will not lay flat, lightly crease the center of the transfer.

5. Lower the heating element and lock it in place for 10 seconds.

6. Open the press without raising the element too quickly.

7. Immediately cool the paper with a rag or chalkboard eraser. If any of the ink splits when opening the press, make sure to press this ink back down onto the cap.

8. Peel off the paper after it has cooled 10-20 seconds.

9. Certain hard-surfaced caps such as golf caps require just the right amount of pressure, temperature and cooling to achieve a good print.

10. If you're printing on a dark front cap, you will get a brighter print if you use less pressure.

Puff Heat Transfers

1. Use on 100% cotton, cotton-polyester blend or 100% polyester fabric. Do not use on waterproof nylon.

2. Set your transfer machine at 375-400° F (191-204° C) with moderate to heavy pressure.

3. Lay the garment over the teflon pad of the heat press. Smooth out wrinkles and remove any lint or foreign material from the surface of the garment. Preheat the garment by lowering the heat press onto the shirt for a few seconds.

4. Place the transfer in the desired print position with the printed side down against the fabric.

5. Lock the heating element into print position for 3 to 5 seconds for a one-color puff transfer or 8 to 12 seconds for a hot-split transfer that is backed in puff ink.

Note: Too much time will cause the puff ink to overheat and collapse. Too little time and the adhesive will not melt and hold the transfer in place. You will need to experiment with these times.

6. Release the heating element and return it to the open position. Immediately reach in and smoothly pull the paper off the transfer. As you pull the paper, the puff ink will expand and puff.

7. Garments decorated with heat transfers should be laundered without the use of bleaching agents.

CHAPTER

6

NYLON JACKETS, BASEBALL CAPS AND OTHER IMPRINTABLES

This chapter covers printing on textiles, garments and imprintables other than T-shirts. Once you know how to print a basic T-shirt, it isn't much harder to print on other substrates. Generally, all you need to know are the specifics about ink selection, curing requirements, mesh recommendations and any peculiar properties of the material.

Nylon Jackets

Everyone likes to make jacket printing into something that it really isn't. Printing jackets isn't that hard! If you know some of the tips and tricks and follow good printing practices, you can print jackets as well the next printer. Following are some key points to successful printing on *water-proofed* nylon jackets.

Problems with Printing on Jackets

Nylon jackets present problems because they generally have a lining in them, are constructed of waterproof material, are much more expensive than most other garments and can't take as much heat as a T-shirt. For these reasons, they are harder to print than T-shirts.

Jacket Material

Most jackets are made from duPont 6,6 nylon. This material can take up to 375° F (191° C) and may be coated to make it "waterproof" or "water

repellent." A water repellent jacket has been lightly treated, while a waterproof jacket is designed to actually prevent water from leaking through for up to 24 hours. The majority of the jackets on the market are water repellent.

If possible, try to buy American-made jackets. They are generally only lightly treated. Imported jackets have a much heavier treatment in order to lower the import duty *and* they will tend to shrink and distort excessively when run through a dryer.

There is also a wide variety of new jacket material on the market. Make sure you know what ink system will work with the new exotic nylons.

Checking for Waterproofing

If you see a note in your supplier's catalog stating that a particular jacket style is "stain resistant" or "waterproof," it's a good indication that the jacket has been heavily treated. The only real way to test for excessive coating is to pour water onto the jacket and see if it actually holds it. A lightly treated jacket will let the water drip through in a matter of minutes. A heavily treated jacket will hold the water all day. If the jacket has been heavily treated, you may need to remove this coating with rubbing alcohol prior to printing (**6.1**). Some manufacturers recommend using acetone, but acetone is so flammable that you really should avoid it.

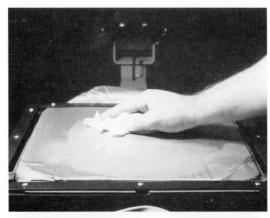

6.1 If the jacket is heavily treated with waterproofing, rub the print area down with rubbing alcohol.

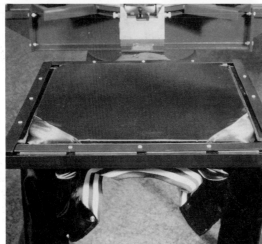

6.2 A good jacket hold-down is very expensive, but well worth the money!

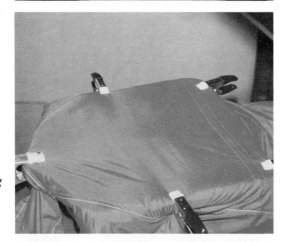

6.3 An optional holding method is to use heavy-duty spring clamps around the jacket.

6.4 The most popular nylon jacket ink system is a special bonding agent that you add to regular plastisol.

Equipment

In order to keep a lined jacket from moving while it is printed, you will need a jacket hold-down (**6.2**). Without a good holddown you might as well give up. There are other ways to hold down a jacket (get your employees to hold it while sitting on the floor, etc., etc.) but if you want consistent results then use a holddown. It will make your quality better and reject rate lower! Pretty simple. If the jacket doesn't have a lining, then regular spray adhesive is all you'll need to hold it in place.

If you don't want to spend $400 on a hold-down for your press, then look at other companies' holding devices. Some manufacturers offer less expensive holddowns that will fit a variety of presses.

One option to using a holddown is to use spring clamps around the outer edge of the jacket (**6.3**). These will make the process go a little slower than a standard holddown would, but will work if you are on a budget. These clamps are available from most hardware stores and have rubber end protectors so they won't damage the jacket.

Use the Correct Screen

You can use the same screens for printing jackets that you use for T-shirts. The only difference is that you will not need to use as low a mesh count for dark jackets since they do not bleed like shirts.

In most cases, you can use a 125 (49 cm) mesh for dark jackets and 180 (70 cm) or higher for light jackets. The tighter the fabric, the better the print. You can use either direct emulsion or capillary direct film for your stencil.

Nylon Ink Systems

This is an area where you want to be very careful. Since nylon is very slippery and tightly woven, you can't use a standard plastisol on it. It will not adhere to the material. There are a number of nylon ink systems on the market, some of which work better than others. Remember, you *do not* want the ink to come off the jacket!

The most popular ink system consists of a regular plastisol with a special bonding agent that is added to the ink (**6.4**). The bonding agent is like a urethane glue that helps the plastisol stick to the nylon and also makes the ink much more durable. Most manufacturers offer these systems. The beauty of them is that you don't have to stock a variety of special inks just for jackets. You can mix the bonding agent with any of your all-purpose plastisols!

6.5

6.6

Since the weight of plastisols vary depending on the color of the ink, you need to add the bonding agent by *weight* when mixing it (**6.5**). If you can't mix by weight then make sure to add more bonding agent to lighter, more opaque colors. Once you add the bonding agent, the mixture must be used within 8-12 hours or it will harden. Just mix what you need for a job. If you add too much bonding agent, it may harden faster, but if you are in doubt as to how much you need to add – add more. Each ink manufacturer has different mixing directions, so be sure to ask for the product's technical data sheet when you order it.

The biggest problem with a plastisol/bonding agent mixture is that the ink becomes much thinner. In fact, it is sometimes too thin to print. If you are printing on a light-colored jacket with a lining, the ink may penetrate through the nylon and print on the lining.

There are a couple of ways to make the ink thicker. You can put the mixture in a refrigerator to make it colder or you can let it sit for a few hours to slowly thicken. In addition to this, some brands of ink are thicker than others and you should try to use a brand that is thicker to start with.

Flash Curing Jackets

A flash-cure unit is a must when printing nylon jackets. Not only do you need it to print multicolor, you also need it to preheat the nylon before the first print. Preheating shrinks the nylon for a tighter fit in the holddown and also softens it and partially burns off sizing, stabilizers and waterproofing. This will help your ink adhere better!

To preheat the jacket, simply place the flash unit over it while it's in the holddown. If you have the unit set 2 in. above the jacket, you should be able to preshrink and preheat it in less than 10 sec (**6.6**).

Running a jacket through the dryer is not the same as preheating it on the holddown. You defeat the purpose of shrinking the jacket tightly *while on the holddown.*

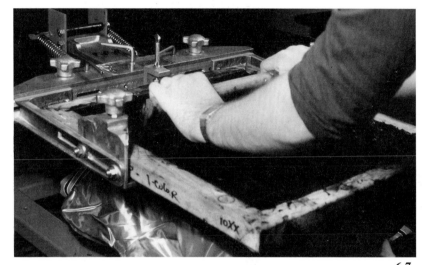

6.7

Printing Technique

It takes a good feel for the squeegee to get a good print. You need to do a stroke that is not too fast or too slow. An even stroke that cleans off the screen is very important (**6.7**). Your screen should obviously be adjusted to sit slightly off-contact *over the jacket* (not just the shirtboard) for the best print quality.

Use a medium squeegee with a very sharp edge. Too much pressure on the squeegee will allow the ink to press out around the stencil, giving a slight ghost to the print. Always try to do just one stroke. If you must do two strokes keep them both in the same direction.

Sometimes a lined jacket will stick to the screen when it's lifted. As the print peels from the screen, you get a ring or circular mark in the image. A good technique is to do a clean stroke and then quickly snap the screen upward. This snap releases the screen *quickly* from the print and gives a sharper image. It's all in the wrist. This snap technique may not be necessary if your ink is flowing correctly and the jacket is releasing on its own during the stroke.

6.5 Make sure to measure the bonding agent/plastisol mixture by weight.

6.6 For better ink adhesion preheat the jacket before you print on it.

6.7 Print with a firm, slow stroke to allow the ink to flow through the mesh onto the garment.

6.8 *You must cure between colors when printing multicolor prints on nylon.*

6.9 *Make sure to increase the belt speed when curing the print. It may require more than one time through the dryer.*

6.10 *When printing a chest print you should raise the print area with a small block of wood.*

6.11 *Special die-cut letters and numbers work well if applied properly.*

Multicolor Printing Techniques

Because nylon is nonabsorbent, you can't print multicolor designs wet-on-wet: you need to flash cure between colors. The flash time can be fairly short (5-10 sec) – just enough to gel the ink so it is dry to the touch (**6.8**). Since nylon shrinks when heated, you must preshrink the jacket under the flash-cure unit before making the first print.

Curing the Print

After printing the jacket, run it through the dryer. It may take more than one trip through to get the ink dry to the touch. Although the plastisol portion of the ink will cure when it goes through the dryer, the *bonding agent* needs 72 hours to *fully cure!* Be very careful that you *do not* give out the jackets for a couple of days after printing. Also, be very careful about stacking them. They may *feel dry* but not actually *be cured.* The best approach is to dry them through the dryer and then hang them on a rack for a few days to fully cure.

Set your dryer belt speed a little faster than normal. The thickness of the material places it closer to the heating elements and can cause it to burn if you run it the same as for a T-shirt (**6.9**).

Problems and Solutions

You may encounter some problems when printing jackets. If the print does not adhere well, the jacket may be heavily treated and require that the waterproofing be removed before printing. If the jackets are already printed or customers are returning them, take all of the jackets to a dry cleaner and ask them to try to remove the print. Believe it or not, dry cleaning will sometimes remove the print. There may be a slight shadow from the previous print. If so, you will need to reprint the design in the same exact location.

Printing on the front of a jacket is difficult because of the snaps, pockets, collar, seams and other obstructions. Raising the print area with a small block of wood or sponge rubber will help to make this task a bit easier (**6.10**).

Applying Heat Transfers to Jackets

We do *not* recommend applying plastisol heat transfers to nylon jackets. They do not adhere well, even if you use the nylon bonding powder that many suppliers carry. One option is to buy specially made die-cut letters and transfers from suppliers who specialize in these products (**6.11**).

Sublimation transfers are excellent for light-colored jackets (especially satin finished polyester jackets) and can be custom made for you or printed from special thermal wax printers using sublimation-coated ribbons. See Chapter 5 for more details on sublimation transfers.

Printing Caps

Caps have become a standard commodity in this industry. They can be decorated in a variety of ways including heat transfers, direct screen printing and embroidery. We will cover direct printing methods here. For information on making heat transfers for caps, see Chapter 5.

Caps are available in different styles and materials, such as polyester baseball caps, poplin golf caps, cotton painters caps and even visors. The difference in printing technique generally has to do with the type of material and how the cap is constructed.

Direct Printing or Heat Transfers?

Direct printing is certainly the quickest decorating method. It does not always produce a sharp edge to the print though, because of the soft printing surface. Direct printing is more difficult when printing multicolor work if you have to flash-cure between colors because it is hard to find a small cap flash curing unit. Direct printing is the only method to use if you are going to print with puff inks. Direct puff prints are far superior to transfer puff prints.

Heat transfers will produce very sharp prints that look good on both light and dark cap fronts. If you use the powdered adhesive mentioned in Chapter 5, you can print fine-detail designs on caps. Transfers will take longer, however, because you have to *make* the transfers first and then *apply* them.

If the job calls for a simple one- or two-color design on a light front cap, or if the job requires puff ink, then use the direct printing method. If the image has lots of colors or is going on a dark-front cap, then make a heat transfer. Your customer really won't care, and you should use the best method for the job.

Direct Printing Caps

The problem with printing directly on the cap front is that you are printing on a round substrate that is soft. A variety of systems are used to print directly on finished caps, including using curved screens, attachments to hold the cap front flat and accessories that rotate a round cap under a flat screen.

Although most systems work fairly well, our favorite – based on *cost of the system* and *ease of use* – is one that holds the front of the cap flat and uses a flat screen. Don't let anyone convince you that printing a round cap with a round screen is easy.

Flat screen systems are available as stand-alone units (**6.12**) or as attachments for your printing press (**6.13**). Flat screen attachments are so inexpensive that one can be placed on each printing arm for high production – while one per-

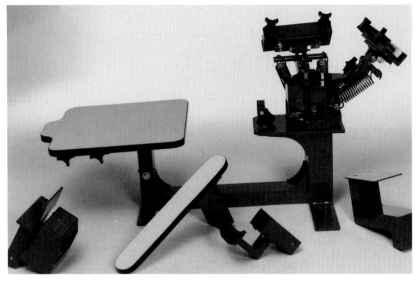

son prints another loads and unloads. Use a frame that has one thin wall (strip of aluminum) so that the image can be positioned close to the edge of the frame (**6.14**). This allows the visor of the cap to stay vertical when the cap is printed. Hold caps in place with spray adhesive and take care when loading them so you don't distort the front.

To achieve the best print quality on light-colored cap fronts use a monofilament mesh count of 200-250 (78-100 cm). By printing through fine mesh with a plastisol ink that has been reduced to a very creamy consistency, using a sharp squeegee and printing with one or two passes in the *same direction,* you can get a very respectable print!

On dark cap front you will have to go to a lower mesh count such as an 86-94 (34-37 cm). Use a *high-opacity low-bleed* plastisol ink and print with two or three strokes in the same direction. The print will not look as sharp as on the light caps. If you're using a puff ink, use the standard 86-94 (34-37 cm) mesh.

Some of the stiffer golf and poplin caps are harder to direct print. They generally have a plastic liner that gets in the way, and they do not always want to lay flat. You may ruin a few before you get just the right technique down with these caps.

6.12 Special printing presses are available that are designed specifically to print on baseball caps, golf caps and sport caps. (Photo courtesy R. Jennings Mfg., Glens Falls, NY.)

6.13 Most manufacturers offer inexpensive attachments for holding a cap front flat during printing.

6.14 Special thin-wall screens are needed for direct printing on baseball caps.

Printing on Panels

Some manufacturers offer "panel programs" where they send the unassembled cap front, you print it flat just like a shirt (**6.15**) and then return it for assembly. This is the perfect way to print caps, but most customers don't want to wait the three- or four-week delivery time.

Corduroy Caps

Corduroy caps present a special problem because of the grooves of the corduroy material. The only effective way to print these caps is to use the direct print method, and by mixing a little puff additive to regular plastisol. Just mix enough so that the print will puff slightly and actually fill in the grooves.

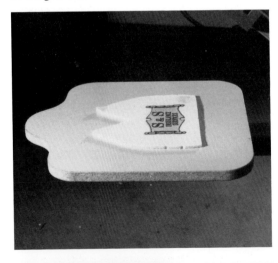

6.15 Some cap manufacturers offer the cap panels to direct print on before the cap is assembled.

6.16 Stack the caps against each other when running them through a standard dryer.

Painters Caps

These are easy to print because they don't have a foam lining and are not stiff. Just use your regular cap attachment and the appropriate mesh for either light or dark material.

Curing and Drying Cap Prints

Caps with bills present some problems. The bill gets in the way when using a flash-cure unit (although some manufacturers do make a small cap heater). Some dryers are designed just for caps, while some multi-purpose dryers have an additional heater on the side for caps. You can also use an industrial heat gun if you are careful.

If you want to run the caps through your regular dryer, try placing them so that the crown is facing up slightly by stacking them against each other (**6.16**).

Art Preparation

The only other helpful tip for cap printing is to make the art simple and readable, and to keep the print area smaller than 4 in. wide x 3 in. high (10.16 x 7.62 cm).

Printing on Fleecewear

Printing fleece is definitely not the same as printing a T-shirt. Because fleece is a much thicker material with a looser knit, more ink needs to lay *on top* of the garment to make the print look sharp and full (**6.17**). For this reason, you will need to modify the artwork, use different meshes at higher tensions, change squeegees, rework your printing technique *and* inform your customers of the differences!

Here are some quick tips for good fleece printing.

Artwork Detail

Keep detail to a minimum for fleece designs. This sounds so simple, but it's hard when the customer brings in the art. If you can, encourage your customers to keep detail to a minimum and use a much coarser than normal halftone dot. Since everything is going to gain in size on the fleece, try to plan for the gain to improve print sharpness. Remember, bold and thick prints are much better than thin and detailed.

If you're printing on raglan-sleeved sweatshirts, remember to check the size of the design. Some sweatshirts have set-in sleeves which leaves more room on the sweatshirt for the artwork.

Screen Making

To achieve a good print on fleece, you need to lay down more ink *without* using too much pressure. This means lowering the mesh counts. If you use a 180 monofilament mesh (69 cm) for light shirts, then go down to a 125 (49 cm). If your nor-

6.17 *Prints on fleece will not look as sharp as normal T-shirt prints. The print on the left is on a sweat-shirt. The one on the right is on a regular T-shirt.*

mal job calls for a 125, lower it to 86 (34 cm) for fleece. Granted, you may lose some detail, but these are the rules.

Also, you will get the best results when using retensionable frames because a higher-tensioned screen transfers the ink with less squeegee pressure. This means that the screens should be at 35-40 newtons and you can marvel at how that sharp print *lays on top* of the fleece.

Squeegee Selection

Use either a medium or soft squeegee blade. A hard blade will require more pressure to get the ink through the screen and will drive it *into* the garment, which is not where you want it!

If the design does not have much detail, you can even dull the edge of the squeegee slightly (a little sandpaper will do).

Inks for Fleece

Hopefully, you have been reducing inks to achieve sharper prints on light shirts. But this isn't going to work on fleece. The ink needs to be a little thicker (straight from the can in many cases). If it is too thin, it will gain and fall into the material. Remember, you want the print to sit on top of the fleece. If the ink is too thick to print without adding reducer, try stirring it first to make it more creamy.

Minimize Bleeding

When printing on a 50/50 fleece, you should use a low-bleed ink. The garment dye may still bleed into the ink (even days or weeks later), so be sure to test. For best results, print, flash cure

and print again (the same color). Or print an underbase of white (either low-bleed or fast fusion) to give you a smooth surface for the top colors.

Use Lots of Spray Adhesive

This is not what the health conscious want to hear, but most of the time, you will have to use spray adhesive after every garment. Another popular method is to use pallet tape or pallet paper which has adhesive on both sides. To use, glue it to the platen and replace it when the adhesive wears out by re-papering the board An alternative is to use a pallet cover which has adhesive on one side and you apply spray adhesive on the other. When the cover gets too loaded with lint, you just strip it off and recover the platen. It's a lot easier than wiping the platens.

Press Set-up and Printing Technique

As usual, you must print off-contact to achieve a clean print. You may need to set the off-contact a little higher than normal to account for the thicker material. Remember, it is very important not to drive the ink too deeply into the garment. Using a lighter stroke (maybe two if needed) is much better than trying to muscle the ink.

Dryer Settings

Proper dryer temperature is important because light-colored (white fleece especially) can scorch and dark 50/50 sweats may bleed. Try to keep the surface temperature of the garment around 325 ° F (160° C).

If you are printing a base of white, the garment may actually move or shrink slightly. Use plenty of spray adhesive and keep the flash-curing time to a minimum. If there is too much movement, pre-flash the garment before printing it.

Communicate with the Customer!

Poor communication can get you in trouble. The customer has certain expectations about the quality of the print. When printing a job for first time fleece customers, make sure to let them know the limitations. The print will probably not look as good on fleece as it does on a shirt. If the job calls for some T-shirts and some sweatshirts, tell them that there will be a difference in print appearance.

Terry-Cloth Towels

Terry-cloth items like towels, bibs and bathrobes present peculiar problems because the surface is so irregular. Don't get too detailed when creating art for terry-cloth fabrics. Keep the art simple and avoid the need for tight registration (**6.18**).

Screen Selection

The best overall mesh for printing on terry-cloth is a 125 monofilament (49 cm). You will need a stencil system that is *water resistant*. Dual-cure photopolymer emulsions will hold up for runs of up to 750 prints before they start to break down. Emulsion companies also offer special water-resistant permanent emulsions that are good choices for longer runs.

Ink Selection

Although a very thin plastisol ink can be used if the image isn't too big, a water-based ink delivers a softer feel. The best choice is a water-in-oil ink that penetrates into the terry-cloth and has a soft hand when dried. These inks will dry in the screen if the right printing technique isn't observed. Also, they will need to be heat cured with air flowing around them in order to hold up when laundered.

Printing Technique

When using any water-based inks, a firm print stroke should be used. Raise the screen and then do a light flood stroke to lay ink over the image area on the screen and keep it from drying. Water-based ink is appropriate mainly for light-colored terry cloth because the ink is not very opaque. For additional information about towel printing, an excellent video tape is available from Mid-America Wholesale "Towels Plus" – see Appendix A.

6.18 Terry-cloth items are harder to print on because of the uneven surface and the fact that you need to use a water-based ink system.

What Else to Print

Printing on unusual textiles can be challenging. The main considerations are what ink to use, what screen mesh is appropriate and how to hold the item in place. Once you find those answers, you can print on almost anything from van tire covers to patches, can coolers, flags, back-packs, fanny-packs, aprons, tote bags and much more. Some manufacturers offer a wide variety of non-standard imprintable items and will give you the printing specifications (**6.19**). Experiment and have fun!

Generally when printing on any material that is more porous or rougher than a standard T-shirt such as aprons, totes, and denim you should use a lower mesh count. This helps deposit more ink into the grooves of the material and gives better coverage. Don't print with ink that is too thin for these items either. If the material is heavy, the ink may bleed too much and give a ragged edge to the print. You can use plastisol on most textile items as long as the material will withstand the curing temperature.

6.19 There is a wide variety of specialty imprintable items that are fairly easy to print on. (Top photo courtesy The Bagworks, Ft. Worth, TX.)

CHAPTER 7

SPECIAL EFFECTS PRINTING

This chapter will deal with all of the terrific special-effects inks such as puff ink, metallic, glitter, suede, shimmer, fragrance and discharge ink. It will also cover how to work with foil and how to create a "hand-done" or wearable art shirt.

You can use special-effects to enhance the appearance of a shirt and turn a boring design into an eye-catching one. Most special-effects inks are actually fairly simple to use. Once you know the correct mesh to use, proper curing techniques and any unusual printing characteristics, you will find that these inks become just one more way to enhance an image on a shirt.

Some topics in this chapter are only covered very briefly to give you an overview of how they are done. For more detailed information on wearable art, shirt-dying treatments and airbrushing, consult the industry trade magazines and other resources listed in the back of this book.

Printing with Puff Ink

Puff ink is by far the most popular special-effects ink. It is used to give a design a more three-dimensional look or to add a raised border or highlights. Puff ink is very simple to use and should be an essential part of your ink inventory.

Puff Ink

Plastisol puff ink is sold either premixed or as a puffing agent you can add to your regular plastisol. Although purchasing the additive will help keep your ink inventory low, it is important to mix it correctly.

If you add too much puffing additive, the ink will actually rise too high and not be durable or abrasion resistant. The best choice is to buy your main puff colors premixed and have some additive on hand for mixing the occasional odd color.

Art Preparation

Puff ink expands in all directions when you heat it, causing the garment to pucker when the ink puffs. Because of this, you need to plan the artwork with this phenomenon in mind. If possible, try to avoid large block design areas. Anything more than 1/8 to ¼ in. wide would be considered a block area.

You may need to change areas larger than this into either a 60% halftone dot, a mezzotint (a random squiggle pattern), stippling or thin lines. When the ink puffs up, these thinner patterns will actually rise and touch, making them appear to be a solid area. The puffing will be more uniform with less puckering (**7.1**).

If you are using a computer graphic system to create a design, you will need to print the block area as a halftone. If the artwork is prepared by hand, you may need to use halftone screen tints and re-cut the solid area using the dots (see Chapter 1).

Heavy solid areas may pucker and puff unevenly.

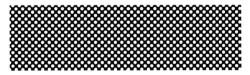

Solid converted to a 60% tint at a 20 line halftone dot will puff more uniformly.

7.1 Artwork for puff printing may need to be modified by converting heavy solid areas into a pattern or texture.

7.2 Be careful when printing tight letters that may close-up when the ink expands in all directions.

Avoid using letters and artwork that will close up when the ink puffs. You may occasionally need to re-work the customer's art so that it will look correct *after it has been puffed.* This may mean going to a thinner lettering style or thinner lines in the artwork (**7.2**).

When creating multicolor overlays do not overlap colors. Either butt register the colors or – better yet – place a small gap between the colors.

Screen Making

A good multipurpose mesh for puff designs is an 86 (34 cm) monofilament. For a thicker puff, you can use a 60 (24 cm) monofilament. In designs with a lot of detail you can go up to a 110 or 125 (43-49 cm) monofilament mesh.

Use a wooden, rigid metal or retensionable frame with direct emulsion or direct capillary film.

Printing Techniques

Unlike general printing, where the ink is driven *into* the garment, with puff printing, the ink should lay *on top* of the garment. This allows more ink to puff up from the garment, giving it a sharp, high-loft look.

To keep the ink on top of the garment, use one or two light print strokes (always in the same

direction). A slightly rounded squeegee may also help. Rather than printing on a hard platen, use a soft printing surface. Putting a piece of 3/16 in. silicone foam rubber (available from local gasket companies) on the platen will soften the printing surface, which will allow more ink on top of the garment. (This tip may help brighten prints on dark garments too!)

Curing Puff Ink

Since puff ink is a plastisol and it will need to be brought to at least 300 ° F (177°C) to cure. Because the ink film will be thick, it may be necessary to run the print through the dryer more than once to get a deep cure *and* to get a good puff. With puff ink, a longer tunnel time is very helpful.

Multicolor Puff Printing

Although puff ink can be printed wet-on-wet in multicolor work, with fair results, flash curing between colors will give the best print quality. This is because the wet-on-wet process tends to transfer the ink layer from the garment to the back of the screens. Printing wet-on-wet also presses the ink into the garment. Both problems prevent good puffing.

Puff ink can be flash dried without puffing it, but you'll need to experiment with the dwell time and distance of your flash-curing unit because there is a very fine line between the temperature that gels the surface of the ink and the temperature that causes the "blowing agent" to puff up. With most flash-cure units, you can achieve the proper gel in less than 10 sec. The ink will turn from a wet look to a lighter, more pastel appearance as it puffs. Curing between colors will keep the ink film smooth and thick, and ensure even puffing of all colors (**7.3**).

A second option for printing multicolor puff designs is to print a base of *white puff ink* through an 86 (34 cm) monofilament, flash cure this puff base and then print the multicolor design with a regular plastisol *directly on top of* the gelled white puff. Use a 180 (70 cm) monofilament for the multicolor screens. If the artwork has been designed for wet-on-wet printing, you could print the top colors without having to flash cure between each color. When the print is run through the dryer, the white puff will rise, making the entire design look like a multicolor puff print.

If the artwork for the white puff ink is "choked" (make the overall edge of the design smaller), the white puff will not show around the top colors and no one will know that you only used one puff color!

If you want to print a multicolor puff design without flash curing, you can maintain fair print quality by staggering the mesh counts. Use a 60

7.3 When printing multicolor puff ink it is necessary to partially cure (but not puff) the first colors. This takes only a few seconds.

7.4 If you apply foil to a puff print with medium heat press pressure it will just stick to the tops of the puff giving the shirt a rich look.

(24 cm) mesh for the first color, 74 (28 cm) for the second, 86 34 cm) for the third, 94 (37 cm) for the fourth, etc. Change your sequence to print as the smallest print area first, to the largest printed last (if possible). Print the most dominant color last since it will have the best and cleanest puff.

If you need a puff ink that is really durable and will take a lot of wear-and-tear and abrasion, try adding a puffing agent to the special athletic plastisols. Athletic plastisols are very stringy and stretchy, and will make the puff prints more durable.

Because puff ink is not very bleed resistant, you may need to print a base of low-bleed white ink, flash cure it and then print the puff ink on top when printing on dark garments.

For extremely high puff, you can also print the ink, flash cure it and then print the puff ink again directly on top. This layering of two cured coats of puff ink makes the puff really stand out from the garment.

Printing with Puff and Foil

Another very popular effect can be achieved by combining puff ink with foil. It is a simple technique that will really make a puff print jump off the shirt (**7.4**)!

The basic principles involve printing a base of plastisol puff that is just for outlines and detail parts of a design. After flash drying the puff ink (without puffing it), print the other standard plastisols wet-on-wet on top of the flash-dried puff. The entire print is then run through the dryer to puff and cure the inks.

Next, take the print to a heat-transfer press and place a sheet of foil over the print. By using very light pressure, the foil is only applied to the top-most areas of the puffed print and the print has a great shine – resulting in a very nice effect.

Other Options

Another option is to print the puff ink *last* in the sequence (after you flash cure the undercolors). This will give a very high puff print on top of the other colors, and the foil will adhere to more of the puff and less of the regular plastisol. Your outlines and detail areas will be more pronounced with this method. If the puff ink is black and a gold foil is used on top, it will give the print a rich look.

Artwork Preparation

For the best results, create the artwork specifically for this type of print. Use the puff portion of the design for outlines and as a texture under other or over colors. When the puff rises it will make any top color look pastel and give it a multi-shade color. Create the puff overlay by using hand stippling and thin lines just for areas where you want puff and where you want the foil to stick (**7.5**). You can create artwork for the other colors just like you do for regular overlays using ruby masking film.

7.5 Create the artwork for the puff/foil combo prints by using thin lines and hand stippling. The puff can be printed under or on top of regular plastisol.

Screen Making

For light-colored shirts, use a 60-86 (24-34 cm) monofilament for the puff print and a 160 - 200 (63-78 cm) for the top colors. For dark shirts, use a 60-86 (24-34 cm) monofilament for the puff print and a 86-125 (34-49 cm) for the top colors. You can use either capillary direct film or direct emulsion for the stencil.

Press Setup

Set up the press the same as for a normal

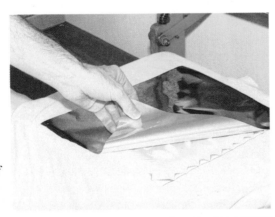

7.6 Place the shirt on the press and a piece of foil over the print with the colored side up.

7.7 Lay a piece of cloth or blank heat transfer paper over the foil to keep it from curling under the heat.

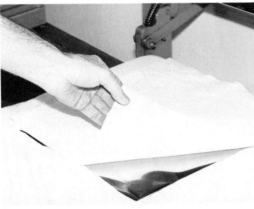

7.8 Let the foil cool completely and peel it away. It only sticks to the tops of the puff ink.

underbase job. The job should be set up so the puff can be flash-dried first *(but not puffed)* and the remaining colors printed lightest to darkest, wet-on-wet. For the best foiling effect, you want a really high loft to the puff print. To achieve this, print the puff ink, flash it, then print and flash again *(without puffing the ink)*, before the other colors are printed on top. Because the finished print will have a heavier ink deposit that a normal design so it should go through the dryer twice to achieve full puffing and curing.

Applying the Foil

This is the fun part. We use a heavyweight hot-stamping foil that is available from companies like Transfermania and Union Ink Co. The foil will cost from $.15 to $.20 cents per 12 x 12 in. (30.48 X 30.48 cm) sheet. Foil is sold in a 200ft roll (60.96 m). The foil is available in a wide variety of colors including pearlescent, rainbow and shimmer.

Set the heat press to 350° F (177° C) with very light pressure. Place the cured print on the heat press platen and lay a sheet of cut foil on top of it (**7.6**). The foil is placed with the *color side up*. Since the foil will curl when it's heated, this is prevented by laying a piece of blank heat-transfer paper or cloth on top of the foil (**7.7**).

Next, lower the heating element so that there is minimal pressure on the foil and leave the press closed for 10-15 sec. When the time is up, raise the press head and quickly cool the foil with a rag or eraser (just like when applying a normal heat transfer). Let the foil cool for 30-60 seconds and peel it off. It will stick to the top areas of the puffed ink and will give the design a rich and shiny look (**7.8**).

If the foil did not stick to enough of the puff ink, use a little more pressure. If the foil sticks to the regular plastisol too much, you will need to reduce the pressure. Don't get frustrated. You will need to play with the settings and times. Just plan to ruin a few shirts until you get it right.

Washing Instructions

To help the print withstand washings, it should be washed inside-out using warm water with a gentle setting, and the dryer setting at warm. You should provide *written* washing instructions to the customer. Although hanging a shirt to dry is preferable, it is not always practical to recommend this. A low clothes dryer setting is an acceptable option. The foil actually washes well although it may dull a little after a few washings.

A sample washing label is provided in Chapter 5 – *Heat Transfers*.

7.9 Foil can also be applied to direct print plastisol and foil adhesive with a heat press.

Other Foil Options

Foil over Direct-Print Plastisol

Although foil looks the most brilliant when applied to a heat transfer, it can also be applied to direct-print plastisol or direct-print foil adhesive (**7.9**). If you're applying foil to adhesive or direct-print plastisol, make sure to print a thick coat of ink to minimize the pitting effect you will get from an uneven ink surface. In the Heat-Transfer Chapter, you were told to apply foil for 2 sec with a heat press. When applying foil to direct prints, you need to increase the time to 10 sec.

Foil and Water-Based Ink

One great property of foil is that is *does not* adhere to water-based ink. This enables you to do a multicolor print with water-based ink and then use plastisol as an accent or outline. The print can then be foiled for 10 sec and the foil will only adhere to the plastisol (**7.10**).

Metallic Ink

Metallic inks are simply finely ground metal flakes that are suspended in a clear plastisol base. They can be used as accents in a design or as the entire print. Metallics are supplied either pre-mixed or as a separate powder and clear base (**7.11**). They are available in a variety of colors, but gold and silver are the most popular.

Print metallics through a 110-125 (43-49 cm) mesh or lower. If the mesh is too fine, you will push the clear base through the screen, but the metallic flakes will get caught in the mesh. Because the flakes are opaque, you can use metallics on both light and dark colored garments. Since the base is plastisol, simply run the shirt through the dryer or flash cure it after printing.

7.10 Since foil will not stick to water-based ink, you can create interesting effects by combining water-based ink and plastisol and then foiling it.

7.11 Metallic inks are finely ground metallic powders that are mixed with a plastisol clear base to give the print a rich look.

One of the biggest problems with metallics is that some brands dull and tarnish *badly* after the first washing. Some brands encapsulate the flakes so they stay brighter after washing. Try different brands and make sure to tell the customer that the print may become fairly dull after the shirt is washed.

7.12 *Glitter inks are glossy mylar flakes that are mixed with clear base plastisol. They are printed through a very coarse mesh and give the design a shiny, reflective look.*

Before

7.13 *Color change inks with either turn to a different color or turn clear when they are heated up. They are a great novelty ink that work best on "concept" or "theme" designs.*

After

Glitter Ink

Unlike the small metal flakes in metallic inks, glitter inks are made of much larger mylar flakes that are suspended in a clear plastisol. Because the flakes are made of mylar the print will always retain its bright, shiny look.

Because the flakes are so big in glitter inks, you need to print through a 30 or 40 (12-16 cm) mesh, and it may require a number of strokes to get a good print.

Because the ink is so thick, you may need to reduce it slightly just like you would a regular plastisol. It also may require more than one trip through the dryer or a longer time under a flash-cure unit because the print will be fairly thick.

Glitter works great as an accent on both light and dark shirts (**7.12**). It can also be used as part of a multicolor design and should be printed last if possible to avoid getting glitter flakes on the bottom of the other screens.

Glitter is available in a wide range of colors including silver, gold, green, red, etc. This ink was very popular in the early 80's and then disappeared from overuse. It has made a comeback with the advent of free-form wearable art shirts and the increased use of foils and other accents.

Color Change Ink

Color change inks are designed to either change color or turn clear when heat is applied to them. They are called Thermochromatic inks. They are great as a novelty ink that makes a design either come to life or reveal itself when the shirt gets hot (**7.13**). Because the ink is fairly expensive, use it as a small accent or novelty part of a design.

7.14

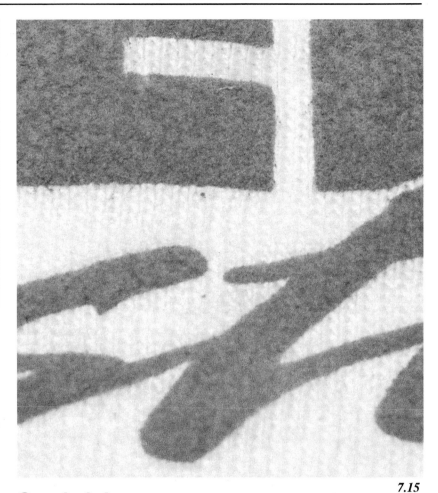

7.15

Thermochromatic ink is supplied a variety of ways. Some suppliers offer it as a premixed water-base formulation while others offer it as an additive for a clear plastisol base. Consult each manufacturer for detailed information and to obtain a *technical data sheet* for specific information on the use of their ink.

Fragrance Ink

This is an ink that you may never use because of the expense but it is great as a novelty or concept ink. Imagine a shirt with flowers or a bowl of fruit you can smell. Fragrance inks are supplied ready-to-use and will withstand up to ten washings before the fragrance disappears. (They lose about 10% of their scent with each washing.) These inks are printed just like all-purpose plastisols and should be used as small parts of a design to minimize the expense.

Shimmer or Crystalina

Crystalina (also known as Shimmer and Yellow Sparkle) is very much like glitter ink except that the mylar flakes are more translucent in a clear base. This ink is designed to overprint other flash-cured colors and requires a coarse mesh such as a 33 or 40 (13-16 cm).

Crystalina ink is a nice accent over colors that gives them a rich-looking pearlescent sparkle. These inks are fairly thick (like glitter) and can be reduced slightly for easier printability (**7.14**). You can create a great effect by printing an underbase of puff ink, flash-drying it, printing with regular plastisol on top, curing it, and then overprinting with a solid coat of shimmer. The entire print is then cured.

Suede Ink

This is terrific stuff! It prints like a puff ink and has a real suede feel to it (**7.15**). Suede ink works really well with designs that are created with it in mind, such as animal or nature prints.

Suede ink is actually made by putting an additive in regular plastisol ink. This means you aren't limited to just brown. You can mix the additive with red, blue, green or whatever color you want. Before mixing, check with your supplier, or the manufacturer, for specific directions. Generally, you mix 20-50% of the suede additive with your regular ink. If you add too much the print will flake and lack durability.

Print suede ink through a 230 (90 cm) mesh. It will take a couple of firm strokes to get good coverage and it also helps to print on a soft printing surface.

It takes a longer than normal tunnel time for the ink to "suede," so run the shirts through the dryer twice and turn the belt speed way down. If you lay down a thick enough coat, you can get excellent coverage on a dark shirt too.

Like puff ink, suede can be flash-dried without puffing it, so you can use it as part of a multi-color design as long as you flash-dry it before printing any other colors.

7.14 Crystalina or Shimmer is an over-print ink that has a pearlescent transparent look to it that accents the color underneath it.

7.15 Suede ink is a plastisol ink additive similar to puff. It is printed through a fairly fine mesh and raises up when run through the dryer to give it a suede feel.

Discharge Ink

Discharge inks are special formulations that remove the dye from the garment (discharge it) and replaces it with an ink color. This ink only works on certain brands of 100% cotton shirts and is designed to provide a softer hand to the print than standard plastisols (**7.16**). Make sure to ask your shirt supplier if their garment will discharge.

Discharge inks are generally used for designs that cover the entire garment (all-over printing) because of the softness of the print. They are also used as spray-on or roll-on inks to provide special free-form background effects to a garment.

Because discharge inks are water-based, they require the use of a durable, water-resistant stencil. They also need to be mixed prior to use and generally will not last longer than 24 hours after mixing.

Print discharge inks through meshes ranging from 60-160 (24-63 cm). The prints *must* be heat cured for *two to three minutes*. They require a longer tunnel time than most small dryers can offer. Another option is to use a standard heat-transfer press for the discharge process. Pressing the garment for 35-45 sec with light pressure at 375° F (190° C) is all that is needed. If you are not sure if your conveyor dryer is discharging the ink properly, use a heat-transfer press to test a shirt to see what the print should look like when the proper heat and time are used.

The brightness of the print will vary from ink-brand to ink-brand and certain brands will have a noticeable rotten-egg odor. Try to purchase a low-odor ink and make sure to use a very heavy stroke to get good penetration.

7.16 Discharge ink removes the dye from the shirt and replaces it with a color. This gives the print a very soft hand. These inks are popular for all-over prints where softness of the ink is important.

7.17 Wearable art is the term coined for free-form hand-done shirts that have an "art-sty" one-of-a-kind look to them.

Wearable Art

An entire book could be written on wearable art shirts, which generally refers to shirts that have been hand decorated with squeeze-bottle ink, hand-applied glitters and other embellishments such as cloth, jewels, foil, puff ink and more (**7.17**).

Wearable art shirts sell for more money than standard screen printed ones because of the time it takes to create each one. Many people start out in this business making wearable art shirts and then progress into screen printing, where they can print the basic design and then decorate the shirt using "wearable art" methods. This combination gives a one-of-a-kind custom look that can be mass produced (**7.18**).

Most arts and crafts stores carry a complete line of hand-applied inks. They are also available in larger quantities for mass production from a handful of industry suppliers (**7.19**).

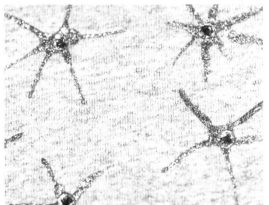

7.18 To mass-produce wearable art shirts you can screen print the basic design and then use hand methods to finish decorating the garment.

7.19 Some manufacturers specialize in supplying everything you need to mass-produce wearable art shirts. (Photo courtesy Transfermania, Hialeah, FL.)

7.20 Shirt treatments such as tie-dye can be combined with screen printing for interesting effects.

7.21 An airbrush sprays paint in a very controllable pattern and is widely used to create lifelike art pieces.

7.22 Airbrushes can be used to create original designs on T-shirts and other clothing items.

7.23 Airbrush Action Magazine is an excellent source of airbrush articles and inspiration. (Photo courtesy Airbrush Action Magazine, Lakewood, NJ.)

Shirt Treatments

Other shirt treatments and dyeing processes such as tie-dyeing, dip-dyeing and marbleizing can be used to achieve interesting effects. You can use these enhancements on the entire garment and then screen print on the shirt (**7.20**). It's a great area in which to be creative!

Airbrushing Shirts

Although airbrushing is not a method of printing a shirt, it is widely used to decorate shirts. You often see artists at fairs and beach resorts "painting" shirts with an airbrush.

In simple terms, an airbrush is a finely tuned paint sprayer that can be adjusted to spray a lot or a little paint or ink (**7.21**). Before you think it sounds like you couldn't have much control with an airbrush look at figure **7.22**). Airbrushing is widely used to create posters and high-end art pieces.

Airbrushes are available for less than $50, and the only other item you need to airbrush shirts is an air compressor. You can use airbrushing to enhance a screen printed design or to personalize a shirt with an individual's name.

To learn more about airbrushing, get a copy of *Airbrush Action Magazine* (**7.23**). It is an excellent source of how-to-do-it articles, video training tapes, seminars and airbrush supplies.

CHAPTER

PRINTING NON-TEXTILES

There is a good market for other printed items besides textiles, and in many cases you can get this from your T-shirt customers. Businesses use posters, decals, bumper stickers and binders to advertise their products (8.1). Politicians can be a good source of printing business during the political season. (But always get paid in advance.) Non-textile items are also good to print when, and if, you have a slow season or are between jobs.

Poster Board

Poster board is available from most screen printing suppliers and art stores. It comes in various weights, colors and finishes. Some jobs may require only a paper-thin poster, while others might require a stiffer and larger cardboard. Most poster board comes in stock sizes and will have to be cut down to the proper size. A good paper cutter will come in handy here or you can pay extra for your supplier to cut it to size.

Decals

Decals are made of pressure-sensitive Mylar™ or vinyl that is sold by the roll or sheet. These materials are available in both clear and opaque colors, and usually come in regular and matte finishes. Decals are normally printed in multiple quantities per sheet, which is referred to as the number up. For example, "6-up" would refer to six of the same design ganged on the screen and printed at the same time. After printing, the sheet is then cut apart on a paper cutter or by hand with scissors or a razor knife.

Bumper Stickers

Stock for bumper stickers is similar to decal material and is sometimes the same. Bumper stickers can also be made from paper stock with a pressure-sensitive backing. The main questions about bumper stickers are how long do you want it to last and should it be removable? If the job is for a short-lived advertising campaign, then removable paper stock is fine. If you are printing someone's store or radio-station name and they want it to stay on a long time, then use a Mylar™ or vinyl stock with a permanent adhesive. Bumper stickers can also be ganged and then cut apart.

8.1 Non-textile items such as posters, decals and bumper stickers are easy to print and can bring additional income.

The Screen

For most non-textile items, you can generally use a 230-305 (90-120 cm) monofilament screen mesh. Ink for these items is thinner and will print better through a finer mesh.

Direct emulsion works well for the stencil but capillary direct film will give a sharper edge. It is a little harder to adhere capillary direct film to fine mesh counts, though, and you may find that a good dual-cure direct emulsion is almost as good and much easier to use!

The Ink

Each substrate has its own type of ink. Your screen printing supplier will be a great help here. For vinyl, you use a vinyl ink; for metal and wood, you can use an enamel, etc. The problem substrates are plastics. There is a very wide variety of plastics from ABS to polystyrene to polypropylene, and *not every plastic ink* will work on every plastic.

You *should not* use plastisol for printing on non-textiles. It does not have any real adhesive properties and needs something to hang onto for it to be durable.

Don't forget the ink additives. Most manufacturers have special thinners, reducers, retarders, etc. that they recommend for use with their products. Since all of these inks will air-dry, you should get the correct reducers and wash-ups. Some inks have a retarder additive that will slow the drying process down a little.

Always test the ink and make sure it will do the job for you before printing the order. Suppliers and ink manufacturers will be glad to answer questions and help you with problems on tricky jobs.

Poster Ink

Poster ink is one of the most widely used screening inks. It is available in both gloss and flat finishes and is soluble in mineral spirits. Always check the instructions on the can or the technical data sheet that is available from your supplier. The drying time is approximately 20-30 minutes. Poster inks dry by the evaporation of their solvent content – usually in 20-30 minutes. There are also some water-soluble poster inks on the market. These are handy because all they require for cleanup is water. If you use a water-soluble ink, be sure your screen and blockout are *not* water soluble.

Enamel Ink

Enamel ink forms a very tough surface and has the highest gloss of commonly available inks. Unlike poster ink, enamels may take up to 24 hr. to dry and it dries by internal reaction with the available air (oxidation). They are one of the most versatile inks and can be used on decals, metal signs, glass, foil, wood, paper, cardboard, leather, Masonite™, etc. Check with your ink supplier for additional information. Always test the ink and the item to be printed for durability and compatibility! Enamels usually clean up with mineral spirits.

Vinyl Ink

Vinyl ink is extremely durable since it actually becomes an integral part of the vinyl or film substrate. It will give the longest-lasting print on decal material. When printed with vinyl ink, the stencil should be made of a lacquer-proof material and blockout, and should be cleaned up with lacquer thinner, methyl ethyl ketone (MEK) or acetone.

Press Setup for Non-Textiles

If you built a T-shirt press then you are all set because it will work just as well for flat objects! Better yet, is printing on the vacuum table explained in the *Heat Transfer* chapter. It will hold down lightweight objects such as decals and bumper stickers.

Actually, you can used a simple pair of screen hinges and a table to print non-textile items because you print one color at a time (**8.2**).

Professional screeners who specialize in printing non-textiles use semi-automatic flat-bed presses (**8.3**).

Registration Guides

In order to ensure that each and every print is printed in the same location, use a registration guide made of thin paper, plastic or cardboard that is taped in place on the printing base. This enables us to always put the stock in the same exact place every time we make a print.

Multicolor printing is similar to transfer printing: you print and dry one color at a time. Registration guides are placed at three points: two at the rear (or back) and one at the side. This is called the three-point system.

You can make your own guides or purchase guides from your screen print supply company (**8.4**).

Off-Contact

Most flat objects should be printed off-contact. This involves placing a few strips of cardboard under the edge of the screen so that when the screen is in the down position, it will actually rest about 1/8 in. (.32 cm) off the printing base. When printing off-contact, the only time the screen should touch the substrate is when the force of the squeegee passes over the screen and

8.2

8.2 *You can print non-textiles on a table with a simple pair of screen hinges.*

8.3 *Professional shops use semi-automatic flat-bed presses to print non-textile items. (Photo courtesy Lawson Products, St. Louis, MO.)*

8.4 *Plastic and metal registration guides can be used to line up the material.*

deposits the ink. Off-contact printing will give a sharper, cleaner print!

Printing

Printing flat objects is about the same process as printing textiles. Use only one stroke – preferably towards you. Two strokes will tend to decrease the sharpness of the print and may cause some ink to leach out under the screen, causing a blurred or smudged print. Remember to use a good, firm stroke and clean the screen with the squeegee. If all the ink doesn't push through to the material below, you will have problems with clogging.

Multicolor

If printing multicolor images, you need to print all of the first color and let it dry. You then place these prints back on the press and print all of the second colors – making sure to put the substrate in the registration guides (for additional information see Chapter 5 - *Heat Transfer.*

Flood Stroke

As with the section on textile and air-dry ink printing, you should use a flood stroke when printing with poster, enamel and vinyl inks. It isn't necessary, but you will have fewer problems with ink drying in the screen!

Simply make a good clean print and then raise the screen and do a light flood stroke across the image area.

Drying

Since air-dry inks are used for non-textiles, and the fact that the print can take a long time to dry, you'll need some kind of rack to set wet prints on. A lot of commercial racks are available, but they are expensive (**8.5**). If the job isn't too large you can just lay the prints on the floor or on tables to dry.

If you have a conveyor dryer with an airflow system, you can turn the heat of the dryer down and run the items through the tunnel with the airflow turned on. It may take a number of trips through the tunnel to get the ink dry.

Cleanup

Make sure to clean your screen and tools immediately after use. Non-textile inks will dry and harden, and you can't leave them like you can with plastisol. Always have plenty of rags handy and be prepared for the ink to start to dry in the screen. A little solvent on a rag should open the clogged area easily.

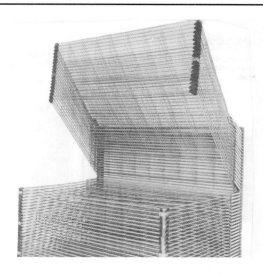

8.5 Special racks can be used to dry air-dry inks.

Ventilation

Non-textile inks generally have a high concentration of solvent and give off a very strong odor. Make sure to have a window open and fans blowing the air away from you. If you are working in your home, you may not want to print with non-textile inks unless you can really ventilate the area. Fumes from the basement will go through your entire house!

Take extreme care when using non-textile inks because of their flammability too! Do not leave garbage cans around that have solvent-soaked rags in them and do not leave the washup and thinners uncapped.

CHAPTER

9

ALL ABOUT GARMENTS

In this chapter we will look at the makeup of the garments we print on. The industry has come a long way from just basic white T-shirts. Now there are hundreds of styles of garments and about as many suppliers.

The *basic* T-shirt is still the staple of the industry. Other shirt styles give you the opportunity to offer more than just T-shirts. You can print a customer's basic T-shirt order and also offer polo shirts, sweatshirts and many other items.

How to Buy Garments

Direct from the Mill

Most shirts are manufactured by major mills such as Hanes, Fruit of the Loom, Lee, Russell, Oneida and others. These mills will generally not sell direct to small printers. Instead, they prefer to sell to local distributors or jobbers who, in turn, will sell you any quantity you want.

Unless you can purchase a case (six dozen) of a particular size and color, book your needs for an entire year, have good credit, etc., etc., it is almost impossible to buy direct. It is not uncommon for certain mills to sell direct to you if you have an unusually large order. They all seem to have two different sales divisions. One side makes sure the local distributors are happy and the other calls on printers to see where the big orders are. Anything to make a sale.

If you want to buy directly from the mill, the best approach is to contact them and get a copy of their current catalog. They may also have color swatches and other sales aids (**9.1**). By requesting a listing of their dealer network, you will know who the distributors are in your area.

Appendix A has an excellent list of garment wholesalers. The back of industry trade maga-

zines usually list smaller mills who have smaller minimum orders and will sell direct to you. Some of these smaller mills will even sew your own label in the shirt (private label). If you are trying to establish a name for yourself and your line of shirts, having *your own* shirt is very impressive.

Wholesalers

This is generally how you will buy shirts. Even large printers who buy direct from the mill will purchase their fill-in from wholesalers. You can call up a wholesaler, order one shirt or 10,000 and they will ship to you the same day. Many of them have millions of shirts in inventory and load UPS trucks until 6:00 pm daily. Of course, they

9.1 All of the major mills offer complete catalogs, color swatches and a dealer listing. (Courtesy Hanes Printables, Winston-Salem, NC.)

9.2 *Wholesale suppliers offer extensive catalogs that show a wide variety of brands and styles.*

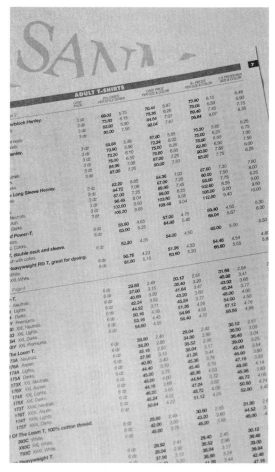

9.3 *Suppliers sell shirts by the single piece, by the half-dozen and in cases of six dozen.*

all have full-color catalogs and toll-free numbers (**9.2**). Wholesalers are very competitive and they all want your business!

Start collecting catalogs today. You will need as many sources as possible for those unusual requests. One thing you will notice when looking at catalogs is that everything is sold by the dozen or ½ dozen. Wholesalers usually offer a case price, ½ dozen price and piece price (**9.3**). Some even offer 100 dozen prices for larger orders.

Let Them Be Your Bank

Another reason for buying from a wholesaler is that you never know what you need to keep in inventory. One day you may have an order for 500 all black XL shirts and the next day an order for 250 light blue in all sizes.

Let the wholesaler be *your* warehouse and your bank. In fact, when a customer calls to see if you have the shirts available, just tell them that you need to check the inventory in the warehouse and you will call them back. Then pick up the phone and call your supplier.

Another benefit of buying from a wholesaler is that you can carry a very minimal inventory of shirts. You will still accumulate shirts from buying extras, and you may want to carry some of the commodity colors (white or maybe the local school colors).

Garment Quality

You should always try to sell the best shirt you can. Regardless of the price you quoted the customer, they will always look to you as the responsible supplier who sells quality. Depending on your situation, you may be better off selling a specific name brand or simply a "high-quality" shirt. If you quote the job with a specific brand and then find that your local supplier is out of the size you need, you may be able to substitute another name brand of equal quality. If shirts are in short supply, sell on the quality of the shirt – not the brand.

100% Cotton or 50/50?

This is always a tough question. Depending on the area of the country you're located in, you will get different answers. For many years, 50/50 blends were the staple because they didn't shrink like cotton. Now, cotton shirts are preshrunk, so this has become less of a factor. Cotton shirts are also more comfortable to wear and cooler.

In most cases, a 50/50 shirt will hold the print better. Cotton fibers fluff up more when a garment is washed which may cause the print to fade a bit more than on 50/50 tees.

Seconds and Irregulars

Different mills have different meanings for seconds and irregular shirts. Generally, the term *irregular* means a garment that is not quite up to specifications, or one that has been repaired or fixed to be almost up to specs.

A *second* usually refers to a shirt that just doesn't meet specifications at all. A second can often be made into an irregular by doing minor repair work such as closing a seam or stitching a hole.

Some seconds cannot be made into an irregular, because they have problems like the wrong size sleeves, color mismatching, excessive shrinkage or large holes.

Other terms used are *graded seconds*, *off-quality*, or *graded imperfects*. Since a mill does not purposely make irregular shirts, they are always offered on an as-available basis.

Some suppliers specialize in selling these off-quality shirts. Check the trade magazines for sources.

How to Return Bad Shirts

When printing, you can have three types of misprints: printing errors that you can't repair, small ink marks or stains that you can remove with a spot removal gun (called "blow out" shirts), and mill defects. Mill defects consist of holes, open seams and other obvious manufacturing problems.

Most suppliers will tell you that they will only take back a shirt with no print on it. Unfortunately, you never seem to find the mill defect until you are folding and packaging the printed shirts. If the print is on the front of the shirt, odds are good that the defect is on the back. The mill should take these shirts back *with or without a print.*

American Made or Imported

Since American-made shirts have good brand recognition, it is best to stick with them. Some customers want the cheapest shirt possible for a promotion or giveaway. In this case, you may want to investigate using an imported shirt from Pakistan, India, China, etc. While you can buy good imported garments, they generally shrink more and are not as smooth as American-made ones. *Make sure your customers know exactly what they are getting if you're using imported or irregular shirts!*

Size Scale

The mills bases their production on projections from wholesalers and market demands. In the old days, the size scale for 12 dozen shirts was called a 2-4-4-2 scale. This meant that there were two dozen small, four dozen medium, four dozen large, and two dozen extra-large shirts.

As the market dictated a looser-fitting and larger-cut garment, the size scale moved up to include more large shirts and fewer smalls.

Some suppliers tack on an "up" charge if you buy out of the size scale. Others add on this charge if the amount of extra-large garments exceeds the number of large on your order.

Pricing

Prices for T-shirts will vary from brand to brand. Generally, you will pay more for dark-colored shirts because it takes longer for the mill to dye them. You will also pay extra for sizes above extra large. A white 100% cotton heavyweight T-shirt sells for $2.50 to $3.00 as of this writing. Dark shirts range from $3.00 to $3.50 each.

How a Shirt Is Made

It isn't really necessary to know how a garment is made. You generally just buy a name-brand shirt and print on it. Understanding how garments are made is more critical if you deal with large corporate accounts or license programs where your customers specify exactly what they want. The following information is also useful when comparing name-brands, off-brands and imported shirts.

Garments are made of twisted strands of yarn that are knitted into fabric. This yarn can be natural material such as vegetable-fiber cotton, man-made material such as the polymer known as polyester, or a combination of both.

Cotton

Cotton can be a curse or a god-send. Some customers think a cotton garment will shrink and not hold its size, regardless of what you tell them about shrinkage control or quality. Other customers know that cotton is a soft, cool material that absorbs moisture and is comfortable to wear. The difference of opinion will vary and often depends on climate conditions and the general quality-consciousness of the market. The undisputed fact is that cotton is easy to print on.

Cotton fibers are long, porous and somewhat hollow, with concentric layers or walls that readily absorb perspiration and draw it away from the body in a process called *wicking.*

The absorbency of the fibers also allows them to accept inks much better than synthetic fibers.

Cotton fibers are noted for their warmth in cold weather, too. The fibers protect against the wind without trapping body moisture. They tend to insulate because of the cushion of air that helps give them a soft feel. Synthetic fabrics, on the other hand, have smooth, slick surfaces that touch the skin and do not insulate well.

In the last few years, the major mills have done an excellent job of producing quality 100% cotton shirts that are shrinkage controlled by chemically treating the cotton with resins and stabilizers or through special processing techniques called "compacting."

The consumer has a much better opinion of cotton than ever before.

Cotton Yarn

Cotton yarn is made by spinning or twisting the fibrous hairs of cotton into lengths of yarn. Before it is spun, the cotton is cleansed of foreign matter, short fibers, seeds and tangles by a method called "carding." The more carding, the better the quality of cotton used in the yarn. Some manufacturers double card the yarn, while other bypass this step entirely!

After the carding process, the cotton is drawn and, if necessary, blended with synthetic fibers. From this process, it may be combed before it is spun into yarn. The combing process removes fibers that are too short and immature and any remaining foreign particles. Cotton that is not combed will not have uniform yarn and will not be quite as smooth.

From combing, the cotton is then reduced in size to a thick cord-like material in a process called "roving." It is then spun into the proper yarn size by twisting the yarn. The more yarn is twisted the stiffer it becomes. The spinning or twisting process draws the fibers down to the predetermined size called the yarn number.

Ring-Spun or Open-End Yarn

Most yarn used in standard-weight garments is called open-end yarn. Some manufacturers have added an additional step in the spinning process that produces a yarn that is more durable and softer. This is called ring-spun and generally produces a better and softer printing surface.

Since a ring-spun yarn will fluff a little more when the garment is washed, the print may fade a little more after the first washing. For best results request that your customers wash their printed shirts inside out *(especially if it is a fine detailed print with high mesh counts and transparent inks)*.

Yarn Number

The yarn number (for cotton and most synthetics) is calculated by a specific weight of yarn to a specific length. The system is based on a "1's" yarn having 840 yards in one pound. *The higher the number, the thinner the yarn.*

Yarns are referred to as *singles* or *doubles*, depending on whether they have a single strand of yarn or a double strand. Yarn used in T-shirts is generally singles and is commonly found in the 24-36 size, also referred to as *24 single* or *36 single*.

Even though the yarn is thicker with a lower number, it does not always mean the shirt is heavier if the material is knitted loosely.

Polyester Yarn

Polyester was commercially introduced in 1953 by duPont. Simply put, it is a man-made fiber derived from coal, air, water and petroleum.

Polyester is made into yarn by cutting the filaments into short staple lengths and then twisting and spinning these filaments into yarn. Polyester fibers are very durable. Due to the fact that they are a slicker, nonporous fiber, they do not absorb moisture or insulate as well as cotton.

Cotton/Polyester Blends

A 50/50 blend shirt is popular because it combines the good qualities of both cotton and polyester. Cotton/polyester blends offer the comfort and moisture absorption of cotton, and the durability and shrinkage resistance of polyester. The blending of the yarn is generally done before the combing and spinning process. This creates what is called an intimate blend.

Knitting

Fabric weaving is done by interlacing yarn at right angles as in yard goods, sheets and most cloth. Knitting is done by interlooping yarn using needles (similar to hand knitting a sweater). T-shirt material is always knitted in what is called a circular knit or a round tube form. This eliminates the need for the garment to have seams down the sides .

Three different stitches are generally used in knitting T-shirt material: jersey, rib and interlock knit.

Jersey knit (also called a plain knit) is used for basic T-shirts. It produces a smooth material with a fine pattern of vertical lines on the outside (wales) and horizontal rows (courses) on the inside (**9.4**).

Rib knit produces wales on both sides of the cloth because every other course loop drops to the back of the knit. This is called a 1x1 rib knit and gives the garment much more elasticity than a jersey knit (**9.5**).

Interlock knit is a special run-resistant knit that combines two inter-knitted 1x1 rib fabrics. It is less elastic than rib or jersey knit and has a smooth surface on both sides. It is used for ladies' tops, some children's garments and better quality shirts. Because of the increased yarn content and more complicated knit, interlock material is more expensive (**9.6**).

Fabric Weight

Fabric weight is determined by the number of yarn used and how tightly or loosely it is knitted. It is common for a manufacturer to indicate the

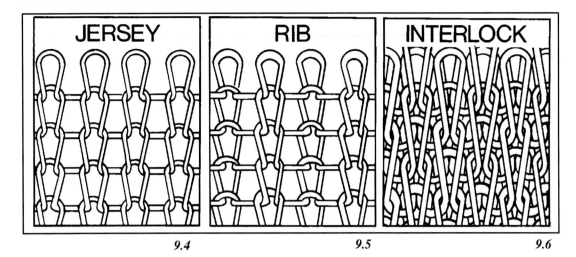

JERSEY	RIB	INTERLOCK
9.4	9.5	9.6

weight of a garment by referring to the yarn size only, such as a *28 single*. This won't always give an accurate comparison. A shirt can be a *34 single* and have more courses and wales than a 28 single – and be a heavier fabric!

Most *lightweight* garments are made of 26 or 28 single yarn, *midweight* of 22 or 24 single yarn and *heavyweight* of 20 or lower yarn.

Generally, material should have a ratio of three courses per inch to two wales per inch. Normal T-shirt jersey material can range from 28 courses by 25 wales to 40 courses by 30 wales. The higher the number, the better the material and the less shrinkage you will have to contend with.

Fabric Finish

After the fabric is knitted, it is referred to as *greige goods*. These are inspected before finishing or dyeing by running the fabric over large light tables.

Bleaching

After inspection, all greige goods are bleached or scoured to help eliminate the color variations in the cotton and allow the yarn to shrink. After bleaching, the greige goods are thoroughly rinsed.

Dyeing

Fabric dyeing is an art in itself that can be very time consuming. Since the dyes used in cotton are different than those used in polyester blends, the two are dyed in different formulations. One stage dyes the cotton portion and the other dyes the polyester.

Knit material is generally dyed in large vats that work under heat and pressure. Dark colors have to stay in the vats longer than lighter colors. As a comparison, light colors may stay in the dye solution for five hours, while dark colors may stay in 16 hours or more. This is the reason dark garments cost more money.

Dyeing is done in batches. Even though the dyer carefully monitors the dye formulations and dye time, colors can vary slightly from batch to batch. Because of this, the various parts of a garment are always made from the same dye batch.

Other Chemicals

After dyeing, the material can be treated with other chemicals such as softeners, fillers and resins to stabilize the fabric, control shrinkage and make the fabric easier to sew.

Calendering and Compacting

After drying, the fabric is calendered – a process that uses steam to bring the fabric to the desired width. This process is sometimes called preshrinking and helps control fabric shrinkage. With current calendering and compacting processes, fabric shrinkage on 100% cotton garments can be held to less than 3%.

Garment Assembly

Cutting and sewing garments is labor-intensive. It is not nearly as automated as you might think. In fact, the actual sewing operations consist of rooms of workers sewing shirts together with industrial sewing machines (**9.7**).

9.7 Although some garment manufacturing processes are automated, much of the assembly work is done in rooms full of operators using industrial sewing machines.

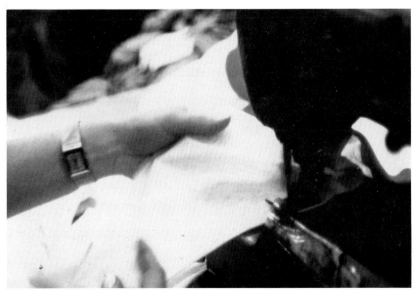

9.8 *Large stacks of fabric are laid out, marked with a pattern and cut with an electric knife.*

Cutting

Finished tubular knitted goods are laid out on long cutting tables and spread to as many as 400 - 500 plys thick. The desired pattern is hand marked on the top ply and specific pieces are cut out using special electric knifes that have extremely sharp blades and operate somewhat like a saber saw (**9.8**). Some of the larger manufacturers now use state-of-the-art *cookie-cutter* type presses to die cut the fabric in a much more automated process.

All Shirts Aren't the Same

Although you may think a shirt is just a shirt, there is a large difference between shirts. Not only does the yarn weight, garment weight and quality of dyeing and shrinkage control play a part, but the actual construction is very important. From simple quality differences such as a *taped neck,* where the neck seam is covered, to making sure the garment is a true full-cut, manufacturers have different quality standards and some cut corners in areas you don't even think about.

Quality Checks

When examining garments, there are a number of areas to check for quality. Start by tugging at a seam to see it if *smiles* or opens up. This can be a sign of too few stitches or loose stitching.

Perform a wash test to check shrinkage. Simply draw a pattern around an unwashed shirt on a piece of paper and then check the washed and dried shirt against the pattern. Only minimal shrinkage should occur, and the shrinkage should be uniform with not too much in any one direction.

Fleecewear

Fleecewear is a term that has been coined for sweatshirt-type material. It is made from specially knitted material that has a smooth outer finish with a soft underside. Originally used for gym clothes and athletic warmups, it has now become another staple of the industry.

Fleecewear is knitted like T-shirt jersey material except three different types of yarn are used: face, tie-in and backing yarn.

Face yarn is used on the front or outside of the garment and is usually tightly woven so it will handle abrasion better. Tie-in yarn is used to connect the face to the backing and is not very visible. Backing yarn is woven in place loosely and made soft by running the fabric through a *napping* machine that uses needles to pull small fibers of the backing yarn loose, giving it a soft, silky feel.

While the most commonly used fiber content is a yarn made of 50% cotton and 50% polyester blend, other materials are also used, including 50% cotton/50% acrylic, 80% polyester/20% cotton, 80% cotton/20% polyester, 90% cotton/10% polyester, 100% cotton, 100% polyester and 100% acrylic.

The fiber content is dictated by the end use of the product. Generally, a 50/50 blend offers the softness of cotton and the shrink resistance of polyester. Garments containing acrylic will hold brighter colors better (fluorescents), but may also be more difficult to print on because they will not take much heat.

Fleecewear Fabric Weight

Fleece fabric weight is measured by the number of ounces of material there are per yard. It can vary from a low of 7 oz per yard for lightweight material to a high of 12 oz per yard for super heavyweight fabric.

Other Garments

Obviously, lots of other garments are on the market. Golf shirts, tank tops, long-sleeve T-shirts and other styles can be printed the same as T-shirts (**9.9**). Don't just think of yourself as a T-shirt printer – think of yourself as selling *imprinted* sportswear!

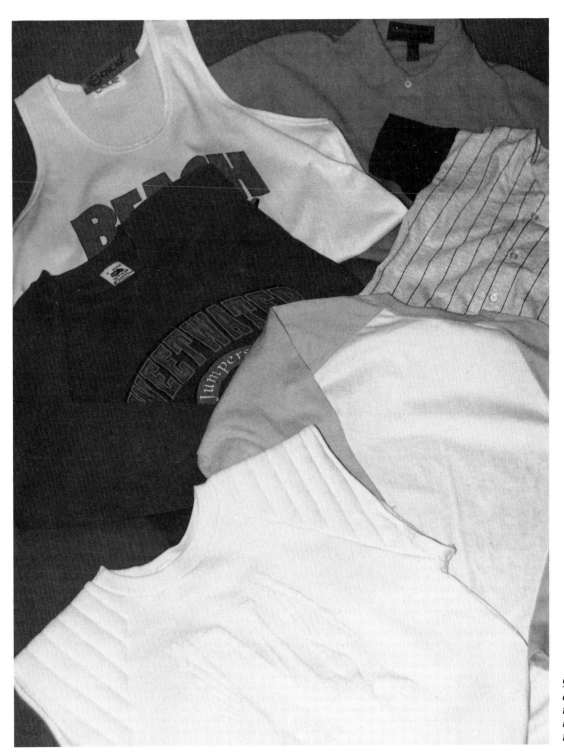

9.9 There are lots of other garments and textile items that can be printed and offered to your customers.

MARKETING AND SELLING

Marketing is how you get your message out or expose your product to potential customers. Selling is turning potential customers into real customers. Nothing that has been covered earlier in this book makes any sense without a marketing and selling effort! This is what running a business is all about (unless you are just going to print a few Christmas presents and polish your equipment while waiting for orders).

Since these two topics are interrelated, we are going to lump together the ideas and suggestions about marketing and selling your products.

The first important point is don't lose sight of what you are selling. *You are not selling screen printing*! You are selling imprinted sportswear, employee ID, promotional products, resort shirts, beach wear, event shirts, souvenirs, etc. You won't make much money just selling screen printing. If you tell customers you sell screen printing, they will want to bring you their shirts to print on. You will make more profit on the shirts you sell than on the designs you print on them. The screen printed design is the magic that makes the shirt worth more money. Just don't tell anyone that.

One thing that will become obvious in the very beginning is that sales will come easily if you have a good marketing plan. If you present your product properly and look like you know what you are doing, then customers will have confidence in your company and be willing to place orders and pay your prices.

If you market your products well in the beginning, you will find you will have steady repeat business as time goes by. The beauty of this business is that 50-75% of your customers will be repeat customers if you do a good job.

Marketing and selling is one area that beginning business people have a hard time with. It is easy to invest all the money in equipment and supplies and leave nothing for marketing. Don't let this happen to you. You are almost better off spending less on equipment and more on your company *package* when you first start out!

Fortunately, marketing doesn't have to be all that expensive. There are literally dozens of ways you can increase your market share without cleaning out your checking account. Here are some very easy, inexpensive and *effective* marketing and selling techniques that we have used over the years.

Marketing 101

24-Hour Marketing

It doesn't matter if you are in line at the grocery store; you should always be in marketing mode. This means networking, talking to people and being the first to strike up a conversation and offer your card. Tell the world what you do for a living. A local screen printer once told us that people look at him like he's an insurance salesman because he is always promoting his products. Everyone knows he is the "shirt person."

Your Company Package Is Everything!

This topic could take up an entire book. For starters, make sure you have an easy-to-remember company name (not too cute, but make it sound big), a *great logo* (aren't you selling your terrific graphics capabilities?), a sharp letterhead and business card, a catalog and price list, a printed order form, etc. (**10.1**). Spend a little extra on good paper and multicolor printing. This is how commercial companies do it. The right image gets

10.1 *The company package is very important. It tells the customer you are a professional and gives them confidence when placing an order with you. The package should include a good looking logo, letterhead, business cards, catalog, order form and more.*

the bigger corporate accounts and will help you get your price! *If you look good, you must be good.*

Your Logo and Name

You should have a name that sounds a little bigger than "Bob and Jane's Screen Printing." At least try to keep it sounding a little bigger so you will get more respect from your suppliers and customers. You may even want to keep it somewhat generic so you can sell other items besides T-shirts.

Spend some time and money to create a logo for your company. It could be a simple graphic that incorporates your company's initials. Just do something that shows you can create good graphics. Then print some shirts and caps with your logo. You need to look the part when making a sales call!

Presenting the Shirts

Do you deliver the shirts in a beat-up box or do you deliver the shirts in a nice clean box with your name on the side and maybe each shirt individually folded? Think about a meal you had at a great restaurant where it was nicely presented. *Presentation is everything* (**10.2**)!

Purchase boxes from a local packaging company and print your logo on the side using a poster ink through a 230 mesh. Some corrugated container companies will also print the boxes for you. If you can't print the boxes then make a label for the side that you spray adhesive in place.

Print a section on the box where you can circle the size of shirts inside. Also consider a slogan about your company and the words "to reorder call toll-free 800-............" Get the idea?

Fold the Shirts

What if every shirt were *individually folded* inside these nice printed boxes. It must be a great order of shirts. They look so professional when folded. What care you took to fold them for the customer. Granted, you will not be folding orders for 10,000 shirts, but how about anything less than 500? Folding shirts doesn't take too long, and you will be *amazed* at the response you'll get from customers. You may lose an account over price, but some will come back later because they like your presentation better than the competition.

Hang Tags and Stickers

If the order isn't too large, consider placing a simple hang tag on the shirts. A hang tag is a small card (like a business card) that is attached to shirts with a thin nylon strap. The card can have information about your company, the artist, the design, how to wash the shirt, how to reorder and anything else that may help increase sales. You can purchase hang tag guns from display companies.

A sticker is another way to say "we care." It could have your toll-free number or tell buyers about the special suede ink or other effect in the design. It could even list washing instructions for a foil print. Anything you can do to make the shirt look like it came from a company that really cares and provides a quality product will help your sales.

10.2 Presenting the shirts individually folded in a printed box and with a hang-tag attached makes a great impression on the customer!

The Paperwork

When you take an order, don't just grab the nearest scrap of paper and scribble notes. Take out your four-part order form and write it up in a professional manner. Use the camera-ready form Appendix B and print the Terms and Conditions of the sale on the back of the form.

Leave the customer a copy and make sure to give the proper copies to the art, purchasing, sales and production departments. Just the psychology of having the distribution of the copies printed on the bottom of the form will make you look like a larger and more sophisticated company.

You can even spice up your printed matter by using the new preprinted laser papers and adding your own copy. From blank multicolor business cards, to letterhead, sales folders and small brochures, these things are hot (**10.3**). All you do is imprint your sales pitch in black ink on the preprinted backgrounds (many have great graphics). You'll look like a major company. Preprinted flyers with perforated Rolodex cards are also available so your mailing can include a phone card for their files.

10.3 Preprinted paper is available for brochures, business cards and flyers that can be imprinted with your information on a laser printer. It is an easy and inexpensive way to add color to your package. (Courtesy Paper Direct, Lyndhurst, NJ)

Use Generic Catalog

No, this is not a plain white catalog. Your T-shirt supplier will sell you his catalog without a name on it for 40-75 cents! You can buy 50 or 5,000. All you have to do is print your name on it and – SHAZAM – you will have an instant 24-page *full-color* catalog of your own! Generic catalogs are available from many industry suppliers and can really make you look professional (**10.4**). This is a standard way of doing business in many other industries too. The T-shirt business did not invent the idea. Appendix A has a listing of sources for generic catalogs.

Start Collecting and Saving Samples

Save at least one print of everything you do. Don't just save prints on test squares. Save printed T-shirts so that customers can see the quality of the garment and printing. Buy blank samples from suppliers. Most will sell you one of anything as a sample for a slightly higher price. When the customer wants to see an XXXL polo shirt with three buttons, you should have one. Remember, since you are selling imprinted garments, your sample case should be full of printed samples.

Your Phone and Fax

When you look up a supplier's phone number and see that they have a *toll-free* line, you automatically think they are *big*! Why would they need an 800 number if they didn't do business nationwide? You too can have an 800 number; in fact, the installation is almost free from some of the telephone line companies. All you pay for are the incoming calls. If you don't want to pay a few cents for someone to call who may buy your products, then maybe you should keep your day job. This is how business works and it is time to start getting the phone to ring so you can sell your products. (It sure beats getting in your car and having the expense of a sales call!).

Along with your toll-free line, you must get a fax number. When customers call to get prices, tell them you will fax a quote immediately. If they ask you to fax them a quote and you don't have a fax machine, it immediately sounds as if you are a *very small* company and may deter them from doing business with you.

If you can't afford a fax (yes, there are lots of other things you need, too), then use a fax service. Just be sure to tell customers to put a cover sheet on their faxes so they will get to you immediately!

If you are working out of your house, you need to have a separate telephone line for your business. Don't let your kids answer and just say "hello." It could be the large corporation you called wanting a quote. Voice mail and answering machines may seem impersonal, but they are better than having no one answering the phone.

10.4 Generic catalogs are available from most suppliers. They are designed to be imprinted with your name and phone number and provide an ideal sales tool.

Get on Bid Lists

This is real easy task. Simply write the city, state, local colleges, large corporations, institutions and anyone else who buys imprinted products on a bid basis, and ask to be placed on the bid list. Don't forget to include your marketing package so that they will know you are a legitimate vendor who can deliver the order at a competitive price.

Computerize Your Marketing Effort

There are terrific sales and marketing software packages that let you keep track of leads and customers. They will print reports showing who you should call back, do mailing lists, create personalized sales letters and much more (**10.5**). You may want to investigate these software packages.

10.5 There are a variety of software programs that help track leads and do follow-up with customers. (Courtesy Telemagic Software, Carlsbad, CA.)

Take Credit Cards

Many of your small customers will want to pay with personal credit cards. Your bank may not set you up as a merchant unless you have excellent personal credit and a store-front. However, there are a number of companies who will set you up as a credit-card merchant for a small fee and an agreement that you lease the electronic data terminal from them. You may have to pay up to 3% of the sale, but it is well worth it. You will find these companies in the Yellow Pages under *Credit Cards & Plans.*

Take Any Size Job

If you're just starting out, take any job that comes in the door. Even if the customer only wants three shirts, tell him you can do it. You may have to assess a minimum order charge and charge extra for setups, but get the order. That same customer will come back to order two dozen and then six dozen and eventually become a steady customer – and he'll tell his friends about your services!

Market Today for Tomorrow's Business

This is *very important.* You should always be making contacts for jobs you may not see for a year. If you don't get a bid this year, find out who did and what the bid was. Then make a note in your database or next-year calendar for next year. If you lose an order because your quote was late, find out when the customer will order next year and plug the information into a recall date in your database or next-year calendar so you can call him back. If a new company breaks ground on a building, don't wait for them to open the doors. Find out who the owner is and make the call *now.* If you call on a large account and they say they are happy with their present supplier, ask them when they generally reorder and make a note to call them back then.

You should always be laying groundwork for jobs that will not materialize until later. Do this even when you are busy. You may be able to prevent slow times by marketing during the busy season.

Display at Local Trade Shows

Sooner or later, you should attend one of the industry trade shows. This is where suppliers try to sell to you. You can also exhibit your products on a local level. There are always home improvement shows, giftware shows, back-to-school shows and other events for specific markets. You can rent a booth to sell imprinted products to these focused customers. How about selling at a fireman's convention? They use up (and burn up) a lot of navy blue shirts! Maybe the local boat show is in town. Offer small quantities of shirts

for the captain and his/her mates. Boaters usually enter fishing tournaments, and they always need caps. You'll be amazed at what a little exposure will do for business.

Read Everything!

How do you find out about new businesses and upcoming special events? You read about them in the paper or business magazines. Read everything you can from the local paper to business journals. Always be on the lookout for a new customer or new idea. When you find someone you want to call on, do it today! Don't wait for your competition to beat you to it.

Subscribe to business papers that list tax licenses for new companies. then, call all the new businesses to make sure they have plenty of employee ID items and uniforms to make their staff look professional.

Contact Ad Agencies and PR Firms

Large corporations appoint advertising agencies and public-relations firms to make their major promotional-product buying decisions. Take an hour right now to go through the Yellow Pages and mail your company package to every agency and PR firm listed. They will definitely want to see a nice package and professional approach.

If you decide to work with ad agencies, be aware that they will be very demanding concerning quality, color matches and prepress samples. They will also ask for you to give them terms because they have to invoice their client and then pay you. This is just how they do business, so if you have a problem with picky customers, ad agencies are not for you.

Increase Your Product Mix with Ad Specialties

You can sell more products to the same customers by adding ad-specialty items to your line. Ad specialties include T-shirts, but also include printed ashtrays, mugs, key chains, etc. You can buy these products at a discount from ad-specialty distributors. Many of them have a generic catalog that you can print your name on (**10.6**). By spending a few dollars for some catalogs, you can instantly increase your product line by about 1,000 items! Appendix A has a listing for ad-specialty distributors.

If you like this type of business you can also become a member of the Advertising Specialty Institute and deal direct with other member companies *and* offer your services to the members.

Stick Your Company Name on Every Shirt!

Want a free ad? Just print your company name (real small) on every shirt you sell. This is called

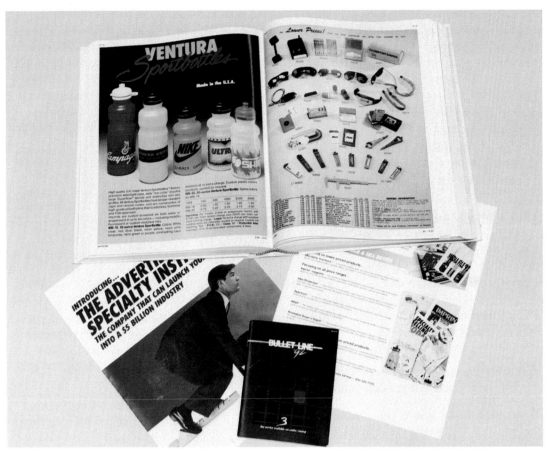

10.6 By becoming an Ad Specialty (ASI) member you gain access to thousands of specialty items and have a wide variety of generic catalogs to imprint with your name. (Courtesy Advertising Specialty Institute, Langhorne, PA. and Winters Associates, Bloomington, IN.)

a "bug" and is just a little one- or two-line name with your toll-free number printed in an inconspicuous place (**10.7**). If the customer doesn't want your name on his garments, how about printing your logo on the bottom of the shirt tail (like a designer shirt!). It will be out of the way and really make the shirt look neat.

Get Free Publicity with a News Release

Newspapers and magazines need to fill the space around the ads. By sending them news about your company and a photograph (a news release) you can get free publicity. So what is newsworthy about your company? How about those 100 reject shirts you sent to the disaster victims? Or the charity event you sponsored by donating caps and shirts. Of course, don't forget to take advantage of the photo of you presenting the products. How about the fact that you just moved to a new location?

Write the news release *as if you were the reporter*. Quote yourself and make it sound important. The more human interest, the better. If you are lucky, one of the larger papers may pick it up and run it nationwide (it better be *real* good).

Don't forget TV. If you are printing a special shirt for a national disaster, call the assignment desk at the local stations and let them know that you have a great human-interest story. Send that special shirt to Willard Scott of the *Today* Show

10.7 If possible try to place your name on every shirt that leaves your shop. This is a free advertisement for your company. Print it below the design and also put on your toll free number or your city name.

(or at least your local weather forecaster). If they use it, write a news release about it. Promote the fact that you are *nationally known*. Get the picture?

Let the Local Quick Printers Sell for You

Your local quick printer can be a valuable referral source. Many people go to quick printers to find out where to get shirts. And a lot of them now have full-color copiers and advertise shirts.

Why not give them a little display, offer them a discount, work up a price list that they can sell from and let them take orders for custom screen printing?

They do the same thing with labels, business cards and business forms. Most quick printers farm out those items. Why not shirts, too?

Telemarketing

This doesn't mean setting up a boiler room. It just means taking time to make a certain number of calls per day. Set your goal (start with just ten calls).

Give Customers a "Call to Action"

The first thing you learn in Sales 101 is to have a *call to action*. Give customers a reason to *buy now* and not later. Offer 10% off on the first order. Give them a *baker's dozen* (one free shirt for every 12 ordered). Offer free freight or a discount if they order caps and shirts. How about "Ginsu" knives if they order this week – just kidding, but you get the idea.

Go after Large Corporate Accounts

This tactic is cheap, but will take much longer than you may think. Get out the phone book again and let your fingers do the selling. Call major corporations (even ones you wouldn't think require shirts) and ask who purchases imprinted sportswear, promotional products or employee identification products for the company. You will be surprised at how easy it is to get the answers. Most of the time you will hear: "All promotional products are purchased through XYZ advertising agency and employee products are purchased by human resources." "Everything is bought through the home office in Sioux City, Iowa." The next question to ask is easy: "Do you have their phone

10.8 Learn how to sell to schools with an industry training course. (Courtesy U.S. Screen Printing Institute, Tempe, AZ.)

numbers and contact names?"

Generally, several departments in a corporation are responsible for buying items. Whether they're buying shirts for the annual picnic, promotional products to give away with their merchandise or employee identification will determine which department does the buying. You could have dozens of sales opportunities with just one company.

Expect to be asked to print a sample or come back later to meet with the buyer or to submit a proposal. Do whatever they ask (within reason). Things do not happen overnight! If a large company is considering you to be a one of their prime vendors, they will want to approve you. This means they will do a credit check and may ask for a financial statement, bank references, etc. This is just how it is done, so don't be put off by it.

Remember, your main contact will generally be a purchasing agent who does not want to lose his or her job because you are a flaky vendor! Treat the PA's right and make sure that you look and act professional and that you have "the package."

Mail Promotional Pieces Every Day

You went to all the trouble to buy generic catalogs and put together a very impressive catalog. Now what do you do? You get out your Yellow Pages (again) and start to address envelopes. Set a goal to mail a certain amount every day. Put these names in a computer database and set a recall date of two weeks after the pieces are mailed.

If you want to do mass mailings, you can buy mailing lists locally or contact a mailing-list company like American Business Lists in Omaha, NE. They will sell labels and floppy disks, or even let you download names off their on-line computer service. You can select any target market in any zip code selection you want.

Sell to Schools

The local school market is wide open. Each campus offers hundreds of sales opportunities because of all the groups, clubs, coaches, special events and class shirts. Just providing shirts for fund-raisers for the various organizations can keep you busy. If you feel uncomfortable about calling on this market, learn more about it through industry training videos (**10.8**).

Yellow Pages

Advertise in the Yellow Pages. Call right now and find out what the ad deadline is for the next book. If you are located in a competitive area, you may need more than just one listing. Try to be listed under more than one heading such as T-shirts, Sporting Goods, Screen Printing, Advertising Specialties, etc.

Price List

You should definitely publish a price list. The price list should include prices for the basic items you sell, such as T-shirts, sweats, caps, jackets, aprons and totes. It should also list other items with a "call for quotation" or some other notation that implies you will print almost anything. Make sure to use the item numbers that are in the generic catalog in your price list. All of your promotional materials must look like part of a total package.

Your price list should include your terms of sales and other pertinent information. Keep it positive. Things like "$20 return check charge," "no collect calls" and "rush jobs 100% extra" all say that you really don't want their business. How about "no order too large or small," "we love rush jobs" (of course you charge extra for them), "we can even work from your rough sketch," etc. These lines tell the customer that you really want his business and will do a great job on the order.

Putting a line on your price list like "orders over 10,000 shirts by special quotation" or "corporate accounts gladly accepted with authorized purchase order" tells customers that you must be big enough to handle and finance any size order – you must be big and professional! Depending on your market, these lines can also make you look too big. Some buyers want a little more personal service that a "small" company can provide.

Also, work up prices for one-color prints on your most common items. Have a separate section for additional colors.

Pricing Strategies

There are two ways to price a job. If you think the customer will become a regular account, then by all means keep the art and screen charges separate. If you include them in the price, then your *reorder* price may be a little too high.

If the job is for a school or club, all they want to know is how much it will cost them per shirt - total! For these jobs, total everything including sales tax and divide by the number of shirts. This way, the person in charge of placing the order can collect money from each club member to cover the costs.

Many printers leave money on the table by not charging enough markup on the garment. Don't make this mistake. If you spend your money to buy the garments and are going to "resell" them to the customer, you are entitled to make a reasonable profit on them!

This leads us to an important point. If you get caught in the trap of doing a lot of *printing only* (on the customer-supplied garments), you may lose out on all of the gravy profits in this business.

Think of ways that you can get the price you want even if the customer says you are too high. Is he comparing the same quality shirts? Will your competition guarantee a specific delivery date? Do you have sources for unusual garments that your competition can't (or won't) print on? Do you offer free delivery? Be sure your customers know all the added benefits of doing business with you.

How about items that cost little but give the order more perceived value? Giving the customer a couple of free baseball caps with each order for six dozen shirts or printing his design on a piece of cloth or test material and framing it for him is a nice touch. You can buy a bandanna for under $1. How about printing a couple of bandannas for *free*? All of these items have a value to the customer and a very low cost to you.

Establishing Your Prices

As the title of this book suggests, we are not only going to teach you how to print shirts, but how to make a profit at the same time. Don't think that just because you know the printing end means that you can skip the rest. Profit is the name of the game, and it can easily get away from you with increased overhead, uncontrolled growth, poor cash flow and lousy management!

Prices are one of the culprits in the "no-profit" syndrome. How? It's easy. Anyone can have a large, busy shop by getting work on price alone. There's no trick to undercutting the next guy and selling everything at reduced rates!

The real trick is to know your costs and sell at a markup that will make you competitive but still give you a reasonable return on your time and money. The best approach is to always try to sell on the quality of the product and your excellent service! This way, price becomes secondary.

Your goal should be to find the right mix of competitive pricing and reasonable profit coupled with a complete product line. Depending on your market area, you might find that while T-shirts are fairly competitive, other textile items such as jackets, caps, fashion items or heat transfers are more profitable.

Setting your prices may not be too hard in the beginning. But before you do, shop the competition and see what the market is charging for various items. By "shopping," we mean literally calling competitors to find out their prices without letting them know who you are. If you think that this is a little unethical, keep in mind that they will also be shopping you! You shop local prices to *keep the market as high as it will take*, *not* to undercut the competitions prices – if they can get a good price, you can too!

Some business books suggest that the only way to establish prices is to look at the history of how much it costs to do each job and add a reasonable markup onto it (**10.9**). In reality, it is the market that drives the prices. Consequently, you must know where your market is. Your goal then, is to determine how to make money at the established market prices by adjusting your overhead

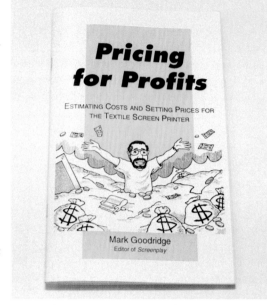

10.9 *There are excellent books that detail how to successfully price your printing for profits. (Courtesy ST Publications, Cincinnati, OH.)*

10.10 *Use these industry average prices as a starting point until you establish history and have a better feel for what your market is charging for jobs.*

and production rates accordingly. This is not to say that you shouldn't know the cost of printing a shirt, but in the beginning you will have little history or experience to go on.

Once you know where the market is, you need to see where you want to be. Try to find a middle ground between the highest and lowest prices. You don't want to be the lowest in the business. *Anyone can give work away.* It is easy to look at your new business and assume you have no real overhead (especially if you are working out of your home). But, if you think that undercutting everyone in town is a smart thing to do, imagine what would happen to pricing if everyone undercut everyone. The market prices would start dropping and no one would make money.

Your goal should be to charge as much as possible and stick to your price by offering quality and service (our two favorite points).

The simplest formula is to take an established markup on the landed cost of the shirt (including freight) and add for the printing. Figure **10.10** has average markups and printing prices that you can start with. Remember, these figures are averages, so adjust them accordingly based on your area and market conditions.

Average Markups and Printing Prices

The best approach to pricing is to offer as many items as you can on your price list (using the same style numbers as the generic catalog you choose) and have all prices *include* a one-color print. At the bottom of your price list show the prices for additional colors AND the extra charge for artwork, screen prep, rushes, flash-curing, special color matches, etc. Using the following formula (do not show this to the customer) you can easily compute the charges for anything you print on. Always charge extra for printing on hard to print items such as jackets, gym bags or any other product where production will be slow and there may be more of a chance for misprints.

Notice that the prices for just one shirt are *very high*! This is to discourage doing just one or two shirts. You may want to charge less for the small quantitites when first starting out.

Quantity (pieces)	1	3	6	12	24	48	72	100	250	500	1000	3000
Printing Chg. (ea.)	$40.00	12.00	6.00	2.75	2.00	.90	.80	.70	.60	.55	.45	.40
Add'l Color (ea.)	$40.00	12.00	6.00	2.75	2.00	.90	.60	.45	.35	.25	.20	.20
Garment M/U%	250%	200%	150%	100%	80%	67%	50%	40%	33%	25%	21%	18%
Profit Margin%*	**71%**	**67%**	**60%**	**50%**	**44%**	**40%**	**33%**	**29%**	**25%**	**20%**	**17%**	**15%**

* Profit margin is figured on shirt mark-up only and is just for reference.

Other Charges

Screen Preparation	$20.00 each
Art Preparation	$20.00 per hour
Computer Graphics	$30.00 per hour
Flash-curing	Add one add'l color
Color matching	$25.00 per color
Jacket printing	Printing price X2
4-Color Process Seps	by quote
Rush charges - 5 Day	25% add'l
Rush charges - 2 Day	50% add'l
Individual packaging	.25 each
Re-order charge	7.50 per screen
(*After 60 days*)	
Ink color change	10.00 per color

Other Charges

Printing on customer garment	Printing price plus
(*Allow for industry standard rejects*)	$1.50 per dz. extra
Specialty Inks	by quotation
(*color-change, puff, suede, etc.*)	
Embroidery and other services available by quotation	

Terms and Conditions
• All Terms and Conditions on back of work order apply.
• 50% deposit with order.
• Printing prices do not include artwork or screen prep.

Sample Job

To understand how to use the Figures in 10.10, let's consider a sample job of printing 250 shirts with a four-color design. The job will be printed on a Hanes Beefy-T at an average cost of $3 per shirt ($36 per dozen).

Shirt Cost	$3.00
Markup (33%)	x 1.33
Unprinted Shirt	$3.99
Printing First Color	.60
Printing Additional Three Colors	1.05
Quote to Customer	**$5.64***

*art and screens separate

Don't be discouraged if someone else will do the same job for $4.75. Larger printers with automatic presses who buy direct from the mill are happy to make their $1.00 per shirt. It is hard to compete on that level, so make sure to stress your quick, personal service and excellent quality.

You will notice in the pricing formulas that when charging for small quantities the prices are very high. You may want to adjust these figures down if your market will not bear these prices. It is not really cost effective to do just one shirt but you will have customers who want to see a sample print first. It is wise to charge for a sample (if you can). The high prices for small quantities force the customer to buy a few more shirts.

There are also inexpensive software programs that have been written by screen printers that help figure prices for you (**10.11**). These programs will print price lists and quotations. They are easy to use and well worth the small expense!

Pricing Preprinted Shirts

If you decide to print stock designs for the local market, your pricing strategy will have to be different. The best you can do is sell the shirt for about one-half of what it will go for on a retail basis. This means that if the shirts retails for $12, then your price would be $6 – regardless of the number of colors or quantity you print. A retail store wants to double its money (keystone) at least. If your shirt has great graphics and lots of special effects like puff and foil, it may retail for $30 and be worth $14 or $15 wholesale.

Profits

After you have been in business for awhile, you should take a close look at the figures to see if you are really making money or just barely making wages for yourself. Obviously, the company needs *profits* to grow and you need wages to live on. Don't expect to have a lot of profits in the beginning. And keep an eye on overhead and costs. Every penny you save in overhead can go directly to the bottom line in the form of *profits*!

10.11 Inexpensive computer programs are available that will figure prices for you and print price lists and quotes. (Courtesy SMR Software division of Northwind, Grand Rapids, MN.)

Specialty Areas

Contract Printing

An easy way to get into this business is by just doing printing for other suppliers, sporting goods stores, T-shirt stores and ad specialty companies. This kind of wholesale printing doesn't require much of a marketing effort and is always done on customer supplied garments. If doing athletic printing you can expect the individual design quantity to be low in this work. The normal team size is around 15. But, there might be 30 teams to a league, and that's 450 shirts or uniforms to letter.

Events

If you have a heat press and a way to make transfers, there could be some good places to make money out there. There are tournaments and events all the time in most sports.

How about Karate and Gymnastics Tournaments, Boat Races, Drag Races, Rodeos, Car Shows? All it takes is to work up a few special designs for the particular event and print them as heat transfers. Take out some shirts, the press, the transfers and you're in business!

Where to Find Customers

Now that you know how to establish prices and are ready to go, the next question is where do you find customers? They are everywhere! This market is so big that almost any company is a prime subject for a sales call!

Look in the paper. Who is doing the most advertising? All those companies could be in need of printed shirts. Look at the custom printed shirts you see people wearing in the malls and in stores. Who prints them? Call the businesses whose names are on the shirts and give them a quote.

LIST OF POTENTIAL CUSTOMERS

BARS
SPEED AND AUTOMOTIVE SHOPS
AD AGENCIES AND PR FIRMS
PROMOTERS
FAMILY REUNIONS
HIGH SCHOOL CLUBS
FRATERNITIES
SORORITIES
SPORTING GOODS STORES
RESTAURANTS
MOTORCYCLE SHOPS
PARKS DEPARTMENTS
THE CITY
GIFT SHOPS
CHURCH GROUPS
DEPARTMENT STORES
T-SHIRT STORES
BEAUTY SALONS
TRAVEL AGENCIES
HEALTH CLUBS
RECORD STORES
HEAD SHOPS
CLOTHING STORES
MUSIC STORES
BANDS AND GROUPS
NIGHTCLUBS
NEWSPAPERS
COLLEGE CLUBS
YMCA
YWCA
BOYS' CLUBS
LITTLE LEAGUE TEAMS
CAR DEALERS
REAL ESTATE COMPANIES
RESORTS

Make the First Sale!

Once you have a price list, a catalog, samples and a toll-free number, go to it and *make that first call!*

CHAPTER 11

THE BUSINESS

After reading the first half of this book, you've probably figured out that with a little time and patience you can learn how to print T-shirts. Hopefully, there will be more orders coming in than you can fill!

But what about the business end of things? There's a lot more to running a business than pulling a squeegee across a screen. Many businesses start up each year and just as many fail. The failures usually occur for the same reason: Lack of business sense and poor marketing and selling!

In this chapter, we will attempt to help you get started on the right foot. This is not everything you need to know about business but a crash course in the basics.

Getting into garment printing is fairly easy. A person can literally set up a simple "garage operation" on a shoestring budget and, with a lot of hard work and ingenuity, make a reasonable profit in the business. In fact, thousands of successful large printers started out just that way.

If you are already selling shirts in a retail T-shirt or sporting goods store, then the move into doing your own printing is fairly straightforward. Chances are you are taking in screen printing orders now and just not getting the service you want from your printer. The next logical step is to bring the production in-house.

Garment printing can be one of the most rewarding businesses around, both financially and emotionally! After all, not too many businesses can make a profit and give the owner the gratification of seeing a total stranger wear a shirt that was printed by his company! That can be almost as rewarding as the money. Face it, the imprinted sportswear industry is a glamorous industry.

Would your friends, family or kids even care if you made "widgets" for a living? But printing on T-shirts . . . now that's something to talk about.

In reality, though, garment printing is a business. And just like any business, it has to be worked at, watched and controlled. Those who get into the business and expect to make *big bucks* overnight will be sadly disappointed. The big bucks will come only if the proper groundwork is laid and the dues are paid. If you talk to successful business people, you will find that they had to work hard to get where they are. Was the hard work worth it? Most will agree that the joy and satisfaction of being your own boss and fulfilling the entrepreneur's dream of building a business from scratch is terrific.

What Type of Business Do You Want?

An important first step is to determine just what type of business you want to have. Obviously, your product will be printed garments, but will it be a full-time venture, a supplement to your present income, a part-time business that will someday replace your regular job or an extension of an existing retail or wholesale business?

Do you plan on doing just athletic printing for sporting goods stores or do you have dreams of creating your own line of shirts? Maybe your plan is to just print on customer-supplied garments.

Income Supplement

Before making a decision about what type of business you want, you need to look at the profit and cash-flow potential of each option.

If your long-range goal is to just supplement your present income, the amount of money you will need to start a business won't be as great as with a full-time venture. The "shoestring" approach will work, and the profit from the business can be taken out sooner if the money doesn't have to be invested back into the business to make it grow. After all, with an income supplementing business, growth is not a major concern. Thousands of printers are grossing $50,000 - 100,000 annually and netting 15-25% of that working out of their homes on a part-time basis!

Part-Time Venture

If your long-range plan is to keep your regular job and start a business on the side with the goal of someday quitting the day job, you can start the business on a shoestring. But all profits will have to be invested in the business to allow it to grow to the point of being able to support you.

Full-Time Business

A full-time business that needs profits to grow and profits to support the owners is much more capital intensive than the two previous part-time endeavors. To support itself and the owners, a full-time business will require plenty of extra money in the bank as a financial cushion until it can start making a profit. And profits will not come overnight. The biggest mistake new business owners make is expecting to be able to live off the business immediately. In the beginning of any new venture, the business needs money to live also.

Supplement to Existing Retail Business

This is probably the easiest approach because the customer base is hopefully already established. Now it is just a matter of learning a new process and trying to gain control of the printing end of the business. Often, you can find the space to print in a back room, so there is no real increase in overhead except for possibly additional employees. See if you can move employees from other departments to train for printing.

Athletic Printing

This is one of the easiest areas to get into because sporting goods stores buy a lot of screen printing on team uniforms. The order sizes are generally small and only one or two color. Also, the sporting goods stores do all the marketing and supply you with their goods to print on.

Sounds easy, but there is a catch. Not only are the order quantities small, but they may have a number of print locations. You may be asked to print numbers on both sides, sponsor name, team name, player's name, sleeve prints, etc. These all have to be coordinated with the proper ink color and the names on the correct size garment. There

is a great margin for error, and the price you can charge is fairly low.

The good news is that even though the individual orders may be small, they can be multiplied by a league of 50 teams–or 50 orders for 15 or 20 uniforms. Of course, they will all need to be done by opening day.

If you can deal with short lead times, occasional reprints, small quantities and fussy customers, then this could be a way to start in this business.

Creating a Line of Shirts

Everyone wants to do this. You have a great idea for a line of shirts and think you can make a lot of money in it. Unfortunately, this area has a lot of competition, and the big money will not come as fast as you think.

Creating your own shirt line requires deep reserves of working capital because of the long lead times between creating the artwork, making the sale, shipping to a store, giving credit terms of 30 or 60 days and paying your bills. If you can finance this type of business, it can be a lucrative area. The competition is fierce, the designs terrific and the buyers sharp. Mediocre graphics and poor quality will not make it here.

Contract Printing

This is actually not a bad way to make a living. Contract printing involves printing on customer-supplied garments form other printers, T-shirt stores, advertising specialty companies or anyone else who will supply the garments. There is minimal marketing expense and no inventory to stock.

There is also less loyalty in contact printing, and you will find yourself competing with large printers that have automatic presses and will print for 25-50 cents per shirt! If you can build up a good volume of steady customers and are happy watching quarters falling into the box at the end of the dryer, then give this a try.

Custom Printing

This can be very profitable and give you immediate cash flow. When printing logos or designs for customers (and when you supply the garments,) always ask for a deposit when you take the order and get the remainder when you deliver the finished job

How Much Money Will It Take?

To reverse the question, how much money do you have? The amount of money you have available will determine how much money it will take. This may sound like a way of avoiding the issue, but let's face facts. If you have $20,000 to spend, then you will probably be tempted to spend most of it. If you only have $500 to spend then that is how much money it will take.

In reality, though, it depends on what your goals are. If the business is going to be a part-time venture or a supplement to your regular income, then it will take less money than if you are going to live off the business from day one.

Business books will tell you that you need to have enough reserves to live for six months to one year. However, if that is what it took before companies opened their doors, then most small businesses would never have started.

Should You Borrow Money for Your Venture?

This is a tough one. It all depends on how much you want to sacrifice. In general, try not to borrow any more than you have to. You are better off starting small and letting the business perpetuate itself than to sign your entire life away. This holds true even if you are expanding your retail business into screen printing.

Legal Forms of Business Organization

There are three possible types of businesses: Sole proprietorship, partnership and corporation. Let's discuss the advantages and disadvantages of each.

Sole Proprietorship

A sole proprietorship is by far the most common business organization.

The major advantages are:

1. Lower taxes than either of the other two types of businesses.

2. Easier and less costly to start.

3. Greater flexibility in management.

4. Less government interference and paper work.

The major disadvantages are:

1. The owner is the key person. If the owner gets ill or dies, the business may fall apart.

2. The owner is totally liable for business losses or debts. The owner's private property and assets could be confiscated as the result of a lawsuit against the business.

Partnership

A partnership is a formal association of two or more persons. In most states, a partnership agreement must be in writing.

The major advantages are:

1. Allows several persons to combine their resources and abilities.

2. Pays no federal income taxes (taxes are paid by the partners).

3. Is relatively free from government interference.

The major disadvantages are:

1. Each partner is liable to the full extent of their personal assets for business debts contracted by themselves or by any other partner.

2. State laws are more stringent than for sole proprietorships.

Corporations

A corporation is a statutory form of organization, a legal entity that may exercise the powers conferred upon it by its charter. The procedures for incorporation are a little complex, and regulations vary from state to state. Before starting a corporation, consult an attorney. If you are a real do-it-yourselfer, there are excellent books and incorporation kits that will help you form your own corporation.

The major advantages are:

1. Stockholders' personal belongings and assets are exempt from levy or confiscation due to corporate financial problems. A corporation can go bankrupt without affecting the stockholders' personal assets.

2. Corporations can act in their own name, sign contracts, bring suit, and own property.

The major disadvantages are:

1. Costly to form. Most attorneys charge $500 and up for the initial setup.

2. Burdensome reports and paperwork for the government.

3. Interstate limitations.

Make sure you weigh the specific advantages and disadvantages of sole proprietorships, partnerships and corporations before making a decision. In general, the smaller and less permanent a business, the more sense it makes to organize on a sole proprietorship basis. If you plan on being a T-shirt tycoon or have people who want to go into business with you, then you should consider a partnership or incorporation.

Business Licenses

State Licenses

Licensing requirements differ from state to state. For many state licenses, you apply to local officials such as the circuit clerk, county clerk, county tax collector or Department of Revenue. Most states will require you to have a state sales tax or privilege license. This is sometimes called a resale permit or license and will entitle you to purchase supplies and merchandise for your business without having to pay sales tax. (In some states, you may have to pay sales tax on some expendable items such as masking tape, mesh, solvents, etc.) You will show this permit to wholesale suppliers, or use the number on their forms to show that you are entitled to purchase goods at wholesale.

This number is usually referred to as your resale number. Don't be afraid to tell a merchant the items you are purchasing are for resale. Check with your state and local government to find out what licenses you need.

*11.1 An excellent book to help with the business side of garment decorating is **Jumping In With Both Feet.** (Photo courtesy SMR Software, Grand Rapids, MN.)*

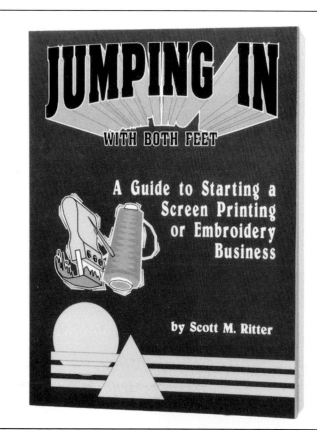

The state may also require you to file your name if you are not going to use your personal name for the business. This is sometimes called a *fictitious name statement* or *DBA*. You also will need an employee withholding tax number and an unemployment number.

Local Licenses

Local licenses are usually issued for the privilege of doing business in their town. The fee is normally only a few dollars and it allows you to collect sales tax on taxable sales. The local license may be called an *occupancy permit.*

Federal Identification Number

This is also called your EIN number. If you are a sole proprietorship, you will use your Social Security Number. If you incorporate, you need to apply for an EIN number. Once you file with the federal government, you will receive quarterly and yearly report forms for withholding tax (941), unemployment tax (940), and income tax (1020).

Accounting

Good accounting is a critical part of business. Start keeping good records from the very beginning, even if you only take in $50 a month to start. Business record books are available from most stationery and office supply stores. There are also excellent, inexpensive accounting software packages and industry-specific programs that handle accounting and production control for screen printers . Playing catch-up in bookkeeping is very hard.

There are also industry specific books that deal with the running of the business and understanding the financial side of the industry (**11.1**).

Two annual statements are customary and will be essential if you have business taxes to pay. The first is an "annual balance sheet," which list the assets and liabilities of the business and thereby calculates its net worth. The second is a "profit and loss statement," which lists the income and expenses of the business and thereby calculates its net profit or loss.

The difference between the two is that the balance sheet reflects the financial condition of the enterprise as of a given date, while the profit and loss statement shows the results of business operations over a given period of time. Standardized forms and instructions for completing both statements are available.

Figure **11.2** shows an average profit and loss

SAMPLE PROFIT AND LOSS STATEMENT

NET SALES	YOUR FIGURES DOLLARS	% OF SALES	AVERAGE FIGURES
COST OF SALES			100%
Cost of Goods Sold			45%
Freight In			5%
Selling Expense			0%
TOTAL COST OF SALES			50%
GROSS PROFIT MARGIN			50%
OPERATING EXPENSES			
Salaries and employee taxes			12%
Rent			4%
Telephone			1%
Advertising			3%
Travel			2%
Utilities			2%
Printing			1%
Postage			1%
Maintenance & Repair			.3%
Office Expense			.4%
Dues and memberships			.2%
Insurance			.8%
Professional fees			1.2%
Automotive Expenses			1.5%
Depreciation			.5%
Interest			1%
Taxes and licenses			
Reserve for bad debts			.5%
TOTAL EXPENSES			33.4%
NET PROFIT BEFORE TAXES			16.6%

statement that only has the percentages of the gross sales. The percentages show what you should be paying for various parts of the income statement based on sales. These figures may vary depending on your business, but in general, the bottom line is what is left for you (before taxes).

In addition, every business should keep a general ledger of assets and liabilities–that is, accounts receivable and merchandise inventory balanced with accounts payable. A cash journal or software program for cash receipts and disbursements is essential for tax purposes, as is a sales and purchases journal.

An accountant is handy to have around, but few small businesses can afford one. There are many bookkeepers and accountants who specialize in small businesses and will come in once a month and see how you are doing for a small fee. They can also help prepare your tax return.

Don't put your bookkeeping off! If your business grows rapidly, you may find you have six months' worth of receipts in a stack and don't know where to start.

Taxes and Other Requirements

The taxes you have to pay differ depending on what type of business you set up. If you are in business for yourself but are not incorporated, then you do not have to pay federal business income tax. You must instead report the gross business earnings on your personal tax return. A formal partnership also pays no federal income tax, but must file an information return upon which each partner's tax is computed. A corporation must pay a federal corporate income tax on its net earning. Then each individual must pay a second tax on his share of the profits.

State business taxes generally follow the same procedures as the federal government. The federal government and many state governments require that you deduct withholding taxes from the wages of all employees to be applied against their personal income taxes. If your business is incorporated, then you yourself are technically an employee, and you must deduct your own withholding taxes as well.

You will have to obtain a federal tax ID number if you have employees. The IRS will send the charts and forms that are needed to figure how much to withhold from an employee's check.

Depending on the amount, the withheld money must be deposited weekly, monthly or quarterly with a commercial bank qualified as a *depository for federal taxes* or mailed to the federal tax department of the federal reserve bank servicing your area.

Don't mess with the IRS! The money you withhold is *their money in trust* until you pay them! Many businesses, both small and large think of this as their own money and forget they owe it to the IRS. The IRS is not like a supplier or a normal creditor who may hound you for payment. You might even forget they exist until you are behind in your payments. But then watch out. They have been known to give a business 24 hours to pay up or have their doors padlocked, their bank account levied upon and their merchandise seized to pay the bill.

The IRS has had so much bad publicity that they now will try and work with a company–the first time! The second time, they aren't so nice.

Most states charge employers state unemployment insurance taxes. In general, the rate is approximately 3% of the wages paid.

All employees must pay social security and medicare taxes. The employer has to match the employee portion. As of this writing, the rate for FICA (social security) is 6.2% and for medicare is 1.45%. If you are an employer, you will have to contribute the same amount. If you are self-employed, you get stuck paying it all yourself!

Besides the withholding, social security, medicare and unemployment taxes, the employer's responsibility to his employees is governed by two laws: Minimum wage and workman's compensation.

Always pay at least minimum wage and overtime when it is due. All it takes is one disgruntled employee to cry wolf to one of the state agencies or labor relations board and you will be in for trouble.

Don't start the bad habit of paying employees in cash! It is so easy to do when your business is small, but as it grows bigger, it becomes harder to change. Remember that it is against the law to not withhold the proper taxes.

The cost of workman's compensation will vary depending on the amount of manual or automatic equipment you have. You can purchase workman's compensation insurance through your state's workman's compensation fund or a private insurance carrier.

Again, don't mess with workman's compensation. If any of your employees ever get hurt on the job – even a slight injury – and they file a complaint, you will have problems if you don't have workman's compensation.

Employee Relations

Don't try to win a popularity contest with your employees. The shop should be a pleasant place to work where your people don't mind coming to work, but they should know you are the boss!

Try to steer clear of hiring relatives and friends. In fact, it should be a rule. You can laugh now, but wait until they don't work out–or forget who the boss is. It is really hard to fire friends or relatives!

Establish definite rules and post them so every employee knows what is expected of them. There are excellent *generic* employee manuals that you can buy and just fill in the blanks with the details about your company.

Don't forget employee welfare. You have an investment in every employee you hire and train. Part of your job is to try and keep happy, long-term employees. To do that, remember that employees appreciate recognition for a job well done and money–in that order! Don't forget that pat on the back and a few extra bucks at Christmas time. Employees also like company parties, picnics, etc. These activities are a good way to get them feeling like they're part of the team!

Check into group insurance plans. Work up a schedule of raises you can live with and let the people who work the hardest work their way up.

Finally, recognize that key employees are worth their weight in gold. It makes it much easier for you to take time off or go out and make calls when you have someone you know and trust in the shop.

If you have to hire a new employee, let him know what is expected of him and what he can expect of you. When firing an employee, make it short and sweet. Try not to degrade or humiliate him in front of his fellow workers.

Leasing Equipment

Experience shows that unless you have a solid track record, it may be hard to qualify for a lease. Beginning business people think of leasing as an easy way to get equipment, and equipment companies perpetuate this belief by running ads that make it all sound so easy. The fact is that leasing is not like renting a TV for a week. A lease is a long-term contract that requires monthly payments and offers no real opportunity to return the equipment if the business doesn't work out. If you have no business credit (or poor business credit), the leasing company will want a complete financial statement from you along with tax returns for the last three years .

If you have limited cash to invest, then a lease does allow the equipment to pay for itself as you use it while you use the cash for working capital.

The Bank

The bank will play a key role in your growth and development. Get started on the right foot. Open a separate business account. Get to know your banker. When you need references, your banker is the one everyone will call. He must be on your side. Even if you have no plans now to borrow money, start laying the groundwork. Get to know the various tellers. Start a savings account at the same branch–anything to get them to know who you are and want your business

The first word of warning is *don't bounce checks!* Nothing is harder to erase from your banker's and suppliers' memory than a bounced check. Granted, it does happen. But if it does, you better have a good reason. Every time you bounce a check, it goes on your record at the bank.

Try to maintain a sizable balance in your account. You may deposit $10,000 in a month, but if you are writing checks for nearly that amount, you may only have an average monthly balance of $500! Bankers like a high average balance.

Unfortunately, it may seem that the time a bank wants to loan you money is when you don't need it! Borrowing money to start a business is possible if you have good personal credit and are already established with the bank. Do your homework first! Show the banker where the money is going to go and explain the market. Show projected first-, second- and third-year sales. Show your banker how you plan to pay the money back! Your banker is a business person, but also has to rely on instincts about you. Look sharp and act like someone who knows where they are going. It is all part of the game of borrowing money.

Insurance

Insurance is necessary in any business. Why work hard to build a business just to lose it in a fire or lawsuit?

Let's discuss the basic types of insurance you will need when starting up. As your business grows, your agent can go over the other types of policies available. Just remember one thing: Don't get too carried away! Make sure your agent has your welfare in mind and not just his pocketbook. Some agents will keep pushing and pushing for you to buy this or that policy, (but buy only what you can afford and need.

When starting out, your basic insurance needs will be fire, liability, contents and workman's compensation.

Fire

Since you will be dealing with solvents and flammable materials, you have a real "exposure" to fire. A fire could happen very quickly and totally wipe you out! If you are working out of your house, you should increase the coverage on the "business" portion of the house or garage. You might even be violating your existing homeowner's fire policy by conducting a business out of a family dwelling. Don't take a chance. Call your insurance agent and tell him what you're doing.

One of your main assets will be screens and artwork. Without these, you could be out of business. Check into a "pattern" floater policy that covers the frames and artwork separately.

Liability

Liability insurance will cover you when someone gets hurt in your shop and decides to sue. You can generally buy a comprehensive liability policy that will cover most situations that might arise.

Contents

This is generally part of a total comprehensive package that includes fire and liability. Estimate the replacement value of your shop's contents and keep an eye on your growth so you can keep the coverage adequate.

Workman's Compensation

As mentioned earlier, if you have employees you must have workman's compensation. This type of insurance is available from your agent or your state compensation fund. The premium is based on the estimated yearly payroll and the rating of the occupation. Don't let your agent group all your employees into one category. The rate is lower for non-production workers such as artists and clerical help.

The only way to get the proper coverage and afford it is to work with your agent. Tell him all about your business, what the risks and exposures are and what you can realistically afford per month. Make sure to review your policies periodically to ensure that you have adequate coverage as your business grows!

Getting Credit

Getting credit is part of growth. At first, no one may be willing to give you credit. Many suppliers will want cash in advance or even a cashiers check when the merchandise is delivered.

Don't get discouraged. Credit can be good and bad. If you stay on a cash basis when you're small, you'll always know where you stand and will have a good idea whether the money in the bank is yours or really belongs to a supplier!

If you are new in business, you may be surprised by the fact that you will often get credit based on how credit worthy *you look* and not on your financial data!

Here are a few suggestions on how to get credit:

1. Establish good relationships with your suppliers. Let them know who you are and find out who they are. Try to always place your order with the same person. Be friendly and get to know them a little. In some cases they might be able to put in a good word for you when it's time for credit decisions.

2. Always act in a professional manner. Know what you want when you order and act like you know a little about the business. Buy a book of purchase orders and fill them out as you place orders. Have the supplier put your purchase order number on the invoice, and mail the supplier a confirmation copy after the order is placed. It may seem too big league if you have a small operation, but as we said earlier, the supplier doesn't know how small you are. All they know is that you operate your business like a professional.

3. Pay your bills on time! If and when you get credit, the bills will usually be due net 30, which means you'll have 30 days to pay from the date of invoice. If you have the money, pay early. It always looks good on your record. If you are going to be late, call the supplier and tell them. They respect honesty and an open line of communication.

Credit is a necessary part of growth. As the size of your orders increase, the amount of cash on hand decrease. You'll be constantly spending the profit from the last order on shirts for the next order. All the money will be tied up in the growth of the business. With credit, you'll be able to use the supplier's money. Generally, you will be able to buy shirts, print them, deliver them and get paid before the bill is due.

Your supplier will be your best source of financing for big orders. Get them involved when you have an order you can't handle. Tell them what you need and see if they will work with you.

Giving Credit

Giving credit is a little different than getting it. You want to get it, but you don't want to give it! Try to stay on a cash basis with your customers as long as possible.

Here are some good rules to establish and follow:

1. *Always* get a 50% deposit with the order. Don't lose sight of the fact that you are a small business person who has to buy the shirts before you get paid. You need the money –and don't be afraid to tell the customer so! It is customary in any custom business to get a deposit. It will give you a good relationship with the customer, too. They'll know you mean business, and you'll know they will pick up the order!

2. If you must extend credit, try to make the terms as short as possible. Some shops have terms of net 10.

3. Don't be afraid to ask for money. If someone owes you money and is late in paying, call them. The person with his hand out will always get paid first.

The Customer

If you are starting out on a shoestring and basically have no money other than a few bucks to buy supplies with, then getting the 50% deposit on the orders will be very useful. That money will enable you to get off the ground and actually buy the shirts. This is called OPM. *Other People's Money*! It is the formula for success used by most businessmen. Large businesses use the bank's money to keep their business going. As a small business, you will use your customer's money. If you can keep the overhead low and do most of the printing yourself, then the constant deposit on orders should keep your cash flow in good shape and allow you to invest the profits back into the business!

Get a Purchase Order

Whenever you do business with large corporations, schools, the government or any place where you are dealing with a purchasing agent or company representative, *always* get a purchase order. This is a legal document that binds them to pay you if you deliver the goods as promised.

Customer Complaints

What if the customer is unhappy? If the ink washed off the shirt, the solution is simple: Replace the entire order. If you missed a few flawed shirts when sorting, then replace them or offer a discount on the goods. If you miss a delivery date for a shirt needed for a specific event, you *eat* the shirts! You customer has no use for them after the event.

What if there is a misspelling? First, find out whose fault it is. You should have a company policy that the customer approves all artwork. With a fax machine at hand, you can simply fax a copy of the art and have them sign and date it to *run as approved.* If you made the spelling mistake, you need to replace the shirts. What if you spelled it just the way it was on their scrap of paper and what if you *kept* the scrap of paper in the file?

They own the shirts! Never throw away any information the customer gives you. You never know when one little piece of paper could be worth thousands of dollars!

Require Customer Approval

Some customers are very picky. You will know who they are. Require these customers to approve the first print. This is not that uncommon in large shops or with big orders. Have them sign the shirt as an indicator of their approval, and don't lose it. Hang it at the end of the dryer for all employees to see and compare the prints to. It is not uncommon to print a pre-production sample on some jobs where color matching is important. You need to charge for this and then credit the charge back against the actual order (if the order hinges on them liking the sample).

Sensitive Jobs

What do you do with the misprinted shirts for the local police department? Don't just throw them away–someone may take them out of the garbage and use them as a false identification for themselves. Instead, cut them up so that no one can use them. You will find certain customers have little patience with you if you let the misprints or a few extras get out to friends or employees. If you constantly strive to do what is best for the customer, you can't go wrong.

The Competition

Don't be afraid of competition. It will always be there and could be helpful. If there are other printers in town, go over and introduce yourself. Their main concern will be that you won't cut prices and bad mouth them–and you shouldn't. That's not good business.

Sometimes large printers don't want to do small-run orders and will refer them to you. That's great! A lot of small accounts will eventually become big accounts. A customer who only buys three dozen shirts every six months might be buying 100 dozen shirts soon!

Service

Besides price and quality, your main concern should be service. If your prices are the same as everyone else but your shop is smaller and you can do the job in less time, chances are you'll get the work. As a small shop, your main goal should be service! It is where you can compete most effectively with the bigger shops.

Watch your service as you grow. Don't get like the big guys. If your service remains quick when you get big, you'll be the guy the competition will worry about.

11.3 The industry has numerous trade magazines that contain articles about screen printing and have supplier ads. Use the forms supplied in Appendix A and request complimentary subscriptions to "the trades."

11.4 All of the trade magazines publish yearly Buyer's Guides that are very helpful when searching for specific products.

Publications

There are numerous trade magazines that deal with imprinted sportswear, screen printing and related fields (**11.3**). If possible, subscribe to them to keep abreast of the most current products and techniques. Consult Appendix A for a complete list including complimentary subscription forms. If you simply request a complimentary subscription, most trade magazines will give you one. In order to qualify for a complimentary subscription, you must fill out a subscription form or request one on your letterhead. You must be a legitimate printer for them to take the request seriously.

Although most screen printing magazines have the same or similar advertisers and similar news and new products information, they each have their own types of articles. Many of the magazines promote their own trade shows and will not promote ones sponsored by the competition. Subscribe to all of the trade magazines to get the big picture.

Buyer's Guides

All of the trade magazines publish annual *Buyer's Guides*. In most cases, they are included as part of your regular subscription (**11.4**). If you are just starting out, make sure to request the most recent buyer's guide to help you find products and services.

Screenprinting and Graphic Imaging Assoc.

The Screenprinting and Graphic Imaging Association (SGIA) is the official trade organization for the screen printing industry. SGIA offers dozens of member services that make membership a real bargain (**11.5**). Along with all of the member services, membership in the SGIA allows you to use the association's logo to tell your customer you are a member of a trade organization. SGIA publishes a complete set of technical guidebooks (also on CD) and has a division called the Screen Printing Technical Foundation (SPTF) that offers workshops and performs research and development for the industry.

SGIA also sponsors a four-day trade show. This show is held once a year at various major cities and is the main convention for the entire screen printing industry. It features social events, seminars, awards programs, hundreds of exhibitors, product demonstrations and a lot more! For more information about SPAI, see Appendix A.

11.5 The Screenprinting and Graphic Imaging Association provides dozens of member services along with Technical Guidebooks and other manuals to help run your business better. (Photo courtesy SGIA, Fairfax, VA.)

Trade Shows

Trade shows have become a large and viable part of most industries. They are a place you can meet hundreds of suppliers in one location. Trade shows are a benefit to both the exhibitors, who can see a lot of customers in a shorter time period, and to buyers, who can see a wide variety of products from different companies in just a few days.

Most trade shows are held in major cities around the country (**11.6**). Shows are generally held in the spring (buying season for the summer) and the fall (buying season for Christmas). Plan to attend at least one trade show per year to keep up with the latest products, trends, styles and techniques. The cost to attend a show is relatively low compared to the benefit you will gain.

Make sure to spend your trade show money wisely. Some industry magazines sponsor smaller, more local shows that have 50-100 exhibitors. Other magazines, like *Impressions*, sponsor shows that have 300-500 exhibitors and give you a better chance to see more companies in one location.

11.6 Industry trade shows are an excellent source for new suppliers and information from the hundreds of exhibitors, seminars and awards displays.(Photos courtesy the Imprinted Sportswear Shows, Dallas, TX.)

General Business Practices

Keep Your Word

Reputation is very important! It goes hand in hand with service, and how you pay your bills. Try to do what you say. If you promise an order by Friday, do your best to have it by Friday. When it comes time to get more credit, get a favor from a supplier or customer or sell your business, your reputation will play an important part!

Watch Growth

Everyone dreams of having a large shop with lots of employees, their own secretary, a nice office, etc. You, too, can have those things–in time! Don't be in too big of a hurry to get the icing on the cake. If you grow too fast, you may find there is no money left to pay the bills and the next thing you know your suppliers have shut you off, the IRS is asking for their money and your employees are wondering if they will get paid. These things all have a direct bearing on service. If you can't get the shirts from normal channels or can't get them printed, your service will suffer. It is a vicious circle that will lead to ruin.

Let the business grow naturally. Take out only the money you absolutely have to have. Leave the rest in the business and try to build up a cash reserve. In some areas of the country, T-shirts may be seasonal. Put away a nest egg for the slow times. If you keep an eye on growth and spending now, you'll get your own secretary and private office later!

Overhead

One of the biggest killers of new businesses is overhead! Having a lot of employees buzzing around looking real busy is great for the ego but hard on the checkbook. Try to do as much of the work yourself as long as you can. When it comes time to hire more employees, make sure you can justify the expense. Consider this: If you increase the payroll $100 per week, you may have to increase sales by $500 per week to pay for it.

Art Ownership, Trade Standards and Copyrights

This section will deal with the color *gray*: The gray area between what you think and what is reality. We might also call this the twilight zone. Who really owns what? You think you own the artwork just because you paid the artist. Wrong! Your customer thinks he owns the screens, camera work and artwork just because he gave you money. Wrong!

Who Owns the Art?

Let's start at the beginning of the process and talk about who owns the art. Although this may seem like a gray area, it is fairly clear if you know the law. It is the misconception that is the problem. Just because you give an artist money doesn't mean you have actually bought the rights to a design. It really is more like paying for a license to use the design. You don't want just a license, though. You want to own the *copyright* to the design.

Copyright Law Overview

Understanding who owns the artwork requires an understanding of the copyright law. The Copyright Law (known at Title 17 of the United States Code) was first adopted in 1790 and has gone through many revisions since then. The last major change went into effect January 1, 1978 with minor revisions in 1989.

Basically, a copyright protects the artists, authors, composers and creators of works of art and published and printed matter from unauthorized publication of their works. Receiving a copyright is much simpler than most people think. A copyright exists *the moment the work is done.* This may sound almost too good to be true, but when an artist draws a design, the copyright is born.

Whether this design belongs to you depends upon the artist's classification. In screen printing, you generally have two classes of artists: In-house artists and independent freelance artists who accept commission work.

Independent Artists

Artists who works on an independent basis *retain ownership of the copyright unless the copyright is transferred in writing and recorded with the copyright office!*

An excerpt of the copyright law - Section 204 reads as follows:

Execution of transfers of copyright ownership
(a) A transfer of copyright ownership, other than by operation of law, is not valid unless an instrument of conveyance, or a note or memorandum of the transfer, is in writing and is signed by the owner of the rights conveyed or such owner's duly authorized agent.

This makes it pretty simple. Unless you receive a written transfer of ownership of the art when you pay the artist, you *have not* purchased the copyright. Figure **11.7** is a *Transfer of Ownership* that you should use for every piece of artwork you purchase from an independent artist!

TRANSFER OF ARTWORK OWNERSHIP
ASSIGNMENT

Received from _____

the sum of _____ Dollars, ($ _____) ,

in full payment for all right, title and interest (including copyright) of every kind

whatsoever for the following work:

_____

_____

_____

(name and description of work)

The undersigned warrants originality, authorship and ownership of the work, that it

has not been heretofore used or published, and that its use or publication will not

infringe upon any copyright, proprietary or other right.

_____   _____
Witness   Artist   Date

_____   _____
Date   Address

                                     _____
                                     City   State   Zip

11.7

In-House Artists

When the artist who creates the design is an employee, the work relationship is called "work for hire" and you, as the employer, own the copyright.

The following excerpt from Section 201 of the Copyright Law explains this:

(b) WORKS MADE FOR HIRE - In the case of a work made for hire, the employer or other person for whom the work was prepared is considered the author for purposes of this title, and, unless the parties have expressly agreed otherwise in a written instrument signed by them, owns all of the rights comprised in the copyright.

What if you commission an independent artist and tell him that you want the piece to be done as a work for hire? Be sure you put *the name of the piece* and the words *work for hire* on the check you pay him with. According to the copyright law, then, you would own the artwork!

In summary, if you had an employee create the art, you own it. If you bought it from an independent artist and got a transfer of ownership, you own it. If you bought it from an independent artist under a *work for hire* relationship, you own it. If you gave a transfer of ownership to the customer, he owns it.

How to Get a Copyright

As previously mentioned , the copyright automatically happens when you create a design. The act of creating it and then putting either a C with a circle around it "©," the word "Copyright" or the abbreviation "Copr." and the name of the copyright owner are all you need.

For greater protection and advantages should you have to sue someone, you may want to register the copyright with the Register of Copyrights, Library of Congress, Washington, DC 20559. In fact, the copyright must be registered before you can file a lawsuit on a copyright infringement.

To register the copyright, you will need a copy of Form VA (for visual arts). Figure **11.8** shows a sample of the six-page form VA. Basically, if you send in Form VA along with $20 and two copies of the work or a photograph, the Library of Congress will "deposit" the work in

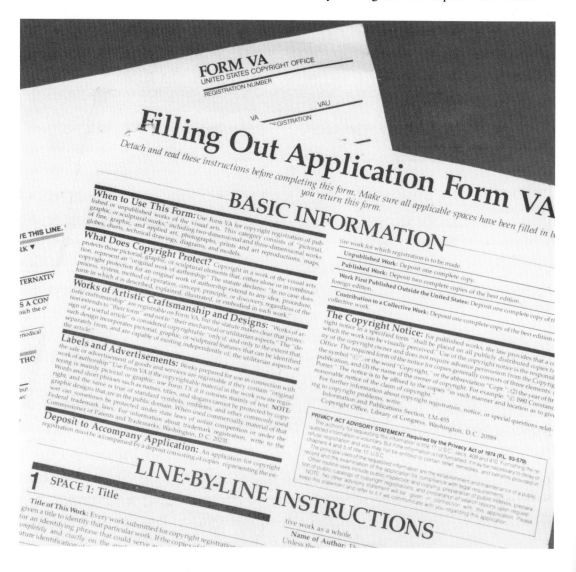

11.8 To copyright a design use form VA from the Copyright Office.

their archives on that date. A copyright will expire 50 years after the owner dies.

If you don't register the work, you can only sue someone for *actual* damages (income or other benefits lost as a result of the infringement). If the work is registered *before* an infringement occurs, you can sue for statutory damages ($50,000 per infringement) and your attorney's fees!

Where to Learn More About Copyrighting

Write or call the Copyright Public Information Office at (202) 707-3000 to receive a Copyright Information Kit or to receive copies of Form VA. The Copyright Office will answer specific questions, but will not give legal advice.

You will probably not want to copyright every design. Some you will create for the customer and gladly give the rights to them. Others that you invest a lot of time in may be worth copyrighting. Some designs you will just want to place the copyright notice on and others you will want to file for better protection. If you have specific questions about the process, consult a copyright, patent or trademark attorney. There are also excellent books on the business side of artwork that are available at bookstores, art stores or industry suppliers (**11.9**).

Who Owns the Camera Work, Computer Graphics and Screens?

Other than the Copyright Law, the industry is governed by what is known as the Trade Standards. These are the established standards that are used by the printing industry. Figure **11.10** shows a modified version of the standards that are used by the National Association of Printers and Lithographers. These standards have been changed slightly to include items of particular interest to screen printers.

If you look at Number 4 and Number 6 you will see that basically *you own everything (!)* unless otherwise agreed to in writing. Unfortunately, customers often think they *own everything* because they paid you for something and expect something in return. What they actually pay you for is *your labor* to make the screen, create computer graphics, do the camera shot, cut the overlay, etc.

All customers really own is what they brought you. If they initially came with a small business card, then when they leave because the price is better somewhere else, all they get is the small business card.

You own *the mechanical* items, like the screen frame, film positive, vellum, drawing or camera shot. The customer may own what is on these items, but you own the physical items.

11.9 The bookstore carries dozens of books about the business and legal side of doing artwork.

Invoicing Is Important

The key to having less confusion is to write invoices properly. You need to specify "screen set-up" or "screen preparation" or "artwork preparation," etc. This way, you are just charging for the labor and not for the physical piece.

Regarding camera shots, you should include a basic shot in the "screen preparation" charge. This way, there is no confusion as to whether you charged for the shot or not.

What if the Customer Claims He Owns the Work?

What if the customer brings you a design to print but doesn't really own the rights? This can happen very easily and if the design is not well known, you are the innocent infringer.

Number 22 of the Trade Standards is called an indemnification. This is also known as a "hold harmless" agreement. Basically, the customer is guaranteeing that he has the rights to the design and will hold you harmless if there is a lawsuit. You should also get a written representation that he does have the rights if you are in doubt.

What if You Change a Design Slightly

We could take up this entire book talking about copyrights. In a nutshell, it is a misconception that if you change a design 20% then you are not breaking the law. In general, what the Copyright Law states is that under a "side-by-side" comparison, are there "substantial similarities." This means that if you alter a design just 20%, then 80% of it is a knock-off!

By no means are we implying that you should copy someone else's work. We are just trying to clear the air on the "20%" rule. There is no 20% rule!

TRADE TERMS, CONDITIONS AND STANDARDS OF THE PRINTING INDUSTRY

1. QUOTATION
A quotation not accepted within thirty (30) days is subject to review.

2. ORDER CANCELLATION
In the case of an order cancellation, if the printer has already commenced working on the order, he shall be entitled to full reimbursement for any costs already incurred, including penalties or restocking charges that sellers suppliers may charge him. This reimbursement shall be taken from the advanced deposit and the balance refunded to the customer.

3. EXPERIMENTAL WORK
Experimental work performed at customer's request, such as sketches, drawings, composition, screens, presswork and materials, will be charged for at current rates and may not be used without consent of the printer.

4. PREPARATORY WORK
Sketches, copy, dummies and all preparatory work created or furnished by the printer, shall remain his exclusive property and no use of same shall be made, nor any ideas obtained therefrom be used, except upon compensation to be determined by the printer.

5. CONDITION OF CUSTOMER SUPPLIED ARTWORK
Estimates for printing are based on customer supplying same size or larger black and white artwork that is "camera ready" and requiring no touch-up or clean-up. Additional time needed to make artwork camera ready shall be billed at current rates.

6. PREPARATORY MATERIALS
Artwork, type, screens, negatives, positives and other items when supplied by the printer shall remain his exclusive property unless otherwise agreed in writing.

7. ALTERATIONS
Alterations represent work performed in addition to the original specifications. Such additional work shall be charged at current rates and be supported with documentation upon request.

8. PROOFS
Proofs shall be submitted with original copy. Corrections are to be made on "master set", returned marked "O.K." or "O.K. with corrections" and signed by customer. If revised proofs are desired, request must be made when proofs are returned. Printer regrets any errors that may occur through production undetected, but cannot be held responsible for errors if the work is printed per customer's O.K. or if changes are communicated verbally. Printer shall not be responsible for errors if the customer has not ordered or has refused to accept proofs or has failed to return proofs with indication of changes or has instructed printer to proceed without submission of proofs.

9. PRESS PROOFS
Unless specifically provided in printer's quotation, press proofs will be charged for at current rates. An inspection sheet of any form can be submitted for customer approval, at no charge, provided customer is available at the press during the time of makeready. Any changes, corrections or lost press time due to customer's change of mind or delay will be charged for at current rates.

10. COLOR PROOFING
Because of differences in equipment, garments, inks and other conditions between color proofing and production pressroom operations, a reasonable variation in color between color proofs and the completed job shall constitute acceptable delivery.

11. OVERRUNS OR UNDERRUNS
Overruns or underruns not to exceed 10% on quantities ordered and/or the percentage agreed upon over or under quantities ordered shall constitute acceptable delivery. Printer will bill for actual quantity delivered within this tolerance. If customer requires guaranteed "no less than" delivery, percentage tolerance of overage must be doubled.

12. CUSTOMER'S PROPERTY
The printer will maintain fire, extended coverage, vandalism, malicious mischief and sprinkler leakage insurance on all property belonging to the customer, while such property is in the printer's possession; printer's liability for such property shall not exceed the amount recoverable from such insurance.

13. DELIVERY
Unless otherwise specified, the price quoted is for a single shipment, without storage, F.O.B. local customer's place of business or F.O.B. printer's platform for out-of-town customers. Proposals are based on continuous and uninterrupted delivery of complete order, unless specifications distinctly state otherwise. Charges related to delivery from customer to printer, or from customer's supplier to printer are not included in any quotations unless specified. Special priority pickup or delivery service will be provided at current rates upon customer's request. Materials delivered from customer or his suppliers are verified with delivery ticket as to cartons, packages or items shown only. The accuracy of quantities indicated on such tickets cannot be verified and printer cannot accept liability for shortage based on supplier's tickets. Title for finished work shall pass to the customer upon delivery to carrier at shipping point or upon mailing of invoices for finished work, whichever occurs first

14. PRODUCTION SCHEDULES
Production schedules will be established and adhered to by customer and printer, provided that neither shall incur any liability or penalty or delays due to state of war, riot, civil disorder, fire, strikes accidents, action of Government or civil authority and acts of God or other causes beyond the control of customer or printer.

15. CUSTOMER-FURNISHED MATERIALS
Garments, stock, camera copy, film, color separations and other customer furnished materials shall be manufactured, packaged and delivered to printer's specifications. Additional cost due to delays or impaired production caused by specification deficiencies shall be charged to the customer.

16. TERMS
An advanced deposit of 50% of the total order price is required on all custom orders. Printer will not commence work until this amount has been paid. Unless otherwise arranged, buyer shall pay the balance due on the order at the time of delivery.

17. GENERAL WARRANTY
Printer shall disclaim any and all express or implied warranties of merchandisability or warranty of fitness for a particular purpose. Although the printer uses quality materials, due to the wide variation in laundering conditions and detergents, printer does not guarantee against fading or shrinkage of garments during laundering.

18. DYE LOT
Due to the practice of batch processing knitted goods when they are dyed, printer cannot guarantee consistency of color on garments from dye lot to dye lot or from one order to the next.

19. SUBSTITUTIONS
Printer reserves the right to substitute materials of equal or better quality with notification, unless advance notification is previously agreed to in writing.

20. REJECTS
Buyer shall have the right to purchase reject material at a reduced cost to be determined by printer. If buyer declines to purchase rejects, printer has the right to sell them as seconds or irregulars in any manner he sees fit. If buyer provided the goods to print on he shall be entitled to all rejects. Reject rates on buyer's goods shall be within excepted industry standards. Printer shall not be obligated to purchase rejects from buyer unless a specific reject rate ceiling is agreed to in writing.

21. PACKAGING
Unless otherwise noted, all items shall be "bulk" packaged. Individual folding, tagging, bagging, etc., shall be charged at current rate.

22. INDEMNIFICATION
The customer shall indemnify and hold harmless the printer from any and all loss, cost, expense and damages on account of any and all manner of claims, demands, actions and proceedings that may be instituted against the printer on grounds alleging that the said printing violates any copyright or any proprietary right of any person, or that it contains any matter that is libelous or scandalous, or invades any person's right to privacy or other personal rights except to the extent that the printer has contributed to the matter. The customer agrees to, at the customer's own expense, promptly defend and continue the defense of any such claim, demand, action or proceeding that may be brought against the printer, provided that the printer shall promptly notify the customer with respect thereto, and provided further that the printer shall give to the customer such reasonable time as the urgency of the situation may permit in which to undertake and continue the defense thereof.

Here are key points to follow:

1. Always purchase *all rights* to designs from freelance artists unless you have a license or royalty arrangement with them.

2. Put the copyright notice on every piece of artwork you purchase or create. This includes design sketches, proofs, comps, etc. Just get a rubber stamp made that you can use to "notice" everything!

3. If you occasionally contract out your printing to outside screen printers, make sure that you have a written agreement that states you are buying all rights to designs they do for you and you are purchasing the camerawork, overlays, etc. They may or may not want you to purchase the screen (if they reclaim or use retensionable frames), so you want to have it understood that after the job is done, the screen is immediately reclaimed. This will prevent a screen printer from going after your account.

4. Print the Trade Standards on the back of your work order and have the customer *sign the work order* when he places the order. Give him a copy of the signed order as confirmation.

5. Quit trying to find ways to change someone else's work so you can claim ownership. Do what they did: Pay for an original piece and protect yourself with proper registration and notices.

Trademarks

Trademarks are another gray area. What appears to be a simple copyright could actually be a trademark. While a copyright gives you the right to control the copying, a trademark tells the world that someone owns the design. Typically, a logo has a trademark, while a general design has a copyright. A design can also have a copyright (for the design) and a trademark (to show ownership).

If you infringe on a trademark and confuse the public, the courts will say you could be prosecuted as infringer. This means that no matter how much you change a trademark, if there is still a likeness or "likelihood of confusion," you lose.

Licensing

Large printers make a lot of their money on licensed products, whether it's major league sports or just universities. Licensing is actually its own industry with trade shows and trade magazines. Appendix A has a listing of licensing agencies and publications.

It may not be as hard as you think to get a license for the local college or team. Many universities work through license brokers who handle a number of schools. They may want an advance against royalties that could range from a few hundred dollars for a local school to hundreds of thousands of dollars for major league sports.

They will also want to approve the garment, the graphics and you. You'll probably have to supply a financial statement and references. Make sure you can produce as promised.

In return, you will pay them 7 ½ -10% for the privilege of selling merchandise with their logo on it. Once you get your first license, the next will come easier because you have a track record.

Walk Before You Run

To many first-time business people, the "trappings" of a business are very important. The new office, secretary, bookkeeper, new car and executive desk are all items that make you feel like an executive. But most of these will have to wait until the business can afford these luxuries. The first priority is to put the money where it will make money. Do the books and answer the phones yourself for a while. It's very important that *you* know the inner workings of the company before you train someone else to do it.

Let the business grow naturally. Always ask the question: "Do I need this item for the survival of the business?" What you will really need in the first few months *and years* of the business is operating capital.

Where to Learn More About Business

How about a local university or junior college? A lot of them have night classes in general business, business law, bookkeeping, etc.

Small Business Administration

Try the local office of the Small Business Administration. They have regular programs including short courses, conferences, problem-solving clinics and workshops tailored to the needs of small businesses. Some of their offerings cover personnel problems, taxation, sales, marketing, manufacturing and inventory control. In most cases, admission fees, if any, are nominal.

Every year, the Small Business Administration gives away millions of leaflets and pamphlets relating to various topics of interest to small businesses. Contact your local office for a catalog of their publications and services.

Recommended Reading

Don't overlook the standard business magazines and newspapers such as *The Wall Street Journal, Barrons, Business Week, Inc., Venture, Forbes* and *Nations Business.* It won't hurt to expand your horizons and find out what the "Business" world is up to. You might even spot a new trend or find potential customers!

How about the library? You can find a wealth of information at your fingertips for free! Go to the bookstore and you will find hundreds of books on business, bookkeeping, marketing, how to run a small business and more.

Recommended Viewing

As a reinforcement to this book you should consider our *Business and Marketing Course* (**11.11**). It is an excellent reference on business and marketing and contains two video tapes and a small manual.

Using Consultants

There are many excellent consultants in this industry who can do everything from conducting a feasibility study to helping you buy equipment and set up the shop to training employees. Consultants generally charge from $500-1,000 per day and can actually save you thousands of dollars. They bring in their years of experience and can see things that you can't.

Don't expect miracles from a consultant, though. Changes can't be made overnight, and you may not get everything you want in a one-day visit. It could take an initial two- or three-day visit and then quarterly follow ups to get the results you are looking for.

Before hiring a consultant, always ask for references and make sure that you both know in advance what the goals are.

*11.11 The **Business and Marketing Course** is an excellent reference on how to run your business and make sales too! (Photo courtesy U.S. Screen Printing Institute, Tempe, AZ.*

CHAPTER

12

SETTING UP A SHOP

Okay, you have read this entire book and think you can print shirts. You have determined that you can make a lot of money because everyone wears printed shirts. You have also figured out that it really won't cost much money to try this venture. Now it's time to set up shop and do it (**12.1**).

Equipment and Supply Needs

In simple terms, you could get into the T-shirt business by buying just one screen, a quart of photoemulsion, one squeegee, a quart of ink and use sunlight to expose the screen and your oven to cure the shirts! To operate on a more professional basis, however, you will need printing equipment and supplies. The amount of money you need to

spend on these items will vary greatly depending on your production goals and ingenuity. Some equipment can be built, while other items will have to be purchased. In general, every shop will need a press, dryer, screen exposing system, screen developing area with running water, basic work area, inks, screens and screen printing tools. Artwork and camera work were not mentioned because they can be done by outside vendors and are not absolute necessities for every shop.

The following lists show what kind of investment it would take to set up four different types of shops. Keep in mind that the dollar figures only cover screen printing equipment and supplies–not office furniture, equipment or supplies. You may need additional money for initial operating expenses, promotion and working capital.

12.1 A typical small shop consists of a printer, dryer, flash-curing unit, exposure unit, washout sink and tools and supplies.

The Starter

This is about as small as you can go. It is designed for the person with practically no money who is looking for a part time business that will need a lot of nurturing to make it into a full-time venture.

EQUIPMENT AND SUPPLIES		LOW	HIGH
Garment Press	- Homemade 1-Color	$ 40	
	- Homemade 4-Color		$150
Dryer	- For Air-Dry Inks	0	
	- Homemade Flash-Cure Unit		250
Art Supplies	- Drawing Board, Tools and Supplies	30	100
Screen Exposure	- Sunlight with Simple Holder	20	
	- Homemade Exposure Box		100
Screen Washout	- Existing Sink or Shower	0	
	- Laundry Tub		75
Basic Supplies	- Ink, Fabric, Frames, Tools, Adhesives, Emulsion, Blockout, Etc.	150	200
Misc. Supplies	- Newspapers, Rags, Aprons, Stir Sticks, Training Books, Etc.	25	100
Other Expenses	- Room Preparation, Plumbing, Wiring, Etc.	0	150
	TOTAL	**$265**	**$1,125**

Realistically, the low-budget shop will only be able to handle one-color work using air-dry inks. This can be very limiting because most printing done in the industry is multicolor with plastisol inks that must be heat cured. The high-budget starter shop has the capability of doing multicolor work with plastisol inks. All of the equipment is homemade and will be adequate for someone starting out. Supplies costs are based on small quantities of basic items that have to be replenished after just a few orders.

With an additional $200-500 in equipment modifications, the starter shop could also handle nylon jackets and baseball caps. By adding heat-transfer paper to the high-budget list of supplies, the starter shop could print heat transfers on either a one- or four-color press.

You could operate either one of these setups out of a small room or bedroom that has a minimum of 100 sq ft (10 x 10-ft room). You would also need a separate screen washout area that has running water. This could be a shower or an outdoor garden hose.

THE SEMI-PROFESSIONAL

This set-up relies on less homemade equipment and more professionally manufactured items. It also offers the capability of handling baseball caps and nylon jackets along with multicolor prints on shirts. The only outside service needed is camera or computer work.

EQUIPMENT AND SUPPLIES		LOW	HIGH
4-Color Press	- Professional Economy Model	$750	
	- Heavy Duty Expandable		$2,500
Press Accessories	- Jacket Attachment	250	450
	- Baseball Cap Attachment	60	100
Dryer	- Economy Flash-Curing Unit	400	
	- Heavy Duty Flash Cure		700
Screen Exposure	- Exposure Unit	450	800
Screen Washout	- Existing Sink	0	
	- Laundry Tub		75
Art Supplies	- Drawing Board, Tools, Etc.	75	200
Printing Supplies	- Inks, Emulsions, Frames, Fabrics, Tools, Etc.	250	500
Misc.Supplies	- Tables, Rags, Aprons, Training Books, Etc.	70	200
Other Expenses	- Room Preparation, Plumbing, Wiring, Etc.	100	500
	TOTAL	**$2,405**	**$6,025**

The quality of the prints will be better with professional equipment because it is manufactured to closer tolerances. Professional equipment will also hold its value if you want to sell it. Because the amount of equipment and supplies listed for the semi-professional shop is greater, this setup has more flexibility in the quantity and type of orders it can produce.

Although you could set up this type of shop in a small room, using a larger area such as a one-car garage would be better because of the increased work space. A 300-500 sq ft room will suffice if extra space is available elsewhere for an office and art department or for computer graphics.

This setup could support a full-time business if there was enough work. It has the capability of growing and possibly seeing a profit in a matter of months. The printing press can be a single station for economy or a multi-station for the high end. The production rate for four-color work will be around 6-8 dozen shirts per hour with one or two people working. With a one-station press, a flash-curing unit will handle the low production easily.

THE PROFESSIONAL SHOP

This shop has everything that is needed to do all types of work including tight registration multicolor jobs. The only outside service that may be needed is camera work.

EQUIPMENT AND SUPPLIES		LOW	HIGH
6-Color Press	- Economy Model	$2,500	
	- Heavy-Duty Model		$4,500
	- Jacket and Cap Holddown	250	500
	- Vacuum Table Attachment	250	350
Dryer	- Small Conveyor (1½ x 6 ft)	2,800	
	- Larger Conveyor (2 x 10 ft)		4,800
	- Economy Flash-Cure Unit	450	
	- Heavy Duty Flash-Cure Unit		800
Heat Transfer	- Cap Heat Transfer Press	400	700
	- Shirt Heat Transfer Press	600	1,000
Exposure System	- Exposure Box	400	
	- Point Light Source		1,500
Screen Washout	- Laundry Tub	75	
	- Professional Sink		600
Art Department	- Drawing Board, Tools and Supplies	100	250
	- Basic Computer Graphics System	3,500	5,500
Supplies	- Inks, Emulsions, Tools, Fabrics, Frames, Etc.	500	1,000
Misc. Equipment	- Tables, Shelves, Aprons, Rags, Etc.	100	500
Other Expenses	- Room Preparation, Wiring, Plumbing, Etc.	200	1000
Training	- Books Only	50	250
	- Seminars or Schools		1000
	TOTAL	**$ 12,175**	**$ 24,250**

The professional shop can do almost any type of work from one-color to multicolor T-shirts, nylon jackets, baseball caps, heat transfers and more. Because of the speed tables on the press and the conveyor dryer, the production rate can be as high as 10-12 dozen multicolor prints per hour or 20-30 dozen one-color prints per hour.

This shop needs at least 400-500 sq ft for the equipment and up to 1,000 sq ft for adequate work room and storage. You may need a separate room for the art and computer department.

THE COMPLETE GARMENT PRINTING SHOP

The following list includes all the equipment and supplies needed to handle all types of jobs without having to use any outside services.

EQUIPMENT AND SUPPLIES		LOW	HIGH
6-Color Press/W Speed Table	- Economy Model - Heavy-Duty Model	$3,000	$4,500
Press Accessories	- Jacket and Cap Holddowns, and Sleeve boards	300	600
Conveyor Dryer	- 2 x 10 feet	4,000	5,000
Flash-Cure Unit	- Economy Model - Heavy-Duty Model w/Auto Cycle	700	1,200
Exposure System	- Small Point Light Source - Two Screen Capacity P.L. Source	1,500	2,000
Heat Transfer	- Cap Heat Press - Shirt Heat Press	400 600	400 1,000
Art Department	- Drawing Board, Tools and Supplies	200	400
Computer Graphics System	- Economy - Complete w/Oversize Laser Printer	3,500	7,000
Screen Washout	- Laundry Tub - Professional Sink	75	700
Supplies	- Inks, Fabric, Tools, Etc.	1,000	2,500
Misc. Equipment and Supplies	- Fixtures, Tables, Etc.	200	400
Other Expenses	- Room Preparation, Wiring, Plumbing, Etc.	500	2000
Training	- Books Only - Seminars or Schools	50	250 1000
	TOTAL	**$16,025**	**$28,950**

With a six-color press, large dryer and complete darkroom, this shop is completely self-contained. Because of the size of the equipment, at least 1,000 sq ft will be necessary and preferably 2,000-3,000 sq ft to allow for adequate work space and room for storage and offices.

Where to Buy Equipment and Supplies

There are dozens of equipment manufacturers and suppliers in the industry. Appendix A has a complete listing of suppliers. Most offer a catalog of their products. A majority of the manufacturers sell their equipment through local screen printing suppliers and many will sell directly to you.

While it may seem more logical to buy direct from the manufacturer, the dealer is often the one who will hold your hand when you are in trouble. By allowing a dealer who sells everything to make you a package deal, you can generally save more money and get help from the dealer when problems arise! If you are in doubt about your dealer's ability or the products he sells, ask for references.

Try not to be oversold by eager sales people. Many a newcomer has spent their life savings (or the second mortgage on the house) only to find that some of the equipment was not necessary *and* that the salesperson did not even advise them to keep enough money for working capital and additional expenses. If you only have $5,000 to spend on everything, for goodness sake leave some in reserve.

Look Out for Hidden Expenses

There are always hidden expenses. No matter how hard you try to budget, something extra will always come up. Generally, freight is always extra on equipment and supply shipments. This can amount to hundreds of dollars on larger orders. Also, you need to know that drivers are *not* required to help you unload heavy pieces. Renting a forklift can be additional expense.

If you're moving into an existing building, make sure the wiring will handle the new equipment. The local building department may require you to bring the wiring up to code *and* have a licensed electrician do the work. Make sure you have 220-volt service if you plan on purchasing a conveyor dryer. Many beginning printers have rented a building and bought equipment only to find that 220-volt service for the dryer wasn't available.

If you are just starting a business, you will have to put down deposits on utilities and phone service. These can run hundreds or even thousands of dollars. Don't make the mistake of telling the power company that you will be running an "energy hog" dryer all day long. The deposit may be based on the anticipated power usage!

Where to Set Up Your Shop

In Your House

If you plan on working out of your home, you need to figure out how much room your shop will take. The garage is probably the most ideal spot. With some inks, ventilation is a must and most garages can be easily ventilated! If you plan to print with nontextile inks such as vinyl or plastic, remember that they have a very strong solvent odor.

The mess is also a consideration. This is not the cleanest business and there will be times when ink will seem to be *everywhere*.

Renting a Building

In retail, location is the most important consideration. In screen printing, location isn't all that important. Because you will generally be going out to see customers and they may not visit the factory, you can rent almost any building that is properly zoned and will allow you to have flammable liquids on the premises. Industrial parks or freestanding buildings are the best options. If you plan to have a retail shop along with your printing business, then location is a very important factor!

Don't forget obvious concerns like running water and an accessible drain for the washout sink. A large overhead door is also nice to keep the shop well ventilated *and* to provide a big enough opening to move the equipment through easily!

The size of the building or shop will depend on your resources and equipment. The equipment lists gave a basic size requirement, but always plan for growth and try to get more space than you need initially. Where are you going to stage orders before they are printed? Where are you going to fold and package?

Wiring

Before you decide to buy a large conveyor dryer, it might be wise to see if the wiring in your house or building will handle it. As mentioned earlier, many older commercial buildings do not have 220 volts.

Most commercial dryers will draw at least 30 amps. Some homes only have 60-amp service.

You will need enough power for the dryer, heat transfer presses, exposure unit, air conditioners, flash-cure units and other equipment that consumes energy. Make sure you have enough power coming into the shop.

If electricity is not your strong suit, then by all means hire a licensed electrician to hook things up for you. Most commercial conveyor dryers have a junction box and are not designed to be

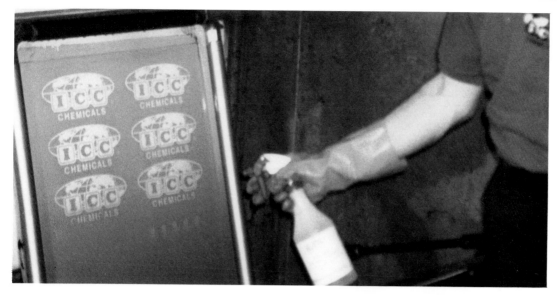

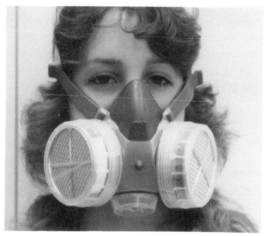

12.2 *Some companies offer specialty chemicals that are less toxic and safer to use. (Photo courtesy Intercontinental Chemical Company, Cleveland, OH.)*

12.3 *Personal protective equipment should be provided to employees to help protect them from harmful chemicals.*

just plugged in. They must be wired into another fused box for protection.

Zoning

This is a gray area if you work out of your house because you may not be zoned for any type of business. You may want to check with the city to see if the zoning is okay. Screening is generally classified as light manufacturing. Before renting a building, make sure allows for screen printing.

If working out of your house, you will have more problems if you have a lot of traffic in and out of your house: such as employees, customers stopping by or delivery trucks. Most cities don't mind a person having an office in their home, or even a small business, but they do mind employees and customers coming to the house.

Your Health and the Environment

Your own health and protection of the environment are of great concern in this industry. For many years no one paid attention to the chemicals that were invading our bodies and the earth. Now that things have changed, this is a hot topic.

What Goes Down the Drain

A very real concern is what goes down the drain. Products are usually referred to as *drain safe* when you can wash them down the drain. Not all obvious products are drain safe. Water-based ink is a good example of a product that sounds safe, but actually has toxic chemicals in it to retard molding and may contain solvents. You would think water-based inks would be drain safe, but in some areas they aren't.

Check with the manufacturers to see which chemicals that you use are drain safe. Some sup-

pliers will put all of their claims in writing and stand behind their compliance with the laws (**12.2**).

Septic Systems

A product can be drain safe but not safe for your septic system. Screen reclaimers and haze removers may be harmful to the proper operation of your septic system. Many manufacturers are replacing older, more hazardous products with newer and safer versions. If you are on a septic system, consult your supplier or the manufacturers about products that will be environmentally safe for you.

Personal Protection

Some chemicals are very harmful if inhaled or if they come in contact with your skin. You should *always* wear personal protective equipment and provide the same for your employees when working with these chemicals–*and insist they use them.* Personal protection equipment usually consists of safety glasses, gloves, aprons and for certain applications, a respirator (**12.3**).

Fire Safety

Safety is always a factor, but in your home, you have more to lose if you have a fire!

Keep *at least* one good fire extinguisher in the shop! Make sure it is designed for use with flammable solvents!

Empty the trash cans often and keep the shop picked-up. A pile of solvent soaked rags is a perfect fire hazard! Invest in a *Safety Kleen* unit for tool clean-up and keep all the solvent containers capped. For added protection, keep your solvents in metal containers designed for this purpose. Your fire inspector will insist on this.

As mentioned earlier, know the limitations of the electrical service and wiring. Everything may seem okay, but wait until you smell something burning in the attic! It may be too late.

In general, whether you are in your home or have a shop, good safety rules are important. You are in an industry where the use of combustible material makes it a definite fire hazard.

Spot-Removal Area

The solvent used in spotting guns is very toxic and can actually kill you if you inhale it in an enclosed area. It is a dry-cleaning solvent called 1,1,1, trichloreothane. This product is being removed from many industrial applications because of its toxicity.

When using a spotting gun, be sure to have adequate ventilation. If possible, use an exhaust system to remove the fumes.

Ventilation

The key to minimizing exposure is to reduce the amount of chemicals you use, use safer (often more expensive) chemicals and have adequate ventilation. This means placing fans to blow exhaust fumes away from you when you are working (**12.4**). If your shop has doors and windows, try to keep them open. By exchanging old air with fresh, you will minimize the exposure to toxic fumes.

You may see fumes coming from the dryer and think that they are coming from the plastisol ink. Actually, it isn't the ink that is smoking; it is the shirt! Shirts have *sizing* and *stabilizers* plus moisture that burns off in the dryer. You may notice a slight odor from shirts that contain polyester. To keep these fumes from burning your eyes, make sure to vent your dryer and ventilate your shop.

Screen Making Department

This will be one of the more hazardous areas in your shop. The chemicals used here may not be drain safe and may be dangerous if inhaled when spraying or wiping reclaimer on screens, you should be in a well-ventilated area or wear a face mask or respirator. Be even more careful with haze and ghost removers.

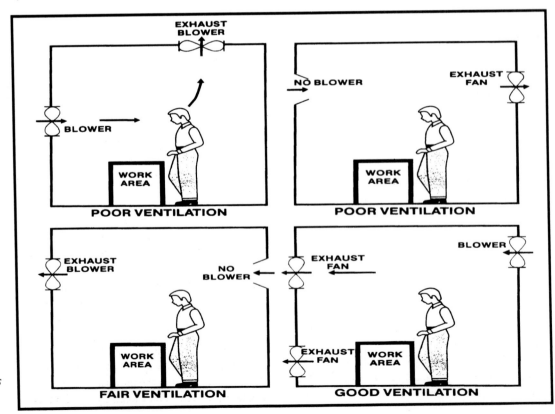

12.4 Proper ventilation is important in keeping harmful fumes away from you.

INTERCONTINENTAL CHEMICAL CORPORATION
4660 Spring Grove Ave., Cincinnati, Ohio 45232 513-541-7100

MATERIAL SAFETY DATA SHEET

(rev. 02/12/91)

PRODUCT IDENTIFICATION.

ICC 846 - CLARIFIER™

HAZARDOUS INGREDIENTS.

ICC 846 contains no haz~ ~nts as defined by the following:

OSHA; 29 CFR 1910.1000
ACGIH
OSHA; IARC; NTP; 29 CFR 1910.1200, Appendix A
OSHA; 29 CFR 1910.1200, Appendix A

PEL's (Permi~
TLV's (™
C~

Vapor Pressure: <1 mmHg. @ 20°C.
Percent Volatile: > 20.
Specific Gravity: > 1.
Appearance: Green liquid.
SCAQMD Rule 1130: 1.2 #/gallon.

MATERIAL SAFETY DATA SHEET
Information in accordance with 29 CFR 1910.1200 (g)(1)

| DATE OF ISSUE: | 07/04/89 | SUPERSEDES: | | MSDS | NBR: | ATEX | 1000 |

SECTION I - GENERAL INFORMATION

MANUFACTURER'S NAME: UNION INK COMPANY, INC.
ADDRESS: 453 BROAD AVENUE
RIDGEFIELD, NJ 07657
EMERGENCY TELEPHONE: 201-945-5766
INFORMATION TELEPHONE: 201-945-5766
PRODUCT CLASS:
TRADE NAME: WATER BASED SCREEN PRINTING INK
AEROTEX COLORS
MANUFACTURER'S CODE: ATEX-1000, -1020, -2011, -2021, -2051, -3006, -3011, -3030, -4020, -5000, -5020
-5035, -5040, -6030, -6081, -7021, -7031, -8000, -9030, -9090

HMIS INFO	
HEALTH	1
FLAMMABILITY	0
REACTIVITY	0

SECTION II - HAZARDOUS INGREDIENTS

This product contains the following toxic chemicals (if any are present they are marked "YES" under the SARA 313 column below) subject to the reporting requirements of Section 313 of the Emergency Planning and Community Right-To-Know Act of 1986 and of 40 CFR 372. This information must be included in all MSDS's that are copied and distributed for this material.

HAZARDOUS INGREDIENTS	CAS NUMBER	%	SARA 313 LISTED	MFR'S SUGG. TLV	OSHA PEL		ACGIH TLV's		L.E.L.	VAPOR PRESS.
					ppm	mg/m	TWA ppm	STEL ppm		mm Hg
NONE										

The remaining [proprietary] ingredients are not found in the most recent Massachusetts, New Jersey, Maryland, Pennsylvania or California Substance Lists, or the Federal Hazardous Substance List or EPA Lists. THE FORMULA, IN ITS ENTIRETY, IS DEEMED "TRADE SECRET" BY THE COMPANY.

SECTION III - PHYSICAL DATA

BOILING RANGE:	212°F.	PER CENT VOLATILE BY WEIGHT:	0
VAPOR DENSITY:	HEAVIER THAN AIR	WEIGHT PER GALLON (LBS.)	8-12
EVAP. RATE:	SLOWER THAN ETHER		

SECTION IV - FIRE AND EXPLOSION DATA

OSHA CLASSIFICATION:

12.5 *A material safety data sheet tells you about each chemical you use and how to safely handle the chemical. You should have an MSDS for each chemical you have on the premises.*

Government Health and Safety Regulations

There are a number of state and federal laws that you should be aware of. The first and most important is the "Right-to-Know" or Hazard Communication Standard. It is an OSHA law that basically says employees have a right to know what chemicals they are working with and be trained in how to properly handle them. If you don't comply with this law, you could face a possible $10,000 fine per infraction.

When you purchase your inks and supplies, the supplier *must* provide a form called a Material Safety Data Sheet (MSDS) that tells you about each hazardous chemical and how to safely handle it (**12.5**). You must put all the MSDS forms (for every hazardous chemical) in a binder where your employees can access them easily.

According to OSHA, you must also train your employees about the hazards through a written training program that you keep on file. A number of companies provide stock programs that you can customize for your shop (**12.6**).

Another law concerns disposing of hazardous waste (solvents, rags, etc.). This law falls under the jurisdiction of the Environmental Protection Agency (EPA). Some states and counties have laws concerning how much solvent you can have in the workplace, statutes covering what you can put in the sewer system and more.

The days of just wiping a screen with paint thinner and throwing the rag away are over! This is against the law. You should try to minimize the

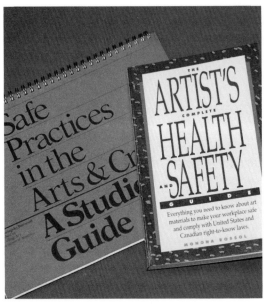

12.6 Prepackaged programs are available that will help you come into compliance with the OSHA Right-to-Know law. (Photo courtesy Union Ink Co., Ridgefield, NJ.)

12.7 A number of books are available that provide information on how to have a safer shop.

use of solvents in your shop and instead use water to wash screens. If you must wipe a screen with solvent, then your best bet may be to run the rag through the dryer when finished. This will dry the wet ink and cause the solvent to evaporate.

Many areas now regulate the amount of Volatile Organic Compounds (VOC's) you release into the air through solvent evaporation and curing. In some states, you need to actually get a permit for each printing press and dryer.

A common practice (as of this writing) is to rent rags from a service and let *them* be responsible for taking care of the hazardous waste you generate! However, *you* are ultimately responsible for the waste you generate, so be careful in selecting a provider.

For additional information about these laws, consult your local supplier and local and state

agencies. Also, the Screen Printing Association International has an excellent section on health and safety in their Technical Guidebooks. Suppliers such as Safety Kleen also offer regional and local seminars on these topics and there are excellent books as well (**12.7**). Appendix A has a listing of health and safety resources.

This is a very important area that will see increased legislation and regulation. Take the time to find out about the state and county laws affecting your business.

Work Flow

If you set up your shop in your garage or a small room, then you have limited layout options. Obviously, you want to have the press by the dryer, the squeegees near the ink and the cleanup area near the ink and press.

If you have more space, then think about how the work will flow. The shirts coming in need to be staged near the press before you print them. After they are printed, they need to be packaged and then shipped.

Many shops have a wet side and a dry side. This means that all ink, screen making and messy items are in part of the shop and all shirts, receiving, shipping and packaging is in the other.

The placement of your washout sink may be dictated by the water and drain source–typically near a restroom. You will also definitely need a darkroom where you can coat and store screens. The ink and cleanup area may need to be near a door to allow for ventilation and easy access if there is a fire. Figure **12.8** and **12.9** show floor plans for a small and large shop.

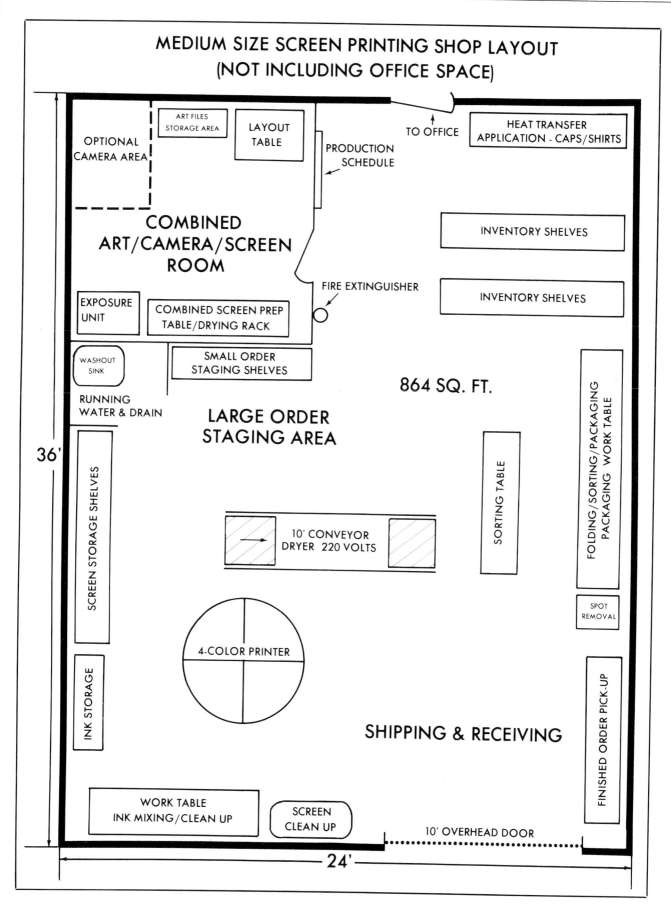

MEDIUM SIZE SCREEN PRINTING SHOP LAYOUT
(NOT INCLUDING OFFICE SPACE)

OPTIONAL CAMERA AREA

ART FILES STORAGE AREA

LAYOUT TABLE

TO OFFICE

HEAT TRANSFER APPLICATION - CAPS/SHIRTS

PRODUCTION SCHEDULE

COMBINED ART/CAMERA/SCREEN ROOM

INVENTORY SHELVES

INVENTORY SHELVES

EXPOSURE UNIT

COMBINED SCREEN PREP TABLE/DRYING RACK

FIRE EXTINGUISHER

WASHOUT SINK

SMALL ORDER STAGING SHELVES

864 SQ. FT.

RUNNING WATER & DRAIN

LARGE ORDER STAGING AREA

36'

SCREEN STORAGE SHELVES

SORTING TABLE

FOLDING/SORTING/PACKAGING PACKAGING WORK TABLE

10' CONVEYOR DRYER 220 VOLTS

SPOT REMOVAL

INK STORAGE

4-COLOR PRINTER

SHIPPING & RECEIVING

FINISHED ORDER PICK-UP

WORK TABLE INK MIXING/CLEAN UP

SCREEN CLEAN UP

10' OVERHEAD DOOR

24'

12.8

MEDIUM TO LARGE
SCREEN PRINTING SHOP LAYOUT
(NOT INCLUDING OFFICE SPACE)

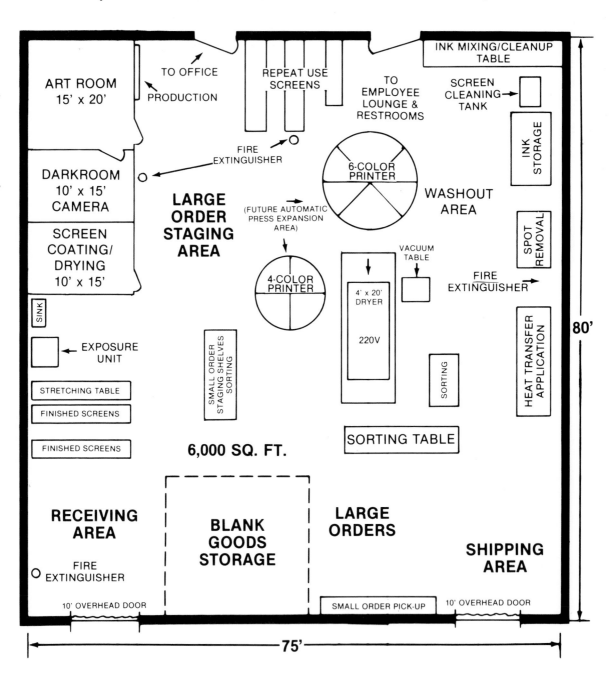

12.9

Everything Takes Longer Than You Think

The first rule of business is that everything takes a little longer than anticipated. This holds true when setting up a shop. If you know the basic rule, at least it is easier to deal with delays. The equipment will generally take longer to arrive than you thought. The supplies may be on backorder. The plumber may be a week late. The electrician may have to make an extra trip out. The trucking company may damage something. One of the orders may get lost by UPS. If this sounds like a scene from "The Out of Towners," that's because it is. But if you just kick back and keep a clear head, you will get through getting everything in place, and the orders rolling out the door.

The biggest problem is that people always take orders before the shop is up and running.

Your customers don't want to hear about the delays mentioned above. Be very careful what you commit to when first setting up. Give yourself a long enough lead time on the first few orders to allow for problems.

Now that we have had all this straight talk, take a look at the various shop setups, analyze the budget (or lack of one) and decide what you want to do. Printing on garments can be a lot of hard work, but the hard work will pay off in profits and the rewarding feeling of being your own boss.

Printing on T-shirts is a glamorous business. You'll be surprised at the orders you will get from friends and people you meet everywhere once they know you are in the "imprinted garment" business. Just watch your growth, keep as much money in reserve as possible, listen to free advice, run the business as a business ***and by all means have fun***!

APPENDIX

SUPPLIER LISTING

The following section is just a small selection of major suppliers. For a detailed listing by product consult one of the buyers' guides published by the trade magazines. This listing has been compiled from industry trade magazines and catalogs. There is no guarantee of accuracy. Most major manufacturers will supply a list of their dealer network so you can find who carries the brand you like in your area.

When calling these suppliers - please tell them you saw their listing in HOW TO PRINT T-SHIRTS FOR FUN AND PROFIT!

CAMERAS

nuArc Co., Inc.
6200 W. Howard St.
Niles, IL 60648-3404
708 967 4400
708 967 9664 (Fax)

CLIP ART

Dynamic Graphics, Inc.
6000 N. Forest Park Drive
Peoria, IL 61614
309 688 8800
800 255 8800
309 688 3075 (Fax)

Smart Designs
310 S. Clark Dr.
Tempe, AZ 85281
602 968 7121
800 959 7627
602 968 8816 (Fax)

U.S.Screen Printing Institute
605 S. Rockford Dr.
Tempe, AZ 85281
602 929 0640
800 624 6532
602 929 0766 (Fax)

Xpres Corp.
111 Cloverleaf Dr.
Winston-Salem, NC 27103
919 768 7400
800 334 0425
919 768 4629 (Fax)

COLOR SEPARATIONS

Coudray Graphic Technologies
825 Capitolio Way
San Luis Obispo, CA 93401
800 826 8372
805 541 1586
805 541 3529 (Fax)

Electronics Design Group
3164 N.1175 East
Layton, UT 84040
800 748 4672

Serichrome Seps
4841 Gretna St.
Dallas, TX 75207
214 631 5400
214 631 6592 (Fax)

COMPUTER

Casey's Page Mill
6528 S. Oneida Court
Englewood, CO 80111-4617
303 220 1463
800 544 5620

Creative Softward Solutions, Inc.
28182 Rubicon Ct.
Laguna Niguel, CA 92656
714 831 9302

International System Solutions, Inc.
2814 W. 15th St.
Panama City, Fl 32401
904 784 1794
904 769 5742 (Fax)

Linographics, Inc.
770 N.Main St.
Orange, CA 92668
714 639 0511
800 854 0273
714 639 3912 (Fax)

Scott M. Ritter Software
Division of Northwind
32 N.W. 4th St.
Grand Rapids, MN 55744
218 326 0890
(Price quotation program)

Smart Designs
310 S. Clark Dr.
Tempe, AZ 85281
602 968 7121
800 959 7627
602 968 8816 (Fax)

Stahl's Lettering
20600 Stephens St.
St.Claire Shores, MI 48080
313 772 6161
800 521 9702
313 521 9702 (Fax)

Xpres Corp.
111 Cloverleaf Dr.
Winston-Salem, NC 27103
919 768 7400 800 334 0425
919 768 4629 (Fax)

Xpres Systems
Southwest Education Bldg.
1425 E. Washington
Phoenix, AZ 85034
602 580 9720
800 995 3242
602 580 9062 (Fax)

COPYRIGHT, TRADEMARK & LICENSING

The Licensing Book and The Licensing Report
Adventure Publishing Group Inc.
1501 Broadway
New York, NY 10036
212 575 4510
212 575 4521 (Fax)

Collegiate Licensing Co.
320 Interstate North, Suite 102
Atlanta, GA 30339
404 956 0520

International Licensing Directory
(U.S.A. Office)
Expocon Management Associates, Inc.
3695 Post Road
Southport, CT 06490
203 256 4700

Licensing Industry Association
c/o Licensing Corporation of America
75 Rockefeller Plaza
New York, NY 10019
212 244 1944

The Licensing Journal
P.O. Box 1169
Three Landmark Square
Stamford, CT 06904-1169
203 358 0848
203 348 2720 (Fax)

Licensing Resource Group
P.O. Box 2778
Iowa City, IA 52224
319 351 1776

Major League Baseball
Office of the Commissioner
350 Park Ave., 29th Fl.
New York, NY 10022
212 339 7800
212 355 0007 (Fax)
(Bob McCandilish-all teams)
(Liz Murphy-local teams)

National Basketball Assoc.
645 5th Ave., 15 Fl.
New York, NY 10022
212 826 7000
212 826 0579 (Fax)
(Attn: Sal Larocca)

Time Warner Sports Merchandising
1325 Avenue of the Americas
New York, NY 10019
212 636 5803
(Attn: Ralph Irizany)

U.S. Copyright Office
Washington, DC 20559
202 707 3000 Public Information
202 707 9100 Forms Hotline
(ask for package #115)

(Address to return forms & applications)
Registrar of Copyrights
Copyright Office
Library of Congress
Washington, D.C. 20559

U.S. Patent & Trademark Office
Arlington, VA 22202
703 308 9000

EMULSION MFG.

Autotype USA
2050 Hammond Dr.
Schaumburg, IL 60173-3810
708 303 5900
800 323 0632
708 303 5225 (Fax)

The Chromaline Corp.
4832 Grand Ave.
Duluth, MN 55807
218 628 2217
800 328 4261
218 628 3245(Fax)

Kiwo, Inc.
P.O. Box 1009
Seabrook, TX 77586
713 474 9777
713 474 7325 (Fax)

Majestech Corp
Route 100
P.O. Box 440
Somers, NY 10589
914 232 7781
800 431 2200
914 232 4004 (Fax)
   Marietta, GA
   404 973 3590
   Brookfield, WI
   414 771 0288
   Canton, OH
   216 477 5578
   Mt. Prospect, IL
   708 296 5090
   Dallax, TX
   214 412 2333

Murakami Screen USA, Inc.
961 Meridian Ave.
Alhambra, CA 91803
818 284 4596
800 562 3534
818 284 5141 (Fax)

Standard Screen Supply
480 Canal St.
New York, NY 10013
212 925 6800
800 221 2697 In-State
212 334 8349 (Fax)

Ulano Corp.
255 Butler St.
Brooklyn, NY 11217
718 622 5200
800 221 0616
718 802 1119 (Fax)

EQUIPMENT MFG.

The following is a list of equipment manufacturers. Contact listing to find closest
distributor.

A & M Printing Equipment
5310 Western Ave.
Connersville, IN 47331
765 825 3444
800 533 4173
765 827 4723 (Fax)

Aaron Worldwide Machine Co.
8057 Raytheon Road #1
San Diego, CA 92111
619 467 1137
619 467 1210 (Fax)

American M & M
6401 W. Chestnut
Morton Grove, IL 60053
708 967 8530
800 876 1600
708 967 8620 (Fax)

Antec, Inc.
P.O.Box 3787
Charlottesville, VA 22903
804 979 8600
800 552 6832 (US)
804 977 1532 (Fax)

Brown Manufacturing
3056 Dixie   Suite C
Grandville, MI 49418
616 249 0200
616 249 3211 (Fax)

BBC Industries/Black Body
1526 Fenpark
Fenton, MO 63026
800 654 4205
314 343 3952 (Fax)

Chaparral Industries, Inc.
3617 E. LaSalle St.
Phoenix, AZ 85040
602 437 4883
800 654 5885 (US)
602 437 2270 (Fax)

Fault Line Graphics
540 E. Thomas St.
Oakview, CA 93022
805 649 2277
888 374 3444
805 649 5004 (Fax)

Hix Corp.
1201 E. 27th St.
Pittsburg, KS 66762
316 231 8568
800 835 0606 (US & Canada)
316 231 1598 (Fax)

Jay Products Co.
(Cylinder Press)
2868 Colerain Ave.
Cincinnati, OH 45225-2278
513 541 2514
800 543 4436 (US)
513 541 2552 (Fax)

Lawson Screen Products
5110 Penrose St.
St. Louis, MO 63115
314 382 9300
800 325 8317
314 382 3012

M & R Printing Equipment, Inc.
1 North 372 Main St.
Glen Ellyn, IL 60137
708 858 6101
800 736 6431
708 858 6134 (Fax)

MBS Inc.
199 7th Ave.
Hawthorne, NJ 07506
201 423 1298
201 427 4835 (fax)

National Screen Printing Equipment, Inc.
1401 N.Broadway
P.O.Box 105
Pittsburg, KS 66762
316 232 1917
800 843 3928
316 232 1941 (Fax)

Odyssey Screen Printing Equipment
P.O. Box 299
Slippery Rock, PA 16057
412 794 6113
800 557 7889
412 794 1218 (Fax)

Print Maker
1118 Burns Ave.
Dallas, TX 75211
888 330 9040
(Bottle printers)

R. Jennings Manufacturing Co.
8 Glen Falls Technical Park
Glen Falls, NY 12801
518 798 2277
518 798 3172 (Fax)

Ranar Mfg., Co.
12912 Venice Blvd.
Los Angeles, CA 90066
310 390 3177
800 735 5411 (In state)
800 421 9910 (US)
310 391 7781 (Fax)

Richmond Graphic Products, Inc.
(Exposure Unit)
204 Hartford Ave.
Providence., RI 02909
401 351 0150
401 351 5490 (Fax)

Striker Products
307 S. Broadway
Pittsburg, KS 66762
316 232 3111
800 669 4356

Tuf Products International
5007 Steffani Ln.
Houston, TX 77041
713 869 7745
713 869 7751 (Fax)

Vastex International, Inc.
R D 1 Box 409D2
Humbolt Industrial Park
Hazelton, PA 18201
717 455 2900
717 455 2927 (Fax)

Workhorse Products
210 Center Court, Giant Trade Center
San Pablo, CA 94806
510 236 2733
800 778 8779
510 236 2723 (Fax)

EQUIPMENT & SUPPLIES

General "consumable" items such as frames, fabric, ink and squeegees. Many of these companies also act as distributors for major lines of equipment.

AA Screen Printing Supplies
1720 Cumberland Point Dr. #21
Marietta, GA 30067
770 850 0110
800 334 4513
770 850 0790 (Fax)

Aegis Supply
5735 Kenwick
San Antonio, TX 78238
210 521 8500
888 397 1212
210 543 0001 (Fax)

A.J.Supply Co.
9263 A3 Ravenna Road
Twinsburg, OH 44087
216 425 7265

The Art Market
1309 West Broad Street
Richmond, VA 23220
804 353 7893
800 541 3696
804 359 2774 (Fax)

Asti Paint Inc.
7408 Gateway East
El Paso, TX 79915
915 594 7304
915 594 7304 (Fax)

Atlantic Screen Supply
20 McDonald Bvld.
I-95 Industrial Park
Aston, PA 19014
610 485 9900
800 834 9910
610 485 1486 (Fax)

A.W.T. World Trade, Inc.
4321 N. Knox Ave.
Chicago, IL 60641
312 777 7100
312 777 7100 (Fax)

Badger Graphic Supply
1225 Delanglade St.
Kaukauna, WI 54130
414 766 9332
414 766 3081 (Fax)

Calcom Graphic Supply
1822 N.E. Grand
Portland, OR 97212
503 281 9698
800 452 7432
503 287 0056(Fax)
Other Locations:
Berkeley, CA, Fullerton, CA,
Seattle, WA

California Shirt Sales
800 S. Raymond Ave.
Fullerton, CA 92631
714 879 8570
800 289 7478
714 992 4855(Fax)
*(See Garments for other
locations)*

Capital Screen Printing Supply
8210 Alpine Ave. Unit J
Sacramento, CA 95826
916 736 3202
800 492 2748
916 736 9516 (Fax)

Central Sign Supply
1741 Guthrie Ave.
Des Moines, IA 50316
515 263 1390
800 999 1390
515 263 1729 (Fax)

Charles M. Jessup Inc.
177 Smith St.
P.O.Box 176
Keasbey, NJ 08832
908 324 0430
800 525 4657
908 324 1616 (Fax)

Clinton Machine & Supply
4675 E. 10th Ct.
Hialeah, FL 33013
305 688 8686
800 330 8386 In-State
800 535 2210 Out-of-State
305 688 6600 (Fax)

CMO Sign Surfaces,Inc.
2941 Walmsley Blvd.
Richmond, VA 23234
804 743 1488
800 888 4844
804 271 4664(Fax)

Coastal Supply Co., Inc.
8650 Argent St.
Santee, CA 92071
619 562 8880
619 562 2772 (Fax)

Commercial Art Supply
935 Erie Blvd., E.
Syracuse, NY 13210
315 474 1000
800 669 2787
315 474 5311 (Fax)
   Rochester, NY 14605
    716 546 2830
    716 546 5957 (Fax)

Commercial Screen Supply
6 Kiddie Dr.
Avon Industrial Park
Avon, MA 02322
508 583 2300
800 227 1449 (US)
508 583 8234 (Fax)

Complete Screen Print Supply
1979 - C Parker Ct.
Stone Mountain, GA 30087
404 972 9166
800 234 0402
404 972 0723 (Fax)

Cudner O'Connor Co.
4035 West Kinzie St.
Chicago, IL 60624
312 826 0200
800 621 7449
312 826 0477 (Fax)

David's Distributing
P.O. Box 324
Glenshaw, PA 15116
412 486 5438
412 486 7081 (Fax)

Dick Blick
P.O. Box 1267
Galesburg, IL 61402-1267
800 447 8192 Order Line
309 343 5785 (Fax)
800 723 2787 Customer Service
800 933 2542 Product Information

Dick Blick East
P.O. Box 26
Allentown, PA 18105
610 965 4026 (Fax)
Other numbers same as Illinois

Dick Blick West
P.O. Box 521
Henderson, NV 89015
702 451 8196 (Fax)
Other numbers same as Illinois

Eagle Screen Print Supply
1949 Lafayette Street
New Orleans, LA 70113
504 525 4000
800 326 INKS
504 522 3535 (Fax)

Ernst W. Dorn Co., Inc
15905 S. Broadway
Gardena, CA 90248
213 770 8080
310 523 3612 (Fax)
   Providence, RI
    401 823 7701
   Chicago, Il
    708 893 0195
   Charlotte, NC
    704 394 0733
   Ft. Worth, TX
    817 595 3676

FranMar Chemical
P. O. Box 97
Normal, IL 61761
309 452 7526
800 538 5069
309 862 1005

Garston Inc.
110 Batson Drive
Manchester, CT 06040
203 649 9626
800 966 9626
203 645 0325 (Fax)
   Wilmington, MA
    508 658 7448
    800 328 7775
    508 657 4622 (Fax)

Global Supply
4337 N. GoldenState Blvd. #109
Fresno, CA 93722
209 276 1877
800 827 7272
209 276 7246 (Fax)

Graphic Art Sign
3401 W.Tillotson
Munice, IN 47306
317 285 5082

Graphic Supply
1131 R South 71st E.Avenue
Tulsa, OK 74112-5601
918 836 6524
800 234 0765
918 835 4371 (Fax)
   Dallas, TX
    800 234 0765

Griffin Supply Co.
633 Middleton St.
P.O.Box 23172
Nashville, TN 32703
615 254 3368

ICC Chemicals,Div.of/
Intercontinental Chemical Corp.
4660 Spring Grove Ave.
Cincinnati, OH 45224
513 541 7100
800 543 2075
513 541 6880 (Fax)

Jay Products Co.
2868 Colerain Ave.
Cincinnati, OH 45225-2278
513 541 2514
800 543 4436 (US)
513 541 2552 (Fax)

Kelley & Green
1540 Euclid Ave.
Bristol, VA 24201
703 669 5181
800 336 8761 (US)
703 669 7500 (Fax)

Lambert Co., Inc.
194 Vanderbilt Ave.
Norwood, MA 02062
617 440 0842
800 292 2900
617 440 0874 (Fax)

Lawson Screen Print Products
5110 Penrose St.
St. Louis, MO 63115
Branches throughout U.S.
314 382 9300
800 325 8317
314 382 3012 (Fax)

Litho-Tech
1921 E. 68th Ave.
Denver, CO 80229-7320
303 288 6837
800 537 6994
303 288 3829 (Fax)

McLogan Supply Co., Inc.
2010 S. Main St.
Los Angeles, CA 90007
(Also in San Diego)
213 749 2262
800 540 4072 (In state)
213 745 6540 (Fax)

McBee Supply
6100 Skyline Suite J
Houston, TX 77081
713 972 1388
800 622 3304
713 972 1385(Fax)

Midwest Sign & Screen Printing
45 E. Maryland Ave.
St. Paul, MN 55117
612 489 9999
800 328 6592 (US)
612 489 0202 (Fax)

Nazdar
1087 N. Northbranch St.
Chicago, IL 60622-4292
Branches throughout U.S.
312 943 8338
800 736 7636
312 943 8215 (Fax)

Neo Sign Supply Co.
6731 South Eastern
Oklahoma City OK 73149
405 672 0555
800 677 3149
405 677 1430

Northland Graphics
P.O. Box 15
Tomahawk, WI 54487
715 453 2166
800 826 0100
715 453 5507 (Fax)

Northwest Graphic Supply
4200 East Lake Street
Minneapolis, MN 55406
612 729 7361
800 221 4079
612 729 6647 (Fax)

One Stop
2935 Walkent Ct.NW
Grand Rapids, MI 49504
616 784 5400
800 968 7550
616 784 1814 (Fax)

Pan Am Supply
2525 N.W. 75th St.
Miami, FL 33147
305 691 0581
800 466 0581
305 691 0587 (Fax)

Pearl Paint
308 Canal St.
New York, NY 10013
212 431 7932
800 221 6845

Pocono Screen Supply
2 Chapel St.
Honesdale, PA 18431
717 253 6375
888 638 4835
717 235 1978 (Fax)

Joseph Podgor Co.
7055 Central Hwy.
Pennsauken, NJ 08109
609 663 7878
800 257 8226
609 663 9467 (Fax)

Printex Ink and Equipment
2123 S. Main ST.
Los Angeles, CA 90007
213 749 1270
213 749 0839 (Fax)

Printer's Source
1204 W. Mountain View Rd. #400
Johnson City, TN 37604
423 854 4557
800 865 7862
423 854 9987 (Fax)

P R Screen Print Supplies
61 Esmeralda Avenue
Ponce De Leon
Guaynabo, PR 00657
809 789 4229
809 720 5166 (Fax)

Reich Supply Company
811 Broad Street
Utica, NY 13501
315 732 6126
800 338 3322
315 732 7841(Fax)

Richardson Industries
535 Enterprise Dr.
Westerville, OH 43081
614 885 3421
800 635 7695
614 885 3725 (Fax)

Screen Printing Products
31-C Beta Court
San Ramon, CA 94583
510 855 9580
510 855 9583 (Fax)

Sericol
1101 W.Cambridge Cir.Dr.
Kansas City, KS 66110
913 342 4060
800 255 4562
913 342 4752 (Fax)

Suncoast Screen Process Supply
2080 Calumet St.
Clearwater, FL 33575
813 441 1321
800 248 3226
813 446 3923 (Fax)

Texas Screen Process Supply Co.
304 N. Walton
Dallas, TX 75226
214 748 3271
800 366 1776 (US)
214 741 6527 (Fax)

Tubelite Co., Inc.
3111 Bellbrook Dr.
P.O. Box 16456
Memphis, TN 38116
901 396 8320
800 238 5280 (US)
901 396 4648 (Fax)
  Phoenix, AZ
    602 484 0122
    800 423 0669
    602 278 2341 (Fax)
  San Leandro, CA
    510 483 8550
    800 562 4285
    510 483 8557 (Fax)
  Apopka, FL
    407 884 0477
    800 432 8526
    407 884 5571 (Fax)
  Medley, FL
    305 883 9070
    800 883 5456
    305 883 9456 (Fax)
  Indianapolis, IN
    317 352 9366
    800 634 5938
    317 352 1637 (Fax)
  Charlotte, NC
    704 875 3117
    800 438 1044
    704 875 8912 (Fax)
  Columbus, OH
    614 443 9734
    800 848 0576
    614 443 0201 (Fax)

TW Graphics Group
7220 E.Slauson
Commerce, CA 90040
213 721 1400
800 734 1704
213 724 2105 (Fax)

Victory Factory
184-10 Jamaica Ave.
Hollis, NY 11423
718 454 2255
718 454 7640 (Fax)

Washington Color & Chemical Co.
401 Evans Black Dr.
Seattle, WA 98188
206 433 8080
800 922 9210 (In state)
800 426 4938 (US)
206 433 8021 (Fax)

GARMENTS

Most garment suppliers carry a full line of imprintable items such as shirts, caps, jackets, tote bags, etc.

A & G, Inc.
2727 W. Roscoe St
Chicago, IL 60618
312 472 0800
800 654 2401 (In state)
800 621 6578 (US)
312 267 7602 (Fax)
   Santa Ana, CA
     800 225 1364
     714 662 0398

A Brand
200 E. Douglas
P.O. Box 195
Jacksonville, IL 62650
217 243 2120
800 252 6436 (In state)
800 637 4328 (US)
217 245 1600 (Fax)

A.Cramer, Inc.
99 Bartholomew Avenue
Hartford, CT 06106
203 951 2036
800 842 6789
203 951 4453 (Fax)

All Texas T's Inc.
4212 Mc Lean
Ft. Worth, TX 76117 1006
817 428 1091
800 367 2600 (US & Canada)
817 428 1092 (Fax)

Alpha Shirt Co.
4309 G.Street
Philadelphia, PA 19124
215 291 0300
800 523 4585 (US)
800 845 4970 (Fax)

The Americana Company
18150 S.Figueroa
Gardena, CA 90248
310 354 1380
800 473 2802
310 354 1386 (Fax)
   Oklahoma City, OK
     405 557 0004
     800 397 5396
     405 525 8115 (Fax)

America's T's
61 Mina Ave
Clifton, NJ 07011
404 924 1325
800 962 9362
404 345 7032 (Fax)
   Atlanta, GA
     800 962 9362

American T-Shirt Company
500 Ala Kawa Street, Bay 114
Honolulu, HI 96817
808 842 4466
808 842 1911 (Fax)

Anvil Knitwear
228 E. 45th St. 4th Floor
New York, NY 10017
212 476 0300
800 223 0332 (US)
212 476 0323 (Fax)

Atlantic Coast Cotton
7930 Notes Drive
Manassas, VA 22110
703 631 7311
800 262 5660
703 368 3527 (Fax)

Atlantic Tees, Inc.
1535 Industrial Drive
Griffin, GA 30223
404 228 0940
800 554 1079
404 228 0995 (Fax)

Aus-Tex Mfg. Co.
400 W.CHURCH
P.O.Box 637
Greenville, TN 37744
615 638 2881
800 264 4649
615 638 3906 (Fax)

Bee Jayes
1720 W. Dewey St.
Bremen, IN 46506
219 546 3731
800 348 2300
219 546 3407 (Fax)

Bodek & Rhodes
225 W.Erie Ave.
Philadelphia, PA 19140
215 425 3855
800 523 2721
215 425 0766 (Fax)

Broder Brothers
1255 La Quinta Drive
Building #130
Orlando, FL 32809
407 240 5590
800 521 0850
407 240 0978 (Fax)
   Plymouth, MI
     313 454 4800
     800 521 0850
     313 521 0851 (Fax)
   Carrolton, TX 75006
     214 242 5858
     800 521 0850
     214 242 5559 (Fax)

Cal Cru Co.,Inc
Hwy 52, P.O.Box 498
Granite Quarry, NC 28072
704 279 5526
800 476 9944 (US)
704 279 8205 (Fax)

California Shirt Sales
800 S.Raymond Ave
Fullerton, CA 92631
714 879 8570
800 289 7478
714 992 4855 (Fax)
   Oakland, CA
     510 430 0486
     800 289 7479
     510 430 9517 (Fax)
   San Diego, CA
     619 452 5051
     800 289 7481
     619 452 6177 (Fax)
   Las Vegas, NV
     702 368 3032
     800 289 7484
     702 368 4131 (Fax)
   Tempe, AZ
     602 966 7750
     800 289 7480
     602 966 0087 (Fax)
   Denver, CO303 289 5456
     800 289 7485
     303 289 3432 (Fax)
   Salt Lake City, UT
     801 977 9800
     800 289 7486
     801 973 4979 (Fax)

Carolina Made, Inc.
400 Indian Trail Road
Indian Trail, NC 28079
704 821 6425
800 222 1409
704 821 6752

Churchwell Imprintables
301-313 E.Bay Street
P.O.Box 1019
Jacksonville, FL 32201
904 356 5721
800 245 0075
904 354 2436 (Fax)

Continental Sportswear
48 Orchard St.
New York City, NY 10002
212 966 3404
800 543 5007
212 941 0438 (Fax)

Cottontops
33305 1st Way, So. B207
Federal Way, WA 98003
206 838 1733
206 874 2118 (Fax)

Davidson Mills
RT 5. Box 457
Winston-Salem, NC 27107
919 764 0092
800 638 2852 (US)

Diamond Head Tee,Inc.
1717 Homerule Street
Honolulu, HI 96819
808 847 1941
808 847 1062 (Fax)

Eisner Brothers
75 Essex Street
New York, NY 10002
212 475 6868
800 426 7700
212 475 6824 (Fax)

Eva Tees
90 Ludlow Street
New York, NY 10002
212 473 1650
800 382 8337
212 353 2910 (Fax)

F & R Sales
1720 Cumberland Pt. #2
Marietta, GA 30067
404 984 0808
800 845 1562 (US)
404 980 1604 (Fax)

F.W.Galliers Co.
25 S.Superior St.
Toledo, OH 43602
800 433 9486
800 537 0152(US)

Foremost Athletic Apparel
1307 E. Maple Rd
Troy, MI 48083
313 689 3850
800 433 9486 (US)
313 689 4653 (Fax)
 Ontario, CA 91761
  714 923 0666
  800 448 6344
  714 923 1973 (Fax)
 Carrolton, TX
  214 242 5858
  800 521 0850
  214 242 5559 (Fax)

Frank L.Robinson Company
1150 S.Flower Street
Los Angeles, CA 90015
213 748 8211
800 367 3572
213 748 5808 (Fax)

Full Line Distributors
2375 Button Gwinnett Dr.,#810
Doraville, GA 30367
404 928 7780
800 633 0654
404 928 6946 (Fax)
 Houston, TX
  713 680 1765
  800 858 9001
  713 680 2452 (Fax)
 Anaheim, CA
  714 693 2424
  800 621 4468
  714 693 0295 (Fax)
 Ambridge, PA
  412 266 4245
  800 323 3166
  412 266 4288
 Hayward, CA
  510 782 3400
  800 582 6660
  510 782 1166 (Fax)

GMP Sales Co., Inc.
49 Orchard Street
New York City, NY 10002
212 226 4340
800 833 7467 (US)
212 431 8693 (Fax)

Golden State T's
981 Stockton
San Jose, CA 95110
408 275 1144
800 892 TEES
408 275 9797 (Fax)

Good Buy Sportswear
2400 31st Street South
P. O. Box 10429
St. Petersburg, FL 33712
813 327 3773
800 282 0974 (US)
813 323 4802 (Fax)

Great American Wearhouse
6750-H jones Mill Court
Norcross, GA 30092
404 447 4660
800 241 1151
404 368 0316 (Fax)

Gulf Coast Sportswear, Inc.
605 109th St.
Arlington, TX 76017
817 640 0831
800 324 4747
817 649 8544 (Fax)

M. Handelsman Co. (Hanco)
1323 S. Michigan Ave.
Chicago, IL 60605
312 427 0784
800 621 4454
312 427 0787 (Fax)

Hanes Printables
Attn: Shirl Brooks
P. O. Box 15901
Winston-Salem, NC 27103
919 519 4562
800 685 7557
910 519 4398 (Fax)

Hawaii Print T's
916 Kaaahi Place
Honolulu, HI 96805
808 847 1967
808 847 1688 (Fax)

Heritage Sportwear, Inc.
102 Reliance Dr.
Hebron, OH 43025
614 928 7771
800 537 2222
614 345 6623 (Fax)

Indiana Tees
5110 West 76th Street
Indianapolis, IN 46268
317 872 4455
800 767 9696
317 875 9311 (Fax)

Irving Grossman & Co.
317-319 Penn Avenue
Scranton, PA 18503
717 342 3248
717 342 3240 (Fax)

J.K.Williams,Inc.
4301 S.Valley View,Unit 11
Las Vegas, NV 89103
702 364 0440
800 767 9784
702 364 0661 (Fax)

J-M Business Enterprises
2244 6th Avenue S.
P.O. Box 3955 Terminal Station
Seattle, WA 98124
206 682 8999
800 678 4200 (US)
206 623 0131 (Fax)
    Ontario, CA
        909 391 0101
        800 447 7794
        909 984 1546 (Fax)
    Richmond, CA
        510 527 7171
        800 852 0824
        510 527 1429 (Fax)

Jewel & Company
9601 Apollo Drive
Landover, MD 20785
301 925 6200
800 638 8583
800 220 7000 (Fax)

Joyce-Munden Sportswear
3735 Kimwell Drive
Winston-Salem, NC 27102
919 765 0234
800 334 8752
919 659 0200 (Fax)

Kaufenberg Enterprises
15801 Graham Street
Huntington Beach, CA 92649
714 891 0054
714 894 8380 (Fax)
    San Diego, CA
        619 571 1013
        619 571 0915 (Fax)

Kay's Enterprises,Inc.
3918 Dunvale Road
Houston, TX 77063
713 780 0808
800 848 5700
713 780 0452 (Fax)

Kayman
1333 Lowrie Ave.
S.San Francisco, CA 94080
415 589 8900
800 488 4800
415 589 5686 (Fax)
    Phoenix, AZ
        602 269 1300
        800 488 4800
        602 269 3799 (Fax)

Anaheim, CA
    714 630 1550
    800 488 4800
    714 630 5506 (Fax)
Denver, CO
    303 375 1400
    800 488 4800
    303 375 0075 (fax)
New Orleans, LA
    504 733 2100
    800 488 4800
    504 733 0665 (Fax)
East Farmingdale, NY
    516 753 2200
    800 488 4800
    516 753 2259 (Fax)

Kelley & Abide
4401 Euphrosine Street
New Orleans, LA 70125
504 822 2700
800 826 5468
504 822 2761 (Fax)

Kellsport
125 Sockanosset Crossroad
Cranston, RI 02920
401 463 7922
800 341 4600
401 463 6242 (Fax)

Kingston Textiles,Inc.
116 Kingston Street
Boston, MA 02111
617 542 8140
800 325 6657
617 482 4093 (Fax)

Leff Brothers
2505 Texas Avenue
Houston, TX 77003
713 223 4365
800 231 7211
713 223 0339 (Fax)

Light Brothers,Inc.
1108 Fifth Avenue
Pittsburg, PA 15219
412 261 3125
412 261 3138 (Fax)

Loving & Associates
409 West 78th Street
Bloomington, MN 55420
612 888 8227
800 328 5927
612 888 8706 (Fax)

Mad Rags Designs, Inc.
544 Windy Point Dr.
Glendale Heights, IL 60139
708 858 5566
800 323 1733

McCreary's Tees
4121 E.Raymond Street
Phoenix, AZ 85040
602 269 6191
800 541 1141
602 269 7138 (Fax)

Mid-America Wholesale
6000 Machester Trafficway Terr.
Kansas City, MO 64130
816 444 9993
800 366 1416 (US)
816 444 8431 (Fax)

Mid-America Tee's,Inc.
1973 Corvair Avenue
Columbus, OH 45207
614 444 5533
800 543 9713
614 444 7004 (Fax)

Midstates
P.O. Box 1153
Milwaukee, WI 53201
414 271 5648
800 558 5648
414 271 6668 (Fax)

MJ Soffe Co.
One Soffe Dr.
Fayettville, NC 28301
919 483 3953
800 444 0337
800 828 0554 (Fax)

Morris Trenk
90 Orchard Street
New York City, NY 10002
212 674 3498
800 257 2500

National Mills
808 E. Jefferson
Pittsburg, KS 66762
316 2311540
800 523 1099
316 232 2583 (Fax)

New England Sportswear
125 Perkins Avenue
Brockton, MA 02402
508 587 6161
800 782 7770
508 584 9338 (Fax)

One Stop
2935 Walkent Court,N.W.
Grand Rapids, MI 49504
616 784 5400
800 968 7550
616 784 1814(Fax)

Oneita Industries
P.O.Drawer 24, Conifer St.
Andrews, SC 29510
803 264 5225
800 7 ONEITA
803 264 4262 (Fax)

Printgear
P.O.Box 71171
N.Charleston, SC 29415
803 747 5433
800 354 9626
803 566 0407(Fax)
   Columbia, OH
     803 771 0392
     800 763 7763
     803 771 6205 (Fax)

Richards Ltd.
2018 Homerule Street
Honolulu, HI 96819
808 847 5778
808 841 1311 (Fax)

SAC Distributors
12420 73rd Court North
Largo, FL 34643
813 536 9112
800 937 8337
813 539 0752

S & S Tees
1103 Westwood Avenue
Addison, IL 60618
708 628 8855
800 523 2155
708 628 8863 (Fax)

San-Mar
P.O. Box 529
Preston, WA 98050
206 727 3230
800 426 6399
800 828 0554 (Fax)

South Carolina Tees,Inc.
P.O.Box 66
Columbia, SC 29202
803 256 1393
800 829 5000
803 771 7635 (Fax)

Southeast T-Shirt Ind.,Inc.
530 N. Beach St
P.O.Box 1970
Daytona, FL 32115
903 252 8600
800 366 8600
903 255 5967 (Fax)

Southern California Tees
P.O.Box 22204
Santa Barbara, CA 93121
805 684 0252
800 726 9001
805 684 0554 (Fax)

Sportcap, Inc.
13401 S. Main St.
Los Angeles, CA 90061
310 538 3312
800 421 5511 (US)
310 324 3898 (Fax)

St. Louis T's
2345 Chaffee Drive
St.Louis, MO 63146
314 991 5080
800 462 1960
314 991 8638 (Fax)

Star Dry Goods Company,Inc.
Turkpike Station, P.O. Box 52
Shrewsbury, MA 01545
508 845 7411
800 343 6142
508 842 7858(Fax)

Stardust
515 Commerce Parkway
Verona, WI 53593
608 845 5600
800 747 4444
608 845 5609(Fax)

Staton Wholesale - All Locations
800-888-8888
800-888-4288 (Fax)
Memphis, TN
Orlando, FL
Elkhart, IN
Baton Rouge, LA
Dayton, NJ
Nashville, TN
Austin, TX
Dallas, TX
Fort Worth, TX
San Antonio, TX

T.C.Distributors
2953 Taylor Drive
Randleman, NC 27317
919 495 7233
800 334 0051
919 495 7283 (Fax)

T-Shirt City,Inc.
4501 W.Mitchell Ave.
Cincinnati, OH 45232
   513 542 3500
   800 543 7230
   800 248 1069 (Fax)
  Ft.Meyers, FL
   813 334 7222
   800 282 9899
   813 334 8845 (Fax)
  Schenectady, NY
   518 356 6900
   800 933 8337
   518 356 4906 (Fax)
  Nashville, TN
   615 242 8383
   800 523 3579
   615 244 1855 (Fax)

Tee Jays Mfg.,Inc.
P.O.Box 2033
Florence, AL 35630
205 767 0560
800 544 8529
205 767 7178(Fax)

Tees 'N Time
10722 Hanna Street
Beltsville, MD 20705
301 937 4154
800 423 9282
301 937 2916(Fax)

Thinc Actionwear,Inc.
1930 N.E.Oregon Street
Portland, OR 97232
503 238 5972
800 841 6295
503 238 4629 (Fax)

Troy Corporation
2701 N.Normandy Avenue
Chicago, IL 60635
312 804 9600
800 888 2400
312 804 0906 (Fax)

United Enterprises,Inc.
5410 West Roosevelt Road
Chicago IL 60650
312 379 1300
800 323 5410
312 238 5410 (Fax)
  Charlotte NC
   704 588 0983
   800 438 4848
   800 237 5410 (Fax)

Virginia T's
2001 Anchor Avenue
P.O. Box 2189
Petersburg, VA 23804
804 862 2600
800 289 8099
804 862 4106 (Fax)
 Jacksonville, FL
  904 783 0884
  800 289 8099
  904 783 1113 (Fax)

Wasatch Import Co.
11000 Wright Rd.
Lynnwood, CA 90262
310 637 6160
800 228 9128
310 637 7346 (Fax)

Wellington House
19520 N.E.San Rafael
Portland, OR 97230
503 661 8693
800 234 4890
503 669 0196 (Fax)

Westark Sales
4551 Grissom #D
Bakersfield, CA 93313
805 837 0429
800 255 6359
805 837 0578 (Fax)
 Lexington, KY
  606 266 4984
  800 755 5578
  606 268 2665 (Fax)

Westark Garment Mfg.,Inc.
P.O.Box 4349, 1612 No.5th
Ft. Smith, AR 72914
501 782 9007
800 782 9007
501 782 5965 (Fax)
 Ridgefield, NJ
  800 877 4272
 Denver, CO
  800 877 4272

Whang Sports Apparel
1501 County Hospital Rd.
P.O.Box 1301
Nashville, TN 37218
615 242 9974
800 251 5102 (US)
615 255 7515 (Fax)

Wholesale Blanks
4201 N.E.12th Terrace
Ft.Lauderdale FL 33334
305 563 4433
800 331 1067
305 565 5542 (Fax)

Whole-Shot Enterprises,Inc.
11361 Sunrise Gold Circle
Rancho Cordova, CA 95742
916 635 9081
800 247 7002
916 635 7546(Fax)

Winkler Northwest, Inc.
P.O. Box 1317
Lynnwood, WA 98046
206 774 5242
800 659 WINK
206 774 6933 (Fax)

Zelinger's
P.O.Box 16447
Denver, CO 80216
303 287 7481
800 822 5520
303 287 0640 (fAX)

GENERIC CATALOGS

Alpha Shirt Co
(See Garments section)

Bodek and Rhodes
(See Garments section)

Broder Brothers
(See Garments section)

California Shirt Sales
(See Garments section)

Good Buy Sportswear
(See Garments section)

Kaymans
(See Garments section)

San-Mar
(See Garments section)

T-Shirt City, Inc.
(See Garments section)

GENERIC, PRE-PRINTED BROCHURE PAPER

Paper Direct
205 Chubb Ave.
Lyndhurst, NJ 07071
800 272 7377

Queblo
1000 Florida Ave.
Hagerstown, MD 21741
800 523 9080
800 554 8779 (Fax)

HEAT TRANSFER - Equipment and Supplies

Air Waves, Inc.
P.O. Box 26137
Columbus, OH 43226-0137
614 841 4100
800 468 7335
614 841 4141 (Fax)

Geo.Knight & Co.,Inc.
54 Lincoln St.
Brockton, MA 02403
800 525 6766
508 587 5108 (Fax)

Hix Corp.
1201 E. 27th St.
Pittsburg, KS 66762
316 231 8568
800 835 0606
316 231 1598 (Fax)

Insta Graphic Systems
13925 E. 166th St.
Cerritos, CA 90702-7900
310 404 3000
800 421 6971
310 404 3010 (Fax)

National Screen Printing Equipment
1401 N. Broadway
P.O. Box 105
Pittsburg, KS 66762
316 232 1917
800 843 3928
316 232 1941 (Fax)

Stahls', Inc.
20600 Stephens St.
St. Claire Shores, MI 48080
313 772 6161
800 521 9702
800 346 2216 (Fax)

Teletrend
1157 Claycraft Rd.
Blacklick, OH 43004
614 861 7913
800 552 8000
614 861 8155 (Fax)

Royal Foil & Transfers
5715 N.W. 84th Ave.
Miami, FL 33166
800 808c3645
305 599 1287 (Fax)

Wildside
1543 Truman St.
San Fernando, CA 91340
818 365 6789
800 421 3130
818 365 6667 (Fax)

HEALTH & SAFETY INFORMATION

J.J. Keller & Associates, Inc.
145 West Wisconsin Ave.
Neenah, WI 54956
414 722 2848
800 558 5011

Lab Safety Supply
P.O. Box 1368
Janesville, WI 53547-1368
800 356 0722 Customer Service
800 356 2501 Safety TechLine
800 543 9910 (Fax)
800 356 0783 Order Line

Safety Kleen
Nationwide
Call 800 323 5740

U.S.Screen Printing Institute
605 S. Rockford Dr.
Tempe, AZ 85281
602 929 0640
800 624 6532
602 929 0766 (Fax)

Union Ink Co., Inc.
453 Broad Avenue
Ridgefield, NJ 07657
201 945 5766
800 526 9455
201 945 4111 (Fax)

SGIA
10015 Main St.
Fairfax, VA 22031
703 385 1335
703 273 0456 (Fax)

INK MANUFACTURERS

Colonial Printing Ink Co.
180 E. Union Ave.
East Rutherford, NJ 07073
201 933 6100
800 999 INKS (In state)
800 274 4657 (US)
201 933 3129 (Fax)

Flexible Products Co.
8155 Cobb Center Dr.
Kennesaw, GA 30144
404 421 3205
800 326 0226
404 590 3625 (Fax)

International Coatings
13929 E. 166th St.
Cerritos, CA 90702-7666
310 926 0747
310 926 9486 (Fax)

J & S Ink, Co.
2290 B W. Airport Blvd.
Sanford, FL 32771
407 324 4200
800 262 3051
407 324 4144 (Fax)
  Las Vegas, NV
   800 574 6526
  Orlando, FL
   800 262 3051

The Nazdar Co.
1087 N. North Branch St.
Chicago, IL 60622-4292
312 943 8338
312 943 8215 (Fax)

Pavonine Products
a division of Union Ink Co.
316 N.Main Street
Lynchburg, OH 45142
513 364 2933
513 364 2108 (Fax)

Pearl Paint
308 Canal St.
New York, NY 10013
212 431 7932
800 221 6845

Rutland Plastics Tech,Inc.
P.O.Box 339
10021 Rodney St.
Pineville, NC 28134
704 553 0046
800 438 5134
704 552 6589

Sericol, Inc.
1101 W. Cambridge Cir Dr.
P.O. Box 2914
Kansas City, KS 66110-0914
913 342 4060
800 255 4562
913 342 4752 (Fax)
  800 255 4562 for all branches
  Kenilworth, NJ
  Anaheim, CA
  Chicago, IL
  Seattle, WA
  Atlanta, GA
  Minneapolis, MN

Union Ink Co., Inc.
453 Broad Avenue
Ridgefield, NJ 07657
201 945 5766
800 526 0455
201 945 4111 (Fax)

MAGAZINES - Airbrush

Airbrush Action
P.O. Box 3000
Denville, NJ 07834-9680
908 364 2111
908 367 5908 (Fax)

MAGAZINES - Awards & Trophies

Awards & Engraving
P.O. Box 1416
Broomfield, CO 80038
303 469 0424
303 469 5730 (Fax)

The Engravers Journal
26 Summit St.
P.O. Box 1230
Brighton, MI 48116
313 227 2614
313 229 8320 (Fax)

The Retailer
4323 N.Golden State Blvd.,#105
Fresno, CA 93722
800 832 9676
209 275 8023 (Fax)

MAGAZINES - Computer

Color Publishing
10 Tara Blvd., 5th Floor
Nashua, NH 03062
603 891 0123
603 891 0539 (Fax)

Computer Artist
P.O. Box 3188
Tulsa, OK 74101
918 831 9405
918 831 9555 (Fax)

Flash Magazine
Riddle Pond Rd.
West Topsham, VT 05086
802 439 6462
802 439 6463 (Fax)

Publish
(Desktop Publishing/Graphics)
P.O. Box 5039
Brentwood, TN 37024-9815
800 685 3435

MAGAZINES - Embroidery

Embroidery Business News
P.O. Box 5400
Scottsdale, AZ 85261
602 990 1101
602 990 0819 (Fax)

Embroidery/Monogram Business
13760 Noel Rd. #500
Dallas, TX 75240
800 527 0207

Stitches Magazine
566 Greenwood Plaza Blvd. #350
Englewood, CO 80111
303 793 0448

MAGAZINES - Miscellaneous

Step-By-Step Graphics
6000 N. Forest Park Dr.
Peoria, IL 61614-3592
309 688 2300
309 698 0831 (Fax)

MAGAZINES - Screen Printing

Impressions Magazine
13760 Noel Rd.,#500
Dallas, TX 75240
214 239 3060
800 527 0207
214 419 7825 (Fax)

Imprintables Today
P.O. Box 5400
Scottsdale, AZ 85261
602 990 1101
602 990 0819 (Fax)

Imprinting Business
3000 Hadley Rd.
South Plainfield, NJ
908 769 1160
908 769 1171(Fax)

The Press Magazine
5660 Greenwood Plaza Blvd. #350
Englewood, CO 80111
303 793 0448
303 793 0454 (Fax)

Printwear Magazine
P.O.Box 1416
Broomfield, CO 80038
303 469 0424
303 469 5730 (Fax)

Screen Print Magazine
407 Gilbert Avenue
Cincinnati, OH 45202
513 421 2050

The Trade Magazine
(West coast)
8580 Hamilton Ave.
Huntington Beach, CA 92646
714 541 9300
714 374 0371 (Fax)

MAGAZINES - Sign

Sign Business
P.O. Box 1416
Broomfield, CO 80038
303 469 0424
303 469 5730 (Fax)

MAGAZINES - Sporting Goods

Retail Focus
1699 Wall Street
Mt. Prospect, IL 60056
800 288 1600

Sport Style
7 East 12th St.
New York, NY 10003
212 630 4000

Sporting Goods Business
P.O. Box 1782
Riverton, NJ 08077-7382
800 964 9494

Sports Trend
6255 Barfield Rd., #200
Atlanta, GA 30328-4300
404 252 8831

Team Sports Business Magazine
P.O. Box 5400
Scottsdale, AZ 85261
602 990 1101
602 990 0819 (Fax)

MAILING LISTS

American Business Lists
P.O.Box 27347
Omaha, NE 68127
402 331 7169
402 331 1505 (Fax)

MISC. IMPRINTABLES

Bag Works,Inc.
Ste.A, 3933 California Pkwy.E.
Ft.Worth, TX 76119
817 536 3892
800 365 7423
800 678 7364 (Fax)

NUMBERING STENCILS

Dalco Athletic Lettering Co.
P.O.Box 550220
Dallas, TX 75355-0220
214 494 1455
800 288 3252 (US)
214 276 9608

Sericol
1101 W.Cambridge Cir.Dr.
Kansas City, KS 66110
913 342 4060
800 255 4562
913 342 4752

Sports I.D., Inc
9703 M-89, P.O. Box 619
Richland, MI 49083
800 435 4384
616 629 4995 (Fax)

PUBLICATIONS & BOOKS

Airbrush Action
P.O. Box 3000
Dept. MM
Denville, NJ 07834-9680
908 364 2111
908 367 5908 (Fax)

ST Publications
407 Gilbert Ave.
Cincinnati, OH 45202
513 421 2050
513 421 5144 (Fax)

Union Ink Company, Inc.
453 Broad Ave.
Ridgefield, N.J. 07657
201 945 5766
800 526 0455
201 945 4111 (Fax)

U.S. Screen Printing Institute
605 S. Rockford Dr.
Tempe, AZ 85281
602 929 0640
800 624 6532
602 929 0766 (Fax)

SCHOOLS & TRAINING

Rochester Institute of Technology
College of Imaging Science
P.O. Box 9887
One Lomb Memorial Dr.
Rochester, NY 14623
716 475 5000

Screen Printing Technical Foundation
10015 Main St.
Fairfax, VA 22031-3489
703 385 1417

U.S. Screen Printing Institute
605 S. Rockford Dr.
Tempe, AZ 85281
602 929 0640
800 624 6532
602 929 0766 (Fax)

SCREEN CLEANING SYSTEMS

Albatross USA, Inc.
36-41 36th St.
Long Island City, NY 11106
800 233 4468
718 392 2899 (Fax)

FranMar Chemical
P. O. Box 97
Normal, IL 61761
309 452 7526
800 538 5069
309 862 1005

Safety Kleen
Nationwide. Call 1-800-323-5740
for closest dealer.

SCREEN FRAMES -
Prestretched

Irish Graphic Products Intl.
250 Tech Way
Grants Pass, OR 97526
503 476 8818
800 247 3977
503 479 1147 (Fax)

Pocono Screen Supply
2 Chapel St.
Honesdale, PA 18431
717 253 6375
888 638 4835
717 235 1978 (Fax)

Silk Screen Frames
1186 Westar Lane
Burlington, WA 98233
360 757 2102
800 574 3477
360 757 4417

Victory Factory
184-10 Jamaica Ave.
Hollis, NY 11423
718 454 2255
718 454 7640 (Fax)

SCREEN FRAMES -
Retensionable

Diamond Chase Company
5162 Oceanus Dr.
Huntington Beach, CA 92649
714 891 3234
714 894 8723(fax)

HIX Corp.
1201 E.27th St.
Pittsburg, KS 66762
316 231 8568
800 835 0606
316 231 1598

Stretch Devices, Inc.
(Newman Roller Frame)
3401 N. I. St.
Philadelphia, PA 19134
215 739 3000
215 739 3011(Fax)

SOURCE DIRECTORIES

Reed Elsevier Company
The Salesman's Guide
RN/WPL Directory
121 Chanlon Rd.
New Providence, NJ 07974
908 464 6800
800 521 8110
908 665 3560 (Fax)

SUBLIMATION EQUIPMENT &
SUPPLIES

Geo.Knight & Co.,Inc.
54 Lincoln St.
Brockton, MA 02403
800 525 6766
508 587 5108 (Fax)

Nova Chrome
3347 Vincent Rd.
Pleasant Hill, CA 94523
510 934 3368
800 788 6682
510 934 7128 (Fax)

Stahl's Lettering
20600 Stephens St.
St.Claire Shores, MI 48080
313 772 6161
800 521 9702
313 521 9702 (Fax)

Xpres Systems
21424 N. Seventh Ave. #10
Phoenix, AZ 85027
602 580 9720
800 995 3242
602 580 9062 (Fax)

Xpres Corp.
111 Cloverleaf Dr.
Winston-Salem, NC 27103
919 768 7400
800 334 0425
919 768 4629

TRADE ORGANIZATIONS

Advertising Specialty Institute
1120 Wheeler Way
Langhorne, PA 19047
800 326 7378
800 829 9240 (Fax)

Embroidery Trade Association
745 N.Gilbert Road, #124-201
Gilbert, AZ 85234
602 497 1274
800 584 7918
602 892 0860 (Fax)

Graphic Artists Guild
11 West 20th St., 8th FL
New York, NY 10011-3704
212 463 7730

Graphic Arts Technical Foundation
4615 Forbes Ave.
Pittsburg, PA 15213
412 621 6941

National Sporting Goods Association
1699 Wall Street
Mt. Prospect, IL 60056
800 288 1600

Personalization Institute
4323 N. Golden State Blvd., #105
Fresno, CA 93722
800 832 9676
209 275 8023 (Fax)

Rochester Institute of Technology
College of Imaging Service
P.O.Box 9887
One Lomb Memorial Drive
Rochester, NY 14623
716 475 5000

Screenprinting & Graphic Imaging Assoc.
10015 Main St.
Fairfax, VA 22031
703 385 1335
703 273 0456 (Fax)

Society of Glass and Ceramic Decorators
888 17th St. N.W., Suite 600
Washington, D.C. 200006
202 728 4132

Speciality Advertising Association
International
3125 Skyway Circle N.
Irving, TX 75038
214 252 0404

Technical Association of the Graphic Arts
P.O.Box 9887
Rochester, NY 14623
716 475 7470

TRADE SHOWS

APEX
Apparel Printing and Embroidery Expo
55 E. Jackson, #1100
Chicago, IL 60604-4188
303 220 4286

Embroidery Expo
P.O. Box 5400
Scottsdale, AZ 85261
602 990 1101
602 990 0819 (Fax)

The Imprinted Sportswear Show
P.O.Box 801402
Dallas, TX 75380
214 239 3060
800 527 0207
214 419 7825 (Fax)

Miller-Freeman
(International Trade Shows)
P.O.Box 801402
Dallas, TX 75380
214 239 3060
800 527 0207
214 419 7825 (Fax)

Sports Expo
National Sporting Goods Association
International
1699 Wall Street
Mt. Prospect, IL 60056
800 288 1600

Screen Graphics & Printwear Shows
P.O.Box 1416
Broomfield, CO 80038
303 469 0424
303 469 5730 (Fax)

Screen Print Show
10015 Main St.
Fairfax, VA 22031-3489
703 385 1335
703 273 0456 (Fax)

Super Show
Sporting Goods Mfg. Association
1450 N.E. 123rd St.
N. Miami, FL 33161
407 842 4100

Imprinted T-Shirt & Actionwear Show
3000 Hadley Rd.
South Plainfield, NJ 07080
908 769 1160
908 769 1171 (Fax)

VIDEO TAPES

Airbrush Action
P.O. Box 3000
Dept. MM
Denville, NJ 07834-9680
908 364 2111
908 367 5908 (Fax)

Screenprinting & Graphic Imaging Asoc.
10015 Main St.
Fairfax, VA 22031
703 385 1335
703 273 0456 (Fax)

ST Publications
407 Gilbert Ave.
Cincinnati, OH 45202
513 421 2050
513 421 5144 (Fax)

U.S.Screen Printing Institute
605 S. Rockford Dr.
Tempe, AZ 85281
602 929 0640
800 624 6532
602929 0766 (Fax)

FOREIGN SUPPLIERS

MAGAZINES

ASIA
Asia Pacific Sign
United Promotions & Publications
46A Horne Road
Singapore 0820
Tel: (65) 2989528
Fax: (65) 2924625

AUSTRALIA
Screen Printer Magazine
Cygnet Publications Pty Ltd.
P.O. Box 1389
West Perth, Western Australia
Australia 6005
61 8 (08) 9322 1168
61 8 (08) 9321 2602 (Fax)

BRAZIL
Silk-Screen
Sao Paulo
Brazil
55 11 941 3400

CANADA
Imprint Canada
3883 Hwy. 7, Suite 214
Woodbridge, Ontario L4L 6C1
905 856 2600
905 856 2667 (Fax)

ENGLAND
Images Magazine
9a Kings Road
Flitwick, Bedfordshire MK45 1ED
01525718890
01525718026 (Fax)

INDIA
Screen Print India
Aditya Publication
Bismillah Building
4th Floor, Room No. 56
Ranade Road
Opp. Dadar (W.R) Station
Bombay 400 028
Tel: 430 3053
Fax: (91) 22 287 4212
Tix: 011-82959 "VYAS IN"

MEXICO
Screen Printing En Espanol
ST Publications
407 Gilbert Ave.
Cincinnati, OH 45202
513 421 2050
513 421 5144 (Fax)

NETHERLANDS
Silkscreen
Uitgeverij Eisma BV
Archimedesweg 20
Postbus 340
8901 BC Leeuwarden (NL)
31 58 152545
31 58 154000 (Fax)

LICENSING - Foreign
International Licensing Directory
A4 Publications Ltd.
Press House, PO Box 12
Church Road
Woldingham Surrey CR3 7YE
Great Britain

SUPPLIERS

CANADA
Behnsen Graphic Supplies
1016 Richards St.
Vancouver, BC
Canada V6B 3B9
604 681 7351
800 663 1215
604 681 6185 (Fax)

Createx
88 Parkland Drive Moncton
New Brunswick, Canada
E1A 3S5
506 383 1563

Discovery Lancer Group
311 Saulteaux Crescent
Winnipeg, Manitoba R3J 3C7
204 889 7422
204 897 3663 (Fax)

Discovery Lancer Group
1-145 Riviera Drive
Markham, Ontario L3R 5J6
905 470 0744
905 470 9454 (Fax)

Graphiques Cosmex Ltee.
491 Deslauriers Street
Ville St-Laurent
Quebec H4N 1W2 Canada
514 745 3446
514 745 3449 (Fax)

Kellsport
5683 CH St.Francois
Montreal, Quebec
Canada H4S 1W6
514 333 3100
800 341 4600
514 333 1845 (Fax)

Metro Graphic Supply
3780 Nopier Street
Burnaby, BC V5C 3E5
604 294 3444
800 294 3468

San Mar - Canada
5949 Ambler Drive
Mississauga , Ontario
Canada L4W 2K2
416 602 6411   800 668 0899
416 602 6435 (Fax)

San Mar - Canada
13120 Bath Gate Place
Richmond, BC
Canada V6V 1Z2
604 273 9101
800 663 2335
604 273 2261 (Fax)

Techno Sport Quebec,Inc.
5-3000 Rue Watt
Sainte Foy, Quebec
Canada G1X 3Y8
418 653 9203
800 463 4456
418 653 4167 (Fax)

Zelco Screen Industries
1907 Triumph Street
Vancouver, BC V5L 1K6 Canada
604 251 5500
604 251 6565 (Fax)

ARGENTINA
Vortex Argentina SA
Riglos 855 Capital Federal
CP1424, Buenos Aires, Argentina
541 925 0044
541 924 2948 (Fax)

AUSTRALIA
Sias Screen Printing
Products Pty.Ltd.
11 Melrose Ct.
Tullamarine,Victoria 3043
03 330 1122
03 335 2592 (Fax)

CHILE
Texur S.A.
S.A. De Productos Para
La Industria Textil Del Sur
Av.Pdte, Edo, Freim. 1751
Casilla 27011 Santiago,Chile
2 737 4117
2 737 4117 (Fax)

DENMARK
Skanflow
Brorupvej 71
Kattrup
8732 Hovedgard
4575662095
4575662094 (Fax)

FRANCE
Sorim Sarl
Z.A.E. Heiden
2 Rue d'Allemagne
F-68310 Wittelsheim
89 57 70 11
89 55 28 30 (Fax)

GERMANY
PROLL GmBH & Co.
Postfach 429
Treuchtlinger Strasse 29
D-8832 Weissenburg 1Bay
141 9060
141 90649 (Fax)

GREECE
A.Kaligos & Co.
P.O.Box 64
95A Papanastasiou St.
544 53 Thessaloniki 920 358
462 243 (Fax)

GUATEMALA
Zimegraph
Av.Bolivar 21-46
Zona 1
Guatmala C.A.
517433
741490 (Fax)

HONG KONG
Grace Screen Supplies Ltd.
Block A Newport Center,3/F
118 Ma Tau Kok Road
Kowloon
362 3060
764 9002 (Fax)

Lancer Group Far East Ltd.
Rm L, 5/F Camelpaint Building
60 Hoi Yuen Road
Kwun Tong, Kowloon
(852)27908313 6
(852)2341 1235 (Fax)

INDIA
Sunglo India Pvt.Ltd.
A/6,Neelam Centre
S.K.Ahire Marg, Worli
Bombay 400025
22 494 8449
22 492 6887 (Fax)

IRELAND
D.O'Sullivan's Print Supplies
Knocksmitten Lane
Western Ind.East
Dublin 12
353 1565788
353 1566326 (Fax)

ISRAEL
Arta Art Graphics Supply
83 Nachlat Binyamin St.
P.O.Box 606
Tel Aviv 61001
03 560 1921
03 560 9722 (Fax)

Target Media & Training
Ghaleb B Akari
P.O. Box 51371
Jerusalem, Israel
02 9958504
02 9958504 (Fax)

ITALY
L.Lamberti S.P.A.
Via Piave 18
21041 Albizzate
0331 986 111
0331 991 212 (Fax)

JAPAN
Yoshikawa Chemical Co.Ltd.
6-27,!-Chome,Kyutaro-Mach
Chuo-Ku, Osaka 541
266 2251
266 2254 (Fax)
Yoshikawa Chemical Co.Ltd.
2-11 Kanda Tsukasa-Cho
Chiyoda-Ku, Tokyo

MALAYSIA
Khai Lien Silk Screen Suppliers
132 Jalan Selar Taman Bukit
Ria, Batu3-1/2 Jalan
Cheras 56100
Kula Lumpur
603 983 7032
603 985 1035 (Fax)

MEXICO
Cosmografica S.A.de C.V.
Norte-45 No.789
Col.Industrial Vallejo
Apartado Postal M-25,86
02300 Mexico D.F
023 24 8131
023 24 7862 (Fax)

NETHERLANDS
Fosfan Products (NZ)
P.O.Box 13035
Onehunga, Auckland
09 579 9576
09 579 9561 (Fax)

NEW ZEALAND
Seritech Ltd.
Unit 2, 91 Shakespeare Rd.
Christchurch, NZ
03 366 2214
03 366 2454 (Fax)

NORWAY
Sandberg & Co. A/S
Aslakveien 20
0753 OSLO 7
02 50 7700
02 52 3623 (Fax)

PUERTO RICO
Yaguez Trading
CARR.No.2 KM 158.8
Frente Res. Sultana Mayaguez, P.R.
00681
809 832 4330

REPUBLIC OF CHINA
Lancer Group China
Room 814 Jinzhong Mansion
No. 37 Dajinzhong Rd.
Guangzhou, Peoples Republic of China
PC 510405
(86)020 86363130
(86) 020 86578756

SINGAPORE
Union Inks & Graphics Pte.Ltd.
No.23 Defu Lane 6 1953
283 8133
283 8122 (Fax)

SOUTH AFRICA
Color Screen
P.O.Box 20992
Durban North
S.A. 4016
31 579 4104
31 579 4197 (Fax)

SPAIN
Seri Service S.L.
c/Treball 70-88
Nave 6
08019 Barcelona
343 266 0780
343 266 1459 (Fax)

SWEDEN
K.E.Levin
Screenmaskiner A/B
Box 9
61053 Enstaberga
01 555 7700
01 555 7685

TAIWAN R.O.C.
Ringhotex Co.Ltd.
P.O.Box 440
Pan Chiao,Taipei
253 6861
253 5144 (Fax)

THAILAND
P.S.I.Marketing Co.Ltd.
53 Soi Ramkamheang 14
Huamark Bangkok 10240
314 7145
318 7625 (Fax)

UNITED ARAB EMIRATES
George & Rubaih Trading
P.O.Box 8340
Dubai
284 455
235 158 (Fax)

UNITED KINGDOM
John T.Keep & Sons Ltd.
P.O.Box 78 Croydon Road
Beckenham Kent BR3 4BL
081 658 7723
081 658 8672 (Fax)

Easy-to-use Information Order Form

It's simple to get information sent to you from the suppliers list. Just copy the letter below onto your **letterhead** or a postcard with your return address. Mail or fax it to the suppliers you are interested in. You can also just copy the listings in the book and tape these to your request as a mailing label. For the best response contact the suppliers in your area and the major manufacturers for their dealer or distributor listing. Remember: you will get better response from a supplier if your request for information looks professional!

The following is a sample letter you can use:

To: _____

Address:_____

City:_____State:_____Zip:_____

Fax:_____

Dear Supplier;

We saw a listing for your products in the book by Scott and Pat Fresener called *How To Print T-Shirts for Fun and Profit*. Please send us a complete catalog of your products and services. Thank you in advance for your prompt response to this request.

We Want To Let You Know What's New

We are constantly adding new products and classes and want to put you on our mailing list. In order to receive more information from us simply send or fax this form back.

Thanks!

Fax or Mail to:
> Scott and Pat Fresener
> U.S. Screen Printing Institute
> 605 S. Rockford Dr.
> Tempe, Az. 85281
> Fax: (602)929-0766

From:
> Company:_____
> Contact:_____
> Address:_____
> City:_____State:_____ Zip:_____
> Phone:_____ Fax:_____

Where did you buy this book?_____

Have you started to print yet?_____

Do you want to receive a full catalog?_____

SGIA International Is Your Leading Source of Information and Education...

Regardless of your production specialty — whether you're a small shop owner or part of a large corporation — Screenprinting & Graphic Imaging Association International offers services tailored to your specific needs. We devote our efforts and resources to addressing your special production interests:

- Ad Specialties
- Binders
- Ceramics & Glass
- Compact Discs
- Containers & 3-D Objects
- Decals & Labels
- Digital Imaging
- Electronics
- Embroidery
- Fine Art & Serigraphs
- Membrane Switches
- Nameplates, Dials, Gauges & Panels
- Pad Printing
- POP & Displays
- Signs & Posters
- Textiles
- *And Much More*

The Association's **NEW STRATEGIC SERVICES** help you succeed in a changing world by providing the vital information you need ... quickly, efficiently and cost-effectively!

- **Improve your processes and expand your production capabilities by using the latest ideas and techniques.** You'll discover valuable, product-specific information in the Association's acclaimed *Technical Guidebook* and in-depth technical, managerial and regulatory information in the new *SGIA Journal* complete with innovative methods to help your business succeed.

- **Save valuable time and money by reducing expensive downtime.** You get immediate access to SGIA's ASSIST Hotline — providing specific answers and practical solutions to your real world problems. Plus, you can access SGIA's *FastFAQ*, an ever-growing list of easy to read answers to frequently asked questions, available on the members-only area of SGIA's website.

- **Identify new business opportunities and markets as you network with your colleagues.** SGIA'98 in Kansas City, October 7-10, is a great place to meet over 14,000 professionals from around the globe. And *Who's Who in SGIA International,* our annual membership directory, makes it easy to contact the industry's finest.

- **Save money on equipment, supplies and services.** SGIA International makes it easy to shop around for the best price and service. With the help of your free *Buyer's Guide,* over 1,000 industry manufacturers, distributors and consultants are as close as your telephone.

- **Generate a steady supply of fresh ideas to boost your company's bottom line.** That's what SGIA International membership is all about...giving you the information you need to make profitable decisions!

Now Everyone Can Participate!

Everyone in your company can keep up-to-date with industry developments and receive all of SGIA International's many benefits by becoming an Additional Contact member. An unlimited number of your company's employees can enroll as Additional Contacts for a reduced membership investment fee of just $95 each in the United States and $125 internationally.

For more details, please refer to Chart B at the right or contact the membership department.

SGIA International Membership Investment Information

Chart A — Membership Investment Schedule

The annual SGIA International membership investment is based on gross annual sales. The annual investment can be calculated using this chart.

Annual Gross Sales Volume

• Printer	United States	International
Less Than $150,000	$300	$200
$150,000 to $249,999	$300	$250
$250,000 to $499,999	$450	$300
$500,000 to $999,999	$600	$350
$1,000,000 to $2,999,999	$700	$400
$3,000,000 plus	$800	$450
• In-Plant Printer	$350	$275

If you are a full-time Educator, please contact SGIA International headquarters for additional information concerning Educational Institution membership.

All fees are shown in US dollars.

Send form and payment to:
**Screenprinting & Graphic Imaging Association International
10015 Main Street
Fairfax, VA 22031-3489 USA**

Investment includes annual subscription US–$30 or International–$35 to the *Tabloid* and annual subscription US–$50 or International–$55 to the *SGIA Journal.*

Chart B — Additional Contacts

United States: $95   International: $125

Individuals of member companies desiring to be an additional contact can receive mailings for a reduced annual fee. Additional contacts receive the same member benefits as the primary contact. Additional contacts cannot be *to separate corporations* even though they are affiliated with the member company. **Indicate full name and address for each additional contact on a separate sheet and attach to the application.**

Geographical restriction for additional contact mailings:

- US members can have additional contacts in the US only.
- International members cannot have additional contacts in the US.

Chart C — Membership Plaque — $40

The universally-recognized insignia on SGIA International's Member Plaque will proudly display your affiliation and make known your dedication to the industry. Membership plaque prices include surface mail.

SGIA Affiliations

Organizations located in Australia, China, Japan, Philippines, South Africa and South Korea must hold membership in their respective national association in order to be accepted for SGIA International membership. For national membership application, dues scale and services information, please make inquiry to the address shown: **Australia:** SCREENPRINTING & GRAPHIC IMAGING ASSOCIATION OF AUSTRALIA INC, 77 Lithgow St, PO Box 58, St Leonards, NSW 2065; **China:** SCREEN PRINTING & GRAHPIC IMAGING ASSOCIATION CHINESE, A36 Qianliang Hutong, Eastern District, Beijing 100010; **Japan:** SCREENPRINTING & GRAPHIC IMAGING ASSOCIATION OF JAPAN, 4-36-12 Hakusan, Bunkyo-ku, Tokyo 112; **Philippines:** SCREENPRINTING & IMAGING GRAPHIC ASSOCIATION OF THE PHILIPPINES, Units 102-103, Integrated Professional Offices Bldg, 14 Quezon Avenue, Bgy. Josefa, Quezon City; **South Africa:** SOUTH AFRICAN SCREEN PRINTING ASSOCIATION, P.O. Box 1084 Honeydew 2040, Printech Avenue, Laser Park; **South Korea:** KOREA SCREEN PRINTING INDUSTRIAL COOPERATIVE, Korea Federation of Small Business Building RM 605, 16-2 Youido Dong, Youngdeungpo-Gu, Seoul, 150-010; SCREEN PRINTING ASSOCIATION OF KOREA, Sam-Poong Bldg, Room 1305, 310-68, 4-Ka, Ulchi-Ro, Chung-ku, Seoul 100-194

Compliments of How To Print T-Shirts for Fun and Profit!

Screenprinting & Graphic Imaging Association International
10015 Main Street, Fairfax, VA 22031-3489 USA

Phone: (703) 385-1335, Fax: (703) 273-0456

E-mail: sgia@sgia.org   Internet: http://www.sgia.org

SGIA

US Fed. ID # 36-2147323

PRINTER MEMBERSHIP APPLICATION

Distributors and Manufacturers, please contact headquarters for membership application.

1. Membership Information (please type or print)

Date _____   No. of Employees _____

Company _____

Name   Mr Ms Mrs   _____
      Circle one   to whom mailings will be addressed

Title _____

Street Address _____

P.O. Box _____City _____

State/Province _____

Country _____ Zip/Mail Code _____

Telephone _____

Fax _____

E-mail address _____

Web address_____

2. Membership Category Definition — Choose one

☐ **Printer**—Any private or commercial firm or organization engaged in the production and/or sale of products produced by graphic imaging.

☐ **In-Plant Printer**—Any graphic imaging operation that: (a) has no commercial graphic sales; and (b) is an imaging applications department or captive operation, which uses the graphic imaging processes in a non-commercial application or (c) is a manufacturer that uses graphic imaging processes as but one of the manufacturing steps for completion of its own products and/or product identification.

3. Production Specialty – Check all that apply

☐ Decal

☐ Industrial Imaging — *Ad Specialties, Binders, Ceramics & Glass, Compact Discs, Containers & 3-D Objects, Electronics, Nameplates, Pad Printing, Panels*

☐ Membrane Switch

☐ Signage & Display — *Banners, Billboards, Fine Art & Serigraphs, POP Displays, Posters, Signs*

☐ Textile — *Caps, Embroidery, Garments, Transfers*

☐ Other _____

4. SGIA International Membership Invoice (must be completed)

Please note the different membership investment rates for US and International members. The various fees for SGIA International membership are listed on the facing page. Please refer to the investment schedule to determine the proper fees for your organization.

Membership Type   ☐ US   ☐ International

| US$ _____ | **A.** Enter appropriate annual investment for membership (See chart A on facing page) |

| US$ _____ | **B.** Additional Contacts (Optional) (See chart B on facing page) |

| US$ _____ | **C.** Membership Plaque $40 (Optional) |

| US$ _____ | **Total Enclosed** Make checks payable to Screenprinting & Graphic Imaging Association International. There will be a US$20 charge for any check returned unpaid by the bank. |

All membership funds must be payable in U.S. currency.

Credit Card Payment

Join by Phone—SGIA International invites you to join via telephone by placing your investment fee on your credit card account. Please have this form and your card at hand when you call the Membership Department at 703-385-1335.

☐ Visa/Mastercard   ☐ Discover   ☐ American Express

Card Number: _____

Expiration Date _____

Name: _____
       Print as appears on card

Card Holder's
Signature: _____

By joining SGIA International, I hereby authorize the Association to send me all appropriate material by mail, fax or other appropriate delivery method.

5. Production Specialty Listing

Membership includes a listing in the SGIA International Membership Directory with your company's production. Use the computer grid below to enter your specialty, using 175 spaces or less, to facilitate computer searching for sales leads. Be specific and complete.

Examples *(you aren't limited by examples)*: pressure sensitives, fleet markings, water decals, signs, displays, banners, flags, T-shirts, 24 sheet posters, heat transfers, dials, panels, circuit boards, glassware, chemical milling, flocking, injection molding, four-color process, UV curing, etc.

Note: Rates and membership investment are those in effect as of September 27, 1997, and are subject to change. Membership fees to the Screenprinting & Graphic Imaging Association International are deductible for USA tax purposes as a business expense to the graphics industry, but are not deductible as charitable contributions. Forms printed October, 1997.

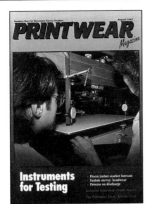

PLACE
STAMP
HERE

SCREENPRINTING
407 GILBERT AVE
CINCINNATI OH 45273-9441

PLACE
STAMP
HERE

SCREENPRINTING
en español
407 GILBERT AVE
CINCINNATI OH 45273-9441

SCREEN EXPOSURE CHART

MESH		DIRECT EMULSION				CAPILLARY DIRECT FILM					DESIGN			LIGHT SOURCE	EXPOSURE TIME
COUNT	COLOR	TYPE	BRAND	COLOR	COATING TECHNIQUE	TYPE	THICKNESS	BRAND	COLOR	WITH EMULSION	AVERAGE	DETAILED			

FOR CONSISTENT SCREEN MAKING — Fill Out Completely For All Variables and Post in Screen Making Department or Put in Binder

(LOGO, NAME, ADDRESS, PHONE)   **WORK ORDER**

COMPANY NAME: _____   INVOICE NO. _____

ADDRESS: _____   JOB NO. _____

TELEPHONE: _____   *ATTACH SEPARATE IMPRINT*

CUSTOMER: _____   *SPECIFICATION SHEET IF MORE*

JOB NAME: _____   *INFORMATION NEEDED.*

FOR GARMENT STYLE AND SIZES SEE SALES ORDER

ARTWORK   **FRONT**   **BACK**
____ EXISTING DESIGN-JOB NO. _____
____ CAMERA READY SUPPLIED
____ ORIGINAL ARTWORK NEEDED
____ CUSTOMER TO APPROVE
____ COLOR SEPARATIONS REQUIRED
____ TOUCH-UP NEEDED
____ ART OR SKETCH ATTACHED
____ COPYRIGHT NEEDED
SPECIAL INSTRUCTIONS: _____
_____
_____

NO. CAMERA SHOTS: _____
ART TIME: _____   DESIGN SIZE _____   DESIGN SIZE _____
OTHER COSTS: _____   LOCATION _____   LOCATION _____

INK, SCREENS AND SQUEEGEES

NO. COLORS	INK TYPE	COLOR	ADDITIVES	COLOR MATCH	FRAME SIZE	MESH	COLOR SEQUENCE	COLOR LOCATION	SQUEEGEE	SCREEN NUMBER
1.										
2.										
3.										
4.										
5.										
6.										

INK SPECIAL INSTRUCTIONS:

____ HOLD FOR RE-ORDER   ____ DIRECT FILM
____ RECLAIM   ____ OTHER _____
____ RE-ORDER SCREENS ON FILE
____ NO. OF RE-MAKES   ____ WATER RESISTANT
____ DIRECT EMULSION   ____ REINFORCE FOR LONG RUN

PRINTING
____ PRESS NUMBER   ____ NO. OF WORKERS
____ MANUAL   ____ SET-UP TIME
____ AUTOMATIC   ____ TEAR-DOWN TIME
____ ACTUAL PRODUCTION TIME   ____ ESTIMATED PRODUCTION TIME
JOB COMMENTS:

NO OF REJECTS: _____

PACKAGING AND SPECIAL INSTUCTIONS
____ BULK FOLD   ____ CUSTOMERS LABEL
____ INDIVIDUAL FOLD   ____ CUSTOMERS PRICE
____ POLY BAG/INDIVIDUAL   ____ CUSTOMER TO APPROVE SAMPLE
____ POLY BAG/½ DOZ.

ORDER DATE _____
DUE DATE _____
TIME _____ A.M.   P.M.

QUALITY CONTROL
ART APPROVED BY _____   PRODUCTION MANAGER _____
SCREENS APPROVED BY _____   PRINTED BY _____
PRINTING APPROVED BY _____   SHIFT _____ DATE _____
FINAL ORDER COUNT _____

JOB # _____

CUSTOMER NAME _____

ADDRESS _____

CITY _____ STATE _____ ZIP _____

PHONE _____ CONTACT _____

JOB ENVELOPE

JOB DESCRIPTION _____

SCREEN NO(S)   _____

                     _____

                     _____

                     _____

                     _____

FIRST ORDER DATE   _____

RE-ORDER DATE   _____

                     _____

                     _____

                     _____

                     _____

**FILE WITH COPY OF WORK ORDER, IMPRINT SPECIFICATION SHEET,
FILM & OVERLAY ENVELOPE, CUSTOMER SUPPLIED ART AND SAMPLE PRINT**

SCREEN STORAGE LOG

PAGE _____

SCREEN NUMBER	CUSTOMER NAME	JOB NAME	MESH	COLOR

LETTERING WORK ORDER

COMPANY NAME *(GROUP, SCHOOL, CLUB, TEAM)*

ADDRESS

CITY   **STATE**   **ZIP CODE**

TELEPHONE NUMBER

WORKORDER OR JOB NO.

ORDER DATE   **DUE DATE**

CONTACT NAME

SAMPLE LETTERING OR PRINTING LOCATIONS

FRONT	BACK

INK COLOR _____   *INK COLOR* _____

	GRMT. STYLE	GRMT. COLOR	DESCRIPTION	NAME	NAME LOC	NUMBER	NO. LOC	SCREEN PRINT	S.P. LOC.
1.									
2.									
3.									
4.									
5.									
6.									
7.									
8.									
9.									
10.									
11.									
12.									
13.									
14.									
15.									
16.									
17.									
18.									
19.									
20.									

LOCATION KEY: FR-FRONT: BK-BACK; F/B-FRONT; RC-RIGHT CHEST; LC-LEFT CHEST
CHECK ALL SPELLING, NUMBERS AND SIZES THOROUGHLY

DRYER TEMPERATURE CHART

SUBSTRATE		INK		SETTINGS			ATTAINED TEMPERATURE		OTHER VARIABLES				
MATERIAL	COLOR	TYPE	COLOR	ELEMENT TEMP.	FORCED AIR	BELT SPEED	AT BELT WITH AIR	WITHOUT AIR	TIME OF DAY	INPUT VOLTAGE	TIME OF YEAR	ELEMENT HEIGHT	OTHER

FOR CONSISTENT CURING AND DRYING — Fill Out All Information and Post Near Dryer or Place on Dryer

Temperature Conversion Table

C°	F°	C°	F°	C°	F°	C°	F°
−75	−103	40	104	155	311	537.8	1000
−73.3	−100	43.3	100	160	320	550	1022
−70	−94	45	113	165	329	593.3	1100
−67.8	−90	48.9	120	165.6	330	600	1112
−65	−85	50	122	170	338	648.9	1200
−62.2	−80	54.4	130	171.1	340	650	1202
−60	−76	55	131	175	347	700	1292
−56.7	−70	60	140	176.7	350	704.4	1300
−55	−67	65	149	180	356	750	1382
−51.1	−60	65.6	150	182.2	360	760	1400
−50	−58	70	158	185	365	800	1472
−45.6	−50	71.1	160	187.8	370	815.6	1500
−45	−49	75	167	190	374	850	1562
−40	−40	76.7	170	193.3	380	871.1	1600
−35	−31	80	176	195	383	900	1652
−34.4	−30	82.2	180	198.9	390	926.7	1700
−30	−22	85	185	200	392	950	1742
−28.9	−20	87.8	190	204.4	400	982.2	1800
−25	−13	90	194	225	437	1000	1832
−23.3	−10	93.3	200	232.2	450	1037.8	1900
−20	−4	95	203	250	482	11050	1922
−17.8	0	98.9	210	260	500	1093.3	2000
−15	5	100	212	275	527	1100	2012
−12.2	10	104.4	220	287.8	550	1148.9	2100
−10	14	105	221	300	572	1150	2102
−6.7	20	110	230	315.6	600	1200	2192
−5	23	115	239	325	617	1204.4	2200
−1.1	30	115.6	240	343.3	650	1250	2282
0	32	120	248	350	662	1260	2300
4.4	40	121.1	250	371.1	700	1300	2372
5	41	125	257	375	707	1315.6	2400
10	50	126.7	260	398.9	750	1350	2462
15	59	130	266	400	752	1371.1	2500
15.6	60	132.2	270	425	797	1400	2552
20	68	135	275	426.7	800	1426.7	2600
21.1	70	137.8	280	450	842	1500	2732
25	77	140	284	454.4	850	1537.8	2800
26.7	80	143.3	290	475	887	1550	2822
30	86	145	293	482.2	900	1593.3	2900
32.2	90	148.9	300	500	932	1600	2912
35	95	150	302	510	950	1648.9	3000
37.8	100	154.4	310	525	977	1650	3002

NOTE: $F° = (C° \times 9/5) + 32$; $C° = (F° - 32) \times 5/9$

METRIC CONVERSION TABLE
UNITS OF MEASURE

INCHES/CENTIMETERS						FEET/METERS					
1 to 50			51 to 100			1 to 50			51 to 100		
Inches		Centimeters	Inches		Centimeters	Feet		Meters	Feet		Meters
0.3937	1	2.54	20.079	51	129.54	3.281	1	0.3048	167.3	51	15.54
0.7874	2	5.08	20.472	52	132.08	6.562	2	0.6096	170.6	52	15.85
1.1811	3	7.62	20.866	53	134.62	9.843	3	0.9144	173.9	53	16.15
1.5748	4	10.16	21.26	54	137.16	13.12	4	1.219	177.2	54	16.46
1.9685	5	12.7	21.654	55	139.7	16.4	5	1.524	180.4	55	16.76
2.3622	6	15.24	22.047	56	142.24	19.69	6	1.829	183.7	56	17.07
2.7559	7	17.78	22.441	57	144.78	22.97	7	2.134	187	57	17.37
3.1496	8	20.32	22.835	58	147.32	26.25	8	2.438	190.3	58	17.68
3.5433	9	22.86	23.228	59	149.86	29.53	9	2.743	193.6	59	17.98
3.937	10	25.4	23.622	60	152.4	32.81	10	3.048	196.9	60	18.29
4.3307	11	27.94	24.016	61	154.94	36.09	11	3.353	200.1	61	18.59
4.7244	12	30.48	24.409	62	157.48	39.37	12	3.658	203.4	62	18.9
5.1181	13	33.02	24.803	63	160.02	42.65	13	3.962	206.7	63	19.2
5.5118	14	35.56	25.197	64	162.56	45.93	14	4.267	210	64	19.51
5.9055	15	38.1	25.591	65	165.1	49.21	15	4.572	213.3	65	19.81
6.2992	16	40.64	25.984	66	167.64	52.49	16	4.877	216.3	66	20.12
6.6020	17	43.18	26.378	67	170.18	55.77	17	5.182	219.8	67	20.42
7.0866	18	45.72	26.772	68	172.72	59.06	18	5.486	223.1	68	20.73
7.4803	19	48.26	27.165	69	175.26	62.34	19	5.791	226.4	69	21.03
7.874	20	50.8	27.559	70	177.8	65.62	20	6.096	229.7	70	21.34
8.2677	21	53.34	27.953	71	180.34	68.9	21	6.401	232.9	71	21.64
8.6614	22	55.88	28.346	72	182.88	72.18	22	6.706	236.2	72	21.95
9.0551	23	58.42	28.42	73	185.42	75.46	23	7.01	239.5	73	22.25
9.4488	24	60.96	29.134	74	187.96	78.74	24	7.315	242.8	74	22.56
9.8425	25	63.5	29.528	75	190.5	82.02	25	7.62	246.1	75	22.86
10.236	26	66.04	29.921	76	193.04	85.3	26	7.925	249.3	76	23.16
10.63	27	68.58	30.315	77	195.58	88.58	27	8.23	252.6	77	23.47
11.024	28	71.12	30.709	78	198.12	91.86	28	8.534	255.9	78	23.77
11.417	29	73.66	31.102	79	200.66	95.14	29	8.839	259.2	79	24.08
11.811	30	76.2	31.496	80	203.2	98.43	30	9.144	262.5	80	24.38
12.205	31	78.74	31.89	81	205.74	101.7	31	9.449	265.7	81	24.69
12.598	32	81.28	32.283	82	208.28	105	32	9.754	269	82	24.99
12.992	33	83.82	32.677	83	210.82	108.3	33	10.06	272.3	83	25.3
13.386	34	86.36	33.071	84	213.36	111.5	34	10.36	275.6	84	25.6
13.78	35	88.9	33.465	85	215.9	114.8	35	10.67	278.9	85	25.91
14.173	36	91.44	33.858	86	218.44	118.1	36	10.97	282.2	86	26.21
14.567	37	93.98	34.252	87	220.98	121.4	37	11.28	285.4	87	26.52
14.961	38	96.52	34.646	88	223.52	124.7	38	11.58	288.7	88	26.82
15.354	39	99.06	35.039	89	226.06	128	39	11.89	292	89	27.13
15.748	40	101.6	35.433	90	228.6	131.2	40	12.19	295.3	90	27.43
16.142	41	104.14	35.827	91	231.14	134.5	41	12.5	298.6	91	27.74
16.535	42	106.68	36.22	92	233.68	137.8	42	12.8	301.8	92	28.04
16.929	43	109.22	36.614	93	236.22	141.1	43	13.11	305.1	93	28.35
17.323	44	111.76	37.008	94	238.76	144.4	44	13.41	308.4	94	28.65
17.717	45	114.3	37.402	95	241.3	147.6	45	13.72	311.7	95	28.96
18.11	46	116.84	37.795	96	243.84	150.9	46	14.02	315	96	29.26
18.504	47	119.38	38.189	97	246.38	154.2	47	14.33	318.2	97	29.57
18.898	48	121.92	38.583	98	248.92	157.5	48	14.63	321.5	98	29.87
19.291	49	124.46	38.976	99	251.46	160.8	49	14.94	324.8	99	30.18
19.685	50	127	39.37	100	254	164	50	15.24	328.1	100	30.48

Numbers in boldface type are the number of units, either linear or metric. When converting the linear system to the metric system, the centimeter or meter equivalent is found in the right column. When converting from the metric system to inches or feet, the linear equivalent is found in the left column.

4-Color Printer Plans

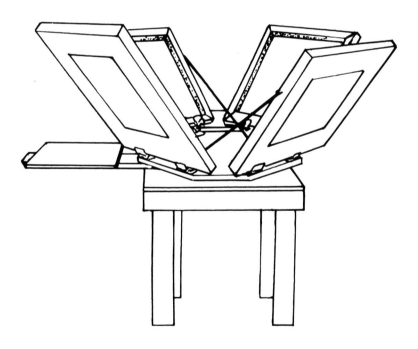

The following pages have plans for a 4-color printer that you can build for around $150. Since we first introduced these plans in 1978 there have been literally thousands of these printers built.

Top View
Without turntable.

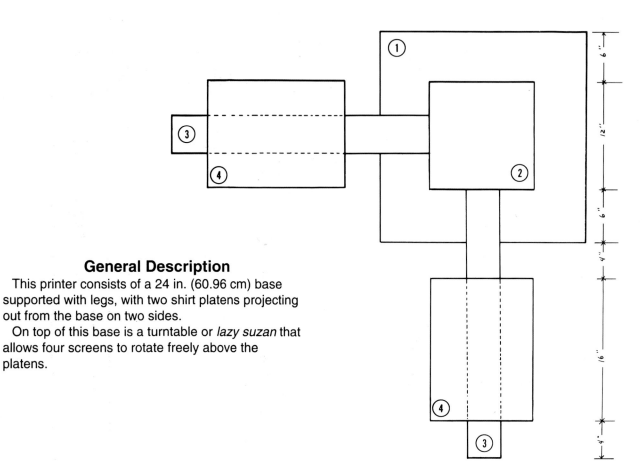

General Description

This printer consists of a 24 in. (60.96 cm) base supported with legs, with two shirt platens projecting out from the base on two sides.

On top of this base is a turntable or *lazy suzan* that allows four screens to rotate freely above the platens.

Materials List

Drawing No.	Quan.	Size	Material	Description
1	1	24 x 24 in. (60.96 x 60.96 cm)	3/4 in. (1.91 cm) Plywood	Base
2	1	12 x 12 in. (30.48 x 30.48 cm)	3/4 in. (1.91 cm) Plywood	Turntable support
3	2	30 in. (76.2 cm)	2 x 4 in. (5.08 x 10.16 cm)	Wooden platen support
4	2	12 x 16 in. (30.48 x 40.64 cm)	5/8 in. (1.60 cm) Plywood	Shirt platen
5	1	24 x 24 in. (60.96 x 60.96 cm) (8 sides)	3/4 in. (1.91 cm) Plywood	Turntable
6	4 pr.		Jiffy Hinges	Screen holder
7	1	8 to 10 in. (20.32 to 25.4 cm)	Lazy Susan turntable	Bearing to allow center to rotate
8	4	12 in. (30.48 cm)	Screen door spring or bungie	Holds screen up
9	4	4 in. (10.16 cm)	C-Clamp	To hold registration guide in place
10	4	2 in. (5.08 cm)	Metal angle	Registration guide
11	4		Box nails or screws	Screen stop
		Assorted wood screws or nails for assembly		

Top View
With turntable and two screens in place.

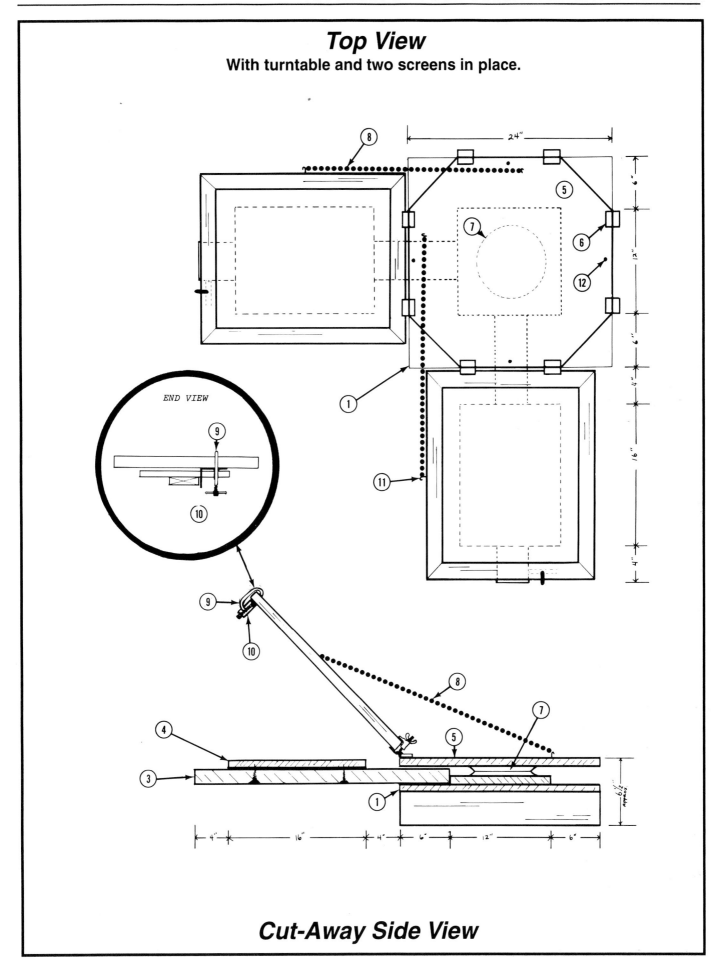

Cut-Away Side View

Homemade Printer Assembly and Set-up

The assembly can be done just by following the basic plans shown.

Here is a basic outline of the steps to follow:

1. Gather all material together. Sand all the edges and spray the wood with polyurethane clear varnish.

2. Assemble a good, sturdy base or build the printer on an existing table. The table should be fairly sturdy because the printer will tend to tip as pressure is applied to the platens with the squeegee. If tipping is a problem, tie a couple of bricks to the opposite side legs.

3. Attach #1 - 2 - 3 to base. Make sure platen supports (3) are attached firmly to top (1). Any "give" here will cause a slight shadow print.

4. Attach shirt platen to support from the bottom with wood screws.

5. Attach a "lazy susan" bearing to base (2). You can also use a bar stool bearing or turntable bearing. These all come as a unit that is ready to be screwed in place. CAUTION: Whatever you use should have no SIDEWAYS play! Any extra sideways play will cause problems in registering the screens.

The thickness or height of the bearing should be between ½ to 1 in. (2.54 to 5.08 cm). The top of the turntable (5) has to turn freely over the platen support (3). When the hinges are attached, they should be the same height as the platen. If the bearing is too short, add an extra filler under the platen.

6. Attach top turntable (5) to "lazy susan".

7. Screw all jiffy hinges in place.

8. Hammer a box nail (12) in line with the edge of the jiffy hinge. This will keep the screen from going up too far when in the up position.

9. Screw the hooks (11) to the turntable and to the screens to be used for the job.

(Note: Jiffy Hinges are special screen holding hinges that are only available from screen print supply companies. They range in price from $15 to $30 per pair.)

This printer is similar in design to the "inexpensive" printer shown on page 69 of this book.

How to Use Your 4-Color Printer

The set-up for this 4-color printer is basically the same as described on page 86 of this book. It is designed to use 18 x 20 in. (45.72 x 50.8 cm) inside dimension screen frames.

The only real difference is that rather than the screen "automatically" registering in place when in the down position, an angle and C-clamp are attached to the end of the screen and registered on the platen.

Set the first color (black) on the printer, square with the platen and clamp it in place with the jiffy hinges.

With the screen in the down position, place the angle under the end of the screen so it is touching the platen support (2 x 4). Secure the angle in this position with the C-clamp.

To hold the screen up, hook the screen door spring or bungie cord to the side of the screen. (The spring may pull the screen to the side slightly so use a sturdy wood frame or retensionable aluminum frames.)

The screen should now register in the exact same place each time it is in the down position.

Now, make the black "line-up" print as described in the book and then rotate the turntable one position, counter-clock-wise.

Attach the second screen (3rd color to be printed) and line this up on the first print. Tighten the jiffy hinges on it and while holding it in register, place the angle and C-clamp on the end. Attach the spring to the side of this screen.

As with the black screen, this screen should line-up in the exact postion everytime it is down!

Repeat the above steps with the other two screens and the run is set-up, ready to go.

Using 2 platens is a must for maximum production.

A minimum of two people – one printing, and one loading and unloading shirts is ideal. While the printer is printing on one platen, the other person is unloading and re-loading the other.

Using the two person method, average production should range between 9 - 12 dozen per hour depending on the difficulty of the design and the speed and endurance of the printers!

Don't underestimate the system used for registration. It will hold the printer in fairly tight registration.

GLOSSARY

The following Glossary contains words and phrases that are commonly used in the garment printing industry. Some words have two meanings, depending on what area of the process is being discussed. In the case of double meanings, the process that the definition pertains to is in parenthesis. The Screen Printing Association also publishes its own English and Spanish Glossary of Terms.

A

Abrasion Resistant The ability of a surface to resist destruction or deterioration through continued friction.

Acetate A synthetic plastic material that serves as the base for most films and can be used to make film positives.

Acetone A solvent that is often an ingredient of lacquer thinner and can be used to remove knife-cut lacquer-adhered stencils or lacquer blockouts.

Actinic Light Light energy in the ultraviolet through blue regions where photostencils are sensitive.

Activator The chemical commonly used in the diffusion-transfer process.

Additive An ingredient that is purposely added to an ink to produce a specific result.

Airbrush A tool used to spray liquids or inks by means of compressed air.

Ambient Temperature The air temperature of the immediate area.

Angle of Attack The angle formed between the squeegee blade and screen fabric before pressure is applied.

B

Baking The heating of an ink or coating to hasten drying.

Base The base of an ink without pigment.

Blockout A liquid that is used to block the areas around the edges of a screen to keep ink from leaking from the screen.

Blend More than one color of ink on the same screen that gives a gradation or blending of one color to another.

Blue Sensitive A term applied to films and emulsions that are primarily sensitive to blue and ultraviolet light and have little sensitivity to other colors.

Bonding Agent An ink additive that improves adhesion characteristics. Generally used to help an ink adhere better to nylon jackets.

Body A term that characterizes the viscosity and flow of an ink.

Build-up (Screen Making) A board that is slightly smaller than the inside dimension of the screen frame used to hold indirect or direct stencils in place during adhering.

Buildup (Printing) The sticking of ink to the bottom of screens when printing wet-on-wet.

Burn To expose a screen.

Burnisher A tool used to push dry-transfer letters from a carrier sheet to an art board.

Butt Cutt See "Perfect Cut."

C

Camera-Ready Artwork that needs no more work or conversion before a final camera shot is made.

Capillary Direct Films Photosensitive films that adhere to wet fabric through capillary action.

Carcinogen A substance that has been found to cause cancer over a period of time.

Carousel A common term applied to a manual multicolor T-shirt printing press where the screens can move or spin horizontally rather than remain in a fixed position.

Catalyst An ink additive that generally enhances the inks adhesion to the substrate.

Centipoise A unit of measure of a liquid's viscosity.

CFM Cubic feet per minute.

Chalking A condition that exists when the ink is not properly bound to the substrate and can be easily rubbed off.

Chase A common term for a metal self-tensioning frame used to hold screen fabric.

Chemistry A common term for the various chemicals used in the darkroom.

Chlorinated Solvents Solvents made up of carbon, hydrogen and chlorine or carbon and chlorine with a high solvent strength for oils and fats.

Choke The reduction of image edges without changing the proportion of the image. Generally done with a camera process or with computer graphics.

Clip Art Artwork that is camera-ready and copyright free for use in designs.

Clogging The drying of ink in the screen.

Coater A special trough for holding emulsion and coating it on screens.

Cold-Peel Transfer A plastisol heat transfer that is peeled after the paper has cooled. Cold-peel transfers generally have a rubbery feel.

Color Separations Film sets that consists of one film positive for each subtractive primary pigment color of magenta, cyan and yellow along with black that has been separated from fully colored artwork and converted into tiny halftone dots.

Color Sequence The printing order of each screen in a multicolor job.

Colorfast The ability of a print to withstand repeated laundering and cleaning.

Composite (Film) The combining of two or more film positives to make one complete film stack for screen exposure.

Conduction The transfer of heat by heating one object and then transferring that heat to another object that the first object comes in contact with.

Convection The transfer of heat by heating the surrounding air and then transferring that heat to an object the air comes in contact with.

Contact Frame Either a glass or glass and vacuum-backed frame for holding film and photoemulsions in perfect contact during exposure.

Contact Printing (Photography) A method of exposing film using an exposure light and contact frame to hold the film.

Contact Screen A film used in the darkroom to convert copy into various textures or a photograph into a halftone.

Continuous Tone (Photography) Tone variations ranging from whites, through gray, all the way to solid blacks.

Contrast The separation of tones in photographs or artwork. The more gradual the separation, the lower the contrast. The sharper the separation, the higher the contrast.

Copy Artwork, copy or other items that are to be used for a camera shot or computer scan.

Copyright The right to prohibit others from copying works of art, books or designs.

Courses The horizontal lines of thread in knitted material.

Crocking The wearing off of a print when rubbed.

Crosslinking The joining together of long chains of molecules causing an ink or substance to solidify.

Curing A reaction - usually chemical - within an ink that promotes polymerization.

Curved Screen Special screens that are used to print on baseball caps or other curved objects.

Cyan A specific blue color that is one of the three subtractive primary pigment colors.

D

Darkroom   A light-tight room that can be used for camera shots or screen coating and drying.

Decoating   The removal of stencils or emulsions from screen fabric. The same as reclaiming.

Deep-Line Cut   A technique used to cut an overlay so that the undercolor and the trap color overlap a great deal.

Degrease   The removal of dirt and oil from the screen fabric prior to applying a stencil.

Density   The degree of blackness or light stopping of a film.

Developer   The chemical used to develop film.

Diazo Emulsion   A light-sensitive emulsion that uses a diazo sensitizer rather than a bichromate sensitizer.

Die-Cuts   Numbers or letters that have been diecut from heat-transfer type material. Generally used for lettering and numbering.

Diffusion Transfer   A photographic process of transferring an image from an exposed donor negative to receiver film or paper in one step using a film processor.

Dimensionally Stable   The ability to resist length, width and thickness changes.

Dot   The individual components of a halftone.

Dot Gain   The spreading or gaining in size of dots during or after they are printed.

Drop Shadow   The effect of making a letter or piece of artwork appear three dimensional by giving it a shadow.

Drying   Changing a wet material such as ink or emulsion into a solid by removing or setting the liquid.

Drying In   The effect of ink that dries in the screen thus causing a loss of detail.

Durometer   The measure of hardness of rubber as in squeegee blades. When applied to screen printing, the durometer is measured on the Shore A scale.

Dual-Cure (Emulsion)   A combination diazo and photopolymer emulsion.

Dwell Time   1. The time between cycles of automatic printing equipment.   2. The amount of time that heat is applied to heat transfers during the application process.

Dye   The colorant used in inks. Dyes are generally soluble in the ink vehicle.

E

Electrostatic Flocking   The use of an electrostatic charge to drive flock fibers into an adhesive that has been printed on a substrate.

Elliptical Dots   Halftone dots that are oval shaped.

Emulsion   A photosensitive coating that is used as the stencil material for screens.

Emulsion Side   (Film) The side of the film that has the emulsion on it.

Enlargement   The increase in size of artwork.

Epoxy   A very generic term for thermosetting resins that have strong adhesive power.

Exposure   (Photography) The act of allowing light to reach the light-sensitive film. (Screen Making) The act of allowing light to reach the light-sensitive photostencil (with a film positive or vellum in place).

Exposure Calculator   A device used to determine the correct exposure time of stencils.

Exposure Time   The amount of time the light is allowed to expose the film or photostencil on the screen.

Exposure Unit   A self-contained system that has a light source and a method of securing the screen.

Extender Base   The base of an ink (without pigment). Usually used to increase the volume of an ink. Also called "Extender," "Transparent Base" and "Halftone Base."

F

Flash-Curing Curing (or semi-curing) a print quickly using a special Flash-Curing unit over the print.

G

Ganging Combining multiple art pieces for one exposure in the camera or to the screen.

Ghosting A double image in a print.

Gray Scale A tool or guide with various tonal ranges that is used to check the reproduction accuracy of a line shot or a halftoned camera shot.

H

Halation (Film) The reflection of light from the back of the film causing unwanted exposure. (Screen Making) The reflection of light from the back of the emulsion or from the fabric causing unwanted exposure in design areas.

Halo Cut An overlay cutting technique that allows ink to print outside of the trap color, thereby creating a halo effect around the design.

Halftone Screen Tints Uniform dot patterns that can be used on artwork to create tints of colors.

Halftoning The conversion of a continuous-tone piece of art or photograph into various sized dots.

Halftone Line Count The number of rows of dots per inch. A measure of coarseness or fineness in halftone dots.

Halftone Screen A film sheet that is printed with dots. In camera work, it is placed over the negative to convert continuous tone copy into a halftone by allowing light to transmit only through the vignetted dots.

Hand The way a print feels when touched.

Heat Curing The curing of textile inks through heat.

Heat-Transfer 1. A design screen printed onto transfer paper. 2. Heat-Transfer application: The process of transferring a heat-transfer from the paper to a substrate through heat and pressure (usually a heat-transfer press is used).

Heat-Transfer Paper Special paper that has release characteristics when printed with heat-transfer inks.

Highlight The lightest portion of a picture.

Highlight Dot (Film) The smallest dot in a positive halftone.

Hot-Peel Transfer A plastisol heat transfer that is peeled immediately after application while the paper is still hot leaving part of the ink on the paper and part of the ink on the garment.

Hot-Split Transfer See *Hot-Peel Transfer*.

Hygroscopic The quality of materials to absorb atmospheric moisture or have an affinity for water.

I

Imprinting Printing a second print on a substrate that has already been printed.

Image Area The area of the positive, negative or screen that has the reproduced artwork.

Index The movement of the platens or shirtboards from one printing station to the next.

Infrared Specific wavelengths on the electromagnetic spectrum that heat any object they strike.

Ink A general term applied to almost any liquid that can be used to make a print.

In-Line Cut An overlay cut that allows the overlay and trap color to overlap slightly.

Inside Cut An overlay cut that allows a slight gap between the overlay and trap color.

K

Keyline The portion of artwork that shows the main outline or design.

Knitting   Material that is made by interlooping yarn.

L

Lacquer Thinner   A blended solvent made up of a mixture of toluene, alcohol, ester, glycol ether and other solvents.

Lens   One or more pieces of optical glass that is ground so that it will collect and focus light rays.

Light Integrator   A device that measures units of light and can control exposure times in screen exposure and film exposure based on light units only.

Line Art   A piece of artwork that has no continuous-tones and is comprised of light and dark areas only with no grays in between. Also called "Line Copy" or "Line Drawing."

Linen Tester   A magnifier used to count the courses and wales of knitted cloth.

Line Shot   A straight camera shot of a line drawing.

Litho Film   The common name given to high-contrast negative-acting film that can be either tray or processor developed.

Logo   Also called "Logotype." - A special symbol, lettering style or graphic that is used in advertising and as a trademark to establish immediate recognition by the customer.

Luminescent   A quality of certain inks to emit light, creating glowing-in-the-dark effects.

M

Magenta   A blue-red color that is one of the three primary pigment colors.

Main Exposure   (Camera) The exposure that establishes the highlight and intermediate tone detail during a halftone exposure.

Mask   Artwork that is usually cut from red overlay film and is used by compositing it with other art films or the film positive to create special effects when shot in the camera.

Masking   A technique used with artwork and camera work where masks are used to either block or permit light to travel through in certain parts of designs.

Masstone   The color of an ink as it is viewed full strength.

Material Safety Data Sheet   (MSDS) Data sheets that are supplied by manufacturers detailing the safe use and handling of specific products and their physical and reactive properties.

Mechanical   A page or design layout that is ready for the camera.

Mesh   Screen fabric.

Mesh Count   A numbering system to denote the number of threads per inch of mesh.

Mesh Determiner   A tool used to determine the mesh count.

Mercury-Vapor Lamp   A screen exposure lamp that is made of mercury enclosed in a quartz tube.

Metal-Halide Lamp   A screen exposure lamp that is made of mercury and metal-halide additives in a quartz tube.

Mezzotint   A randomly-textured special-effects pattern.

Micro Adjustment   The fine-tuning adjustments on a press that allow for precise movements in all directions.

Midtone   The middle areas of gray in a continuous-tone photograph, halftone photograph or other type of artwork. Midtones are halfway between the lightest highlights and the darkest shadows.

Migration   The movement of ink into another ink, coating or substrate causing unwanted muddying of colors.

Mill Defect   A flaw or defect in a shirt that came from the mill.

Mineral Spirits   An aliphatic solvent that has a mild odor and is commonly used to clean plastisol ink from screens. Also called "Paint Thinner."

Misprint   A print that is not up to quality standards. Also called a "Reject."

Mock Full-Color Process The process of achieving a full-color process look in a design using hand-separated artwork.

Moire (Pronounced "moray") An optical pattern created when two sets of lines, patterns, screens or halftones overlap.

Monofilament Screen mesh that is woven from a single strand of thread.

Multifilament Screen mesh that is woven from twisted strands of thread.

N

Name Drop Imprinting a special name on an already printed shirt in order to make it appear to be more customized for a specific location or city.

Negative A photographic image where the dark areas of the original are light and the light areas of the original are dark.

Newtons Per Centimeter (N/CM) The measure of the amount of deflection of a weighted object placed on a tensioned screen fabric.

O

Off-Contact Printing The process of printing with the screen sitting slightly above the substrate so that the only time it touches the substrate is as the print stroke is made.

On-Contact Printing The process of printing with the screen sitting flat on the substrate.

Opacity The hiding power of an ink.

Opaque Light proof.

Ortho Film A common term used to denote negative-acting film that is sensitive to green, blue and ultraviolet spectrums.

Overexposure The exposing of a screen or camera shot longer than recommended.

Overcut An overlay cutting term for cutting past intersecting corners of a design area.

Overlay A mechanical film or vellum that is used to create additional colors in a design.

Overprinting The printing a color directly on another color, whether the undercolor is wet or dry.

Oxidation (Inks) The drying of inks by absorbing oxygen. (Darkroom) The deterioration of chemistry by coming in contact with oxygen.

P

Panchromatic Photographic film that is sensitive to all colors and must be handled in darkness.

Paper Thermometers Heat-sensitive paper that indicates achieved temperature on substrates. Available in various temperature ranges.

Pasteup Artwork that consists of various components of art, type and design that has been pasted together (usually on a master carrier sheet) to create a "whole" design.

Perfect Cut An overlay cut that is prepared by cutting the film portion exactly against the edge of the trapping color. Also known as a "Butt" cut.

Phosphorescent Ink Ink that will glow in the dark.

Photopolymer Emulsions that have a higher solids content and shorter exposure times than most general emulsions.

Photostencil Any stencil system that is light sensitive and reproduces the artwork through exposure.

Picking The pulling of an order prior to printing or shipping to check it for the proper quantity of size and color.

Pigment The particles in ink that give it color.

Pigment Emulsion Inks Inks that contain a pigment mixed with an emulsified vehicle. This includes water-in-oil inks, oil-in-water inks and some water-based inks.

Pinholes 1. (Film) Small imperfections in film. 2. (Screen Making) Openings in the non-design areas of the mesh where the stencil has not bridged across the weave allowing unwanted ink to pass through during printing.

Plastisol A printing ink most commonly used on garments that contains a plasticizer and resin and will not air dry or air cure.

Plate   A common offset-printing term that has come to be known as the positive or printing screen in the screen printing industry.

Platen   1. (Printing) The item that holds the substrate or garment during printing. Also called a "Shirtboard." 2. (Heat-Transfer) The base or heating element of a heat transfer press.

Plugging   The clogging of screens.

Point   (Artwork) A unit of measure used to denote the height of type. There are approximately 72 points per inch.

Point Light Source   A light source that has a single point or filament.

Polymerization   (Ink) The joining of small molecules to form larger molecules of the same substance. These long chains of molecules then join with other chains in what is called cross-linking.

Positive   A term given to almost any media that is used to block the light in the design areas during screen exposure.

Post Hardening   The re-exposing of a screen after it has been developed to aid in further hardening of the emulsion.

Posterization   A special effect done to a piece of art that compresses all of the tonal values into a smaller range of tones.

Powdered Adhesive   A thermoplastic material that is used on the back of plastisol transfers and patches to help them adhere better.

Preregistration   The registering of screens and artwork together before exposure.

Prestretched Screens   Screens that are purchased with fabric already stretched on them.

Pretreatment   The preparing of the screen fabric for the stencil system by degreasing, roughening or coating with an adhering fluid.

Primary Colors   The primary colors of light are red, green and blue. Primary pigment colors are yellow, magenta and cyan. (Black & white often included.)

Printability   The ability of a substrate to accept printing ink and produce an accurate reproduction of the image.

Printing Screen   The carrier or holder for the screen fabric.

Process Camera   A graphic-arts camera designed to shoot large-format film of flat objects.

Process Colors   The process ink colors for full-color process printing of yellow, magenta and cyan.

Proof   A sample print.

Progressive Proof   A successive print of each individual color in a multicolor design followed by printing other colors on top, one at a time. Used to compare what happens when each new color is introduced.

Proportional Scale   A scale for determining the percentage of enlargement or reduction of artwork.

PSI   Pounds per square inch. The measurement of pressure exerted.

Puff Ink   An ink that expands when heated and gives an embossed or three-dimensional effect.

Puff Additive   A puffing agent that can be added to ink to make it puff up when heated.

Pyrometer   A heat-measuring device.

Q

Quartz-Iodine Lamps   An improved tungsten bulb that has a tungsten filament surrounded by a quartz envelope. Also called "Quartz-Halogen."

R

Ream   A standard count for paper. Usually 500 sheets.

Rear Clamps   Screen clamps that hold the screen from the rear only.

Reclaiming   The removing of the stencil from the screen fabric.

Reclaiming Solution   A liquid or powder that is used to dissolve the stencil system from the printing screen.

Red Overlay Film Red film that is adhered to a clear carrier and cut and stripped away to make masks and overlays.

Reducer An additive that will reduce the viscosity of ink.

Reflective Artwork Artwork that is opaque and is reproduced by reflecting light from it.

Reflective Ink An ink that has tiny glass beads that reflect light back to its source.

Register The accurate alignment of colors on a multicolor design.

Registration Targets Small crosshairs that are used on artwork (trap color - usually first film positive) and overlays to keep them in register.

Reject See "Misprint."

Repeatability The ability to repeat a job or process over and over with the same consistent results.

Resolution The ability to resolve or reproduce fine lines or detail in a design.

Resolving Power The ability of a lens or photographic emulsion to accurately reproduce fine detail.

Retarder An additive that slows the drying time of ink.

Retensionable Frames Screen frames that can be retensioned between jobs in order to stretch the fabric at high tension.

Reverse The production of artwork that reverses the dark and light areas of a design (same as negative).

Rheology The properties and relationship of ink viscosity and flow.

Right-Reading A camera shot that reads correctly (same as original art) from emulsion side.

S

Safelight A light that will not expose photographic films or emulsions. Safelight colors vary depending on the light sensitivity of the material being used.

Sandwich The combining of films (usually camera positives and negatives) in register and securing them together.

Sawtooth The jagged edge (sawtooth edge) created when the photographic stencil does not bridge across the weave of the mesh. The sawtooth edge is actually mesh marks.

Scoop Coater See "Coater."

Screen The common name given to the complete frame with mesh.

Screen Angles The angles at which halftone screens are used when shooting color separations to minimize the moire effect.

Screen Clamps Screen holding devices.

Screen Cutting (Screen burning) The common term for exposing a stencil on a screen.

Screen Opener A solvent used to open up clogged screens.

Scumming The blockage of the image area by unexposed emulsion or an emulsion and water mixture, usually caused by improper or lack-of blotting the screen after washout.

Secondary Colors Colors created by overprinting primary colors.

Self-Tensioning See *Retensionable Frame.*

Sensitizer A chemical used to sensitize emulsion.

Shadow Dot The halftone dot in the shadow (darkest) portion of a halftone.

Shirtboard The common term used for the item that holds the shirt in place while printing.

Side Clamps Screen clamps that hold the screen or printing machine during the print stroke.

Simulated Process Color A special computer and camera effect that creates a full-color process look by using posterization and grayscale techniques.

Snap-off The ease at which the mesh snaps off the substrate as the print stroke is made when printing off contact.

Soft-Hand (Direct Printing) A soft feel to the print. (Transfers) A special heat transfer that does not have the traditional rubbery feel.

Soft-Hand Additive An extender base designed to be added to plastisol to make it print and flow better and give a softer hand to the print.

Solvent A substance used to dissolve, thin or reduce another substance.

Special-Effects Screens Texture or halftone screens that can be used to give continuous-tone or line artwork a different look.

Spread The expanding of the size of the image edge. Generally done with a camera process or in computer graphics.

Split Fountain See *Blend*.

Spot-Curing The process of either a fully curing or partially curing ink between colors or after the final print is made.

Squeegee The tool used to push the ink through the screen.

Staging Area A designated area that is used to hold orders that are ready to be printed.

Stencil The medium used to create an image on the printing screen.

Step-and-Repeat (Camera) The shooting of multiple exposures of the same copy on one piece of film. (Screen Making) The exposing of multiple art images on the same screen. The technique is used to eliminate the need for multiple camera shots of the same piece of artwork.

Step Test A multiple exposure test to determine correct exposure time for film or photographic emulsions.

Stretching The stretching of the fabric on the screen frame.

Strike A sample print or test print. Also sometimes the same as *Stroke*.

Stroke A single pull of the squeegee across the screen while pulling ink in front of it and applying downward pressure.

Sublimation Transfer A heat transfer printed with special sublimation dyes that form a molecular bond with synthetic substrates such as nylon and polyester when heat is applied.

Substrate The item or surface being printed.

Subtractive Color Theory The pigment color theory that states the subtractive primary colors of magenta, cyan and yellow are produced by subtracting one or more additive primary colors.

Square Dots Halftone dots that are square like a checkerboard.

T

Tack The stickiness or adhesive nature of certain inks.

Temperature Tapes See *Paper Thermometers*.

Tension The tightness of screen fabric when stretched.

Tension Meter An instrument used to measure the tautness of screen fabric in Newtons per Centimeter (N/CM.)

Thermoplastic A plastic that is solid or fairly rigid at room temperature that has the ability to become liquid again under heat.

Thermosetting The process of becoming permanently solid with the application of heat.

Thixotropic The ability of a liquid to thin down when shaken or stirred and set-up slightly when standing still.

Tint A variation of a color by adding white to it or printing it as halftone dots.

Tonal Range The difference between the lightest tone and the darkest tone in a design.

Toxicity The hazard rating given to substance in threshold limit value in parts per million (TLV-PPM).

Translucent The ability to allow light to pass through without the ability to be seen through.

Transparent The ability to allow light to pass through and to be seen through.

Trap   Artwork that is an outline around other color areas.

U

Ultraviolet   The section of the electromagnetic spectrum in the 200–400 nanometer region that is used to expose screens and cure certain types of inks.

Underbase   A solid area of ink (generally white) that is printed and cured on a dark shirt and acts as a base for colors printed on top of it.

Underlay   See *Underbase*.

Undercolor Removal   The removing of colors from underneath other colors. Generally done if the undercolor is not necessary to the design or if the process will help produce cleaner prints. Helps reduce buildup. Usually done under black.

Undercutting   The overexposure of photostencils causing light to expose around the film and under the image edges.

Undertone   The appearance of a thin or transparent ink film when viewed on a white background.

V

Vacuum Blanket   The rubber used on vacuum frame to create a tight seal around the screen frame or stencil before and during exposure.

Vacuum Easel   A vacuum-backed negative holder of a camera or contact printing setup.

Vacuum Frame   The equipment that holds the screen and film positive in almost perfect contact by means of a vacuum.

Vacuum Table   A flat table with tiny holes in the top that hold the substrate in place during printing by use of a vacuum.

Vehicle   (Ink) The base used in ink to make it printable.

Vellum Paper   1. (Art Preparation) Special transparent drawing paper that has a smooth surface and will not bleed. 2. (Screen Making) Transparent paper that is run through a laser printer or copier and can be used to expose a screen.

Vignette   An area of artwork or dot pattern that gradually shades off into the background.

Viscosity   The flow or fluidity of inks.

W

Wales   The vertical rows of loops on knitted material.

Warp   The threads that run the length of the screen fabric.

Washout   The developing of the photostencil.

Washup   The process of cleaning the ink from the screen. Also a common term that denotes the solvent used to washup a screen.

Water-Based Ink   An ink whose vehicle's binder is soluble in water.

Water-in-Oils Inks   A textile ink that is made of water, pigments, solvents and a vehicle that is usually oil.

Weaving   The fabric-making process of interlacing yarn at right angles.

Weft   The threads that run the width of the screen fabric.

Work Hardening   Using a screen and retensioning a number of times between jobs until the fabric has achieved the highest tension possible.

Working Head of Ink   The ink pushed in front of the squeegee.

Well   The non-print area of the screen frame between the design and the inside of the frame where the ink and squeegee sit.

Wet Film Thickness   (Screen Making) The thickness of direct emulsion measured in mils immediately after application.

Wet-on-Dry   The process of printing one color of ink and drying it first before printing a second color.

Wet-on-Wet   Printing succesive colors of ink without curing or drying in between.

Wet Sample   A sample of wet ink that is saved in a small jar or container for future reference.

Wicking (Printing) The bleeding of inks or ink additives into the surrounding garment fibers.

Wick (Garments) The nature of a fiber to draw moisture away from the body.

Y

Yield Value The term used to describe the flow characteristics of printing ink.

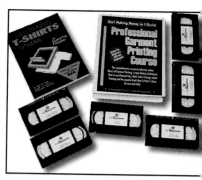

Educational Products and Services for Screen Printers, Artists, and Garment Decorators.

- Books
- Video Training Tapes
- Video Training Courses
- Hands-On Workshops
- On-Site Consulting

www.usscreen.com

1998 Product Catalog

U.S. Screen Printing

INSTITUTE

Since 1979

Welcome to our latest collection of products and educational services for screen printers. Over the years I have strived to provide the best training materials anywhere and to help the industry standardize and grow through the exchange of information.

To keep us at the leading edge we have established a FREE internet service to the industry called the T-Net Site. Since it's inception it has had over 150,000 accesses by screeners who utilize the Message Board and Classified Ad section along with the dozens of articles and industry information to help them run their business better.

This new catalog contains information on all of our products including our ever popular and updated book, *How To Print T-Shirts for Fun and Profit!* We have added a number of NEW items including a variety of Video Courses such as *Creating and Selling Your Preprint Line*, *How To Do Award Winning Process Color*, *The T-Shirt Printer's Business and Marketing Course*, our revised *Dark Shirt Printing Made Easy*, and the hot new *Index Color Separations* and *Corel 8.0* training videos.

Since 1979 we have been providing top notch training to screen printers and have had over 10,000 students! We have also increased our on-site consulting and training.

Education is the key to better quality and increased profits. We want to be your number one source for educational products and services! I look forward to hearing from you and seeing you at one of our classes or at a trade show.

Sincerely,

Scott Fresener

Scott Fresener
Director

The U.S. Screen Printing Institute

Corporate Office & Training Center
605 S. Rockford Dr. • Tempe, Arizona 85281 USA

Hours

9:00 a.m. - 5:00 p.m. (MST) Monday - Friday

Note: Arizonans never change their clocks.
We are the same time as California (PST) in the summer.

Phones

Main Line and Technical Support (602)929-0640
Toll Free Order Line 1/800-624-6532
Fax (602)929-0766

E-Mail

sales@usscreen.com

Internet Address

Our complete catalog and other industry resources are available at our World Wide Web site called *The T-Net* at:
http://www.usscreen.com/

We Accept

and Discover and Bravo Cards

ABOUT THE INSTITUTE

The U.S. Screen Printing Institute offers intensive professional training courses and workshops on screen printing, and garment decorating. The Institute was established in 1979 by Scott and Pat Fresener, authors of the industry's standard reference works, *The Encyclopedia of Garment Printing*, and *How To Print T-Shirts for Fun and Profit*. The Freseners are considered the leading industry experts.

Scott and Pat started in screen printing in 1970 when they began a small garment printing business out of their garage. This business grew to be a large company with automatic equipment and gave the Freseners experience in both technical areas and business management. The lack of standardization and training programs prompted the Freseners to write their books and start giving classes.

Scott Fresener, the Institute's Director, has contributed over 250 articles to industry trade magazines and is a popular guest speaker at major industry trade shows. He is also a contributor to the Screen Printing Association's Academy of Screen Printing Technical Guidebook and a lifetime member of the Academy of Screen Printing Technology.

The Freseners and the Institute have received dozens of industry awards and are two-time winners of the coveted *Magnus Award* by the Screenprinting and Graphic Imaging Association for outstanding service to the industry. They are also two-time winners of *Impressions Magazine's* **Quest for the Best** award for the best training courses and books in the industry.

In 1995, Scott and his son Michael established the first industry specific internet World Wide Web site and became the first internet provider to the industry. In 1996, Scott was awarded the *Parmele Award* by the Screenprinting and Graphic Imaging Association. This is the highest award you can receive from them and is given for outstanding lifetime service and major contributions to the industry.

The Freseners truly care about the industry that they have been so active in and tirelessly strive to keep their school's classes and products the best anywhere!

Member

Screenprinting & Graphic Imaging
Association International

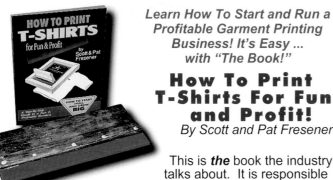

Learn How To Start and Run a Profitable Garment Printing Business! It's Easy ... with "The Book!"

How To Print T-Shirts For Fun and Profit!
By Scott and Pat Fresener

This is *the* book the industry talks about. It is responsible for getting thousands of T-Shirt printers into the profitable garment printing business! Every successful shop has a "well used" copy of this book. **How To Print T-Shirts For Fun And Profit** has literally become "the Bible" of the industry. It is written in an *easy-to-follow* step-by-step manner by industry experts Scott and Pat Fresener who have been in the industry since 1970.

This book covers everything from A to Z about screen printing T-Shirts and Heat Transfers, and includes sections on printing Nylon Jackets, Baseball Caps and more. It tells you how to set-up a shop, where to find customers, how to run your business, PLUS it contains a complete suppliers listing, dozens of charts and forms AND plans to build your own equipment including a 4-color printer for under $150!

- **300 photos**
- **260 pages**
- **50 charts and diagrams**
- **Equipment plans**
- **Suppliers list**

Every Shop Should Have A Copy of This Book!

$29.95
ITEM # B-HTP
Softcover, 260 pages, 8 1/2" x 11"

Totally revised and updated!

Business and Marketing Course
with Scott Fresener

Running a business in a professional manner and good marketing are the keys to being a success and this course covers it all! Whether you are just getting into the business or are trying to make a profit in an existing business, this course is a must. It covers everything from creating your own catalog, to how to price your work, getting the larger accounts, getting credit, giving credit, all about the industry, trade shows, trade magazines and more. It also covers copyrights and trademarks, licensing, and trade standards. It is a great morale booster with terrific tips and ideas on how to package your company for success.

This course is a video seminar featuring Scott Fresener. It consists of two indepth videos and a workbook with samples, forms, resources and more. Packaged in a sturdy binder.

A Must for Every Shop!   ITEM # VC-BUSCOURSE   **$129.95**
(PAL FORMAT $149.95)

PERFECT FOR THE BEGINNER! GREAT FOR NEW EMPLOYEES!

Introductory Garment Printing Course

Just starting out? Need a quick reference for new employees? This is it! This introductory course includes two excellent video tapes - *Basics of Garment Printing* and *Multicolor Printing*. It also includes the popular 260 page manual *How To Print T-Shirts for Fun and Profit*.

The entire course is packaged in a durable vinyl video album case that holds both tapes and the book. Learn the basics all the way through multicolor printing. It's easy with this course.

Item # VC-INTROSET   **$99.95**
(PAL FORMAT $119.95)

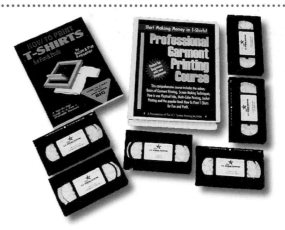

Six Videos and a Book in one great course!

Professional Garment Printing Course

This is a complete course that will teach you everything you need to know to start a successful garment printing company. The **Professional Garment Printing Course** includes five of our most popular video titles: *Basics of Garment Printing*, *Multicolor Printing*, *Screen Making Techniques*, *How To Use Plastisol Inks* and *Jacket Printing*. It also includes a copy of *How To Print T-Shirts for Fun and Profit*. Great for beginners. An excellent reference set. Perfect to train employees. Packed in sturdy video albums.

Item # VC-PROSET   **$249.95**
(PAL FORMAT $309.95)

Order Toll Free 1/800-624-6532. We Accept COD, Company or Personal Check and

T-Shirt Graphics With CorelDRAW 8.0 By Scott Fresener

Corel Draw 8.0 is the HOTTEST Windows based drawing program around and it is time to upgrade now. If you want to learn how to do T-Shirt graphics with Corel and learn 100's of tips and tricks that ARE NOT in the manual, then you need this program.

Learn all about the new drag and drop features, how to adjust bitmaps in Corel, all about the new tools, lots of undocumented tips, how to fix problems, proper scanning techniques, doing spot color and process color separations, creating underbases for dark shirts, proper trapping, using halftones, doing hot special effects and a lot more! Six hours of video instruction featuring Scott Fresener. Each tape is fully indexed so it is easy to review specific sections.

Three-tape set includes a large wall chart cheat sheet for easy reference!

Item # VC-COREL8 **$199.95**
(PAL FORMAT $229.95)

T-Shirt Graphics With Corel Draw 7.0

A great step-by-step that covers everything. Includes wall chart. Three tapes.

Item # VC-COREL7 **$179.95**
(PAL FORMAT $209.95)

T-Shirt Graphics With Corel Draw 5.0

Three-tape set that covers everything the manual doesn't tell. Includes wall chart.

Item # VC-COREL **$129.95**
(PAL FORMAT $159.95)

T-Shirt Graphics With Adobe Photoshop 4.0 By Scott Fresener

Adobe Photoshop 4.0 is the number one image manipulation program! Now you can do your own process color separations IN HOUSE and save thousands of dollars every year. Why send out your process jobs when you can learn what the separators know. With this step-by-step course you'll learn all about image manipulation, halftones, color correction, proper scanning, unsharp masking, special effects filters, creating process separations AND spot color separations, how to create a white plate, basic dark shirt separations, adjusting separations for specific inks, undercolor removal, tone curve and levels adjustments, action palette, and EVERYTHING THE MANUAL DOESN'T TELL YOU!

This course also covers the tools and fundamentals of Adobe Photoshop and is designed for the beginner AND power user alike. Each section is fully indexed for easy replay. This is the course you will constantly refer back to as a refresher. ***Three tapes, 4-1/2 hours and large wall chart cheat sheet.***

Item # VC-PHOTO4 **$149.95**
(PAL FORMAT $179.95)

T-Shirt Graphics With Adobe Photoshop 3.0

Still a great version of Photoshop, this tape teaches how to use the program and do your own separations in-house. Three tape set.

$129.95
Item # VC-PHOTO
(PAL FORMAT $159.95)

Creating and Selling a Successful Preprint Line

A hot new product from U.S. Screen! Are you looking to start your own line of shirts. Don't do anything until you see this course! It will teach you how to find and what to pay reps, what types of designs sell where, dealing with large and small accounts, how to keep the cash flowing, where to get business, how to package and present your line for maximum sales, how to price the shirts and much more!

This video course is a live seminar and includes two video tapes and a workbook full of forms, procedures and ideas.

ITEM # VC-PREPRINT **$129.95**
(PAL FORMAT $149.95)

Selling To The School Market

What a package! This combination two-tape video set and booklet will teach you all the secrets of selling to the school market. From how to get in the back door to who to contact, direct mail that works, how to sell fund raisers, how to get paid and much more!

The pricing and marketing strategy is worth the price of the set - even if you don't sell to the school market! Includes booklet of samples, contracts, special school order forms, direct mail pieces and much more. Two and one-half hours of great information!

ITEM # VC-SCHOOL **$99.95**
(PAL FORMAT $119.95)

The Industry's Number One Source for Educational Products and Services!

INDEX SEPARATIONS
For Screen Printers
Video Training Course

The Hot method for creating very bright separations that work on both dark and light shirts!

Index separations is the process you have been hearing about. Finally there is a comprehensive training course that teaches everything there is to know about doing index color separations that are bright and work on both dark and light shirts.

Index Separations are easy to do in Adobe Photoshop. By converting the image to Index Color you can print the file as a bitmap random dither rather than a halftone dot. This makes the design much easier to screen print and the colors are much brighter than process color. In fact, Index Color is the perfect way to finally use all of the Corel Draw Clip Art (PC users). *No additional software is needed with our course!*

You'll learn this and more:

• What indexed color is and where it works the best.
• Using Adobe Photoshop to create files.
• Choosing the correct color palette.
• Exporting images to MAC or PC illustration programs.
• How to proof your designs.
• All about printing and inks.
• Creating underbases for dark shirts.
• Dozens of tricks of the pro's.
• Combining spot color with index color.
• Image resolution, screen meshes....and more!

You Get All This:

• **Two Step-By-Step Video Tapes**
  In sturdy album binder. Fully indexed.
• **Reference Manual**
  Perfect reference book.
• **Work Files (MAC or PC)**
  Sample files, separations and color tables.
• **Resolution and Print Test Film**
  Test image resolution, screen mesh and dot gain.
• **Sample Prints**
  Compare the work files and video with the actual sample print on both light and dark backgrounds
• **Large Wall Chart Cheat Sheet**

Great on light and dark shirts! Very easy-to-make underbases.

Perfect for simple designs and clip art with gradations and fills. Works great with Corel Draw clip art!

Now Available in Spanish!

$349.95

English - Item # VC-INDEXKIT
Spanish - Item # VC-INDEXKIT-SP
(PAL VERSION $369.95)

The easy way to learn at your own pace. Great for experienced printers and newcomers.

Understand The Entire Screen Printing Process!
Basics of Garment Screen Printing

This is a great "primer" tape for that new employee and for anyone thinking of getting into the business! You can see what processes are involved in T-Shirt printing before you take the plunge! Topics include an overview of artwork preparation, screen making, inks, printing techniques and more.

By Scott and Pat Fresener
minutes.

English ITEM # VC-BASIC $39.95 (PAL $49.95)
Spanish ITEM # VC-BASIC-SP $49.95 (PAL $59.95)

Print Multi-Color Work With Confidence!
Multi-Color Printing

If you are doing or want to do multi-color printing then you need this tape in your library! It covers the important aspects of printing multi-color designs on garments in a step-by-step manner utilizing professional techniques used in the industry.

Topics include art & overlay preparation, screen set-up and mesh selection, color sequence, ink usage, wet-on-wet and flash-cure printing, overprinting, troubleshooting and much more.
By Scott and Pat Fresener
30 minutes.

English ITEM #VC-MULTI $39.95 (PAL $49.95)
Spanish ITEM #VC-MULT-SP $49.95 (PAL $59.95)

Easy Screen Making!
Screen Making Techniques

This terrific video is a must for every screen making department - whether you are using wooden hand-stretched frames or the latest retensionable frames. It covers all about frames, mesh, emulsions, direct film, exposure, wash-out, screen prep, reclaiming, troubleshooting and much more. This presentation was videotaped live at the U.S. Screen Printing Institute and features Bob Alabaster.
Two tape set - 180 minutes.

ITEM # VC-SCREEN $79.95 set (PAL $99.95)

How To Use Plastisol Inks

Questions on how to use your inks? The answers are here! This tape was shot live at the U.S. Screen Printing Institute and features Scott Fresener lecturing and demonstrating the use of Plastisol Inks.

How To Use Plastisol Inks is a how-to-do-it video cassette covering the important aspects of using plastisol ink in the garment screen printing shop.

Topics include types of plastisol, using additives and reducers properly, curing techniques, using high opacity and low-bleed inks, troubleshooting and much more.
5 minutes.

ITEM # VC-INKS $39.95 (PAL $49.95)

An Important Topic!
Health and Safety in the Screening Shop

It's time to think about the health and safety of you and your employees in the screen printing shop AND complying with the law. This video cassette covers all of the important points of both OSHA and EPA regulations and how you can come into compliance with regulations that effect your business.
This video tape was filmed live at the U.S. Screen Printing Institute and features Bob Alabaster.
75 minutes

ITEM # VC-HEALTH $39.95 (PAL $49.95)

Learn from a Pro!
Hiring And Training A Sales Staff

This step-by-step tape covers all aspects of dealing with a sales staff. Taught by industry veteran, Steve Mertens, it is based on his 20 years of experience running his own company and as a sales rep himself. This tapes format is a live lecture.
Topics covered include the interview process, compensation, training, sales management, when to hire and much more.

Two tape set - 150 minutes

ITEM # VC-SALES $79.95 set (PAL $99.95)

New Ergonomic Video......
Power Printing Through Full Body Force

Are you tired of being sore at the end of the day? Does fatigue have an effect on production? This video features industry ergonomics expert, Cathy Coulson, of Squeegee Plus® and will teach you the proper printing technique to minimize stress and increase production.
0 minutes.

English ITEM # VC-POWER $39.95 (PAL $49.95)

Making Plastisol transfers.
Heat Transfer Production

Transfers are useful when you need to print more colors than your press allows, for "event" and concession work, and in other ventures where a large pre-printed inventory would be required and therefore prohibitive. This step-by-step video shows you how easy it is to make your own transfers!

Topics include hot and cold split transfers, sublimations, all about papers and inks, curing and drying, mesh and stencil systems, multi-color transfers, puff and foil, cap transfers, art requirements and much more.
30 minutes.

English ITEM # VC-TRANS $39.95 (PAL $49.95)
Spanish ITEM # VC-TRANS-SP $49.95 (PAL $59.95)

Art Preparation
Manual Techniques For Screen Printing

Art Prep is a step-by-step video tape that covers all aspects of creating artwork for screen printing using traditional hand and camera techniques including cutting overlays, using halftone dots, working with clip art and more. It is designed for non- artists as well as artists who want to learn how to apply their knowledge to the screen printing process. There is also a brief overview of computer graphics. This presentation was videotaped live at the U.S. Screen Printing Institute and features instructor Bob Alabaster.

Two Tape Set - 180 minutes.

ITEM # VC-ART $79.95 set (PAL $99.95)

It's Not Difficult!
Jacket Printing

Jackets can be very profitable! Now you can quit turning down those jacket orders. If you already print jackets this video will help you minimize your mistakes and teach you how to do top quality work. Salvaging just one or two jackets could pay for this tape!

Topics include screen making and art requirements, nylon inks, multicolor prints, printing lined jackets, troubleshooting and more.

By Scott Fresener
30 minutes.

ITEM # VC-JACK $39.95 (PAL $49.95)

Learn to do great effects!
Special Effects That Make Shirts Sell!

Do you like what you see in the airport gift shops and resorts. Do you wish you could do great foil, glitter and puff prints? This tape tells it all. It covers how to use these inks to make your designs jump off the shirt. Learn the secrets to great puff and foil and other outstanding ink effects. Increase what you charge for shirts by using these special effects inks. This tape is a live lecture featuring Dawn Fayen from Creative Spirit, Inc. - with shirts in all the major airports and gift shops.

40 minutes.

ITEM VC-SPECIAL $39.95 (PAL $49.95)

Spanish Videos

We ship same-day VIA UPS. If there is no Order Form in this catalog please call and we will fax you one.

U.S. Screen Printing
INSTITUTE

The U.S. Screen Printing Institute offers the most comprehensive hands-on workshops in the industry and has had over 10,000 students since 1979. The Institute was voted the Number One training program in the industry by the 1992 and 1994 *Impression's Magazine Quest-for-the-Best* reader's poll.

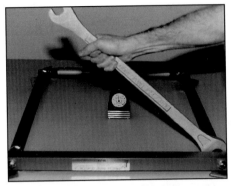

INFORMATION ABOUT THE INSTITUTE

COME TO SUNNY ARIZONA!
The Institute is located in Tempe, Arizona, a beautiful suburb of Phoenix and the home of Arizona State University. Tempe has gained a reputation as a first class community with dozens of golf courses, shopping areas, night clubs and tourist attractions, PLUS unbeatable winter weather!

Tempe is only four hours by car to the Grand Canyon and six hours by car to Las Vegas.

HOUSING
Students stay at a variety of motels and hotels including the Holiday Inn in Tempe, Arizona. Transportation is provided free between the Holiday Inn and the school.

TRANSPORTATION
Students coming to Tempe can take any major airline into Sky Harbor International Airport in Phoenix. If staying at the Holiday Inn, they offer free airport pickup by baggage claim. Phoenix also has an excellent airport shuttle service called the Super Shuttle, there is no need to rent a car.

ABOUT THE FACILITIES
In order to provide the best possible learning environment, the facility contains the latest in equipment including four and six color printers, exposure units, wash-out sinks, computer graphics systems, dryers and flash curing units, heat transfer presses and much more.

The walls of the classrooms are covered with dozens of printed samples - many from former students! Every effort is made to make the students stay comfortable, including providing FREE coffee and refreshments during class.

WHY ATTEND A CLASS?
A typical response from former students is they wish they had attended a class sooner. It is easy to get caught up in the day-to-day running of a business or to try to start a business and figure you will learn as you go. Our

courses are COMMERCIAL CLASSES that teach you the latest techniques used by professional screen printing shops around the world. We will save you countless hours of trial and error. What may take you months to learn on your own will take only days in one of our classes.

If you are already printing and want to be one step ahead of the competition then our classes will show you how the big printers do things! Just a few of the tips from one of our classes will more than pay for your trip. Our hands-on computer classes will teach the latest high-end separation and printing techniques.

CLASS MATERIALS
All class participants receive Hanes shirts to print on, free subscription forms for trade magazines, notepad, pencil, and apron (that can be printed also). Attendees of class #101 also receive a copy of *How To Print T-shirts For Fun And Profit* and a screen.

STUDENT DISCOUNTS
Students of the Institute receive special discounts on other educational products. The Institute can often help obtain equipment and supply discounts from industry suppliers.

CERTIFICATE OF COMPLETION
Every student receives a Certificate of Completion at the end of each class. We have had many former students comment that they have made more money with this certificate than with their college diploma!

IT'S EASY TO LEARN
The U.S. Screen Printing Institute uses an interactive approach to teaching. By combining audio-visuals, lecture, question and answers, problem solving, peer interaction, and hands-on sessions, the students learn AND RETAIN a great amount of information in a short time period!

This approach coupled with a relaxed, casual teaching environment full of hundreds of samples, the latest equipment and patient, professional instructors with years of actual field experience makes the total learning experience easy and enjoyable.

Would you like your entire staff trained? The Institute also offers private on-site consulting and training. Call for details.

Classes are held monthly and fill up rapidly! Don't be left out. Call 1/800-624-6532 for class dates and availability.

Register by phone or simply fax the attached registration form.

CLASS #201
All NEW Class!

2-Days $495 per person
(Discounts for groups and couples.)

High-End Color Separations and Printing Workshop

Classes taught by Scott and Mike Fresener.

Class Hours:
Day 1 - 9:00 am - 5:00 pm
Day 2 - 9:00 am - 5:00 pm

Partial Course Contents

Introduction to the Processes
You will get a complete overview of each process and the problems associated with them. You will learn all of the important terminology.

Artwork Requirements
Since a good portion of high-end work is from customer supplied art or computer file, you will learn what types of artwork is the best and how to specify and demand the type of file format, resolution, size and specifics for files that are supplied. You will also learn the requirements when doing artwork in-house.

Computer Systems
Even though attendees will be expected to have some computer knowledge, there will be an overview of hardware needs and requirements (both MAC and PC). Peripherals will be discussed along with important features to look for in scanners, laser printers, dry film imaging systems and imagesetters.

System Calibration
Learn about calibrating your complete system including the monitor, scanner, printer and doing calibration test prints to calibrate to your ink and screens!

Proper Scanning Techniques
You will learn about scanning techniques for each process including scan resolution and color adjustment, plus see how to make a marginal piece of art look good with the proper scan.

Image Manipulation in Adobe Photoshop 4.01
Learn the secrets to image manipulation in Photoshop including proper tone curve and level adjustments, setting the black and white point and density range, adjusting for hue error, correct unsharp masking and image sharpening, general image touchup techniques, working with layers, exporting images to drawing programs for text and additional graphics and much more.

Working with Service Bureaus
Depending on what computer equipment you have, for very high-end work you may want to have scans and films done by a service bureau. You will learn how to deal with service bureaus, how to specify your exact needs and how to save money by giving them PRN files.

General Screen Printing and Screen Making Equipment Requirements
You will learn what types of screen making and screen printing works best for high-end work and where your shops weaknesses are. You will learn about proper tension, mesh counts, how to hold fine detail, what stencil systems work best, proper ink usage, correct press setup and color sequences and proper printing techniques for high-end work.

Process Color on Light Shirts
Learn how to use Adobe Photoshop to separate RGB images into CMYK. Learn the proper settings for Printing Inks Setup and Separation Setup including using industry specific ink brands, adjusting the black ink and total ink limit settings, dot gain adjustments, and more.

Learn about undercolor removal, creating spot colors, dealing with out-of-gamut colors, creating a white plate for pastel shirts, calibrating your system for the proper gray balance, how to maintain detail in the shadow areas and of course how to match the original art! You will also learn the proper angles and line counts to minimzie moire, what meshes work best, and the printing sequence for the process colors and spot colors.

You will work through complete process jobs (from scan to screens) and print one of the jobs as a reference print PLUS will leave with the computer files you worked on.

Index Color on Light and Dark Shirts
Index color will soon be the most popular color separation method. You will learn how to pick the correct colors, what resolution to use, how to create detailed underbased and highlights for dark shirts, all about inks, mesh, color sequence and printing techniques plus dozens of closely guarded secrets of the pros. Learn how to get bright, soft prints that work on both light and dark shirts plus how to use index images with drawing programs.

You will work through complete jobs from scan to screens and will print one of the jobs as a reference plus receive copies of the computer files you worked on.

Simulated and Real Process Color on Dark Shirts
The is what everyone wants to do - create photo realistic images with a soft feel. You will learn that including: how to create halftone spot colors, detailed underbases, great highlights, realistic fleshtones, using CMYK and spot colors, and how to preview the image right on the computer. You will also learn the proper mesh selection, inks, correct angles and line counts, special printing techniques and color sequences and how to do eight and ten color designs with only ONE FLASH CURE!

You will work through simulated process on dark jobs and one real process color on dark job (from scan to screens) and will print one of the jobs as a reference and will take home the computer files you worked on in class.

Optional Software Programs
You will learn about third party software programs that can be used to speed up some of the processes.

Plus More!
You will also learn about the state of the industry, trends in art preparation, separation techniques, plus printing tips and techniques, production considerations, improving setup times and much more!

Computer Training is Hands-On!
The classroom is equipment with the latest Windows based IBM Compatible computers. Two people will share a computer *(there is an additional fee of $175 to have your own private computer in class.)* If you are an Apple Macintosh user everything you learn is transferrable since Adobe Photoshop is identical on both the PC and MAC platform.

ABOUT THIS CLASS
Are you struggling trying to compete on quality and high-end work? Is your art department taking much too long and achieving marginal results? Are you ready to move up to real high quality photorealism on shirts? Are you looking for a more profitable market niche? Do you want to bring color separtions in-house to have more control and increase profits? Are you just tired of "slapping ink on shirts?"

If so, this class is for you. It will teach all of the important aspects of doing very high-end award winning light and dark shirt prints. In the U.S. Screen Printing Institute's new Computer Graphic Training Center you will learn from industry expert, Scott Fresener, how to do use Adobe Photoshop and a drawing program to create stunning color separations that print like the original! You will also learn all about proper screen making, inks, and printing requirements to reproduce these separations faithfully on a shirt.

Who Should Attend?
Although the majority of this class is hands-on color separation training that is perfect for in-house and freelance artists, this class is also great for production managers, general manager, owners and even sales people who need to understand what is involved in doing high-end printing.

Prerequisites: Attendees must have a working knowledge of computer graphics (MAC or PC). A working knowledge of Adobe Photoshop is helpful but not necessary. Attendees must have a working knowledge of the garment printing process. This course is not for total beginners. Class #101 and #201 can be taken back-to-back for a thorough understanding of the printing and computer separation process.

INSTITUTE REGISTRATION AND INFORMATION

PHONE REGISTRATION

Our classes are VERY popular. They generally fill up two and three weeks before the class date. We will gladly accept phone registrations. They are taken on a first come, first served basis. Registration can be made by phoning toll-free at 1/800-624-6532 between the hours of 9:00 a.m. and 5:00 p.m. (mst) Monday through Friday. You can also fax your registration to (602)929-0766.

VERIFY CLASS AVAILABILITY

Since the classes fill up rapidly, you should ALWAYS make a phone reservation first to make sure there is room in the class. In this age of non-refundable and restricted airline tickets it is wise to check class availability first before making the rest of your travel plans.

REGISTRATION CONFIRMATION

A phone registration should be confirmed by mail with a registration form and full payment of class fees. When you sign-up we will immediately confirm your registration in writing to you with a letter outlining details about the school, the location, housing, transportation, what to bring, what to wear and what to expect.

REGISTRATION FEES

In order to guarantee your place in class, full payment must accompany your registration. A phone registration does not guarantee your place in class.

Purchase orders are only accepted from institutions, insurance companies, rehabilitation centers, government agencies and major corporations.

LATE REGISTRATION

Although the classes always fill up, there are occasional last minute cancellations. We can also put you on a class waiting list in case the class is full.

If you are a last minute registrant it may be necessary to overnight your payment to guarantee your place in class.

CANCELLATIONS AND REFUNDS

Our classes are very popular and are generally full. All advance payments are fully refundable if cancellation is made ten working days before the class start date. After that time, class fees are non-refundable but may be transferred to a different class provided that notice is received at least three business days before class start date. If a three business day notice is not given, fees are forfeited.

If for any reason a class is cancelled, students will be notified within ten days of the class date and full refunds sent.

CLASS FEES AND DISCOUNTS

The registration fee is $495 per-person, per-class. We offer discounts if more than one person from the same company attends, or if you take the two classes back-to-back.

Discount fees are as follows:
1 person - class 101 and 201 combined $895.00
2 people (same company) - class 101 $895.00
2 people (same company) - class 201 $895.00
2 people (same company) - both classes $1,695.00

Private computer for class 201 $175 additional fee.

TAX DEDUCTION

According to Treasury Regulation 1.162-5, registration fees, travel, meals, lodging, etc., are tax deductible as educational expenses if the instruction is TO MAINTAIN OR IMPROVE SKILLS necessary to employment or required by an employer or by law. If you HAVE NOT started your business prior to attending one of these classes it may NOT be possible to deduct these expenses. Consult your accountant or CPA for additional information.

HOTEL ACCOMMODATIONS

Hotel accommodations are not included in the class fees. Reservations should be made directly with the hotel as far in advance as possible. Students must tell the hotel they are attending the U.S. Screen Printing Institute in order to get the special class discount.

If you are arriving after 6:00 p.m. make sure to guarantee the room with prepayment or credit card.

If for some reason our official hotel does not have vacancies please call the school at once so alternate arrangements can be made.

THE OFFICIAL HOTEL IS:

HOLIDAY INN - TEMPE
915 E. Apache Blvd.
Tempe, Arizona 85281
(602)968-3451 or 1/800-553-1826

Winter room rate (January 1 - April 30)
$78.00 per night plus tax

Summer/Fall rate (May 1 - December 31)
$63.00 per night plus tax
(Room rate is for single occupancy. Add $10.00 for additional person. Rate includes airport transportation The Holiday Inn is only two miles from the school and convenient to shopping, restaurants and entertainment.)

WE ACCEPT:

PLUS Discover and Bravo Cards

To register, simply copy this form and fax it to (602)929-0766 or call Toll Free 1/800-624-6532.

REGISTRATION FORM

U.S. Screen Printing Institute
605 S. Rockford Dr.
Tempe, AZ 85281
1/800-624-6532 Fax (602)929-0766

Mail or fax registration. Print or type clearly. If registering within two weeks of a class date please call to check space availability. A confirmation letter will be mailed after receipt of this form. Please note the Cancellation Policy in the Institute's registration information.

COMPANY: _____

ADDRESS: _____

CITY: _____ STATE: ____ ZIP: _____

DAYTIME PHONE: (____) _____ FAX: (____) _____

CONTACT: _____

TOTAL CLASS FEES

$ _____

COURSE NO.	ATTENDEE NAME(S)	DATES	FEE

PAYMENT INFORMATION

REGISTRATION DATE _____

[ ] Enclosed is CK/MO # _____ Amount $ _____

[ ] Purchase Order # _____
     (Dealers, government agencies and institutions only)

[ ] Bill to my Visa, Mastercard, Discover or American Express Card
     (circle one)

Card No. _____

Expiration Date _____

Cardholders Name _____

Cardholders Signature
X _____

250

INDEX

About the Authors

Scott and Pat Fresener entered the screen printing industry in 1969 when they started a T-shirt printing business out of their garage with a $500 investment. This business grew to be a large company with automatic equipment.

The lack of standardization and training in the industry prompted the Freseners to sell their printing business and write the original version of this book in 1979. That same year they founded *The U.S. Screen Printing Institute*. The original version of this book sold over 100,000 copies in 15 years and their school has had over 10,000 students!

In 1985 they authored the industry's most respected technical manual *The Encyclopedia of Garment Printing*.

In 1986 Scott and Pat were voted *"the most influential couple of the last ten years"* by an **Impressions Magazine** readers poll. They have also received the coveted *Service to the Industry* and *Leadership Awards* from industry publications and trade associations. In October of 1986 the Screen printing and Graphic Imaging Association, awarded Scott *The Magnus*, for his outstanding service to the industry. In 1992, the Fresener's school was also awarded *The Magnus* for its contributions to the industry.

A 1992 **Impressions Magazine** *Quest for the Best* readers poll voted the Fresener's school and books as the number one technical products in the industry and Scott was voted one of the top two consultants.

Scott is a popular guest speaker at industry trade shows in this country and abroad, and has written hundreds of articles for trade magazines. Scott and Pat also have produced dozens of how-to-do-it training videos for screen printers.

In 1996, Scott was awarded the highest honor you can receive from the Screenprinting and Graphic Imaging Association, *The Parmele Award*, for his outstanding lifetime contributions to the industry.

The Freseners have three grown children, two who work in the business. They also raise and show Labrador Retrievers and are very active in the dog community. In fact they often take most of the dogs to work. The joke around the office is that you had better like dogs if you are going to work for the Freseners.

Scott and Pat Fresener have always felt that the way to strengthen an industry is through education and the exchange of ideas and constantly strive to improve the industry with their products and services.